MEMOIRS OF GENERAL
W. T. SHERMAN
By William T. Sherman

VOLUME I

VOLUME I.

GENERAL W. T. SHERMAN
HIS COMRADES IN ARMS,
VOLUNTEERS AND REGULARS.

Nearly ten years have passed since the close of the civil war in America, and yet no satisfactory history thereof is accessible to the public; nor should any be attempted until the Government has published, and placed within the reach of students, the abundant materials that are buried in the War Department at Washington. These are in process of compilation; but, at the rate of progress for the past ten years, it is probable that a new century will come before they are published and circulated, with full indexes to enable the historian to make a judicious selection of materials.

What is now offered is not designed as a history of the war, or even as a complete account of all the incidents in which the writer bore a part, but merely his recollection of events, corrected by a reference to his own memoranda, which may assist the future historian when he comes to describe the whole, and account for the motives and reasons which influenced some of the actors in the grand drama of war.

I trust a perusal of these pages will prove interesting to the survivors, who have manifested so often their intense love of the "cause" which moved a nation to vindicate its own authority; and, equally so, to the rising generation, who therefrom may learn that a country and government such as ours are worth fighting for, and dying for, if need be.

If successful in this, I shall feel amply repaid for departing from the usage of military men, who seldom attempt to publish their own deeds, but rest content with simply contributing by their acts to the honor and glory of their country.

WILLIAM T. SHERMAN,
General

St. Louis, Missouri, January 21, 1875.

PREFACE TO THE SECOND EDITION.

Another ten years have passed since I ventured to publish my Memoirs, and, being once more at leisure, I have revised them in the light of the many criticisms public and private.

My habit has been to note in pencil the suggestions of critics, and to examine the substance of their differences; for critics must differ from the author, to manifest their superiority.

Where I have found material error I have corrected; and I have added two chapters, one at the beginning, another at the end, both of the most general character, and an appendix.

I wish my friends and enemies to understand that I disclaim the character of historian, but assume to be a witness on the stand before the great tribunal of history, to assist some future Napier, Alison, or Hume to comprehend the feelings and thoughts of the actors in the grand conflicts of the recent past, and thereby to lessen his labors in the compilation necessary for the future benefit of mankind.

In this free country every man is at perfect liberty to publish his own thoughts and impressions, and any witness who may differ from me should publish his own version of facts in the truthful narration of which he is interested. I am publishing my own memoirs, not theirs, and we all know that no three honest witnesses of a simple brawl can agree on all the details. How much more likely will be the difference in a great battle covering a vast space of broken ground, when each division, brigade, regiment, and even company, naturally and honestly believes that it was the focus of the whole affair! Each of them won the battle. None ever lost. That was the fate of the old man who unhappily commanded.

In this edition I give the best maps which I believe have ever been prepared, compiled by General O. M. Poe, from personal knowledge and official surveys, and what I chiefly aim to establish is the true cause of the results which are already known to the whole world; and it may be a relief to many to know that I shall publish no other, but, like the player at cards, will "stand;" not that I have accomplished perfection, but because I can do no better with the cards in hand. Of omissions there are plenty, but of wilful perversion of facts, none.

In the preface to the first edition, in 1875, I used these words: "Nearly ten years have passed since the close of the civil war in America, and yet no satisfactory history thereof is accessible to the public; nor should any be attempted until the Government has published, and placed within the reach of students, the abundant materials that are buried in the War Department at Washington. These are in process of compilation; but, at the rate of progress for the past ten years, it is probable that a new century will come before they are published and circulated, with full indexes to enable the historian to make a judicious selection of materials"

Another decade is past, and I am in possession of all these publications, my last being Volume XI, Part 3, Series 1, the last date in which is August 30, 1862. I am afraid that if I assume again the character of prophet, I must extend the time deep into the next century, and pray meanwhile that the official records of the war, Union and Confederate, may approach completion before the "next war," or rather that we, as a people, may be spared another war until the last one is officially recorded. Meantime the rising generation must be content with memoirs and histories compiled from the best sources available.

In this sense I offer mine as to the events of which I was an eye-witness and participant, or for which I was responsible.

WILLIAM T. SHERMAN,
General (retired).

St. Louis, Missouri, March 30, 1885.

MEMOIRS OF
GENERAL WILLIAM T. SHERMAN.

CHAPTER I.
FROM 1820 TO THE MEXICAN WAR.

1820-1846.

According to Cothren, in his "History of Ancient Woodbury, Connecticut," the Sherman family came from Dedham, Essex County, England. The first recorded name is of Edmond Sherman, with his three sons, Edmond, Samuel, and John, who were at Boston before 1636; and farther it is distinctly recorded that Hon. Samuel Sherman, Rev. John, his brother, and Captain John, his first cousin, arrived from Dedham, Essex County, England, in 1634. Samuel afterward married Sarah Mitchell, who had come (in the same ship) from England, and finally settled at Stratford, Connecticut. The other two (Johns) located at Watertown, Massachusetts.

From Captain John Sherman are descended Roger Sherman, the signer of the Declaration of Independence, Hon. William M. Evarts, the Messrs. Hoar, of Massachusetts,

2

and many others of national fame. Our own family are descended from the Hon. Samuel Sherman and his son; the Rev. John, who was born in 1650-'51; then another John, born in 1687; then Judge Daniel, born in 1721; then Taylor Sherman, our grandfather, who was born in 1758. Taylor Sherman was a lawyer and judge in Norwalk, Connecticut, where he resided until his death, May 4, 1815; leaving a widow, Betsey Stoddard Sherman, and three children, Charles R. (our father), Daniel, and Betsey.

When the State of Connecticut, in 1786, ceded to the United States her claim to the western part of her public domain, as defined by her Royal Charter, she reserved a large district in what is now northern Ohio, a portion of which (five hundred thousand acres) composed the "Fire-Land District," which was set apart to indemnify the parties who had lost property in Connecticut by the raids of Generals Arnold, Tryon, and others during the latter part of the Revolutionary War.

Our grandfather, Judge Taylor Sherman, was one of the commissioners appointed by the State of Connecticut to quiet the Indian title, and to survey and subdivide this Fire-Land District, which includes the present counties of Huron and Erie. In his capacity as commissioner he made several trips to Ohio in the early part of this century, and it is supposed that he then contracted the disease which proved fatal. For his labor and losses he received a title to two sections of land, which fact was probably the prime cause of the migration of our family to the West. My father received a good education, and was admitted to the bar at Norwalk, Connecticut, where, in 1810, he, at twenty years of age, married Mary Hoyt, also of Norwalk, and at once migrated to Ohio, leaving his wife (my mother) for a time. His first purpose was to settle at Zanesville, Ohio, but he finally chose Lancaster, Fairfield County, where he at once engaged in the practice of his profession. In 1811 he returned to Norwalk, where, meantime, was born Charles Taylor Sherman, the eldest of the family, who with his mother was carried to Ohio on horseback.

Judge Taylor Sherman's family remained in Norwalk till 1815, when his death led to the emigration of the remainder of the family, viz., of Uncle Daniel Sherman, who settled at Monroeville, Ohio, as a farmer, where he lived and died quite recently, leaving children and grandchildren; and an aunt, Betsey, who married Judge Parker, of Mansfield, and died in 1851, leaving children and grandchildren; also Grandmother Elizabeth Stoddard Sherman, who resided with her daughter, Mrs. Betsey Parker, in Mansfield until her death, August 1,1848.

Thus my father, Charles R. Sherman, became finally established at Lancaster, Ohio, as a lawyer, with his own family in the year 1811, and continued there till the time of his death, in 1829. I have no doubt that he was in the first instance attracted to Lancaster by the natural beauty of its scenery, and the charms of its already established society. He continued in the practice of his profession, which in those days was no sinecure, for the ordinary circuit was made on horseback, and embraced Marietta, Cincinnati, and Detroit. Hardly was the family established there when the War of 1812 caused great alarm and distress in all Ohio. The English captured Detroit and the shores of Lake Erie down to the Maumee River; while the Indians still occupied the greater part of the State. Nearly every man had to be somewhat of a soldier, but I think my father was only a commissary; still, he seems to have caught a fancy for the great chief of the Shawnees, "Tecumseh."

Perry's victory on Lake Erie was the turning-point of the Western campaign, and General Harrison's victory over the British and Indians at the river Thames in Canada ended the war in the West, and restored peace and tranquillity to the exposed settlers of Ohio. My father at once resumed his practice at the bar, and was soon recognized as an able and successful lawyer. When, in 1816, my brother James was born, he insisted on engrafting the Indian name "Tecumseh" on the usual family list. My mother had already named her first son after her own brother Charles; and insisted on the second son taking the name of her other brother James, and when I came along, on the 8th of February, 1820, mother having no more brothers, my father succeeded in his original purpose, and named me William Tecumseh.

The family rapidly increased till it embraced six boys and five girls, all of whom attained maturity and married; of these six are still living.

In the year 1821 a vacancy occurred in the Supreme Court of Ohio, and I find this petition:

Somerset, Ohio, July 6, 1821.

May it please your Excellency:

We ask leave to recommend to your Excellency's favorable notice Charles R. Sherman, Esq., of Lancaster, as a man possessing in an eminent degree those qualifications so much to be desired in a Judge of the Supreme Court.

From a long acquaintance with Mr. Sherman, we are happy to be able to state to your Excellency that our minds are led to the conclusion that that gentleman possesses a disposition noble and generous, a mind discriminating, comprehensive, and combining a heart pure, benevolent and humane. Manners dignified, mild, and complaisant, and a firmness not to be shaken and of unquestioned integrity.

But Mr. Sherman's character cannot be unknown to your Excellency, and on that acquaintance without further comment we might safely rest his pretensions.

We think we hazard little in assuring your Excellency that his appointment would give almost universal satisfaction to the citizens of Perry County.

With great consideration, we have the honor to be

Your Excellency's most obedient humble servants,

CHARLES A. HOOD,
GEORGE TREAT,
PETER DITTOR,
P. ODLIN,
J. B. ORTEN,
T. BECKWITH,
WILLIAM P. DORST,
JOHN MURRAY,
JACOB MOINS,
B. EATON,
DANIEL GRIGGS,
HENRY DITTOE,
NICHOLAS McCARTY.

His Excellency ETHAN A. BROWN,
Governor of Ohio, Columbus.

He was soon after appointed a Judge of the Supreme Court, and served in that capacity to the day of his death.

My memory extends back to about 1827, and I recall him, returning home on horseback, when all the boys used to run and contend for the privilege of riding his horse from the front door back to the stable. On one occasion, I was the first, and being mounted rode to the stable; but "Old Dick" was impatient because the stable-door was not opened promptly, so he started for the barn of our neighbor Mr. King; there, also, no one was in waiting to open the gate, and, after a reasonable time, "Dick" started back for home somewhat in a hurry, and threw me among a pile of stones, in front of preacher Wright's house, where I was picked up apparently a dead boy; but my time was not yet, and I recovered, though the scars remain to this day.

The year 1829 was a sad one to our family. We were then ten children, my eldest brother Charles absent at the State University, Athens, Ohio; my next brother, James, in a store at Cincinnati; and the rest were at home, at school. Father was away on the circuit. One day Jane Sturgeon came to the school, called us out, and when we reached home all was lamentation: news had come that father was ill unto death, at Lebanon, a hundred miles away. Mother started at once, by coach, but met the news of his death about Washington, and returned home. He had ridden on horseback from Cincinnati to Lebanon to hold court, during a hot day in June. On the next day he took his seat on the bench, opened court in the forenoon, but in the afternoon, after recess, was seized with a severe chill and had to adjourn the court. The best medical aid was called in, and for three days with apparent success, but the fever then assumed a more dangerous type, and he gradually yielded to it, dying on the sixth day, viz., June 24, 1829.

My brother James had been summoned from Cincinnati, and was present at his bedside, as was also Henry Stoddard, Esq., of Dayton, Ohio, our cousin. Mr. Stoddard once told me that the cause of my father's death was cholera; but at that time, 1829, there was no Asiatic cholera in the United States, and the family, attributed his death to exposure to the hot sun of June, and a consequent fever, "typhoid."

From the resolutions of the bench, bar, and public generally, now in my possession, his death was universally deplored; more especially by his neighbors in Lancaster, and by the Society of Freemasons, of which he was the High-Priest of Arch Chapter No. 11.

His death left the family very poor, but friends rose up with proffers of generous care and assistance; for all the neighbors knew that mother could not maintain so large a family without help. My eldest brother, Charles, had nearly completed his education at the university at Athens, and concluded to go to his uncle, Judge Parker, at Mansfield, Ohio, to study law. My eldest sister, Elizabeth, soon after married William J. Reese, Esq.; James was already in a store at Cincinnati; and, with the exception of the three youngest children, the rest of us were scattered. I fell to the charge of the Hon. Thomas Ewing, who took me to his family, and ever after treated me as his own son.

I continued at the Academy in Lancaster, which was the best in the place; indeed, as good a school as any in Ohio. We studied all the common branches of knowledge, including Latin, Greek, and French. At first the school was kept by Mr. Parsons; he was succeeded by Mr. Brown, and he by two brothers, Samuel and Mark How. These were all excellent teachers, and we made good progress, first at the old academy and afterward at a new school-house, built by Samuel How, in the orchard of Hugh Boyle, Esq.

Time passed with us as with boys generally. Mr. Ewing was in the United States Senate, and I was notified to prepare for West Point, of which institution we had little knowledge, except that it was very strict, and that the army was its natural consequence. In 1834 I was large for my age, and the construction of canals was the rage in Ohio. A canal was projected to connect with the great Ohio Canal at Carroll (eight miles above Lancaster), down the valley of the Hock Hocking to Athens (forty-four miles), and thence to the Ohio River by slack water.

Preacher Carpenter, of Lancaster, was appointed to make the preliminary surveys, and selected the necessary working party out of the boys of the town. From our school were chosen _____Wilson, Emanuel Geisy, William King, and myself. Geisy and I were the rod-men. We worked during that fall and next spring, marking two experimental lines, and for our work we each received a silver half-dollar for each day's actual work, the first money any of us had ever earned.

In June, 1835, one of our school-fellows, William Irvin, was appointed a cadet to West Point, and, as it required sixteen years of age for admission, I had to wait another year. During the autumn of 1835 and spring of 1836 I devoted myself chiefly to mathematics and French, which were known to be the chief requisites for admission to West Point.

Some time in the spring of 1836 I received through Mr. Ewing, then at Washington, from the Secretary of War, Mr. Poinsett, the letter of appointment as a cadet, with a list of the articles of clothing necessary to be taken along, all of which were liberally provided by

Mrs. Ewing; and with orders to report to Mr. Ewing, at Washington, by a certain date, I left Lancaster about the 20th of May in the stage-coach for Zanesville. There we transferred to the coaches of the Great National Road, the highway of travel from the West to the East. The stages generally travelled in gangs of from one to six coaches, each drawn by four good horses, carrying nine passengers inside and three or four outside.

In about three days, travelling day and night, we reached Frederick, Maryland. There we were told that we could take rail-cars to Baltimore, and thence to Washington; but there was also a two-horse hack ready to start for Washington direct. Not having full faith in the novel and dangerous railroad, I stuck to the coach, and in the night reached Gadsby's Hotel in Washington City.

The next morning I hunted up Mr. Ewing, and found him boarding with a mess of Senators at Mrs. Hill's, corner of Third and C Streets, and transferred my trunk to the same place. I spent a week in Washington, and think I saw more of the place in that time than I ever have since in the many years of residence there. General Jackson was President, and was at the zenith of his fame. I recall looking at him a full hour, one morning, through the wood railing on Pennsylvania Avenue, as he paced up and down the gravel walk on the north front of the White House. He wore a cap and an overcoat so full that his form seemed smaller than I had expected. I also recall the appearance of Postmaster-General Amos Kendall, of Vice-President Van Buren, Messrs. Calhoun, Webster, Clay, Cass, Silas Wright, etc.

In due time I took my departure for West Point with Cadets Belt and Bronaugh. These were appointed cadets as from Ohio, although neither had ever seen that State. But in those days there were fewer applicants from Ohio than now, and near the close of the term the vacancies unasked for were usually filled from applicants on the spot. Neither of these parties, however, graduated, so the State of Ohio lost nothing. We went to Baltimore by rail, there took a boat up to Havre de Grace, then the rail to Wilmington, Delaware, and up the Delaware in a boat to Philadelphia. I staid over in Philadelphia one day at the old Mansion House, to visit the family of my brother-in-law, Mr. Reese. I found his father a fine sample of the old merchant gentleman, in a good house in Arch Street, with his accomplished daughters, who had been to Ohio, and whom I had seen there. From Philadelphia we took boat to Bordentown, rail to Amboy, and boat again to New York City, stopping at the American Hotel. I staid a week in New York City, visiting my uncle, Charles Hoyt, at his beautiful place on Brooklyn Heights, and my uncle James, then living in White Street. My friend William Scott was there, the young husband of my cousin, Louise Hoyt; a neatly-dressed young fellow, who looked on me as an untamed animal just caught in the far West— "fit food for gunpowder," and good for nothing else.

About June 12th I embarked in the steamer Cornelius Vanderbilt for West Point; registered in the office of Lieutenant C. F. Smith, Adjutant of the Military Academy, as a new cadet of the class of 1836, and at once became installed as the "plebe" of my fellow-townsman, William Irvin, then entering his Third Class.

Colonel R. E. De Russy was Superintendent; Major John Fowle, Sixth United States Infantry, Commandant. The principal Professors were: Mahan, Engineering; Bartlett, Natural Philosophy; Bailey, Chemistry; Church, Mathematics; Weir, Drawing; and Berard, French.

The routine of military training and of instruction was then fully established, and has remained almost the same ever since. To give a mere outline would swell this to an inconvenient size, and I therefore merely state that I went through the regular course of four years, graduating in June, 1840, number six in a class of forty-three. These forty-three were all that remained of more than one hundred which originally constituted the class. At the Academy I was not considered a good soldier, for at no time was I selected for any office, but remained a private throughout the whole four years. Then, as now, neatness in dress and form, with a strict conformity to the rules, were the qualifications required for office, and I suppose I was found not to excel in any of these. In studies I always held a respectable reputation with the professors, and generally ranked among the best, especially in drawing, chemistry, mathematics, and natural philosophy. My average demerits, per annum, were about one hundred and fifty, which. reduced my final class standing from number four to six.

In June, 1840, after the final examination, the class graduated and we received our diplomas. Meantime, Major Delafield, United States Engineers, had become Superintendent; Major C. F. Smith, Commandant of Cadets; but the corps of professors and assistants remained almost unchanged during our whole term. We were all granted the usual furlough of three months, and parted for our homes, there to await assignment to our respective corps and regiments. In due season I was appointed and commissioned second-lieutenant, Third Artillery, and ordered to report at Governor's Island, New York Harbor, at the end of September. I spent my furlough mostly at Lancaster and Mansfield, Ohio; toward the close of September returned to New York, reported to Major Justin Dimock, commanding the recruiting rendezvous at Governor's Island, and was assigned to command a company of recruits preparing for service in Florida. Early in October this company was detailed, as one of four, to embark in a sailing-vessel for Savannah, Georgia, under command of Captain and Brevet Major Penrose. We embarked and sailed, reaching Savannah about the middle of October, where we transferred to a small steamer and proceeded by the inland route to St. Augustine, Florida. We reached St. Augustine at the same time with the Eighth Infantry, commanded by Colonel and Brevet Brigadier-General William J. Worth. At that time General Zachary Taylor was in chief command in Florida, and had his headquarters at Tampa Bay. My regiment, the Third Artillery, occupied the posts along the Atlantic coast of Florida, from St. Augustine south to Key Biscayne, and my own company, A, was at Fort Pierce, Indian River. At St. Augustine I was detached from the company of recruits, which was designed for the Second Infantry, and was ordered to join my proper company at Fort Pierce. Colonel William Gates commanded the regiment, with Lieutenant William Austine Brown as adjutant of the regiment. Lieutenant Bragg commanded the post of St. Augustine with his own company, E, and G (Garner's), then commanded by Lieutenant Judd. In, a few days I embarked in the little steamer William Gaston down the coast, stopping one day at New Smyrna, held by John R. Vinton's company (B), with which was serving Lieutenant William H. Shover.

In due season we arrived off the bar of Indian River and anchored. A whale-boat came off with a crew of four men, steered by a character of some note, known as the Pilot Ashlock. I transferred self and baggage to this boat, and, with the mails, was carried through the surf over the bar, into the mouth of Indian River Inlet. It was then dark; we transferred to a smaller boat, and the same crew pulled us up through a channel in the middle of Mangrove Islands, the roosting-place of thousands of pelicans and birds that rose in clouds and circled above our heads. The water below was alive with fish, whose course through it could be seen by the phosphoric wake; and Ashlock told me many a tale of the Indian war then in progress, and of his adventures in hunting and fishing, which he described as the best in the world. About two miles from the bar, we emerged into the lagoon, a broad expanse of shallow water that lies parallel with the coast, separated from it by a narrow strip of sand, backed by a continuous series of islands and promontories, covered with a dense growth of mangrove and saw-palmetto. Pulling across this lagoon, in about three more miles we approached the lights of Fort Pierce. Reaching a small wharf, we landed, and were met by the officers of the post, Lieutenants George Taylor and Edward J. Steptoe, and Assistant-Surgeon James Simons. Taking the mail-bag, we walked up a steep sand-bluff on which the fort was situated, and across the parade-ground to the officers' quarters. These were six or seven log-houses, thatched with palmetto-leaves, built on high posts, with a porch in front, facing the water. The men's quarters were also of logs forming the two sides of a rectangle, open toward the water; the intervals and flanks were closed with log stockades. I was assigned to one of these rooms, and at once began service with my company, A, then commanded by Lieutenant Taylor.

The season was hardly yet come for active operations against the Indians, so that the officers were naturally attracted to Ashlock, who was the best fisherman I ever saw. He soon initiated us into the mysteries of shark-spearing, trolling for red-fish, and taking the sheep's-head and mullet. These abounded so that we could at any time catch an unlimited quantity at pleasure. The companies also owned nets for catching green turtles. These nets had meshes about a foot square, were set across channels in the lagoon, the ends secured to stakes driven into the mad, the lower line sunk with lead or stone weights and the upper line floated with

7

cork. We usually visited these nets twice a day, and found from one to six green turtles entangled in the meshes. Disengaging them, they were carried to pens, made with stakes stuck in the mud, where they were fed with mangrove-leaves, and our cooks had at all times an ample supply of the best of green turtles. They were so cheap and common that the soldiers regarded it as an imposition when compelled to eat green turtle steaks, instead of poor Florida beef, or the usual barrelled mess-pork. I do not recall in my whole experience a spot on earth where fish, oysters, and green turtles so abound as at Fort Pierce, Florida.

In November, Major Childs arrived with Lieutenant Van Vliet and a detachment of recruits to fill our two companies, and preparations were at once begun for active operations in the field. At that time the Indians in the Peninsula of Florida were scattered, and the war consisted in hunting up and securing the small fragments, to be sent to join the others of their tribe of Seminoles already established in the Indian Territory west of Arkansas. Our expeditions were mostly made in boats in the lagoons extending from the "Haul-over," near two hundred miles above the fort, down to Jupiter Inlet, about fifty miles below, and in the many streams which emptied therein. Many such expeditions were made during that winter, with more or less success, in which we succeeded in picking up small parties of men, women, and children. On one occasion, near the "Haul-over," when I was not present, the expedition was more successful. It struck a party of nearly fifty Indians, killed several warriors, and captured others. In this expedition my classmate, lieutenant Van Vliet, who was an excellent shot, killed a warrior who was running at full speed among trees, and one of the sergeants of our company (Broderick) was said to have dispatched three warriors, and it was reported that he took the scalp of one and brought it in to the fort as a trophy. Broderick was so elated that, on reaching the post, he had to celebrate his victory by a big drunk.

There was at the time a poor, weakly soldier of our company whose wife cooked for our mess. She was somewhat of a flirt, and rather fond of admiration. Sergeant Broderick was attracted to her, and hung around the mess-house more than the husband fancied; so he reported the matter to Lieutenant Taylor, who reproved Broderick for his behavior. A few days afterward the husband again appealed to his commanding officer (Taylor), who exclaimed: "Haven't you got a musket? Can't you defend your own family?" Very soon after a shot was heard down by the mess-house, and it transpired that the husband had actually shot Broderick, inflicting a wound which proved mortal. The law and army regulations required that the man should be sent to the nearest civil court, which was at St. Augustine; accordingly, the prisoner and necessary witnesses were sent up by the next monthly steamer. Among the latter were lieutenant Taylor and the pilot Ashlock.

After they had been gone about a month, the sentinel on the roof-top of our quarters reported the smoke of a steamer approaching the bar, and, as I was acting quartermaster, I took a boat and pulled down to get the mail. I reached the log-but in which the pilots lived, and saw them start with their boat across the bar, board the steamer, and then return. Ashlock was at his old post at the steering-oar, with two ladies, who soon came to the landing, having passed through a very heavy surf, and I was presented to one as Mrs. Ashlock, and the other as her sister, a very pretty little Minorcan girl of about fourteen years of age. Mrs. Ashlock herself was probably eighteen or twenty years old, and a very handsome woman. I was hurriedly informed that the murder trial was in progress at St. Augustine; that Ashlock had given his testimony, and had availed himself of the chance to take a wife to share with him the solitude of his desolate hut on the beach at Indian River. He had brought ashore his wife, her sister, and their chests, with the mail, and had orders to return immediately to the steamer (Gaston or Harney) to bring ashore some soldiers belonging to another company, E (Braggs), which had been ordered from St. Augustine to Fort Pierce. Ashlock left his wife and her sister standing on the beach near the pilot-hut, and started back with his whale-boat across the bar. I also took the mail and started up to the fort, and had hardly reached the wharf when I observed another boat following me. As soon as this reached the wharf the men reported that Ashlock and all his crew, with the exception of one man, had been drowned a few minutes after I had left the beach. They said his surf-boat had reached the steamer, had taken on board a load of soldiers, some eight or ten, and had started back through the surf, when on the bar a heavy breaker upset the boat, and all were lost except the boy who pulled the bow-oar, who clung to the rope or painter, hauled himself to the upset boat, held on, drifted with it outside the breakers, and was finally beached near a mile down the coast. They reported also that the steamer had got up anchor, run in as close to the bar as she could, paused awhile, and then had started down the coast.

I instantly took a fresh crew of soldiers and returned to the bar; there sat poor Mrs. Ashlock on her chest of clothes, a weeping widow, who had seen her husband perish amid sharks and waves; she clung to the hope that the steamer had picked him up, but, strange to say, he could not swim, although he had been employed on the water all his life.

Her sister was more demonstrative, and wailed as one lost to all hope and life. She appealed to us all to do miracles to save the struggling men in the waves, though two hours had already passed, and to have gone out then among those heavy breakers, with an inexperienced crew, would have been worse than suicide. All I could do was to reorganize the guard at the beach, take the two desolate females up to the fort, and give them the use of my own quarters. Very soon their anguish was quieted, and they began to look, for the return of their steamer with Ashlock and his rescued crew. The next day I went again to the beach with Lieutenant Ord, and we found that one or two bodies had been washed ashore, torn all to pieces by the sharks, which literally swarmed the inlet at every new tide. In a few days the weather moderated, and the steamer returned from the south, but the surf was so high that she anchored a mile off. I went out myself, in the whale or surf boat, over that terrible bar with a crew of, soldiers, boarded the steamer, and learned that none other of Ashlock's crew except the one before mentioned had been saved; but, on the contrary, the captain of the steamer had sent one of his own boats to their rescue, which was likewise upset in the surf, and, out of the three men in her, one had drifted back outside the breakers, clinging to the upturned boat, and was picked up. This sad and fatal catastrophe made us all afraid of that bar, and in returning to the shore I adopted the more prudent course of beaching the boat below the inlet, which insured us a good ducking, but was attended with less risk to life.

I had to return to the fort and bear to Mrs. Ashlock the absolute truth, that her husband was lost forever.

Meantime her sister had entirely recovered her equilibrium, and being the guest of the officers, who were extremely courteous to her, she did not lament so loudly the calamity that saved them a long life of banishment on the beach of Indian River. By the first opportunity they were sent back to St. Augustine, the possessors of all of Ashlock's worldly goods and effects, consisting of a good rifle, several cast-nets, hand-lines, etc., etc., besides some three hundred dollars in money, which was due him by the quartermaster for his services as pilot. I afterward saw these ladies at St. Augustine, and years afterward the younger one came to Charleston, South Carolina, the wife of the somewhat famous Captain Thistle, agent for the United States for live-oak in Florida, who was noted as the first of the troublesome class of inventors of modern artillery. He was the inventor of a gun that "did not recoil at all," or "if anything it recoiled a little forward."

One day, in the summer of 1841, the sentinel on the housetop at Fort Pierce called out, "Indians! Indians!" Everybody sprang to his gun, the companies formed promptly on the parade-ground, and soon were reported as approaching the post, from the pine-woods in rear, four Indians on horseback. They rode straight up to the gateway, dismounted, and came in. They were conducted by the officer of the day to the commanding officer, Major Childs, who sat on the porch in front of his own room. After the usual pause, one of them, a black man named Joe, who spoke English, said they had been sent in by Coacoochee (Wild Cat), one of the most noted of the Seminole chiefs, to see the big chief of the post. He gradually unwrapped a piece of paper, which was passed over to Major Childs, who read it, and it was in the nature of a "Safe Guard" for "Wild Cat" to come into Fort Pierce to receive provisions and assistance while collecting his tribe, with the purpose of emigrating to their reservation west of Arkansas. The paper was signed by General Worth, who had succeeded General Taylor, at Tampa Bay, in command of all the troops in Florida. Major Childs inquired, "Where is Coacoochee?" and was answered, "Close by," when Joe explained that he had been sent in by his chief to see if the paper was all right. Major Childs said it was "all right," and that Coacoochee ought to come in himself. Joe offered to go out and bring him in, when Major Childs ordered me to take eight or ten mounted men and go out to escort him in. Detailing ten men to saddle up, and taking Joe and one Indian boy along on their own ponies, I started out under their guidance.

We continued to ride five or six miles, when I began to suspect treachery, of which I had heard so much in former years, and had been specially cautioned against by the older officers; but Joe always answered, "Only a little way." At last we approached one of those close hammocks, so well known in Florida, standing like an island in the interminable pine-forest, with a pond of water near it. On its edge I noticed a few Indians loitering, which Joe pointed out as the place. Apprehensive of treachery, I halted the guard, gave orders to the sergeant to watch me closely, and rode forward alone with the two Indian guides. As we neared the hammock, about a dozen Indian warriors rose up and waited for us. When in their midst I inquired for the chief, Coacoochee. He approached my horse and, slapping his breast, said, "Me Coacoochee." He was a very handsome young Indian warrior, not more than twenty-five years old, but in his then dress could hardly be distinguished from the rest. I then explained to him, through Joe, that I had been sent by my "chief" to escort him into the fort. He wanted me to get down and "talk" I told him that I had no "talk" in me, but that, on his reaching the post, he could talk as much as he pleased with the "big chief," Major Childs. They all seemed to be indifferent, and in no hurry; and I noticed that all their guns were leaning against a tree. I beckoned to the sergeant, who advanced rapidly with his escort, and told him to secure the rifles, which he proceeded to do. Coacoochee pretended to be very angry, but I explained to him that his warriors were tired and mine were not, and that the soldiers would carry the guns on their horses. I told him I would provide him a horse to ride, and the sooner he was ready the better for all. He then stripped, washed himself in the pond, and began to dress in all his Indian finery, which consisted of buckskin leggins, moccasins, and several shirts. He then began to put on vests, one after another, and one of them had the marks of a bullet, just above the pocket, with the stain of blood. In the pocket was a one-dollar Tallahassee Bank note, and the rascal had the impudence to ask me to give him silver coin for that dollar. He had evidently killed the wearer, and was disappointed because the pocket contained a paper dollar instead of one in silver. In due time he was dressed with turban and ostrich-feathers, and mounted the horse reserved for him, and thus we rode back together to Fort Pierce. Major Childs and all the officers received him on the porch, and there we had a regular "talk." Coacoochee "was tired of the war." "His people were scattered and it would take a 'moon' to collect them for emigration," and he "wanted rations for that time," etc., etc.

All this was agreed to, and a month was allowed for him to get ready with his whole band (numbering some one hundred and fifty or one hundred and sixty) to migrate. The "talk" then ceased, and Coacoochee and his envoys proceeded to get regularly drunk, which was easily done by the agency of commissary whiskey. They staid at Fort Pierce daring the night, and the next day departed. Several times during the month there came into the post two or more of these same Indians, always to beg for something to eat or drink, and after a full month Coacoochee and about twenty of his warriors came in with several ponies, but with none of their women or children. Major Childs had not from the beginning the least faith in his sincerity; had made up his mind to seize the whole party and compel them to emigrate. He arranged for the usual council, and instructed Lieutenant Taylor to invite Coacoochee and his uncle (who was held to be a principal chief) to his room to take some good brandy, instead of the common commissary whiskey. At a signal agreed on I was to go to the quarters of Company A, to dispatch the first-sergeant and another man to Lieutenant Taylor's room, there to seize the two chiefs and secure them; and with the company I was to enter Major Childs's room and secure the remainder of the party. Meantime Lieutenant Van Vliet was ordered to go to the quarters of his company, F, and at the same signal to march rapidly to the rear of the officers' quarters, so as to catch any who might attempt to escape by the open windows to the rear.

All resulted exactly as prearranged, and in a few minutes the whole party was in irons. At first they claimed that we had acted treacherously, but very soon they admitted that for a month Coacoochee had been quietly removing his women and children toward Lake Okeechobee and the Everglades; and that this visit to our post was to have been their last. It so happened that almost at the instant of our seizing these Indians a vessel arrived off the bar with reenforcements from St. Augustine. These were brought up to Fort Pierce, and we marched that night and next day rapidly, some fifty miles, to Lake Okeechobee, in hopes to capture the balance of the tribe, especially the families, but they had taken the alarm and escaped. Coacoochee and his warriors were sent by Major Childs in a schooner to New Orleans en route to their reservation, but General Worth recalled them to Tampa Bay, and by sending out Coacoochee himself the women and children came in voluntarily, and then all were shipped to their destination. This was a heavy loss to the Seminoles, but there still remained in the Peninsula a few hundred warriors with their families scattered into very small parcels, who were concealed in the most inaccessible hammocks and swamps. These had no difficulty in finding plenty of food anywhere and everywhere. Deer and wild turkey were abundant, and as for fish there was no end to them. Indeed, Florida was the Indian's paradise, was of little value to us, and it was a great pity to remove the Seminoles at all, for we could have collected there all the Choctaws, Creeks, Cherokees, and Chickasaws, in addition to the Seminoles. They would have thrived in the Peninsula, whereas they now occupy lands that are very valuable, which are coveted by their white neighbors on all sides, while the Peninsula, of Florida still remains with a population less than should make a good State.

During that and preceding years General W. S. Harney had penetrated and crossed through the Everglades, capturing and hanging Chekika and his band, and had brought in many prisoners, who were also shipped West. We at Fort Pierce made several other excursions to Jupiter, Lake Worth, Lauderdale, and into the Everglades, picking up here and there a family, so that it was absurd any longer to call it a "war." These excursions, however, possessed to us a peculiar charm, for the fragrance of the air, the abundance of game and fish, and just enough of adventure, gave to life a relish. I had just returned to Lauderdale from one of these scouts with Lieutenants Rankin, Ord, George H. Thomas, Field, Van Vliet, and others, when I received notice of my promotion to be first lieutenant of Company G, which occurred November 30, 1841, and I was ordered to return to Fort Pierce, turn over the public property for which I was accountable to Lieutenant H. S. Burton, and then to join my new company at St. Augustine.

I reached St. Augustine before Christmas, and was assigned to command a detachment of twenty men stationed at Picolata, on the St. John's River, eighteen miles distant. At St. Augustine were still the headquarters of the regiment, Colonel William Gates, with Company E, Lieutenant Bragg, and Company G, Lieutenant H. B. Judd. The only buildings at Picolata were the one occupied by my detachment, which had been built for a hospital, and the dwelling of a family named Williams, with whom I boarded. On the other hand, St. Augustine had many pleasant families, among whom was prominent that of United States Judge Bronson. I was half my time in St. Augustine or on the road, and remember the old place with pleasure. In February we received orders transferring the whole regiment to the Gulf posts, and our company, G, was ordered to escort Colonel Gates and his family across to the Suwanee River, en route for Pensacola. The company, with the colonel and his family, reached Picolata (where my detachment joined), and we embarked in a steamboat for Pilatka. Here Lieutenant Judd discovered that he had forgotten something and had to return to St. Augustine, so that I commanded the company on the march, having with me Second-Lieutenant George B. Ayres. Our first march was to Fort Russell, then Micanopy, Wacahoota, and Wacasassee, all which posts were garrisoned by the Second or Seventh Infantry. At Wacasassee we met General Worth and his staff, en route for Pilatka. Lieutenant Judd overtook us about the Suwanee, where we embarked on a small boat for Cedar Keys, and there took a larger one for Pensacola, where the colonel and his family landed, and our company proceeded on in the same vessel to our post—Fort Morgan, Mobile Point.

This fort had not been occupied by troops for many years, was very dirty, and we found little or no stores there. Major Ogden, of the engineers, occupied a house outside the fort. I was quartermaster and commissary, and, taking advantage of one of the engineer schooners engaged in bringing materials for the fort, I went up to Mobile city, and, through the agency of Messrs. Deshon, Taylor, and Myers, merchants, procured all essentials for the troops, and returned to the post. In the course of a week or ten days arrived another company, H, commanded by Lieutenant James Ketchum, with Lieutenants Rankin and Sewall L. Fish, and an assistant surgeon (Wells.) Ketchum became the commanding officer, and Lieutenant Rankin quartermaster. We proceeded to put the post in as good order as possible; had regular guard-mounting and parades, but little drill. We found magnificent fishing with the seine on the outer beach, and sometimes in a single haul we would take ten or fifteen barrels of the best kind of fish, embracing pompinos, red-fish, snappers, etc.

We remained there till June, when the regiment was ordered to exchange from the Gulf posts to those on the Atlantic, extending from Savannah to North Carolina. The brig Wetumpka was chartered, and our company (G) embarked and sailed to Pensacola, where we took on board another company (D) (Burke's), commanded by Lieutenant H. S. Burton, with Colonel Gates, the regimental headquarters, and some families. From Pensacola we sailed for Charleston, South Carolina. The weather was hot, the winds light, and we made a long passage but at last reached Charleston Harbor, disembarked, and took post in Fort Moultrie.

Soon after two other companies arrived, Bragg's (B) and Keyes's (K). The two former companies were already quartered inside of Fort Moultrie, and these latter were placed in gun-sheds, outside, which were altered into barracks. We remained at Fort Moultrie nearly five years, until the Mexican War scattered us forever. Our life there was of strict garrison duty, with plenty of leisure for hunting and social entertainments. We soon formed many and most pleasant acquaintances in the city of Charleston; and it so happened that many of the families resided at Sullivan's Island in the summer season, where we could reciprocate the hospitalities extended to us in the winter.

During the summer of 1843, having been continuously on duty for three years, I applied for and received a leave of absence for three months, which I spent mostly in Ohio. In November I started to return to my post at Charleston by way of New Orleans; took the stage to Chillicothe, Ohio, November 16th, having Henry Stanberry, Esq., and wife, as travelling companions, We continued by stage. next day to Portsmouth, Ohio.

At Portsmouth Mr. Stanberry took a boat up the river, and I one down to Cincinnati. There I found my brothers Lampson and Hoyt employed in the "Gazette" printing-office, and spent much time with them and Charles Anderson, Esq., visiting his brother Larz, Mr. Longworth, some of his artist friends, and especially Miss Sallie Carneal, then quite a belle, and noted for her fine voice,

On the 20th I took passage on the steamboat Manhattan for St. Louis; reached Louisville, where Dr. Conrad, of the army, joined me, and in the Manhattan we continued on to St. Louis, with a mixed crowd. We reached the Mississippi at Cairo the 23d, and St. Louis, Friday, November 24, 1843. At St. Louis we called on Colonel S. W. Kearney and Major Cooper, his adjutant-general, and found my classmate, Lieutenant McNutt, of the ordnance, stationed at the arsenal; also Mr. Deas, an artist, and Pacificus Ord, who was studying law. I spent a week at St. Louis, visiting the arsenal, Jefferson Barracks, and most places of interest, and then became impressed with its great future. It then contained about forty thousand people, and my notes describe thirty-six good steamboats receiving and discharging cargo at the levee.

I took passage December 4th in the steamer John Aull for New Orleans. As we passed Cairo the snow was falling, and the country was wintery and devoid of verdure. Gradually, however, as we proceeded south, the green color came; grass and trees showed the change of latitude, and when in the course of a week we had reached New Orleans, the roses were in full bloom, the sugar-cane just ripe, and a tropical air prevalent. We reached New Orleans December 11, 1843, where I spent about a week visiting the barracks, then occupied by the Seventh Infantry; the theatres, hotels, and all the usual places of interest of that day.

On the 16th of December I continued on to Mobile in the steamer Fashion by way of Lake Pontchartrain; saw there most of my personal friends, Mr. and Mrs. Bull, Judge Bragg and his brother Dunbar, Deshon, Taylor, and Myers, etc., and on the 19th of December took passage in the steamboat Bourbon for Montgomery, Alabama, by way of the Alabama River. We reached Montgomery at noon, December 23d, and took cars at 1 p. m. for Franklin, forty miles, which we reached at 7 p. m., thence stages for Griffin, Georgia, via La

Grange and Greenville. This took the whole night of the 23d and the day of the 24th. At Griffin we took cars for Macon, and thence to Savannah, which we reached Christmas-night, finding Lieutenants Ridgley and Ketchum at tea, where we were soon joined by Rankin and Beckwith.

On the 26th I took the boat for Charleston, reaching my post, and reported for duty Wednesday morning, December 27, 1843.

I had hardly got back to my post when, on the 21st of January, 1844, I received from Lieutenant R. P. Hammond, at Marietta, Georgia, an intimation that Colonel Churchill, Inspector-General of the Army, had applied for me to assist him in taking depositions in upper Georgia and Alabama; concerning certain losses by volunteers in Florida of horses and equipments by reason of the failure of the United States to provide sufficient forage, and for which Congress had made an appropriation. On the 4th of February the order came from the Adjutant-General in Washington for me to proceed to Marietta, Georgia, and report to Inspector-General Churchill. I was delayed till the 14th of February by reason of being on a court-martial, when I was duly relieved and started by rail to Augusta, Georgia, and as far as Madison, where I took the mail-coach, reaching Marietta on the 17th. There I reported for duty to Colonel Churchill, who was already engaged on his work, assisted by Lieutenant R. P. Hammond, Third Artillery, and a citizen named Stockton. The colonel had his family with him, consisting of Mrs. Churchill, Mary, now Mrs. Professor Baird, and Charles Churchill, then a boy of about fifteen years of age.

We all lived in a tavern, and had an office convenient. The duty consisted in taking individual depositions of the officers and men who had composed two regiments and a battalion of mounted volunteers that had served in Florida. An oath was administered to each man by Colonel Churchill, who then turned the claimant over to one of us to take down and record his deposition according to certain forms, which enabled them to be consolidated and tabulated. We remained in Marietta about six weeks, during which time I repeatedly rode to Kenesaw Mountain, and over the very ground where afterward, in 1864, we had some hard battles.

After closing our business at Marietta the colonel ordered us to transfer our operations to Bellefonte, Alabama. As he proposed to take his family and party by the stage, Hammond lent me his riding-horse, which I rode to Allatoona and the Etowah River. Hearing of certain large Indian mounds near the way, I turned to one side to visit them, stopping a couple of days with Colonel Lewis Tumlin, on whose plantation these mounds were. We struck up such an acquaintance that we corresponded for some years, and as I passed his plantation during the war, in 1864, I inquired for him, but he was not at home. From Tumlin's I rode to Rome, and by way of Wills Valley over Sand Mountain and the Raccoon Range to the Tennessee River at Bellefonte, Alabama. We all assembled there in March, and continued our work for nearly two months, when, having completed the business, Colonel Churchill, with his family, went North by way of Nashville; Hammond, Stockton, and I returning South on horseback, by Rome, Allatoona, Marietta, Atlanta, and Madison, Georgia. Stockton stopped at Marietta, where he resided. Hammond took the cars at Madison, and I rode alone to Augusta, Georgia, where I left the horse and returned to Charleston and Fort Moultrie by rail.

Thus by a mere accident I was enabled to traverse on horseback the very ground where in after-years I had to conduct vast armies and fight great battles. That the knowledge thus acquired was of infinite use to me, and consequently to the Government, I have always felt and stated.

During the autumn of 1844, a difficulty arose among the officers of Company B, Third Artillery (John R. Yinton's), garrisoning Augusta Arsenal, and I was sent up from Fort Moultrie as a sort of peace-maker. After staying there some months, certain transfers of officers were made, which reconciled the difficulty, and I returned to my post, Fort Moultrie. During that winter, 1844-'45, I was visiting at the plantation of Mr. Poyas, on the east branch of the Cooper, about fifty miles from Fort Moultrie, hunting deer with his son James, and Lieutenant John F. Reynolds, Third Artillery. We had taken our stands, and a deer came out of the swamp near that of Mr. James Poyas, who fired, broke the leg of the deer, which turned back into the swamp and came out again above mine. I could follow his course by the cry of the hounds, which were in close pursuit. Hastily mounting my horse, I struck across the pine-woods to head the deer off, and when at full career my horse leaped a fallen log and his fore-foot caught one of those hard, unyielding pineknots that brought him with violence to the ground. I got up as quick as possible, and found my right arm out of place at the shoulder, caused by the weight of the double-barrelled gun.

Seeing Reynolds at some distance, I called out lustily and brought him to me. He soon mended the bridle and saddle, which had been broken by the fall, helped me on my horse, and we followed the coarse of the hounds. At first my arm did not pain me much, but it soon began to ache so that it was almost unendurable. In about three miles we came to a negro hut, where I got off and rested till Reynolds could overtake Poyas and bring him back. They came at last, but by that time the arm was so swollen and painful that I could not ride. They rigged up an old gig belonging to the negro, in which I was carried six miles to the plantation of Mr. Poyas, Sr. A neighboring physician was sent for, who tried the usual methods of setting the arm, but without success; each time making the operation more painful. At last he sent off, got a set of double pulleys and cords, with which he succeeded in extending the muscles and in getting the bone into place. I then returned to Fort Moultrie, but being disabled, applied for a short leave and went North.

I started January 25,1845; went to Washington, Baltimore, and Lancaster, Ohio, whence I went to Mansfield, and thence back by Newark to Wheeling, Cumberland, Baltimore, Philadelphia, and New York, whence I sailed back for Charleston on the ship Sullivan, reaching Fort Moultrie March 9, 1845.

About that time (March 1, 1845) Congress had, by a joint resolution, provided for the annexation of Texas, then an independent Republic, subject to certain conditions requiring the acceptance of the Republic of Texas to be final and conclusive. We all expected war as a matter of course. At that time General Zachary Taylor had assembled a couple of regiments of infantry and one of dragoons at Fort Jessup, Louisiana, and had orders to extend military protection to Texas against the Indians, or a "foreign enemy," the moment the terms of annexation were accepted. He received notice of such acceptance July 7th, and forthwith proceeded to remove his troops to Corpus Christi, Texas, where, during the summer and fall of 1845, was assembled that force with which, in the spring of 1846, was begun the Mexican War.

Some time during that summer came to Fort Moultrie orders for sending Company E, Third Artillery, Lieutenant Bragg, to New Orleans, there to receive a battery of field-guns, and thence to the camp of General Taylor at Corpus Christi. This was the first company of our regiment sent to the seat of war, and it embarked on the brig Hayne. This was the only company that left Fort Moultrie till after I was detached for recruiting service on the 1st of May, 1846.

Inasmuch as Charleston afterward became famous, as the spot where began our civil war, a general description of it, as it was in 1846, will not be out of place.

The city lies on a long peninsula between the Ashley and Cooper Rivers—a low, level peninsula, of sand. Meeting Street is its Broadway, with King Street, next west and parallel, the street of shops and small stores. These streets are crossed at right angles by many others, of which Broad Street was the principal; and the intersection of Meeting and Broad was the heart of the city, marked by the Guard-House and St. Michael's Episcopal Church. The Custom-House, Post-Office, etc., were at the foot of Broad Street, near the wharves of the Cooper River front. At the extremity of the peninsula was a drive, open to the bay, and faced by some of the handsomest houses of the city, called the "Battery." Looking down the bay on the right, was James Island, an irregular triangle of about seven miles, the whole island in cultivation with sea-island cotton. At the lower end was Fort Johnson, then simply the station of Captain Bowman, United States Engineers, engaged in building Fort Sumter. This fort (Sumter) was erected on an artificial island nearly in mid-channel, made by dumping rocks, mostly brought as ballast in cotton-ships from the North. As the rock reached the surface it was levelled, and made the foundation of Fort Sumter. In 1846 this fort was barely above the water. Still farther out beyond James Island, and separated from it by a wide space of salt marsh with crooked channels, was Morris Island, composed of the sand-dunes thrown up by the wind and the sea, backed with the salt marsh. On this was the lighthouse, but no people.

On the left, looking down the bay from the Battery of Charleston, was, first, Castle Pinckney, a round brick fort, of two tiers of guns, one in embrasure, the other in barbette, built on a marsh island, which was not garrisoned. Farther down the bay a point of the mainland reached the bay, where there was a group of houses, called Mount Pleasant; and at the extremity of the bay, distant six miles, was Sullivan's Island, presenting a smooth sand-beach to the sea, with the line of sand-hills or dunes thrown up by the waves and winds, and the usual backing of marsh and crooked salt-water channels.

At the shoulder of this island was Fort Moultrie, an irregular fort, without ditch or counterscarp, with a brick scarp wall about twelve feet high, which could be scaled anywhere, and this was surmounted by an earth parapet capable of mounting about forty twenty-four and thirty-two pounder smooth-bore iron guns. Inside the fort were three two-story brick barracks, sufficient to quarter the officers and men of two companies of artillery.

At sea was the usual "bar," changing slightly from year to year, but generally the main ship-channel came from the south, parallel to Morris Island, till it was well up to Fort Moultrie, where it curved, passing close to Fort Sumter and up to the wharves of the city, which were built mostly along the Cooper River front.

Charleston was then a proud, aristocratic city, and assumed a leadership in the public opinion of the South far out of proportion to her population, wealth, or commerce. On more than one occasion previously, the inhabitants had almost inaugurated civil war, by their assertion and professed belief that each State had, in the original compact of government, reserved to itself the right to withdraw from the Union at its own option, whenever the people supposed they had sufficient cause. We used to discuss these things at our own mess-tables, vehemently and sometimes quite angrily; but I am sure that I never feared it would go further than it had already gone in the winter of 1832-'33, when the attempt at "nullification" was promptly suppressed by President Jackson's famous declaration, "The Union must and shall be preserved!" and by the judicious management of General Scott.

Still, civil war was to be; and, now that it has come and gone, we can rest secure in the knowledge that as the chief cause, slavery, has been eradicated forever, it is not likely to come again.

CHAPTER II.
EARLY RECOLLECTIONS of CALIFORNIA.

1846-1848.

In the spring of 1846 I was a first lieutenant of Company C,1, Third Artillery, stationed at Fort Moultrie, South Carolina. The company was commanded by Captain Robert Anderson; Henry B. Judd was the senior first-lieutenant, and I was the junior first-lieutenant, and George B. Ayres was the second-lieutenant. Colonel William Gates commanded the post and regiment, with First-Lieutenant William Austine as his adjutant. Two other companies were at the post, viz., Martin Burke's and E. D. Keyes's, and among the officers were T. W. Sherman, Morris Miller, H. B. Field, William Churchill, Joseph Stewart, and Surgeon McLaren.

The country now known as Texas had been recently acquired, and war with Mexico was threatening. One of our companies (Bragg's), with George H. Thomas, John F. Reynolds, and Frank Thomas, had gone the year previous and was at that time with General Taylor's army at Corpus Christi, Texas.

In that year (1846) I received the regular detail for recruiting service, with orders to report to the general superintendent at Governor's Island, New York; and accordingly left Fort Moultrie in the latter part of April, and reported to the superintendent, Colonel R. B.

Mason, First Dragoons, at New York, on the 1st day of May. I was assigned to the Pittsburg rendezvous, whither I proceeded and relieved Lieutenant Scott. Early in May I took up my quarters at the St. Charles Hotel, and entered upon the discharge of my duties. There was a regular recruiting-station already established, with a sergeant, corporal, and two or three men, with a citizen physician, Dr. McDowell, to examine the recruits. The threatening war with Mexico made a demand for recruits, and I received authority to open another sub-rendezvous at Zanesville, Ohio, whither I took the sergeant and established him. This was very handy to me, as my home was at Lancaster, Ohio, only thirty-six miles off, so that I was thus enabled to visit my friends there quite often.

In the latter part of May, when at Wheeling, Virginia, on my way back from Zanesville to Pittsburg, I heard the first news of the battle of Palo Alto and Resaca de la Palma, which occurred on the 8th and 9th of May, and, in common with everybody else, felt intensely excited. That I should be on recruiting service, when my comrades were actually fighting, was intolerable, and I hurried on to my post, Pittsburg. At that time the railroad did not extend west of the Alleghanies, and all journeys were made by stage-coaches. In this instance I traveled from Zanesville to Wheeling, thence to Washington (Pennsylvania), and thence to Pittsburg by stage-coach. On reaching Pittsburg I found many private letters; one from Ord, then a first-lieutenant in Company F, Third Artillery, at Fort McHenry, Baltimore, saying that his company had just received orders for California, and asking me to apply for it. Without committing myself to that project, I wrote to the Adjutant-General, R. Jones, at Washington, D. C., asking him to consider me as an applicant for any active service, and saying that I would willingly forego the recruiting detail, which I well knew plenty of others would jump at. Impatient to approach the scene of active operations, without authority (and I suppose wrongfully), I left my corporal in charge of the rendezvous, and took all the recruits I had made, about twenty-five, in a steamboat to Cincinnati, and turned them over to Major N. C. McCrea, commanding at Newport Barracks. I then reported in Cincinnati, to the superintendent of the Western recruiting service, Colonel Fanning, an old officer with one arm, who inquired by what authority I had come away from my post. I argued that I took it for granted he wanted all the recruits he could get to forward to the army at Brownsville, Texas, and did not know but that he might want me to go along. Instead of appreciating my volunteer zeal, he cursed and swore at me for leaving my post without orders, and told me to go back to Pittsburg. I then asked for an order that would entitle me to transportation back, which at first he emphatically refused, but at last he gave the order, and I returned to Pittsburg, all the way by stage, stopping again at Lancaster, where I attended the wedding of my schoolmate Mike Effinger, and also visited my sub-rendezvous at Zanesville. R. S. Ewell, of my class, arrived to open a cavalry rendezvous, but, finding my depot there, he went on to Columbus, Ohio. Tom Jordan afterward was ordered to Zanesville, to take charge of that rendezvous, under the general War Department orders increasing the number of recruiting-stations. I reached Pittsburg late in June, and found the order relieving me from recruiting service, and detailing my classmate H. B. Field to my place. I was assigned to Company F, then under orders for California. By private letters from Lieutenant Ord, I heard that the company had already started from Fort McHenry for Governor's Island, New York Harbor, to take passage for California in a naval transport. I worked all that night, made up my accounts current, and turned over the balance of cash to the citizen physician, Dr. McDowell; and also closed my clothing and property returns, leaving blank receipts with the same gentleman for Field's signature, when he should get there, to be forwarded to the Department at Washington, and the duplicates to me. These I did not receive for more than a year. I remember that I got my orders about 8 p. m. one night, and took passage in the boat for Brownsville, the next morning traveled by stage from Brownsville to Cumberland, Maryland, and thence by cars to Baltimore, Philadelphia, and New York, in a great hurry lest the ship might sail without me. I found Company F at Governor's Island, Captain C. Q. Tompkins in command, Lieutenant E. O. C. Ord senior first-lieutenant, myself junior first-lieutenant, Lucien Loeser and Charles Minor the second-lieutenants.

The company had been filled up to one hundred privates, twelve non-commissioned officers, and one ordnance sergeant (Layton), making one hundred and thirteen enlisted men and five officers. Dr. James L. Ord had been employed as acting assistant surgeon to accompany the expedition, and Lieutenant H. W. Halleck, of the engineers, was also to go along. The United States store-ship Lexington was then preparing at the Navy-Yard, Brooklyn, to carry us around Cape Horn to California. She was receiving on board the necessary stores for the long voyage, and for service after our arrival there. Lieutenant-Commander Theodorus Bailey was in command of the vessel, Lieutenant William H. Macomb executive officer, and Passed-Midshipmen Muse, Spotts, and J. W. A. Nicholson, were the watch-officers; Wilson purser, and Abernethy surgeon. The latter was caterer of the mess, and we all made an advance of cash for him to lay in the necessary mess-stores. To enable us to prepare for so long a voyage and for an indefinite sojourn in that far-off country, the War Department had authorized us to draw six months' pay in advance, which sum of money we invested in surplus clothing and such other things as seemed to us necessary. At last the ship was ready, and was towed down abreast of Fort Columbus, where we were conveyed on board, and on the 14th of July, 1846, we were towed to sea by a steam-tug, and cast off: Colonel R. B. Mason, still superintendent of the general recruiting service, accompanied us down the bay and out to sea, returning with the tug. A few other friends were of the party, but at last they left us, and we were alone upon the sea, and the sailors were busy with the sails and ropes. The Lexington was an old ship, changed from a sloop-of-war to a store-ship, with an after-cabin, a "ward-room," and "between-decks." In the cabin were Captains Bailey and Tompkins, with whom messed the purser, Wilson. In the ward-room were all the other officers, two in each state-room; and Minor, being an extra lieutenant, had to sleep in a hammock slung in the ward-room. Ord and I roomed together; Halleck and Loeser and the others were scattered about. The men were arranged in bunks "between-decks," one set along the sides of the ship, and another, double tier, amidships. The crew were slung in hammocks well forward. Of these there were about fifty. We at once subdivided the company into four squads, under the four lieutenants of the company, and arranged with the naval officers that our men should serve on deck by squads, after the manner of their watches; that the sailors should do all the work aloft, and the soldiers on deck.

On fair days we drilled our men at the manual, and generally kept them employed as much as possible, giving great attention to the police and cleanliness of their dress and bunks; and so successful were we in this, that, though the voyage lasted nearly two hundred days, every man was able to leave the ship and march up the hill to the fort at Monterey, California, carrying his own knapsack and equipments.

The voyage from New York to Rio Janeiro was without accident or any thing to vary the usual monotony. We soon settled down to the humdrum of a long voyage, reading some, not much; playing games, but never gambling; and chiefly engaged in eating our meals regularly. In crossing the equator we had the usual visit of Neptune and his wife, who, with a large razor and a bucket of soapsuds, came over the sides and shaved some of the greenhorns; but naval etiquette exempted the officers, and Neptune was not permitted to come aft of the mizzen-mast. At last, after sixty days of absolute monotony, the island of Raza, off Rio Janeiro, was descried, and we slowly entered the harbor, passing a fort on our right hand, from which came a hail, in the Portuguese language, from a huge speaking-trumpet, and our officer of the deck answered back in gibberish, according to a well-understood custom of the place. Sugar-loaf Mountain, on the south of the entrance, is very remarkable and well named; is almost conical, with a slight lean. The man-of-war anchorage is about five miles inside the heads, directly in front of the city of Rio Janeiro. Words will not describe the beauty of this perfect harbor, nor the delightful feeling after a long voyage of its fragrant airs, and the entire contrast between all things there and what we had left in New York.

We found the United Staten frigate Columbia anchored there, and after the Lexington was properly moored, nearly all the officers went on shore for sight-seeing and enjoyment. We landed at a wharf opposite which was a famous French restaurant, Farroux, and after ordering supper we all proceeded to the Rua da Ouvador, where most of the shops were, especially those for making feather flowers, as much to see the pretty girls as the flowers which they so skillfully made; thence we went to the theatre, where, besides some opera, we witnessed the audience and saw the Emperor Dom Pedro, and his Empress, the daughter of the King of Sicily. After the theatre, we went back to the restaurant, where we had an excellent supper, with fruits of every variety and excellence, such as we had never seen before, or even knew the names of. Supper being over, we called for the bill, and it was rendered in French, with Brazilian currency. It footed up some twenty-six thousand reis. The figures alarmed us, so we all put on the waiters' plate various coins in gold, which he took to the counter and returned the change, making the total about sixteen dollars. The millreis is about a dollar, but being a paper-money was at a discount, so as only to be worth about fifty-six cents in coin.

The Lexington remained in Rio about a week, during which we visited the Palace, a few miles in the country, also the Botanic Gardens, a place of infinite interest, with its specimens of tropical fruits, spices; etc., etc., and indeed every place of note. The thing I best recall is a visit Halleck and I made to the Corcovado, a high mountain whence the water is conveyed for the supply of the city. We started to take a walk, and passed along the aqueduct, which approaches the city by a aeries of arches; thence up the point of the hill to a place known as the Madre, or fountain, to which all the water that drips from the leaves is conducted by tile gutters, and is carried to the city by an open stone aqueduct.

Here we found Mr. Henry A. Wise, of Virginia, the United States minister to Brazil, and a Dr. Garnett, United States Navy, his intended son-in-law. We had a very interesting conversation, in which Mr. Wise enlarged on the fact that Rio was supplied from the "dews of heaven," for in the dry season the water comes from the mists and fogs which hang around the Corcovado, drips from the leaves of the trees, and is conducted to the Madre fountain by miles of tile gutters. Halleck and I continued our ascent of the mountain, catching from points of the way magnificent views of the scenery round about Rio Janeiro. We reached near the summit what was called the emperor's coffee-plantation, where we saw coffee-berries in their various stages, and the scaffolds on which the berries were dried before being cleaned. The coffee-tree reminded me of the red haw-tree of Ohio, and the berries were somewhat like those of the same tree, two grains of coffee being inclosed in one berry. These were dried and cleaned of the husk by hand or by machinery. A short, steep ascent from this place carried us to the summit, from which is beheld one of the most picturesque views on earth. The Organ Mountains to the west and north, the ocean to the east, the city of Rio with its red-tiled houses at our feet, and the entire harbor like a map spread out, with innumerable bright valleys, make up a landscape that cannot be described by mere words. This spot is universally visited by strangers, and has often been described. After enjoying it immeasurably, we returned to the city by another route, tired but amply repaid by our long walk.

In due time all had been done that was requisite, and the Lexington put to sea and resumed her voyage. In October we approached Cape Horn, the first land descried was Staten Island, white with snow, and the ship seemed to be aiming for the channel to its west, straits of Le Maire, but her course was changed and we passed around to the east. In time we saw Cape Horn; an island rounded like an oven, after which it takes its name (Ornos) oven. Here we experienced very rough weather, buffeting about under storm stay-sails, and spending nearly a month before the wind favored our passage and enabled the course of the ship to be changed for Valparaiso. One day we sailed parallel with a French sloop-of-war, and it was sublime to watch the two ships rising and falling in those long deep swells of the ocean. All the time we were followed by the usual large flocks of Cape-pigeons and albatrosses of every color. The former resembled the common barn-pigeon exactly, but are in fact gulls of beautiful and varied colors, mostly dove-color. We caught many with fishing-lines baited with pork. We also took in the same way many albatrosses. The white ones are very large, and their down is equal to that of the swan. At last Cape Horn and its swelling seas were left behind, and we reached Valparaiso in about sixty days from Rio. We anchored in the open roadstead, and spent there about ten days, visiting all the usual places of interest, its foretop, main-top, mizzen-top, etc. Halleck and Ord went up to Santiago, the capital of Chili, some sixty miles inland, but I did not go. Valparaiso did not impress me favorably at all. Seen from the sea, it looked like a long string of houses along the narrow beach, surmounted with red banks of earth, with little verdure, and no trees at all. Northward the space widened out somewhat, and gave room for a plaza, but the mass of houses in that quarter were poor. We were there in November, corresponding to our early spring, and we enjoyed the large strawberries which abounded. The Independence frigate, Commodore Shubrick, came in while we were there, having overtaken us, bound also for California. We met there also the sloop-of-war levant, from California, and from the officers heard of many of the events that had transpired about the time the navy, under Commodore Sloat, had taken possession of the country.

All the necessary supplies being renewed in Valparaiso, the voyage was resumed. For nearly forty days we had uninterrupted favorable winds, being in the "trades," and, having settled down to sailor habits, time passed without notice. We had brought with us all the books we could find in New York about California, and had read them over and over again: Wilkes's "Exploring Expedition;" Dana's "Two Years before the Mast;" and Forbes's "Account of the Missions." It was generally understood we were bound for Monterey, then the capital of Upper California. We knew, of course, that General Kearney was enroute for the same country overland; that Fremont was therewith his exploring party; that the navy had already taken possession, and that a regiment of volunteers, Stevenson's, was to follow us from New York; but nevertheless we were impatient to reach our destination. About the middle of January the ship began to approach the California coast, of which the captain was duly cautious, because the English and Spanish charts differed some fifteen miles in the longitude, and on all the charts a current of two miles an hour was indicated northward along the coast. At last land was made one morning, and here occurred one of those accidents so provoking after a long and tedious voyage. Macomb, the master and regular navigator, had made the correct observations, but Nicholson during the night, by an observation on the north star, put the ship some twenty miles farther south than was the case by the regular reckoning, so that Captain Bailey gave directions to alter the course of the ship more to the north, and to follow the coast up, and to keep a good lookout for Point Pinos that marks the location of Monterey Bay. The usual north wind slackened, so that when noon allowed Macomb to get a good observation, it was found that we were north of Ano Nuevo, the northern headland of Monterey Bay. The ship was put about, but little by little arose one of those southeast storms so common on the coast in winter, and we buffeted about for several days, cursing that unfortunate observation on the north star, for, on first sighting the coast, had we turned for Monterey, instead of away to the north, we would have been snugly anchored before the storm. But the southeaster abated, and the usual northwest wind came out again, and we sailed steadily down into the roadstead of Monterey Bay. This is shaped somewhat like a fish hook, the barb being the harbor, the point being Point Pinos, the southern headland. Slowly the land came out of the water, the high mountains about Santa Cruz, the low beach of the Saunas, and the strongly-marked ridge terminating in the sea in a point of dark pine-trees. Then the line of whitewashed houses of adobe, backed by the groves of dark oaks, resembling old apple-trees; and then we saw two vessels anchored close to the town. One was a small merchant-brig and another a large ship apparently dismasted. At last we saw a boat coming out to meet us, and when it came alongside, we were surprised to find Lieutenant Henry Wise, master of the Independence frigate, that we had left at Valparaiso. Wise had come off to pilot us to our anchorage. While giving orders to the man at the wheel, he, in his peculiar fluent style, told to us, gathered about him, that the Independence had sailed from Valparaiso a week after us and had been in Monterey a week; that the Californians had broken out into an insurrection; that the naval fleet under Commodore Stockton was all down the coast about San Diego; that General Kearney had reached the country, but had had a severe battle at San Pascual, and had been worsted, losing several officers and men, himself and others wounded; that war was then going on at Los Angeles; that the whole country was full of guerrillas, and that recently at Yerba Buena the alcalde, Lieutenant Bartlett, United States Navy, while out after cattle, had been lassoed, etc., etc. Indeed, in the short space of time that Wise was piloting our ship in, he told us more news than we could have learned on shore in a week, and, being unfamiliar with the great distances, we imagined that we should have to debark and begin fighting at once. Swords were brought out, guns oiled and made ready, and every thing was in a bustle when the old Lexington dropped her anchor on January 26, 1847, in Monterey

Bay, after a voyage of one hundred and ninety-eight days from New York. Every thing on shore looked bright and beautiful, the hills covered with grass and flowers, the live-oaks so serene and homelike, and the low adobe houses, with red-tiled roofs and whitened walls, contrasted well with the dark pine-trees behind, making a decidedly good impression upon us who had come so far to spy out the land. Nothing could be more peaceful in its looks than Monterey in January, 1847. We had already made the acquaintance of Commodore Shubrick and the officers of the Independence in Valparaiso, so that we again met as old friends. Immediate preparations were made for landing, and, as I was quartermaster and commissary, I had plenty to do. There was a small wharf and an adobe custom-house in possession of the navy; also a barrack of two stories, occupied by some marines, commanded by Lieutenant Maddox; and on a hill to the west of the town had been built a two-story block-house of hewed logs occupied by a guard of sailors under command of Lieutenant Baldwin, United States Navy. Not a single modern wagon or cart was to be had in Monterey, nothing but the old Mexican cart with wooden wheels, drawn by two or three pairs of oxen, yoked by the horns. A man named Tom Cole had two or more of these, and he came into immediate requisition. The United States consul, and most prominent man there at the time, was Thomas O. Larkin, who had a store and a pretty good two-story house occupied by his family. It was soon determined that our company was to land and encamp on the hill at the block-house, and we were also to have possession of the warehouse, or custom-house, for storage. The company was landed on the wharf, and we all marched in full dress with knapsacks and arms, to the hill and relieved the guard under Lieutenant Baldwin. Tents and camp-equipage were hauled up, and soon the camp was established. I remained in a room at the customhouse, where I could superintend the landing of the stores and their proper distribution. I had brought out from New York twenty thousand dollars commissary funds, and eight thousand dollars quartermaster funds, and as the ship contained about six months' supply of provisions, also a saw-mill, grist-mill, and almost every thing needed, we were soon established comfortably. We found the people of Monterey a mixed set of Americans, native Mexicans, and Indians, about one thousand all told. They were kind and pleasant, and seemed to have nothing to do, except such as owned ranches in the country for the rearing of horses and cattle. Horses could be bought at any price from four dollars up to sixteen, but no horse was ever valued above a doubloon or Mexican ounce (sixteen dollars). Cattle cost eight dollars fifty cents for the best, and this made beef net about two cents a pound, but at that time nobody bought beef by the pound, but by the carcass.

Game of all kinds—elk, deer, wild geese, and ducks—was abundant; but coffee, sugar, and small stores, were rare and costly.

There were some half-dozen shops or stores, but their shelves were empty. The people were very fond of riding, dancing, and of shows of any kind. The young fellows took great delight in showing off their horsemanship, and would dash along, picking up a half-dollar from the ground, stop their horses in full career and turn about on the space of a bullock's hide, and their skill with the lasso was certainly wonderful. At full speed they could cast their lasso about the horns of a bull, or so throw it as to catch any particular foot. These fellows would work all day on horseback in driving cattle or catching wildhorses for a mere nothing, but all the money offered would not have hired one of them to walk a mile. The girls were very fond of dancing, and they did dance gracefully and well. Every Sunday, regularly, we had a baile, or dance, and sometimes interspersed through the week.

I remember very well, soon after our arrival, that we were all invited to witness a play called "Adam and Eve." Eve was personated by a pretty young girl known as Dolores Gomez, who, however, was dressed very unlike Eve, for she was covered with a petticoat and spangles. Adam was personated by her brother—the same who has since become somewhat famous as the person on whom is founded the McGarrahan claim. God Almighty was personated, and heaven's occupants seemed very human. Yet the play was pretty, interesting, and elicited universal applause. All the month of February we were by day preparing for our long stay in the country, and at night making the most of the balls and parties of the most primitive kind, picking up a smattering of Spanish, and extending our acquaintance with the people and the costumbrea del pais. I can well recall that Ord and I, impatient to look inland, got permission and started for the Mission of San Juan Bautista. Mounted on horses, and with our carbines, we took the road by El Toro, quite a prominent hill, around which passes the road to the south, following the Saunas or Monterey River. After about twenty miles over a sandy country covered with oak-bushes and scrub, we entered quite a pretty valley in which there was a ranch at the foot of the Toro. Resting there a while and getting some information, we again started in the direction of a mountain to the north of the Saunas, called the Gavillano. It was quite dark when we reached the Saunas River, which we attempted to pass at several points, but found it full of water, and the quicksands were bad. Hearing the bark of a dog, we changed our course in that direction, and, on hailing, were answered by voices which directed us where to cross. Our knowledge of the language was limited, but we managed to understand, and to founder through the sand and water, and reached a small adobe-house on the banks of the Salinas, where we spent the night: The house was a single room, without floor or glass; only a rude door, and window with bars. Not a particle of food but meat, yet the man and woman entertained us with the language of lords put themselves, their house, and every thing, at our "disposition," and made little barefoot children dance for our entertainment. We made our supper of beef, and slept on a bullock's hide on the dirt-floor. In the morning we crossed the Salinas Plain, about fifteen miles of level ground, taking a shot occasionally at wild-geese, which abounded there, and entering the well-wooded valley that comes out from the foot of the Gavillano. We had cruised about all day, and it was almost dark when we reached the house of a Senor Gomez, father of those who at Monterey had performed the parts of Adam and Eve. His house was a two-story adobe, and had a fence in front. It was situated well up among the foot-hills of the Gavillano, and could not be seen until within a few yards. We hitched our horses to the fence and went in just as Gomez was about to sit down to a tempting supper of stewed hare and tortillas. We were officers and caballeros and could not be ignored. After turning our horses to grass, at his invitation we joined him at supper. The allowance, though ample for one, was rather short for three, and I thought the Spanish grandiloquent politeness of Gomez, who was fat and old, was not over-cordial. However, down we sat, and I was helped to a dish of rabbit, with what I thought to be an abundant sauce of tomato. Taking a good mouthful, I felt as though I had taken liquid fire; the tomato was chile colorado, or red pepper, of the purest kind. It nearly killed me, and I saw Gomez's eyes twinkle, for he saw that his share of supper was increased.—I contented myself with bits of the meat, and an abundant supply of tortillas. Ord was better case-hardened, and stood it better. We staid at Gomez's that night, sleeping, as all did, on the ground, and the next morning we crossed the hill by the bridle-path to the old Mission of San Juan Bautista. The Mission was in a beautiful valley, very level, and bounded on all sides by hills. The plain was covered with wild-grasses and mustard, and had abundant water. Cattle and horses were seen in all directions, and it was manifest that the priests who first occupied the country were good judges of land. It was Sunday, and all the people, about, a hundred, had come to church from the country round about. Ord was somewhat of a Catholic, and entered the church with his clanking spars and kneeled down, attracting the attention of all, for he had on the uniform of an American officer. As soon as church was out, all rushed to the various sports. I saw the priest, with his gray robes tucked up, playing at billiards, others were cock fighting, and some at horse-racing. My horse had become lame, and I resolved to buy another. As soon as it was known that I wanted a horse, several came for me, and displayed their horses by dashing past and hauling them up short. There was a fine black stallion that attracted my notice, and, after trying him myself, I concluded a purchase. I left with the seller my own lame horse, which he was to bring to me at Monterey, when I was to pay him ten dollars for the other. The Mission of San Juan bore the marks of high prosperity at a former period, and had a good pear-orchard just under the plateau where stood the church. After spending the day, Ord and I returned to Monterey, about thirty-five miles, by a shorter route, Thus passed the month of February, and, though there were no mails or regular expresses, we heard occasionally from Yerba Buena and Sutter's Fort to the north, and from the army and navy about Los Angeles at the south. We also knew that a quarrel had grown up at Los Angeles, between General Kearney, Colonel Fremont, and Commodore Stockton, as to the right to control affairs in California. Kearney had with him only the fragments of the two companies of dragoons, which had come across from New Mexico with him, and had been handled very roughly by Don Andreas Pico, at San Pascual, in which engagement Captains Moore and Johnson, and Lieutenant Hammond, were killed, and Kearney himself wounded. There remained with him Colonel Swords, quartermaster; Captain H. S. Turner, First Dragoons; Captains Emory and Warner, Topographical Engineers; Assistant Surgeon Griffin, and Lieutenant J. W. Davidson. Fremont had marched down from the north with a battalion of volunteers; Commodore Stockton had marched up from San Diego to Los Angeles, with General Kearney, his dragoons, and a battalion of sailors and marines, and was soon joined there by Fremont, and they jointly received the surrender of the insurgents under Andreas Pico. We also knew that General R. B. Mason had been ordered to California; that Colonel John D. Stevenson was coming out to California with a regiment of New York Volunteers; that Commodore Shubrick had orders also from the Navy Department to control matters afloat; that General Kearney, by virtue of his rank, had the right to control all the land-forces in the service of the United States; and that Fremont claimed the same right by virtue of a letter he had received from Colonel Benton, then a Senator, and a man of great influence with Polk's Administration. So that among the younger officers the query was very natural, "Who the devil is Governor of California?" One day I was on board the Independence frigate, dining with the ward-room officers, when a war-vessel was reported in the offing, which in due time was made out to be the Cyane, Captain DuPont. After dinner we were all on deck to watch the new arrival, the ships meanwhile exchanging signals, which were interpreted that General Kearney was on board. As the Cyane approached, a boat was sent to meet her, with Commodore Shubrick's flag-officer, Lieutenant Lewis, to carry the usual messages, and to invite General Kearney to come on board the Independence as the guest of Commodore Shubrick. Quite a number of officers were on deck, among them Lieutenants Wise, Montgomery Lewis, William Chapman, and others, noted wits and wags of the navy. In due time the Cyane anchored close by, and our boat was seen returning with a stranger in the stern-sheets, clothed in army blue. As the boat came nearer, we saw that it was General Kearney with an old dragoon coat on, and an army-cap, to which the general had added the broad vizor, cut from a full-dress hat, to shade his face and eyes against the glaring sun of the Gila region. Chapman exclaimed: "Fellows, the problem is solved; there is the grand-vizier (visor) by G-d! He is Governor of California."

All hands received the general with great heartiness, and he soon passed out of our sight into the commodore's cabin. Between Commodore Shubrick and General Kearney existed from that time forward the greatest harmony and good feeling, and no further trouble existed as to the controlling power on the Pacific coast. General Kearney had dispatched from San Diego his quartermaster, Colonel Swords, to the Sandwich Islands, to purchase clothing and stores for his men, and had come up to Monterey, bringing with him Turner and Warner, leaving Emory and the company of dragoons below. He was delighted to find a full strong company of artillery, subject to his orders, well supplied with clothing and money in all respects, and, much to the disgust of our Captain Tompkins, he took half of his company clothing and part of the money held by me for the relief of his worn-out and almost naked dragoons left behind at Los Angeles. In a few days he moved on shore, took up his quarters at Larkin's house, and established his headquarters, with Captain Turner as his adjutant general. One day Turner and Warner were at my tent, and, seeing a store-bag full of socks, drawers, and calico shirts, of which I had laid in a three years' supply, and of which they had none, made known to me their wants, and I told them to help themselves, which Turner and Warner did. The latter, however, insisted on paying me the cost, and from that date to this Turner and I have been close friends. Warner, poor fellow, was afterward killed by Indians. Things gradually came into shape, a semi-monthly courier line was established from Yerba Buena to San Diego, and we were thus enabled to keep pace with events throughout the country. In March Stevenson's regiment arrived. Colonel Mason also arrived by sea from Callao in the store-ship Erie, and P. St. George Cooke's battalion of Mormons reached San Luis Rey. A. J. Smith and George Stoneman were with him, and were assigned to the company of dragoons at Los Angeles. All these troops and the navy regarded General Kearney as the rightful commander, though Fremont still remained at Los Angeles, styling himself as Governor, issuing orders and holding his battalion of California Volunteers in apparent defiance of General Kearney. Colonel Mason and Major Turner were sent down by sea with a paymaster, with muster-rolls and orders to muster this battalion into the service of the United States, to pay and then to muster them out; but on their reaching Los Angeles Fremont would not consent to it, and the controversy became so angry that a challenge was believed to have passed between Mason and Fremont, but the duel never came about. Turner rode up by land in four or five days, and Fremont, becoming alarmed, followed him, as we supposed, to overtake him, but he did not succeed. On Fremont's arrival at Monterey, he camped in a tent about a mile out of town and called on General Kearney, and it was reported that the latter threatened him very severely and ordered him back to Los Angeles immediately, to disband his volunteers, and to cease the exercise of authority of any kind in the country. Feeling a natural curiosity to see Fremont, who was then quite famous by reason of his recent explorations and the still more recent conflicts with Kearney and Mason, I rode out to his camp, and found him in a conical tent with one Captain Owens, who was a mountaineer, trapper, etc., but originally from Zanesville, Ohio. I spent an hour or so with Fremont in his tent, took some tea with him, and left, without being much impressed with him. In due time Colonel Swords returned from the Sandwich Islands and relieved me as quartermaster. Captain William G. Marcy, son of the Secretary of War, had also come out in one of Stevenson's ships as an assistant commissary of subsistence, and was stationed at Monterey and relieved me as commissary, so that I reverted to the condition of a company-officer. While acting as a staff officer I had lived at the custom-house in Monterey, but when relieved I took a tent in line with the other company-officers on the hill, where we had a mess.

Stevenson'a regiment reached San Francisco Bay early in March, 1847. Three companies were stationed at the Presidio under Major James A. Hardier one company (Brackett's) at Sonoma; three, under Colonel Stevenson, at Monterey; and three, under Lieutenant-Colonel Burton, at Santa Barbara. One day I was down at the headquarters at Larkin's horse, when General Kearney remarked to me that he was going down to Los Angeles in the ship Lexington, and wanted me to go along as his aide. Of course this was most agreeable to me. Two of Stevenson's companies, with the headquarters and the colonel, were to go also. They embarked, and early in May we sailed for San Pedro. Before embarking, the United States line-of-battle-ship Columbus had reached the coast from China with Commodore Biddle, whose rank gave him the supreme command of the navy on the coast. He was busy in calling in—"lassooing "—from the land-service the various naval officers who under Stockton had been doing all sorts of military and civil service on shore. Knowing that I was to go down the coast with General Kearney, he sent for me and handed me two unsealed parcels addressed to Lieutenant Wilson, United States Navy, and Major Gillespie, United States Marines, at Los Angeles. These were written orders pretty much in these words: "On receipt of this order you will repair at once on board the United States ship Lexington at San Pedro, and on reaching Monterey you will report to the undersigned.-JAMES BIDDLE." Of course, I executed my part to the letter, and these officers were duly "lassooed." We sailed down the coast with a fair wind, and anchored inside the kelp, abreast of Johnson's house. Messages were forthwith dispatched up to Los Angeles, twenty miles off, and preparations for horses made for us to ride up. We landed, and, as Kearney held to my arm in ascending the steep path up the bluff, he remarked to himself, rather than to me, that it was strange that Fremont did not want to return north by the Lexington on account of sea-sickness, but preferred to go by land over five hundred miles. The younger officers had been discussing what the general would do with Fremont, who was supposed to be in a state of mutiny. Some, thought he would be tried and shot, some that he would be carried back in irons; and all agreed that if any one else than Fremont had put on such airs, and had acted as he had done, Kearney would have shown him no mercy, for he was regarded as the strictest sort of a disciplinarian. We had a pleasant ride across the plain which lies between the seashore and Los Angeles, which we reached in about three hours, the infantry following on foot. We found Colonel P. St. George Cooke living at the house of a Mr. Pryor, and the company of dragoons, with A. J. Smith, Davidson, Stoneman, and Dr. Griffin, quartered in an adobe-house close by. Fremont held his court in the only two-story frame-house in the place. After sometime spent at Pryor's house, General Kearney ordered me to call on Fremont to notify him of his arrival, and that he desired to see him. I walked round to the house which had been pointed out to me as his, inquired of a man at the door if the colonel was in, was answered "Yea," and was conducted to a large room on the second floor, where very soon Fremont came in, and I delivered my message. As I was on the point of leaving, he inquired where I was going to, and I answered that I was going back to Pryor's house, where the general was, when he remarked that if I would wait a moment he would go along. Of course I waited, and he soon joined me, dressed much as a Californian, with the peculiar high, broad-brimmed hat, with a fancy cord, and we walked together back to Pryor's, where I left him with General Kearney. We spent several days very pleasantly at Los Angeles, then, as now, the chief pueblo of the south, famous for its grapes, fruits, and wines. There was a hill close to the town, from which we had a perfect view of the place. The surrounding country is level, utterly devoid of trees, except the willows and cotton-woods that line the Los Angeles Creek and the acequias, or ditches, which lead from it. The space of ground cultivated in vineyards seemed about five miles by one, embracing the town. Every house had its inclosure of vineyard, which resembled a miniature orchard, the vines being very old, ranged in rows, trimmed very close, with irrigating ditches so arranged that a stream of water could be diverted between each row of vines. The Los Angeles and San Gabriel Rivers are fed by melting snows from a range of mountains to the east, and the quantity of cultivated land depends upon the amount of water. This did not seem to be very large; but the San Gabriel River, close by, was represented to contain a larger volume of water, affording the means of greatly enlarging the space for cultivation. The climate was so moderate that oranges, figs, pomegranates, etc.... were generally to be found in every yard or inclosure.

At the time of our visit, General Kearney was making his preparations to return overland to the United States, and he arranged to secure a volunteer escort out of the battalion of Mormons that was then stationed at San Luis Rey, under Colonel Cooke and a Major Hunt. This battalion was only enlisted for one year, and the time for their discharge was approaching, and it was generally understood that the majority of the men wanted to be discharged so as to join the Mormons who had halted at Salt Lake, but a lieutenant and about forty men volunteered to return to Missouri as the escort of General Kearney. These were mounted on mules and horses, and I was appointed to conduct them to Monterey by land. Leaving the party at Los Angeles to follow by sea in the Lexington, I started with the Mormon detachment and traveled by land. We averaged about thirty miles a day, stopped one day at Santa Barbara, where I saw Colonel Burton, and so on by the usually traveled road to Monterey, reaching it in about fifteen days, arriving some days in advance of the Lexington. This gave me the best kind of an opportunity for seeing the country, which was very sparsely populated indeed, except by a few families at the various Missions. We had no wheeled vehicles, but packed our food and clothing on mules driven ahead, and we slept on the ground in the open air, the rainy season having passed. Fremont followed me by land in a few days, and, by the end of May, General Kearney was all ready at Monterey to take his departure, leaving to succeed him in command Colonel R. B. Mason, First Dragoons. Our Captain (Tompkins), too, had become discontented at his separation from his family, tendered his resignation to General Kearney, and availed himself of a sailing-vessel bound for Callao to reach the East. Colonel Mason selected me as his adjutant-general, and on the very last day of May General Kearney, with his Mormon escort, with Colonel Cooke, Colonel Swords (quartermaster), Captain Turner, and a naval officer, Captain Radford, took his departure for the East overland, leaving us in full possession of California and its fate. Fremont also left California with General Kearney, and with him departed all cause of confusion and disorder in the country. From that time forth no one could dispute the authority of Colonel Mason as in command of all the United States forces on shore, while the senior naval officer had a like control afloat. This was Commodore James Biddle, who had reached the station from China in the Columbus, and he in turn was succeeded by Commodore T. Ap Catesby Jones in the line-of-battle-ship Ohio. At that time Monterey was our headquarters, and the naval commander for a time remained there, but subsequently San Francisco Bay became the chief naval rendezvous.

Colonel R. B. Mason, First Dragoons, was an officer of great experience, of stern character, deemed by some harsh and severe, but in all my intercourse with him he was kind and agreeable. He had a large fund of good sense, and, during our long period of service together, I enjoyed his unlimited confidence. He had been in his day a splendid shot and hunter, and often entertained me with characteristic anecdotes of Taylor, Twiggs, Worth, Harvey, Martin Scott, etc., etc, who were then in Mexico, gaining a national fame. California had settled down to a condition of absolute repose, and we naturally repined at our fate in being so remote from the war in Mexico, where our comrades were reaping large honors. Mason dwelt in a house not far from the Custom-House, with Captain Lanman, United States Navy; I had a small adobe-house back of Larkin's. Halleck and Dr. Murray had a small log-house not far off. The company of artillery was still on the hill, under the command of Lieutenant Ord, engaged in building a fort whereon to mount the guns we had brought out in the Lexington, and also in constructing quarters out of hewn pine-logs for the men. Lieutenant Minor, a very clever young officer, had taken violently sick and died about the time I got back from Los Angeles, leaving Lieutenants Ord and Loeser alone with the company, with Assistant-Surgeon Robert Murray. Captain William G. Marcy was the quartermaster and commissary. Naglee's company of Stevenson's regiment had been mounted and was sent out against the Indians in the San Joaquin Valley, and Shannon's company occupied the barracks. Shortly after General Kearney had gone East, we found an order of his on record, removing one Mr. Nash, the Alcalde of Sonoma, and appointing to his place ex-Governor L. W. Boggs. A letter came to Colonel and Governor Mason from Boggs, whom he had personally known in Missouri, complaining that, though he had been appointed alcalde, the then incumbent (Nash) utterly denied Kearney's right to remove him, because he had been elected by the people under the proclamation of Commodore Sloat, and refused to surrender his office or to account for his acts as alcalde. Such a proclamation had been made by Commodore Sloat shortly after the first occupation of California, announcing that the people were free and enlightened American citizens, entitled to all the rights and privileges as such, and among them the right to elect their own officers, etc. The people of Sonoma town and valley, some forty or fifty immigrants from the United States, and very few native Californians, had elected Mr. Nash, and, as stated, he refused to recognize the right of a mere military commander to eject him and to appoint another to his place. Neither General Kearney nor Mason had much respect for this land of "buncombe," but assumed the true doctrine that California was yet a Mexican province, held by right of conquest, that the military commander was held responsible to the country, and that the province should be held in statu quo until a treaty of peace. This letter of Boggs was therefore referred to Captain Brackett, whose company was stationed at Sonoma, with orders to notify Nash that Boggs was the rightful alcalde; that he must quietly surrender his office, with the books and records thereof, and that he must account for any moneys received from the sale of town-lots, etc., etc.; and in the event of refusal he (Captain Brackett) must compel him by the use of force. In due time we got Brackett's answer, saying that the little community of Sonoma was in a dangerous state of effervescence caused by his orders; that Nash was backed by most of the Americans there who had come across from Missouri with American ideas; that as he (Brackett) was a volunteer officer, likely to be soon discharged, and as he designed to settle there, he asked in consequence to be excused from the execution of this (to him) unpleasant duty. Such a request, coming to an old soldier like Colonel Mason, aroused his wrath, and he would have proceeded rough-shod against Brackett, who, by-the-way, was a West Point graduate, and ought to have known better; but I suggested to the colonel that, the case being a test one, he had better send me up to Sonoma, and I would settle it quick enough. He then gave me an order to go to Sonoma to carry out the instructions already given to Brackett.

I took one soldier with me, Private Barnes, with four horses, two of which we rode, and the other two we drove ahead. The first day we reached Gilroy's and camped by a stream near three or four adobe-huts known as Gilroy's ranch. The next day we passed Murphy's, San Jose, and Santa Clara Mission, camping some four miles beyond, where a kind of hole had been dug in the ground for water. The whole of this distance, now so beautifully improved and settled, was then scarcely occupied, except by poor ranches producing horses and cattle. The pueblo of San Jose was a string of low adobe-houses festooned with red peppers and garlic; and the Mission of Santa Clara was a dilapidated concern, with its church and orchard. The long line of poplar-trees lining the road from San Jose to Santa Clara bespoke a former period when the priests had ruled the land. Just about dark I was lying on the ground near the well, and my soldier Barnes had watered our horses and picketed them to grass, when we heard a horse crushing his way through the high mustard-bushes which filled the plain, and soon a man came to us to inquire if we had seen a saddle-horse pass up the road. We explained to him what we had heard, and he went off in pursuit of his horse. Before dark he came back unsuccessful, and gave his name as Bidwell, the same gentleman who has since been a member of Congress, who is married to Miss Kennedy, of Washington City, and now lives in princely style at Chico, California.

He explained that he was a surveyor, and had been in the lower country engaged in surveying land; that the horse had escaped him with his saddle-bags containing all his notes and papers, and some six hundred dollars in money, all the money he had earned. He spent the night with us on the ground, and the next morning we left him there to continue the search for his horse, and I afterward heard that he had found his saddle-bags all right, but never recovered the horse. The next day toward night we approached the Mission of San Francisco, and the village of Yerba Buena, tired and weary—the wind as usual blowing a perfect hurricane, and a more desolate region it was impossible to conceive of. Leaving Barnes to work his way into the town as best he could with the tired animals, I took the freshest horse and rode forward. I fell in with Lieutenant Fabius Stanley, United States Navy, and we rode into Yerba Buena together about an hour before sundown, there being nothing but a path from the Mission into the town, deep and heavy with drift-sand. My horse could hardly drag one foot after the other when we reached the old Hudson Bay Company's house, which was then the store of Howard and Mellus. There I learned where Captain Folsom, the quartermaster, was to be found. He was staying with a family of the name of Grimes, who had a small horse back of Howard's store, which must have been near where Sacramento Street now crosses Kearney. Folsom was a classmate of mine, had come out with Stevenson's regiment as quartermaster, and was at the time the chief-quartermaster of the department. His office was in the old custom-horse standing at the northwest corner of the Plaza. He had hired two warehouses, the only ones there at the time, of one Liedsdorff, the principal man of Yerba Buena, who also owned the only public-house, or tavern, called the City Hotel, on Kearney Street, at the southeast corner of the Plaza. I stopped with Folsom at Mrs. Grimes's, and he sent my horse, as also the other three when Barnes had got in after dark, to a coral where he had a little barley, but no hay. At that time nobody fed a horse, but he was usually turned out to pick such scanty grass as he could find on the side-hills. The few government horses used in town were usually sent out to the Presidio, where the grass was somewhat better. At that time (July, 1847), what is now called San Francisco was called Yerba Buena. A naval officer, Lieutenant Washington A. Bartlett, its first alcalde, had caused it to be surveyed and laid out into blocks and lots, which were being sold at sixteen dollars a lot of fifty vuras square; the understanding being that no single person could purchase of the alcalde more than one in-lot of fifty varas, and one out-lot of a hundred varas. Folsom, however, had got his clerks, orderlies, etc., to buy lots, and they, for a small consideration, conveyed them to him, so that he was nominally the owner of a good many lots. Lieutenant Halleck had bought one of each kind, and so had Warner. Many naval officers had also invested, and Captain Folsom advised me to buy some, but I felt actually insulted that he should think me such a fool as to pay money for property in such a horrid place as Yerba Buena, especially ridiculing his quarter of the city, then called Happy Valley. At that day Montgomery Street was, as now, the business street, extending from Jackson to Sacramento, the water of the bay leaving barely room for a few houses on its east side, and the public warehouses were on a sandy beach about where the Bank of California now stands, viz., near the intersection of Sansome and California, Streets. Along Montgomery Street were the stores of Howard & Mellus, Frank Ward, Sherman & Ruckel, Ross & Co., and it may be one or two others. Around the Plaza were a few houses, among them the City Hotel and the Custom-House, single-story adobes with tiled roofs, and they were by far the most substantial and best houses in the place. The population was estimated at about four hundred, of whom Kanakas (natives of the Sandwich Islands) formed the bulk.

At the foot of Clay Street was a small wharf which small boats could reach at high tide; but the principal landing-place was where some stones had fallen into the water, about where Broadway now intersects Battery Street. On the steep bluff above had been excavated, by the navy, during the year before, a bench, wherein were mounted a couple of navy-guns, styled the battery, which, I suppose, gave name to the street. I explained to Folsom the object of my visit, and learned from him that he had no boat in which to send me to Sonoma, and that the only, chance to get there was to borrow a boat from the navy. The line-of-battle-ship Columbus was then lying at anchor off the town, and he said if I would get up early the next morning I could go off to her in one of the market-boats.

Accordingly, I was up bright and early, down at the wharf, found a boat, and went off to the Columbus to see Commodore Biddle. On reaching the ship and stating to the officer of the deck my business, I was shown into the commodore's cabin, and soon made known to him my object. Biddle was a small-sized man, but vivacious in the extreme. He had a perfect contempt for all humbug, and at once entered into the business with extreme alacrity. I was somewhat amused at the importance he attached to the step. He had a chaplain, and a private secretary, in a small room latticed off from his cabin, and he first called on them to go out, and, when we were alone, he enlarged on the folly of Sloat's proclamation, giving the people the right to elect their own officers, and commended Kearney and Mason for nipping that idea in the bud, and keeping the power in their own hands. He then sent for the first lieutenant (Drayton), and inquired if there were among the officers on board any who had ever been in the Upper Bay, and learning that there was a midshipman (Whittaker) he was sent for. It so happened that this midshipman had been on a frolic on shore a few nights before, and was accordingly much frightened when summoned into the commodore's presence, but as soon as he was questioned as to his knowledge of the bay, he was sensibly relieved, and professed to know every thing about it.

Accordingly, the long boat was ordered with this midshipman and eight sailors, prepared with water and provisions for several days absence. Biddle then asked me if I knew any of his own officers, and which one of them I would prefer to accompany me. I knew most of them, and we settled down on Louis McLane. He was sent for, and it was settled that McLane and I were to conduct this important mission, and the commodore enjoined on us complete secrecy, so as to insure success, and he especially cautioned us against being pumped by his ward-room officers, Chapman, Lewis, Wise, etc., while on board his ship. With this injunction I was dismissed to the wardroom, where I found Chapman, Lewis, and Wise, dreadfully exercised at our profound secrecy. The fact that McLane and I had been closeted with the commodore for an hour, that orders for the boat and stores had been made, that the chaplain and clerk had been sent out of the cabin, etc., etc., all excited their curiosity; but McLane and I kept our secret well. The general impression was, that we had some knowledge about the fate of Captain Montgomery's two sons and the crew that had been lost the year before. In 1846 Captain Montgomery commanded at Yerba Buena, on board the St. Mary sloop-of-war, and he had a detachment of men stationed up at Sonoma. Occasionally a boat was sent up with provisions or intelligence to them. Montgomery had two sons on board his ship, one a midshipman, the other his secretary. Having occasion to send some money up to Sonoma, he sent his two sons with a good boat and crew. The boat started with a strong breeze and a very large sail, was watched from the deck until she was out of sight, and has never been heard of since. There was, of coarse, much speculation as to their fate, some contending that the boat must have been capsized in San Pablo Bay, and that all were lost; others contending that the crew had murdered the officers for the money, and then escaped; but, so far as I know, not a man of that crew has ever been seen or heard of since. When at last the boat was ready for us, we started, leaving all hands, save the commodore, impressed with the belief that we were going on some errand connected with the loss of the missing boat and crew of the St. Mary. We sailed directly north, up the bay and across San Pablo, reached the month of Sonoma Creek about dark, and during the night worked up the creek some twelve miles by means of the tide, to a landing called the Embarcadero. To maintain the secrecy which the commodore had enjoined on us, McLane and I agreed to keep up the delusion by pretending to be on a marketing expedition to pick up chickens, pigs, etc., for the mess of the Columbus, soon to depart for home.

Leaving the midshipman and four sailors to guard the boat, we started on foot with the other four for Sonoma Town, which we soon reached. It was a simple open square, around which were some adobe-houses, that of General Vallejo occupying one side. On another was an unfinished two-story adobe building, occupied as a barrack by Bracken's company. We soon found Captain Brackett, and I told him that I intended to take Nash a prisoner and convey him back to Monterey to answer for his mutinous behavior. I got an old sergeant of his company, whom I had known in the Third Artillery, quietly to ascertain the whereabouts of Nash, who was a bachelor, stopping with the family of a lawyer named Green. The sergeant soon returned, saying that Nash had gone over to Napa, but would be back that evening; so McLane and I went up to a farm of some pretensions, occupied by one Andreas Hoepner, with a pretty Sitka wife, who lived a couple of miles above Sonoma, and we bought of him some chickens, pigs, etc. We then visited Governor Boggs's family and that of General Vallejo, who was then, as now, one of the most prominent and influential natives of California. About dark I learned that Nash had come back, and then, giving Brackett orders to have a cart ready at the corner of the plaza, McLane and I went to the house of Green. Posting an armed sailor on each side of the house, we knocked at the door and walked in. We found Green, Nash, and two women, at supper. I inquired if Nash were in, and was first answered "No," but one of the women soon pointed to him, and he rose. We were armed with pistols, and the family was evidently alarmed. I walked up to him and took his arm, and told him to come along with me. He asked me, "Where?" and I said, "Monterey." "Why?" I would explain that more at leisure. Green put himself between me and the door, and demanded, in theatrical style, why I dared arrest a peaceable citizen in his house. I simply pointed to my pistol, and told him to get out of the way, which he did. Nash asked to get some clothing, but I told him he should want for nothing. We passed out, Green following us with loud words, which brought the four sailors to the front-door, when I told him to hush up or I would take him prisoner also. About that time one of the sailors, handling his pistol carelessly, discharged it, and Green disappeared very suddenly. We took Nash to the cart, put him in, and proceeded back to our boat. The next morning we were gone.

Nash being out of the way, Boggs entered on his office, and the right to appoint or remove from civil office was never again questioned in California during the military regime. Nash was an old man, and was very much alarmed for his personal safety. He had come across the Plains, and had never yet seen the sea. While on our way down the bay, I explained fully to him the state of things in California, and he admitted he had never looked on it in that light before, and professed a willingness to surrender his office; but, having gone so far, I thought it best to take him to Monterey. On our way down the bay the wind was so strong, as we approached the Columbus, that we had to take refuge behind Yerba Buena Island, then called Goat Island, where we landed, and I killed a gray seal. The next morning, the wind being comparatively light, we got out and worked our way up to the Columbus, where I left my prisoner on board, and went on shore to find Commodore Biddle, who had gone to dine with Frank Ward. I found him there, and committed Nash to his charge, with the request that he would send him down to Monterey, which he did in the sloop-of-war Dale, Captain Selfridge commanding. I then returned to Monterey by land, and, when the Dale arrived, Colonel Mason and I went on board, found poor old Mr. Nash half dead with sea-sickness and fear, lest Colonel Mason would treat him with extreme military rigor. But, on the contrary, the colonel spoke to him kindly, released him as a prisoner on his promise to go back to Sonoma, surrender his office to Boggs, and account to him for his acts while in office. He afterward came on shore, was provided with clothing and a horse, returned to Sonoma, and I never have seen him since.

Matters and things settled down in Upper California, and all moved along with peace and harmony. The war still continued in Mexico, and the navy authorities resolved to employ their time with the capture of Mazatlan and Guaymas. Lower California had already been occupied by two companies of Stevenson's regiment, under Lieutenant-Colonel Burton, who had taken post at La Paz, and a small party of sailors was on shore at San Josef, near Cape

San Lucas, detached from the Lexington, Lieutenant-Commander Bailey. The orders for this occupation were made by General Kearney before he left, in pursuance of instructions from the War Department, merely to subserve a political end, for there were few or no people in Lower California, which is a miserable, wretched, dried-up peninsula. I remember the proclamation made by Burton and Captain Bailey, in taking possession, which was in the usual florid style. Bailey signed his name as the senior naval officer at the station, but, as it was necessary to put it into Spanish to reach the inhabitants of the newly-acquired country, it was interpreted, "El mas antiguo de todos los oficiales de la marina," etc., which, literally, is "the most ancient of all the naval officers," etc., a translation at which we made some fun.

The expedition to Mazatlan was, however, for a different purpose, viz., to get possession of the ports of Mazatlan and Guaymas, as a part of the war against Mexico, and not for permanent conquest.

Commodore Shubrick commanded this expedition, and took Halleck along as his engineer-officer. They captured Mazatlan and Guaymas, and then called on Colonel Mason to send soldiers down to hold possession, but he had none to spare, and it was found impossible to raise other volunteers either in California or Oregon, and the navy held these places by detachments of sailors and marines till the end of the war. Burton also called for reenforcements, and Naglee'a company was sent to him from Monterey, and these three companies occupied Lower California at the end of the Mexican War. Major Hardie still commanded at San Francisco and above; Company F, Third Artillery, and Shannon's company of volunteers, were at Monterey; Lippett's company at Santa Barbara; Colonel Stevenson, with one company of his regiment, and the company of the First Dragoons, was at Los Angeles; and a company of Mormons, reenlisted out of the Mormon Battalion, garrisoned San Diego—and thus matters went along throughout 1847 into 1848. I had occasion to make several trips to Yerba Buena and back, and in the spring of 1848 Colonel Mason and I went down to Santa Barbara in the sloop-of-war Dale.

I spent much time in hunting deer and bear in the mountains back of the Carmel Mission, and ducks and geese in the plains of the Salinas. As soon as the fall rains set in, the young oats would sprout up, and myriads of ducks, brant, and geese, made their appearance. In a single day, or rather in the evening of one day and the morning of the next, I could load a pack-mule with geese and ducks. They had grown somewhat wild from the increased number of hunters, yet, by marking well the place where a flock lighted, I could, by taking advantage of gullies or the shape of the ground, creep up within range; and, giving one barrel on the ground, and the other as they rose, I have secured as many as nine at one discharge. Colonel Mason on one occasion killed eleven geese by one discharge of small shot. The seasons in California are well marked. About October and November the rains begin, and the whole country, plains and mountains, becomes covered with a bright-green grass, with endless flowers. The intervals between the rains give the finest weather possible. These rains are less frequent in March, and cease altogether in April and May, when gradually the grass dies and the whole aspect of things changes, first to yellow, then to brown, and by midsummer all is burnt up and dry as an ashheap.

When General Kearney first departed we took his office at Larkin's; but shortly afterward we had a broad stairway constructed to lead from the outside to the upper front porch of the barracks. By cutting a large door through the adobe-wall, we made the upper room in the centre our office; and another side-room, connected with it by a door, was Colonel Mason's private office.

I had a single clerk, a soldier named Baden; and William E. P. Hartnell, citizen, also had a table in the same room. He was the government interpreter, and had charge of the civil archives. After Halleck's return from Mazatlan, he was, by Colonel Mason, made Secretary of State; and he then had charge of the civil archives, including the land-titles, of which Fremont first had possession, but which had reverted to us when he left the country.

I remember one day, in the spring of 1848, that two men, Americans, came into the office and inquired for the Governor. I asked their business, and one answered that they had just come down from Captain Sutter on special business, and they wanted to see Governor Mason in person. I took them in to the colonel, and left them together. After some time the colonel came to his door and called to me. I went in, and my attention was directed to a series of papers unfolded on his table, in which lay about half an ounce of placer gold. Mason said to me, "What is that?" I touched it and examined one or two of the larger pieces, and asked, "Is it gold?" Mason asked me if I had ever seen native gold. I answered that, in 1844, I was in Upper Georgia, and there saw some native gold, but it was much finer than this, and that it was in phials, or in transparent quills; but I said that, if this were gold, it could be easily tested, first, by its malleability, and next by acids. I took a piece in my teeth, and the metallic lustre was perfect. I then called to the clerk, Baden, to bring an axe and hatchet from the backyard. When these were brought, I took the largest piece and beat it out flat, and beyond doubt it was metal, and a pure metal. Still, we attached little importance to the fact, for gold was known to exist at San Fernando, at the south, and yet was not considered of much value. Colonel Mason then handed me a letter from Captain Sutter, addressed to him, stating that he (Sutter) was engaged in erecting a saw-mill at Coloma, about forty miles up the American Fork, above his fort at New Helvetia, for the general benefit of the settlers in that vicinity; that he had incurred considerable expense, and wanted a "preemption" to the quarter-section of land on which the mill was located, embracing the tail-race in which this particular gold had been found. Mason instructed me to prepare a letter, in answer, for his signature. I wrote off a letter, reciting that California was yet a Mexican province, simply held by us as a conquest; that no laws of the United States yet applied to it, much less the land laws or preemption laws, which could only apply after a public survey. Therefore it was impossible for the Governor to promise him (Sutter) a title to the land; yet, as there were no settlements within forty miles, he was not likely to be disturbed by trespassers. Colonel Mason signed the letter, handed it to one of the gentlemen who had brought the sample of gold, and they departed. That gold was the first discovered in the Sierra Nevada, which soon revolutionized the whole country, and actually moved the whole civilized world. About this time (May and June, 1848), far more importance was attached to quicksilver. One mine, the New Almaden, twelve miles south of San Jose, was well known, and was in possession of the agent of a Scotch gentleman named Forties, who at the time was British consul at Tepic, Mexico. Mr. Forties came up from San Blas in a small brig, which proved to be a Mexican vessel; the vessel was seized, condemned, and actually sold, but Forties was wealthy, and bought her in. His title to the quicksilver-mine was, however, never disputed, as he had bought it regularly, before our conquest of the country, from another British subject, also named Forties, a resident of Santa Clara Mission, who had purchased it of the discoverer, a priest; but the boundaries of the land attached to the mine were even then in dispute. Other men were in search of quicksilver; and the whole range of mountains near the New Almaden mine was stained with the brilliant red of the sulphuret of mercury (cinnabar). A company composed of T. O. Larkin, J. R. Snyder, and others, among them one John Ricord (who was quite a character), also claimed a valuable mine near by. Ricord was a lawyer from about Buffalo, and by some means had got to the Sandwich Islands, where he became a great favorite of the king, Kamehameha; was his attorney-general, and got into a difficulty with the Rev. Mr. Judd, who was a kind of prime-minister to his majesty. One or the other had to go, and Ricord left for San Francisco, where he arrived while Colonel Mason and I were there on some business connected with the customs. Ricord at once made a dead set at Mason with flattery, and all sorts of spurious arguments, to convince him that our military government was too simple in its forms for the new state of facts, and that he was the man to remodel it. I had heard a good deal to his prejudice, and did all I could to prevent Mason taking him, into his confidence. We then started back for Monterey. Ricord was along, and night and day he was harping on his scheme; but he disgusted Colonel Mason with his flattery, and, on reaching Monterey, he opened what he called a law-office, but there were neither courts nor clients, so necessity forced him to turn his thoughts to something else, and quicksilver became his hobby. In the spring of 1848 an appeal came to our office from San Jose, which compelled the Governor to go up in person. Lieutenant Loeser and I, with a couple of soldiers, went along. At San Jose the Governor held some kind of a court, in which Ricord and the alcalde had a warm dispute about a certain mine which Ricord, as a member of the Larkin Company, had opened within the limits claimed by the New Almaden Company. On our way up we had visited the ground, and were therefore better prepared to understand the controversy. We had found at New Almaden Mr. Walkinshaw, a fine Scotch gentleman, the resident agent of Mr. Forbes. He had built in the valley, near a small stream, a few board-houses, and some four or five furnaces for the distillation of the mercury. These were very simple in their structure, being composed of whalers' kettles, set in masonry. These kettles were filled with broken ore about the size of McAdam-stone, mingled with lime. Another kettle, reversed, formed the lid, and the seam was luted with clay. On applying heat, the mercury was volatilized and carried into a chimney-stack, where it condensed and flowed back into a reservoir, and then was led in pipes into another kettle outside. After witnessing this process, we visited the mine itself, which outcropped near the apex of the hill, about a thousand feet above the furnaces. We found wagons hauling the mineral down the hill and returning empty, and in the mines quite a number of Sonora miners were blasting and driving for the beautiful ore (cinnabar). It was then, and is now, a most valuable mine. The adit of the mine was at the apex of the hill, which drooped off to the north. We rode along this hill, and saw where many openings had been begun, but these, proving of little or no value, had been abandoned. Three miles beyond, on the west face of the hill, we came to the opening of the "Larkin Company." There was evidence of a good deal of work, but the mine itself was filled up by what seemed a land-slide. The question involved in the lawsuit before the alcalde at San Jose was, first, whether the mine was or was not on the land belonging to the New Almaden property; and, next, whether the company had complied with all the conditions of the mite laws of Mexico, which were construed to be still in force in California.

These laws required that any one who discovered a valuable mine on private land should first file with the alcalde, or judge of the district, a notice and claim for the benefits of such discovery; then the mine was to be opened and followed for a distance of at least one hundred feet within a specified time, and the claimants must take out samples of the mineral and deposit the same with the alcalde, who was then required to inspect personally the mine, to see that it fulfilled all the conditions of the law, before he could give a written title. In this case the alcalde had been to the mine and had possession of samples of the ore; but, as the mouth of the mine was closed up, as alleged, from the act of God, by a land-slide, it was contended by Ricord and his associates that it was competent to prove by good witnesses that the mine had been opened into the hill one hundred feet, and that, by no negligence of theirs, it had caved in. It was generally understood that Robert J. Walker, United States Secretary of the Treasury, was then a partner in this mining company; and a vessel, the bark Gray Eagle, was ready at San Francisco to sail for New York with the title-papers on which to base a joint-stock company for speculative uses. I think the alcalde was satisfied that the law had been complied with, that he had given the necessary papers, and, as at that time there was nothing developed to show fraud, the Governor (Mason) did not interfere. At that date there was no public house or tavern in San Jose where we could stop, so we started toward Santa Cruz and encamped about ten miles out, to the west of the town, where we fell in with another party of explorers, of whom Ruckel, of San Francisco, was the head; and after supper, as we sat around the camp-fire, the conversation turned on quicksilver in general, and the result of the contest in San Jose in particular. Mason was relating to Ruckel the points and the arguments of Ricord, that the company should not suffer from an act of God, viz., the caving in of the mouth of the mine, when a man named Cash, a fellow who had once been in the quartermaster's employ as a teamster, spoke up: "Governor Mason, did Judge Ricord say that?" "Yes," said the Governor; and then Cash related how he and another man, whose name he gave, had been employed by Ricord to undermine a heavy rock that rested above the mouth of the mine, so that it tumbled down, carrying with it a large quantity of earth, and completely filled it up, as we had seen; "and," said Cash, "it took us three days of the hardest kind of work." This was the act of God, and on the papers procured from the alcalde at that time, I understand, was built a huge speculation, by which thousands of dollars changed hands in the United States and were lost. This happened long before the celebrated McGarrahan claim, which has produced so much noise, and which still is being prosecuted in the courts and in Congress.

On the next day we crossed over the Santa Cruz Mountains, from which we had sublime views of the scenery, first looking east toward the lower Bay of San Francisco, with the bright plains of Santa Clara and San Jose, and then to the west upon the ocean, the town of Monterey being visible sixty miles off. If my memory is correct, we beheld from that mountain the firing of a salute from the battery at Monterey, and counted the number of guns from the white puffs of smoke, but could not hear the sound. That night we slept on piles of wheat in a mill at Soquel, near Santa Cruz, and, our supplies being short, I advised that we should make an early start next morning, so as to reach the ranch of Don Juan Antonio Vallejo, a particular friend, who had a large and valuable cattle-ranch on the Pajaro River, about twenty miles on our way to Monterey. Accordingly, we were off by the first light of day, and by nine o'clock we had reached the ranch. It was on a high point of the plateau, overlooking the plain of the Pajaro, on which were grazing numbers of horses and cattle. The house was of adobe, with a long range of adobe-huts occupied by the semi-civilized Indians, who at that time did all the labor of a ranch, the herding and marking of cattle, breaking of horses, and cultivating the little patches of wheat and vegetables which constituted all the farming of that day. Every thing about the house looked deserted, and, seeing a small Indian boy leaning up against a post, I approached him and asked him in Spanish, "Where is the master?" "Gone to the Presidio" (Monterey). "Is anybody in the house?" "No." "Is it locked up?" "Yes." "Is no one about who can get in?" "No." "Have you any meat?" "No." "Any flour or grain?" "No." "Any chickens?" "No." "Any eggs?" "No." "What do you live on?" "Nada" (nothing). The utter indifference of this boy, and the tone of his answer "Nada," attracted the attention of Colonel Mason, who had been listening to our conversation, and who knew enough of Spanish to catch the meaning, and he exclaimed with some feeling, "So we get nada for our breakfast." I felt mortified, for I had held out the prospect of a splendid breakfast of meat and tortillas with rice, chickens, eggs, etc., at the ranch of my friend Josh Antonio, as a justification for taking the Governor, a man of sixty years of age, more than twenty miles at a full canter for his breakfast. But there was no help for it, and we accordingly went a short distance to a pond, where we unpacked our mules and made a slim breakfast; on some scraps of hard bread and a bone of pork that remained in our alforjas. This was no uncommon thing in those days, when many a ranchero with his eleven leagues of land, his hundreds of horses and thousands of cattle, would receive us with all the grandiloquence of a Spanish lord, and confess that he had nothing in his house to eat except the carcass of a beef hung up, from which the stranger might cut and cook, without money or price, what he needed. That night we slept on Salinas Plain, and the next morning reached Monterey. All the missions and houses at that period were alive with fleas, which the natives looked on as pleasant titillators, but they so tortured me that I always gave them a wide berth, and slept on a saddle-blanket, with the saddle for a pillow and the serape, or blanket, for a cover. We never feared rain except in winter. As the spring and summer of 1848 advanced, the reports came faster and faster from the gold-mines at Sutter's saw-mill. Stories reached us of fabulous discoveries, and spread throughout the land. Everybody was talking of "Gold! gold!" until it assumed the character of a fever. Some of our soldiers began to desert; citizens were fitting out trains of wagons and packmules to go to the mines. We heard of men earning fifty, five hundred, and thousands of dollars per day, and for a time it seemed as though somebody would reach solid gold. Some of this gold began to come to Yerba Buena in trade, and to disturb the value of merchandise, particularly of mules, horses, tin pans, and articles used in mining: I of course could not escape the infection, and at last convinced Colonel Mason that it was our duty to go up and see with our own eyes, that we might report the truth to our Government. As yet we had no regular mail to any part of the United States, but mails had come to us at long intervals, around Cape Horn, and one or two overland. I well remember the first overland mail. It was brought by Kit Carson in saddle-bags from Taos in New Mexico. We heard of his arrival at Los Angeles, and waited patiently for his arrival at headquarters. His fame then was at its height, from the publication of Fremont's books, and I was very anxious to see a man who had achieved such feats of daring among the wild animals of the Rocky Mountains, and still wilder Indians of the Plains. At last his arrival was reported at the tavern at Monterey, and I hurried to hunt him up. I cannot express my surprise at beholding a small, stoop-shouldered man, with reddish hair, freckled face, soft blue eyes, and nothing to indicate extraordinary courage or daring. He spoke but little, and answered questions in monosyllables. I asked for his mail, and he picked up his light saddle-bags containing the great overland mail, and we walked together to headquarters, where he delivered his parcel into Colonel Mason's own hands. He spent some days in Monterey, during which time we extracted with difficulty some items of his personal history. He was then by commission a lieutenant in the regiment of Mounted Rifles serving in Mexico under Colonel Sumner, and, as he could not reach his regiment from California, Colonel Mason ordered that for a time he should be assigned to duty with A. J. Smith's company, First Dragoons, at Los Angeles. He remained at Los Angeles some months, and was then sent back to the United Staten with dispatches, traveling two thousand miles almost alone, in preference to being encumbered by a large party.

Toward the close of June, 1848, the gold-fever being at its height, by Colonel Mason's orders I made preparations for his trip to the newly-discovered gold-mines at Sutter's Fort. I selected four good soldiers, with Aaron, Colonel Mason's black servant, and a good outfit of horses and pack-mules, we started by the usually traveled route for Yerba Buena. There Captain Fulsom and two citizens joined our party. The first difficulty was to cross the bay to Saucelito. Folsom, as quartermaster, had a sort of scow with a large sail, with which to discharge the cargoes of ships, that could not come within a mile of the shore. It took nearly the whole day to get the old scow up to the only wharf there, and then the water was so shallow that the scow, with its load of horses, would not float at the first high tide, but by infinite labor on the next tide she was got off and safely crossed over to Saucelito. We followed in a more comfortable schooner. Having safely landed our horses and mules, we picked up and rode to San Rafael Mission, stopping with Don Timoteo Murphy. The next day's journey took us to Bodega, where lived a man named Stephen Smith, who had the only steam saw-mill in California. He had a Peruvian wife, and employed a number of absolutely naked Indians in making adobes. We spent a day very pleasantly with him, and learned that he had come to California some years before, at the personal advice of Daniel Webster, who had informed him that sooner or later the United States would be in possession of California, and that in consequence it would become a great country. From Bodega we traveled to Sonoma, by way of Petaluma, and spent a day with General Vallejo. I had been there before, as related, in the business of the alcalde Nash. From Sonoma we crossed over by way of Napa, Suisun, and Vaca's ranch, to the Puta. In the rainy season, the plain between the Puta and Sacramento Rivers is impassable, but in July the waters dry up; and we passed without trouble, by the trail for Sutter's Embarcadero. We reached the Sacramento River, then full of water, with a deep, clear current. The only means of crossing over was by an Indian dugout canoe. We began by carrying across our packs and saddles, and then our people. When all things were ready, the horses were driven into the water, one being guided ahead by a man in the canoe. Of course, the horses and mules at first refused to take to the water, and it was nearly a day's work to get them across, and even then some of our animals after crossing escaped into the woods and undergrowth that lined the river, but we secured enough of them to reach Sutter's Fort, three miles back from the embcarcadero, where we encamped at the old slough, or pond, near the fort. On application, Captain Butter sent some Indians back into the bushes, who recovered and brought in all our animals. At that time there was not the sign of a habitation there or thereabouts, except the fort, and an old adobe-house, east of the fort, known as the hospital. The fort itself was one of adobe-walls, about twenty feet high, rectangular in form, with two-story block houses at diagonal corners. The entrance was by a large gate, open by day and closed at night, with two iron ship's guns near at hand. Inside there was a large house, with a good shingle-roof, used as a storehouse, and all round the walls were ranged rooms, the fort wall being the outer wall of the house. The inner wall also was of adobe. These rooms were used by Captain Sutter himself and by his people. He had a blacksmith's shop, carpenter's shop, etc., and other rooms where the women made blankets. Sutter was monarch of all he surveyed, and had authority to inflict punishment even unto death, a power he did not fail to use. He had horses, cattle, and sheep, and of these he gave liberally and without price to all in need. He caused to be driven into our camp a beef and some sheep, which were slaughtered for our use. Already the goldmines were beginning to be felt. Many people were then encamped, some going and some coming, all full of gold-stories, and each surpassing the other. We found preparations in progress for celebrating the Fourth of July, then close at hand, and we agreed to remain over to assist on the occasion; of course, being the high officials, we were the honored guests. People came from a great distance to attend this celebration of the Fourth of July, and the tables were laid in the large room inside the storehouse of the fort. A man of some note, named Sinclair, presided, and after a substantial meal and a reasonable supply of aguardiente we began the toasts. All that I remember is that Folsom and I spoke for our party; others, Captain Sutter included, made speeches, and before the celebration was over Sutter was enthusiastic, and many others showed the effects of the aguardiente. The next day (namely, July 5, 1848) we resumed our journey toward the mines, and, in twenty-five miles of as hot and dusty a ride as possible, we reached Mormon Island. I have heretofore stated that the gold was first found in the tail-race of the stew-mill at Coloma, forty miles above Sutter's Fort, or fifteen above Mormon Island, in the bed of the American Fork of the Sacramento River. It seems that Sutter had employed an American named Marshall, a sort of millwright, to do this work for him, but Marshall afterward claimed that in the matter of the saw-mill they were copartners. At all events, Marshall and the family of Mr. Wimmer were living at Coloma, where the pine-trees afforded the best material for lumber. He had under him four white men, Mormons, who had been discharged from Cooke's battalion, and some Indians. These were engaged in hewing logs, building a mill-dam, and putting up a saw-mill. Marshall, as the architect, had made the "tub-wheel," and had set it in motion, and had also furnished some of the rude parts of machinery necessary for an ordinary up-and-down saw-mill.

Labor was very scarce, expensive, and had to be economized. The mill was built over a dry channel of the river which was calculated to be the tail-race. After arranging his head-race, dam and tub-wheel, he let on the water to test the goodness of his machinery. It worked very well until it was found that the tail-race did not carry off the water fast enough, so he put his men to work in a rude way to clear out the tail-race. They scratched a kind of ditch down the middle of the dry channel, throwing the coarser stones to one side; then, letting on the water again, it would run with velocity down the channel, washing away the dirt, thus saving labor. This course of action was repeated several times, acting exactly like the long Tom afterward resorted to by the miners. As Marshall himself was working in this ditch, he observed particles of yellow metal which he gathered up in his hand, when it seemed to have suddenly flashed across his mind that it was gold. After picking up about an ounce, he hurried down to the fort to report to Captain Sutter his discovery. Captain Sutter himself related to me Marshall's account, saying that, as he sat in his room at the fort one day in February or March, 1848, a knock was heard at his door, and he called out, "Come in." In walked Marshall, who was a half-crazy man at best, but then looked strangely wild. "What is the matter, Marshall!" Marshall inquired if any one was within hearing, and began to peer about the room, and look under the bed, when Sutter, fearing that some calamity had befallen the party up at the saw-mill, and that Marshall was really crazy, began to make his way to the door, demanding of Marshall to explain what was the matter. At last he revealed his discovery, and laid before Captain Sutter the pellicles of gold he had picked up in the ditch. At first, Sutter attached little or no importance to the discovery, and told Marshall to go back to the mill, and say nothing of what he had seen to Mr. Wimmer, or any one else. Yet, as it might add value to the location, he dispatched to our headquarters at Monterey, as I have already related, the two men with a written application for a preemption to the quarter-section of land at Coloma. Marshall returned to the mill, but could not keep out of his wonderful ditch, and by some means the other men employed there learned his secret. They then wanted to gather the gold, and Marshall threatened to shoot them if they attempted it; but these men had sense enough to know that if "placer"-gold existed at Coloma, it would also be found farther down-stream, and they gradually "prospected" until they reached Mormon Island, fifteen miles below, where they discovered one of the richest placers on earth. These men revealed the fact to some other Mormons who were employed by Captain Sutter at a grist-mill he was building still lower down the American Fork, and six miles above his fort. All of them struck for higher wages, to which Sutter yielded, until they asked ten dollars a day, which he refused, and the two mills on which he had spent so much money were never built, and fell into decay.

In my opinion, when the Mormons were driven from Nauvoo, Illinois, in 1844, they cast about for a land where they would not be disturbed again, and fixed on California. In the year 1845 a ship, the Brooklyn, sailed from New York for California, with a colony of

Mormons, of which Sam Brannan was the leader, and we found them there on our arrival in January, 1847. When General Kearney, at Fort Leavenworth, was collecting volunteers early in 1846, for the Mexican War, he, through the instrumentality of Captain James Allen, brother to our quartermaster, General Robert Allen, raised the battalion of Mormons at Kanesville, Iowa, now Council Bluffs, on the express understanding that it would facilitate their migration to California. But when the Mormons reached Salt Lake, in 1846, they learned that they had been forestalled by the United States forces in California, and they then determined to settle down where they were. Therefore, when this battalion of five companies of Mormons (raised by Allen, who died on the way, and was succeeded by Cooke) was discharged at Los Angeles, California, in the early summer of 1847, most of the men went to their people at Salt Lake, with all the money received, as pay from the United States, invested in cattle and breeding-horses; one company reenlisted for another year, and the remainder sought work in the country. As soon as the fame of the gold discovery spread through California, the Mormons naturally turned to Mormon Island, so that in July, 1848, we found about three hundred of them there at work. Sam Brannan was on hand as the high-priest, collecting the tithes. Clark, of Clark's Point, an early pioneer, was there also, and nearly all the Mormons who had come out in the Brooklyn, or who had staid in California after the discharge of their battalion, had collected there. I recall the scene as perfectly to-day as though it were yesterday. In the midst of a broken country, all parched and dried by the hot sun of July, sparsely wooded with live-oaks and straggling pines, lay the valley of the American River, with its bold mountain-stream coming out of the Snowy Mountains to the east. In this valley is a flat, or gravel-bed, which in high water is an island, or is overflown, but at the time of our visit was simply a level gravel-bed of the river. On its edges men were digging, and filling buckets with the finer earth and gravel, which was carried to a machine made like a baby's cradle, open at the foot, and at the head a plate of sheet-iron or zinc, punctured full of holes. On this metallic plate was emptied the earth, and water was then poured on it from buckets, while one man shook the cradle with violent rocking by a handle. On the bottom were nailed cleats of wood. With this rude machine four men could earn from forty to one hundred dollars a day, averaging sixteen dollars, or a gold ounce, per man per day. While the' sun blazed down on the heads of the miners with tropical heat, the water was bitter cold, and all hands were either standing in the water or had their clothes wet all the time; yet there were no complaints of rheumatism or cold. We made our camp on a small knoll, a little below the island, and from it could overlook the busy scene. A few bush-huts near by served as stores, boardinghouses, and for sleeping; but all hands slept on the ground, with pine-leaves and blankets for bedding. As soon as the news spread that the Governor was there, persons came to see us, and volunteered all kinds of information, illustrating it by samples of the gold, which was of a uniform kind, "scale-gold," bright and beautiful. A large variety, of every conceivable shape and form, was found in the smaller gulches round about, but the gold in the river-bed was uniformly "scale-gold." I remember that Mr. Clark was in camp, talking to Colonel Mason about matters and things generally, when he inquired, "Governor, what business has Sam Brannan to collect the tithes here?" Clark admitted that Brannan was the head of the Mormon church in California, and he was simply questioning as to Brannan's right, as high-priest, to compel the Mormons to pay him the regular tithes. Colonel Mason answered, "Brannan has a perfect right to collect the tax, if you Mormons are fools enough to pay it." "Then," said Clark, "I for one won't pay it any longer." Colonel Mason added: "This is public land, and the gold is the property of the United States; all of you here are trespassers, but, as the Government is benefited by your getting out the gold, I do not intend to interfere." I understood, afterward, that from that time the payment of the tithes ceased, but Brannan had already collected enough money wherewith to hire Sutter's hospital, and to open a store there, in which he made more money than any merchant in California, during that summer and fall. The understanding was, that the money collected by him as tithes was the foundation of his fortune, which is still very large in San Francisco. That evening we all mingled freely with the miners, and witnessed the process of cleaning up and "panning" out, which is the last process for separating the pure gold from the fine dirt and black sand.

The next day we continued our journey up the valley of the American Fork, stopping at various camps, where mining was in progress; and about noon we reached Coloma, the place where gold had been first discovered. The hills were higher, and the timber of better quality. The river was narrower and bolder, and but few miners were at work there, by reason of Marshall's and Sutter's claim to the site. There stood the sawmill unfinished, the dam and tail-race just as they were left when the Mormons ceased work. Marshall and Wimmer's family of wife and half a dozen children were there, guarding their supposed treasure; living in a house made of clapboards. Here also we were shown many specimens of gold, of a coarser grain than that found at Mormon Island. The next day we crossed the American River to its north side, and visited many small camps of men, in what were called the "dry diggings." Little pools of water stood in the beds of the streams, and these were used to wash the dirt; and there the gold was in every conceivable shape and size, some of the specimens weighing several ounces. Some of these "diggings" were extremely rich, but as a whole they were more precarious in results than at the river. Sometimes a lucky fellow would hit on a "pocket," and collect several thousand dollars in a few days, and then again he would be shifting about from place to place, "prospecting," and spending all he had made. Little stores were being opened at every point, where flour, bacon, etc., were sold; every thing being a dollar a pound, and a meal usually costing three dollars. Nobody paid for a bed, for he slept on the ground, without fear of cold or rain. We spent nearly a week in that region, and were quite bewildered by the fabulous tales of recent discoveries, which at the time were confined to the several forks of the American and Yuba Rivers.' All this time our horses had nothing to eat but the sparse grass in that region, and we were forced to work our way down toward the Sacramento Valley, or to see our animals perish. Still we contemplated a visit to the Yuba and Feather Rivers, from which we had heard of more wonderful "diggings;" but met a courier, who announced the arrival of a ship at Monterey, with dispatches of great importance from Mazatlan. We accordingly turned our horses back to Sutter's Fort. Crossing the Sacramento again by swimming our horses, and ferrying their loads in that solitary canoe, we took our back track as far as the Napa, and then turned to Benicia, on Carquinez Straits. We found there a solitary adobe-house, occupied by Mr. Hastings and his family, embracing Dr. Semple, the proprietor of the ferry. This ferry was a ship's-boat, with a latteen-sail, which could carry across at one time six or eight horses.

It took us several days to cross over, and during that time we got well acquainted with the doctor, who was quite a character. He had come to California from Illinois, and was brother to Senator Semple. He was about seven feet high, and very intelligent. When we first reached Monterey, he had a printing-press, which belonged to the United States, having been captured at the custom-house, and had been used to print custom-house blanks. With this Dr. Semple, as editor, published the Californian, a small sheet of news, once a week; and it was a curiosity in its line, using two v's for a w, and other combinations of letters, made necessary by want of type. After some time he removed to Yerba Buena with his paper, and it grew up to be the Alta California of today. Foreseeing, as he thought, the growth of a great city somewhere on the Bay of San Francisco, he selected Carquinez Straits as its location, and obtained from General Vallejo a title to a league of land, on condition of building up a city thereon to bear the name of Vallejo's wife. This was Francisca Benicia; accordingly, the new city was named "Francisca." At this time, the town near the mouth of the bay was known universally as Yerba Buena; but that name was not known abroad, although San Francisco was familiar to the whole civilized world. Now, some of the chief men of Yerba Buena, Folsom, Howard, Leidesdorf, and others, knowing the importance of a name, saw their danger, and, by some action of the ayuntamiento, or town council, changed the name of Yerba Buena to "San Francisco." Dr. Semple was outraged at their changing the name to one so like his of Francisca, and he in turn changed his town to the other name of Mrs. Vallejo, viz., "Benicia;" and Benicia it has remained to this day. I am convinced that this little circumstance was big with consequences. That Benicia has the best natural site for a commercial city, I am, satisfied; and had half the money and half the labor since bestowed upon San Francisco been expended at Benicia, we should have at this day a city of palaces on the Carquinez Straits. The name of "San Francisco," however, fixed the city where it now is; for every ship in 1848-'49, which cleared from any part of the world, knew the name of

San Francisco, but not Yerba Buena or Benicia; and, accordingly, ships consigned to California came pouring in with their contents, and were anchored in front of Yerba Buena, the first town. Captains and crews deserted for the gold-mines, and now half the city in front of Montgomery Street is built over the hulks thus abandoned. But Dr. Semple, at that time, was all there was of Benicia; he was captain and crew of his ferry boat, and managed to pass our party to the south side of Carquinez Straits in about two days.

Thence we proceeded up Amador Valley to Alameda Creek, and so on to the old mission of San Jose; thence to the pueblo of San Jose, where Folsom and those belonging in Yerba Buena went in that direction, and we continued on to Monterey, our party all the way giving official sanction to the news from the gold-mines, and adding new force to the "fever."

On reaching Monterey, we found dispatches from Commodore Shubrick, at Mazatlan, which gave almost positive assurance that the war with Mexico was over; that hostilities had ceased, and commissioners were arranging the terms of peace at Guadalupe Hidalgo. It was well that this news reached California at that critical time; for so contagious had become the "gold-fever" that everybody was bound to go and try his fortune, and the volunteer regiment of Stevenson's would have deserted en masse, had the men not been assured that they would very soon be entitled to an honorable discharge.

Many of our regulars did desert, among them the very men who had escorted us faithfully to the mines and back. Our servants also left us, and nothing less than three hundred dollars a month would hire a man in California; Colonel Mason's black boy, Aaron, alone of all our then servants proving faithful. We were forced to resort to all manner of shifts to live. First, we had a mess with a black fellow we called Bustamente as cook; but he got the fever, and had to go. We next took a soldier, but he deserted, and carried off my double-barreled shot-gun, which I prized very highly. To meet this condition of facts, Colonel Mason ordered that liberal furloughs should be given to the soldiers, and promises to all in turn, and he allowed all the officers to draw their rations in kind. As the actual valve of the ration was very large, this enabled us to live. Halleck, Murray, Ord, and I, boarded with Dona Augustias, and turned in our rations as pay for our board.

Some time in September, 1848, the official news of the treaty of peace reached us, and the Mexican War was over. This treaty was signed in May, and came to us all the way by land by a courier from Lower California, sent from La Paz by Lieutenant-Colonel Burton. On its receipt, orders were at once made for the muster-out of all of Stevenson's regiment, and our military forces were thus reduced to the single company of dragoons at Los Angeles, and the one company of artillery at Monterey. Nearly all business had ceased, except that connected with gold; and, during that fall, Colonel Mason, Captain Warner, and I, made another trip up to Sutter's Fort, going also to the newly-discovered mines on the Stanislaus, called "Sonora," named from the miners of Sonora, Mexico, who had first discovered them. We found there pretty much the same state of facts as before existed at Mormon Island and Coloma, and we daily received intelligence of the opening of still other mines north and south.

But I have passed over a very interesting fact. As soon as we had returned from our first visit to the gold-mines, it became important to send home positive knowledge of this valuable discovery. The means of communication with the United States were very precarious, and I suggested to Colonel Mason that a special courier ought to be sent; that Second-Lieutenant Loeser had been promoted to first-lieutenant, and was entitled to go home. He was accordingly detailed to carry the news. I prepared with great care the letter to the adjutant-general of August 17, 1848, which Colonel Mason modified in a few Particulars; and, as it was important to send not only the specimens which had been presented to us along our route of travel, I advised the colonel to allow Captain Folsom to purchase and send to Washington a large sample of the commercial gold in general use, and to pay for the same out of the money in his hands known as the "civil fund," arising from duties collected at the several ports in California. He consented to this, and Captain Folsom bought an oyster-can full at ten dollars the ounce, which was the rate of value at which it was then received at the custom house. Folsom was instructed further to contract with some vessel to carry the messenger to South America, where he could take the English steamers as far east as Jamaica, with a conditional charter giving increased payment if the vessel could catch the October steamer. Folsom chartered the bark La Lambayecana, owned and navigated by Henry D. Cooke, who has since been the Governor of the District of Columbia. In due time this vessel reached Monterey, and Lieutenant Loeser, with his report and specimens of gold, embarked and sailed. He reached the South American Continent at Payta, Peru, in time; took the English steamer of October to Panama, and thence went on to Kingston, Jamaica, where he found a sailing vessel bound for New Orleans. On reaching New Orleans, he telegraphed to the War Department his arrival; but so many delays had occurred that he did not reach Washington in time to have the matter embraced in the President's regular message of 1848, as we had calculated. Still, the President made it the subject of a special message, and thus became "official" what had before only reached the world in a very indefinite shape. Then began that wonderful development, and the great emigration to California, by land and by sea, of 1849 and 1850.

As before narrated, Mason, Warner, and I, made a second visit to the mines in September and October, 1848. As the winter season approached, Colonel Mason returned to Monterey, and I remained for a time at Sutter's Fort. In order to share somewhat in the riches of the land, we formed a partnership in a store at Coloma, in charge of Norman S. Bestor, who had been Warner's clerk. We supplied the necessary money, fifteen hundred dollars (five hundred dollars each), and Bestor carried on the store at Coloma for his share. Out of this investment, each of us realized a profit of about fifteen hundred dollars. Warner also got a regular leave of absence, and contracted with Captain Sutter for surveying and locating the town of Sacramento. He received for this sixteen dollars per day for his services as surveyor; and Sutter paid all the hands engaged in the work. The town was laid off mostly up about the fort, but a few streets were staked off along the river bank, and one or two leading to it. Captain Sutter always contended, however, that no town could possibly exist on the immediate bank of the river, because the spring freshets rose over the bank, and frequently it was necessary to swim a horse to reach the boat-landing. Nevertheless, from the very beginning the town began to be built on the very river-bank, viz., First, Second, and Third Streets, with J and K Streets leading back. Among the principal merchants and traders of that winter, at Sacramento, were Sam Brannan and Hensley, Reading & Co. For several years the site was annually flooded; but the people have persevered in building the levees, and afterward in raising all the streets, so that Sacramento is now a fine city, the capital of the State, and stands where, in 1848, was nothing but a dense mass of bushes, vines, and submerged land. The old fort has disappeared altogether.

During the fall of 1848, Warner, Ord, and I, camped on the bank of the American River, abreast of the fort, at what was known as the "Old Tan-Yard." I was cook, Ord cleaned up the dishes, and Warner looked after the horses; but Ord was deposed as scullion because he would only wipe the tin plates with a tuft of grass, according to the custom of the country, whereas Warner insisted on having them washed after each meal with hot water. Warner was in consequence promoted to scullion, and Ord became the hostler. We drew our rations in kind from the commissary at San Francisco, who sent them up to us by a boat; and we were thus enabled to dispense a generous hospitality to many a poor devil who otherwise would have had nothing to eat.

The winter of 1848 '49 was a period of intense activity throughout California. The rainy season was unfavorable to the operations of gold-mining, and was very hard upon the thousands of houseless men and women who dwelt in the mountains, and even in the towns. Most of the natives and old inhabitants had returned to their ranches and houses; yet there were not roofs enough in the country to shelter the thousands who had arrived by sea and by land. The news had gone forth to the whole civilized world that gold in fabulous quantities was to be had for the mere digging, and adventurers came pouring in blindly to seek their fortunes, without a thought of house or food. Yerba Buena had been converted into San Francisco. Sacramento City had been laid out, lots were being rapidly sold, and the town was being built up as an entrepot to the mines. Stockton also had been chosen as a convenient point for trading with the lower or southern mines. Captain Sutter was the sole proprietor of the former, and Captain Charles Weber was the owner of the site of Stockton, which was as yet known as "French Camp."

38

CHAPTER III.
EARLY RECOLLECTIONS OF CALIFORNIA—(CONTINUED).

1849-1850.

The department headquarters still remained at Monterey, but, with the few soldiers, we had next to nothing to do. In midwinter we heard of the approach of a battalion of the Second Dragoons, under Major Lawrence Pike Graham, with Captains Rucker, Coutts, Campbell, and others, along. So exhausted were they by their long march from Upper Mexico that we had to send relief to meet them as they approached. When this command reached Los Angeles, it was left there as the garrison, and Captain A. J. Smith's company of the First Dragoons was brought up to San Francisco. We were also advised that the Second Infantry, Colonel B. Riley, would be sent out around Cape Horn in sailing-ships; that the Mounted Rifles, under Lieutenant-Colonel Loring, would march overland to Oregon; and that Brigadier-General Persifer F. Smith would come out in chief command on the Pacific coast. It was also known that a contract had been entered into with parties in New York and New Orleans for a monthly line of steamers from those cities to California, via Panama. Lieutenant-Colonel Burton had come up from Lower California, and, as captain of the Third Artillery, he was assigned to command Company F, Third Artillery, at Monterey. Captain Warner remained at Sacramento, surveying; and Halleck, Murray, Ord, and I, boarded with Dona Augustias. The season was unusually rainy and severe, but we passed the time with the usual round of dances and parties. The time fixed for the arrival of the mail-steamer was understood to be about January 1, 1849, but the day came and went without any tidings of her. Orders were given to Captain Burton to announce her arrival by firing a national salute, and each morning we listened for the guns from the fort. The month of January passed, and the greater part of February, too. As was usual, the army officers celebrated the 22d of February with a grand ball, given in the new stone school-house, which Alcalde Walter Colton had built. It was the largest and best hall then in California. The ball was really a handsome affair, and we kept it up nearly all night. The next morning we were at breakfast: present, Dona Augustias, and Manuelita, Halleck, Murray, and myself. We were dull and stupid enough until a gun from the fort aroused us, then another and another. "The steamer" exclaimed all, and, without waiting for hats or any thing, off we dashed. I reached the wharf hatless, but the dona sent my cap after me by a servant. The white puffs of smoke hung around the fort, mingled with the dense fog, which hid all the water of the bay, and well out to sea could be seen the black spars of some unknown vessel. At the wharf I found a group of soldiers and a small row-boat, which belonged to a brig at anchor in the bay. Hastily ordering a couple of willing soldiers to get in and take the oars, and Mr. Larkin and Mr. Hartnell asking to go along, we jumped in and pushed off. Steering our boat toward the spars, which loomed up above the fog clear and distinct, in about a mile we came to the black hull of the strange monster, the long-expected and most welcome steamer California. Her wheels were barely moving, for her pilot could not see the shore-line distinctly, though the hills and Point of Pines could be clearly made out over the fog, and occasionally a glimpse of some white walls showed where the town lay. A "Jacob's ladder" was lowered for us from the steamer, and in a minute I scrambled up on deck, followed by Larkin and Hartnell, and we found ourselves in the midst of many old friends. There was Canby, the adjutant-general, who was to take my place; Charley Hoyt, my cousin; General Persifer F. Smith and wife; Gibbs, his aide-de-camp; Major Ogden, of the Engineers, and wife; and, indeed, many old Californians, among them Alfred Robinson, and Frank Ward with his pretty bride. By the time the ship was fairly at anchor we had answered a million of questions about gold and the state of the country; and, learning that the ship was out of fuel, had informed the captain (Marshall) that there was abundance of pine-wood, but no willing hands to cut it; that no man could be hired at less than an ounce of gold a day, unless the soldiers would volunteer to do it for some agreed-upon price. As for coal, there was not a pound in Monterey, or anywhere else in California. Vessels with coal were known to be en route around Cape Horn, but none had yet reached California.

The arrival of this steamer was the beginning of a new epoch on the Pacific coast; yet there she lay, helpless, without coal or fuel. The native Californians, who had never seen a steamship, stood for days on the beach looking at her, with the universal exclamation, "Tan feo!"—how ugly!—and she was truly ugly when compared with the clean, well-sparred frigates and sloops-of-war that had hitherto been seen on the North Pacific coast. It was first supposed it would take ten days to get wood enough to prosecute her voyage, and therefore all the passengers who could took up their quarters on shore. Major Canby relieved me, and took the place I had held so long as adjutant-general of the Department of California. The time seemed most opportune for me to leave the service, as I had several splendid offers of employment and of partnership, and, accordingly, I made my written resignation; but General Smith put his veto upon it, saying that he was to command the Division of the Pacific, while General Riley was to have the Department of California, and Colonel Loring that of Oregon. He wanted me as his adjutant-general, because of my familiarity with the country, and knowledge of its then condition: At the time, he had on his staff Gibbs as aide-de-camp, and Fitzgerald as quartermaster. He also had along with him quite a retinue of servants, hired with a clear contract to serve him for a whole year after reaching California, every one of whom deserted, except a young black fellow named Isaac. Mrs. Smith, a pleasant but delicate Louisiana lady, had a white maid-servant, in whose fidelity she had unbounded confidence; but this girl was married to a perfect stranger, and off before she had even landed in San Francisco. It was, therefore, finally arranged that, on the California, I was to accompany General Smith to San Francisco as his adjutant-general. I accordingly sold some of my horses, and arranged for others to go up by land; and from that time I became fairly enlisted in the military family of General Persifer F. Smith.

I parted with my old commander, Colonel Mason, with sincere regret. To me he had ever been kind and considerate, and, while stern, honest to a fault, he was the very embodiment of the principle of fidelity to the interests of the General Government. He possessed a native strong intellect, and far more knowledge of the principles of civil government and law than he got credit for. In private and public expenditures he was extremely economical, but not penurious. In cases where the officers had to contribute money for parties and entertainments, he always gave a double share, because of his allowance of double rations. During our frequent journeys, I was always caterer, and paid all the bills. In settling with him he required a written statement of the items of account, but never disputed one of them. During our time, California was, as now, full of a bold, enterprising, and speculative set of men, who were engaged in every sort of game to make money. I know that Colonel Mason was beset by them to use his position to make a fortune for himself and his friends; but he never bought land or town-lots, because, he said, it was his place to hold the public estate for the Government as free and unencumbered by claims as possible; and when I wanted him to stop the public-land sales in San Francisco, San Jose, etc., he would not; for, although he did not believe the titles given by the alcaldes worth a cent, yet they aided to settle the towns and public lands, and he thought, on the whole, the Government would be benefited thereby. The same thing occurred as to the gold-mines. He never took a title to a town lot, unless it was one, of no real value, from Alcalde Colton, in Monterey, of which I have never heard since. He did take a share in the store which Warner, Beator, and I, opened at Coloma, paid his share of the capital, five hundred dollars, and received his share of the profits, fifteen hundred dollars. I think also he took a share in a venture to China with Larkin and others; but, on leaving California, he was glad to sell out without profit or loss. In the stern discharge of his duty he made some bitter enemies, among them Henry M. Naglee, who, in the newspapers of the day, endeavored to damage his fair name. But, knowing him intimately, I am certain that he is entitled to all praise for having so controlled the affairs of the country that, when his successor arrived, all things were so disposed that a civil form of government was an easy matter of adjustment. Colonel Mason was relieved by General Riley some time in April, and left California in the steamer of the 1st May for Washington and St. Louis, where he died of cholera in the summer of 1850, and his body is buried in Bellefontaine Cemetery. His widow afterward married Major (since General) Don Carlos Buell, and is now living in Kentucky.

In overhauling the hold of the steamer California, as she lay at anchor in Monterey Bay, a considerable amount of coal was found under some heavy duplicate machinery. With this, and such wood as had been gathered, she was able to renew her voyage. The usual signal was made, and we all went on board. About the 1st of March we entered the Heads, and anchored off San Francisco, near the United States line-of-battle-ship Ohio, Commodore T. Catesby Jones. As was the universal custom of the day, the crew of the California deserted her; and she lay for months unable to make a trip back to Panama, as was expected of her. As soon as we reached San Francisco, the first thing was to secure an office and a house to live in. The weather was rainy and stormy, and snow even lay on the hills back of the Mission. Captain Folsom, the quartermaster, agreed to surrender for our office the old adobe custom house, on the upper corner of the plaza, as soon as he could remove his papers and effects down to one of his warehouses on the beach; and he also rented for us as quarters the old Hudson Bay Company house on Montgomery Street, which had been used by Howard & Mellua as a store, and at that very time they were moving their goods into a larger brick building just completed for them. As these changes would take some time, General Smith and Colonel Ogden, with their wives, accepted the hospitality offered by Commodore Jones on board the Ohio. I opened the office at the custom house, and Gibbs, Fitzgerald, and some others of us, slept in the loft of the Hudson Bay Company house until the lower part was cleared of Howard's store, after which General Smith and the ladies moved in. There we had a general mess, and the efforts at house-keeping were simply ludicrous. One servant after another, whom General Smith had brought from New Orleans, with a solemn promise to stand by him for one whole year, deserted without a word of notice or explanation, and in a few days none remained but little Isaac. The ladies had no maid or attendants; and the general, commanding all the mighty forces of the United States on the Pacific coast, had to scratch to get one good meal a day for his family! He was a gentleman of fine social qualities, genial and gentle, and joked at every thing. Poor Mrs. Smith and Mrs. Ogden did not bear it so philosophically. Gibbs, Fitzgerald, and I, could cruise around and find a meal, which cost three dollars, at some of the many restaurants which had sprung up out of red-wood boards and cotton lining; but the general and ladies could not go out, for ladies were rara aves at that day in California. Isaac was cook, chamber-maid, and everything, thoughtless of himself, and struggling, out of the slimmest means, to compound a breakfast for a large and hungry family. Breakfast would be announced any time between ten and twelve, and dinner according to circumstances. Many a time have I seen General Smith, with a can of preserved meat in his hands, going toward the house, take off his hat on meeting a negro, and, on being asked the reason of his politeness, he would answer that they were the only real gentlemen in California. I confess that the fidelity of Colonel Mason's boy "Aaron," and of General Smith's boy "Isaac," at a time when every white man laughed at promises as something made to be broken, has given me a kindly feeling of respect for the negroes, and makes me hope that they will find an honorable "status" in the jumble of affairs in which we now live.

That was a dull hard winter in San Francisco; the rains were heavy, and the mud fearful. I have seen mules stumble in the street, and drown in the liquid mud! Montgomery Street had been filled up with brush and clay, and I always dreaded to ride on horseback along it, because the mud was so deep that a horse's legs would become entangled in the bushes below, and the rider was likely to be thrown and drowned in the mud. The only sidewalks were made of stepping-stones of empty boxes, and here and there a few planks with barrel-staves nailed on. All the town lay along Montgomery Street, from Sacramento to Jackson, and about the plaza. Gambling was the chief occupation of the people. While they were waiting for the cessation of the rainy season, and for the beginning of spring, all sorts of houses were being put up, but of the most flimsy kind, and all were stores, restaurants, or gambling -saloons. Any room twenty by sixty feet would rent for a thousand dollars a month. I had, as my pay, seventy dollars a month, and no one would even try to hire a servant under three hundred dollars. Had it not been for the fifteen hundred dollars I had made in the store at Coloma, I could not have lived through the winter. About the 1st of

April arrived the steamer Oregon; but her captain (Pearson) knew what was the state of affairs on shore, and ran his steamer alongside the line-of-battle-ship Ohio at Saucelito, and obtained the privilege of leaving his crew on board as "prisoners" until he was ready to return to sea. Then, discharging his passengers and getting coal out of some of the ships which had arrived, he retook his crew out of limbo and carried the first regular mail back to Panama early in April. In regular order arrived the third steamer, the Panama; and, as the vessels were arriving with coal, The California was enabled to hire a crew and get off. From that time forward these three ships constituted the regular line of mail-steamers, which has been kept up ever since. By the steamer Oregon arrived out Major R. P. Hammond, J. M. Williams, James Blair, and others; also the gentlemen who, with Major Ogden, were to compose a joint commission to select the sites for the permanent forts and navyyard of California. This commission was composed of Majors Ogden, Smith, and Leadbetter, of, the army, and Captains Goldsborough, Van Brunt, and Blunt, of the navy. These officers, after a most careful study of the whole subject, selected Mare Island for the navy-yard, and "Benicia" for the storehouses and arsenals of the army. The Pacific Mail Steamship Company also selected Benicia as their depot. Thus was again revived the old struggle for supremacy of these two points as the site of the future city of the Pacific. Meantime, however, San Francisco had secured the name. About six hundred ships were anchored there without crews, and could not get away; and there the city was, and had to be.

Nevertheless, General Smith, being disinterested and unprejudiced, decided on Benicia as the point where the city ought to be, and where the army headquarters should be. By the Oregon there arrived at San Francisco a man who deserves mention here—Baron Steinberger. He had been a great cattle-dealer in the United States, and boasted that he had helped to break the United States Bank, by being indebted to it five million dollars! At all events, he was a splendid looking fellow, and brought with him from Washington a letter to General Smith and another for Commodore Jones, to the effect that he was a man of enlarged experience in beef; that the authorities in Washington knew that there existed in California large herds of cattle, which were only valuable for their hides and tallow; that it was of great importance to the Government that this beef should be cured and salted so as to be of use to the army and navy, obviating the necessity of shipping salt-beef around Cape Horn. I know he had such a letter from the Secretary of War, Marcy, to General Smith, for it passed into my custody, and I happened to be in Commodore Jones's cabin when the baron presented the one for him from the Secretary of the Navy. The baron was anxious to pitch in at once, and said that all he needed to start with were salt and barrels. After some inquiries of his purser, the commodore promised to let him have the barrels with their salt, as fast as they were emptied by the crew. Then the baron explained that he could get a nice lot of cattle from Don Timoteo Murphy, at the Mission of San Rafael, on the north aide of the bay, but he could not get a boat and crew to handle them. Under the authority from the Secretary of the Navy, the commodore then promised him the use of a boat and crew, until he (the baron) could find and purchase a suitable one for himself. Then the baron opened the first regular butcher-shop in San Francisco, on the wharf about the foot of Broadway or Pacific Street, where we could buy at twenty-five or fifty cents a pound the best roasts, steaks, and cuts of beef, which had cost him nothing, for he never paid anybody if he could help it, and he soon cleaned out poor Don Timoteo out. At first, every boat of his, in coming down from the San Rafael, touched at the Ohio, and left the best beefsteaks and roasts for the commodore, but soon the baron had enough money to dispense with the borrowed boat, and set up for himself, and from this small beginning, step by step, he rose in a few months to be one of the richest and most influential men in San Francisco; but in his wild speculations he was at last caught, and became helplessly bankrupt. He followed General Fremont to St. Louis in 1861, where I saw him, but soon afterward he died a pauper in one of the hospitals. When General Smith had his headquarters in San Francisco, in the spring of 1849, Steinberger gave dinners worthy any baron of old; and when, in after-years, I was a banker there, he used to borrow of me small sums of money in repayment for my share of these feasts; and somewhere among my old packages I hold one of his confidential notes for two hundred dollars, but on the whole I got off easily. I have no doubt that, if this man's history could be written out, it would present phases as wonderful as any of romance; but in my judgment he was a dangerous man, without any true-sense of honor or honesty.

Little by little the rains of that season grew less and less, and the hills once more became green and covered with flowers. It became perfectly evident that no family could live in San Francisco on such a salary as Uncle Sam allowed his most favored officials; so General Smith and Major Ogden concluded to send their families back to the United States, and afterward we men-folks could take to camp and live on our rations. The Second Infantry had arrived, and had been distributed, four companies to Monterey, and the rest somewhat as Stevenson's regiment had been. A. J. Smith's company of dragoons was sent up to Sonoma, whither General Smith had resolved to move our headquarters. On the steamer which sailed about May 1st (I think the California), we embarked, the ladies for home and we for Monterey. At Monterey we went on shore, and Colonel Mason, who meantime had been relieved by General Riley, went on board, and the steamer departed for Panama. Of all that party I alone am alive.

General Riley had, with his family, taken the house which Colonel Mason had formerly used, and Major Canby and wife had secured rooms at Alvarado's. Captain Bane was quartermaster, and had his family in the house of a man named Garner, near the redoubt. Burton and Company F were still at the fort; the four companies of the Second Infantry were quartered in the barracks, the same building in which we had had our headquarters; and the company officers were quartered in hired buildings near by. General Smith and his aide, Captain Gibbs, went to Larkin's house, and I was at my old rooms at Dona Augustias. As we intended to go back to San Francisco by land and afterward to travel a good deal, General Smith gave me the necessary authority to fit out the party. There happened to be several trains of horses and mules in town, so I purchased about a dozen horses and mules at two hundred dollars a head, on account of the Quartermaster's Department, and we had them kept under guard in the quartermaster's corral.

I remember one night being in the quarters of Lieutenant Alfred Sully, where nearly all the officers of the garrison were assembled, listening to Sully's stories. Lieutenant Derby, "Squibob," was one of the number, as also Fred Steele, "Neighbor" Jones, and others, when, just after "tattoo," the orderly-sergeants came to report the result of "tattoo" roll-call; one reported five men absent, another eight, and so on, until it became certain that twenty-eight men had deserted; and they were so bold and open in their behavior that it amounted to defiance. They had deliberately slung their knapsacks and started for the gold-mines. Dr. Murray and I were the only ones present who were familiar with the country, and I explained how easy they could all be taken by a party going out at once to Salinas Plain, where the country was so open and level that a rabbit could not cross without being seen; that the deserters could not go to the mines without crossing that plain, and could not reach it before daylight. All agreed that the whole regiment would desert if these men were not brought back. Several officers volunteered on the spot to go after them; and, as the soldiers could not be trusted, it was useless to send any but officers in pursuit. Some one went to report the affair to the adjutant-general, Canby, and he to General Riley. I waited some time, and, as the thing grew cold, I thought it was given up, and went to my room and to bed.

About midnight I was called up and informed that there were seven officers willing to go, but the difficulty was to get horses and saddles. I went down to Larkin's house and got General Smith to consent that we might take the horses I had bought for our trip. It was nearly three o'clock a.m. before we were all mounted and ready. I had a musket which I used for hunting. With this I led off at a canter, followed by the others. About six miles out, by the faint moon, I saw ahead of us in the sandy road some blue coats, and, fearing lest they might resist or escape into the dense bushes which lined the road, I halted and found with me Paymaster Hill, Captain N. H. Davis, and Lieutenant John Hamilton. We waited some time for the others, viz., Canby, Murray, Gibbs, and Sully, to come up, but as they were not in sight we made a dash up the road and captured six of the deserters, who were Germans, with heavy knapsacks on, trudging along the deep, sandy road. They had not expected pursuit, had not heard our horses, and were accordingly easily taken. Finding myself the senior officer present, I ordered Lieutenant Hamilton to search the men and then to march them back to Monterey, suspecting, as was the fact, that the rest of our party had taken a

43

road that branched off a couple of miles back. Daylight broke as we reached the Saunas River, twelve miles out, and there the trail was broad and fresh leading directly out on the Saunas Plain. This plain is about five miles wide, and then the ground becomes somewhat broken. The trail continued very plain, and I rode on at a gallop to where there was an old adobe-ranch on the left of the road, with the head of a lagoon, or pond, close by. I saw one or two of the soldiers getting water at the pond, and others up near the house. I had the best horse and was considerably ahead, but on looking back could see Hill and Davis coming up behind at a gallop. I motioned to them to hurry forward, and turned my horse across the head of the pond, knowing the ground well, as it was a favorite place for shooting geese and ducks. Approaching the house, I ordered the men who were outside to go in. They did not know me personally, and exchanged glances, but I had my musket cocked, and, as the two had seen Davis and Hill coming up pretty fast, they obeyed. Dismounting, I found the house full of deserters, and there was no escape for them. They naturally supposed that I had a strong party with me, and when I ordered them to "fall in" they obeyed from habit. By the time Hill and Davis came up I had them formed in two ranks, the front rank facing about, and I was taking away their bayonets, pistols, etc. We disarmed them, destroying a musket and several pistols, and, on counting them, we found that we three had taken eighteen, which, added to the six first captured, made twenty-four. We made them sling their knapsacks and begin their homeward march. It was near night when we got back, so that these deserters had traveled nearly forty miles since "tattoo" of the night before. The other party had captured three, so that only one man had escaped. I doubt not this prevented the desertion of the bulk of the Second Infantry that spring, for at that time so demoralizing was the effect of the gold-mines that everybody not in the military service justified desertion, because a soldier, if free, could earn more money in a day than he received per month. Not only did soldiers and sailors desert, but captains and masters of ships actually abandoned their vessels and cargoes to try their luck at the mines. Preachers and professors forgot their creeds and took to trade, and even to keeping gambling-houses. I remember that one of our regular soldiers, named Reese, in deserting stole a favorite double-barreled gun of mine, and when the orderly-sergeant of the company, Carson, was going on furlough, I asked him when he came across Reese to try and get my gun back. When he returned he told me that he had found Reese and offered him a hundred dollars for my gun, but Reese sent me word that he liked the gun, and would not take a hundred dollars for it. Soldiers or sailors who could reach the mines were universally shielded by the miners, so that it was next to useless to attempt their recapture. In due season General Persifer Smith, Gibbs, and I, with some hired packers, started back for San Francisco, and soon after we transferred our headquarters to Sonoma. About this time Major Joseph Hooker arrived from the East—the regular adjutant-general of the division—relieved me, and I became thereafter one of General Smith's regular aides-de-camp.

As there was very little to do, General Smith encouraged us to go into any business that would enable us to make money. R. P. Hammond, James Blair, and I, made a contract to survey for Colonel J. D. Stevenson his newly-projected city of "New York of the Pacific," situated at the month of the San Joaquin River. The contract embraced, also, the making of soundings and the marking out of a channel through Suisun Bay. We hired, in San Francisco, a small metallic boat, with a sail, laid in some stores, and proceeded to the United States ship Ohio, anchored at Saucelito, where we borrowed a sailor-boy and lead-lines with which to sound the channel. We sailed up to Benicia, and, at General Smith's request, we surveyed and marked the line dividing the city of Benicia from the government reserve. We then sounded the bay back and forth, and staked out the best channel up Suisun Bay, from which Blair made out sailing directions. We then made the preliminary surveys of the city of "New York of the Pacific," all of which were duly plotted; and for this work we each received from Stevenson five hundred dollars and ten or fifteen lots. I sold enough lots to make up another five hundred dollars, and let the balance go; for the city of "New York of the Pacific" never came to any thing. Indeed, cities at the time were being projected by speculators all round the bay and all over the country.

While we were surveying at "New York of the Pacific," occurred one of those little events that showed the force of the gold-fever. We had a sailor-boy with us, about seventeen years old, who cooked our meals and helped work the boat. Onshore, we had the sail spread so as to shelter us against the wind and dew. One morning I awoke about daylight, and looked out to see if our sailor-boy was at work getting breakfast; but he was not at the fire at all. Getting up, I discovered that he had converted a tule-bolsa into a sail boat, and was sailing for the gold-mines. He was astride this bolsa, with a small parcel of bread and meat done up in a piece of cloth; another piece of cloth, such as we used for making our signal-stations, he had fixed into a sail; and with a paddle he was directing his precarious craft right out into the broad bay, to follow the general direction of the schooners and boats that he knew were ascending the Sacramento River. He was about a hundred yards from the shore. I jerked up my gun, and hailed him to come back. After a moment's hesitation, he let go his sheet and began to paddle back. This bolsa was nothing but a bundle of tule, or bullrush, bound together with grass-ropes in the shape of a cigar, about ten feet long and about two feet through the butt. With these the California Indiana cross streams of considerable size. When he came ashore, I gave him a good overhauling for attempting to desert, and put him to work getting breakfast. In due time we returned him to his ship, the Ohio. Subsequently, I made a bargain with Mr. Hartnell to survey his ranch at Cosnmnes River, Sacramento Valley. Ord and a young citizen, named Seton, were associated with me in this. I bought of Rodman M. Price a surveyor's compass, chain, etc., and, in San Francisco, a small wagon and harness. Availing ourselves of a schooner, chartered to carry Major Miller and two companies of the Second Infantry from San Francisco to Stockton, we got up to our destination at little cost. I recall an occurrence that happened when the schooner was anchored in Carquinez Straits, opposite the soldiers' camp on shore. We were waiting for daylight and a fair wind; the schooner lay anchored at an ebb-tide, and about daylight Ord and I had gone ashore for something. Just as we were pulling off from shore, we heard the loud shouts of the men, and saw them all running down toward the water. Our attention thus drawn, we saw something swimming in the water, and pulled toward it, thinking it a coyote; but we soon recognized a large grizzly bear, swimming directly across the channel. Not having any weapon, we hurriedly pulled for the schooner, calling out, as we neared it, "A bear! a bear!" It so happened that Major Miller was on deck, washing his face and hands. He ran rapidly to the bow of the vessel, took the musket from the hands of the sentinel, and fired at the bear, as he passed but a short distance ahead of the schooner. The bear rose, made a growl or howl, but continued his course. As we scrambled up the port-aide to get our guns, the mate, with a crew, happened to have a boat on the starboard-aide, and, armed only with a hatchet, they pulled up alongside the bear, and the mate struck him in the head with the hatchet. The bear turned, tried to get into the boat, but the mate struck his claws with repeated blows, and made him let go. After several passes with him, the mate actually killed the bear, got a rope round him, and towed him alongside the schooner, where he was hoisted on deck. The carcass weighed over six hundred pounds. It was found that Major Miller's shot had struck the bear in the lower jaw, and thus disabled him. Had it not been for this, the bear would certainly have upset the boat and drowned all in it. As it was, however, his meat served us a good turn in our trip up to Stockton. At Stockton we disembarked our wagon, provisions, and instruments. There I bought two fine mules at three hundred dollars each, and we hitched up and started for the Coaumnes River. About twelve miles off was the Mokelumne, a wide, bold stream, with a canoe as a ferry-boat. We took our wagon to pieces, and ferried it and its contents across, and then drove our mules into the water. In crossing, one mule became entangled in the rope of the other, and for a time we thought he was a gone mule; but at last he revived and we hitched up. The mules were both pack-animals; neither had ever before seen a wagon. Young Seton also was about as green, and had never handled a mule. We put on the harness, and began to hitch them in, when one of the mules turned his head, saw the wagon, and started. We held on tight, but the beast did not stop until he had shivered the tongue-pole into a dozen fragments. The fact was, that Seton had hitched the traces before he had put on the blind-bridle. There was considerable swearing done, but that would not mend the pole. There was no place nearer than Sutter's Fort to repair damages, so we were put to our wits' end. We first sent back a mile or so, and bought a raw-hide. Gathering up the fragments of the pole and cutting the hide into strips, we finished it in the rudest manner. As long as the hide was green, the pole was very shaky; but gradually the sun dried the hide, tightened it, and the pole actually held for about a month. This cost us nearly a day of delay; but, when damages were repaired, we harnessed up again, and reached the crossing of the Cosumnes, where our survey was to begin. The expediente, or title-papers, of the ranch described it as containing nine or eleven leagues on the Cosumnes, south side, and between the San Joaquin River and Sierra Nevada Mountains. We began at the place where the road crosses the Cosumnes, and laid down a line four miles south, perpendicular to the general direction of the stream; then, surveying up the stream, we marked each mile so as to admit of a subdivision of one mile by four. The land was dry and very poor, with the exception of here and there some small pieces of bottom land, the great bulk of the bottom-land occurring on the north side of the stream. We continued the survey up some twenty miles into the hills above the mill of Dailor and Sheldon. It took about a month to make this survey, which, when finished, was duly plotted; and for it we received one-tenth of the land, or two subdivisions. Ord and I took the land, and we paid Seton for his labor in cash. By the sale of my share of the land, subsequently, I realized three thousand dollars. After finishing Hartnell's survey, we crossed over to Dailor's, and did some work for him at five hundred dollars a day for the party. Having finished our work on the Cosumnes, we proceeded to Sacramento, where Captain Sutter employed us to connect the survey of Sacramento City, made by Lieutenant Warner, and that of Sutterville, three miles below, which was then being surveyed by Lieutenant J. W. Davidson, of the First Dragoons. At Sutterville, the plateau of the Sacramento approached quite near the river, and it would have made a better site for a town than the low, submerged land where the city now stands; but it seems to be a law of growth that all natural advantages are disregarded wherever once business chooses a location. Old Sutter's embarcadero became Sacramento City, simply because it was the first point used for unloading boats for Sutter's Fort, just as the site for San Francisco was fixed by the use of Yerba Buena as the hide-landing for the Mission of "San Francisco de Asis."

I invested my earnings in this survey in three lots in Sacramento City, on which I made a fair profit by a sale to one McNulty, of Mansfield, Ohio. I only had a two months' leave of absence, during which General Smith, his staff, and a retinue of civil friends, were making a tour of the gold-mines, and hearing that he was en route back to his headquarters at Sonoma, I knocked off my work, sold my instruments, and left my wagon and mules with my cousin Charley Hoyt, who had a store in Sacramento, and was on the point of moving up to a ranch, for which he had bargained, on Bear Creek, on which was afterward established Camp "Far West." He afterward sold the mules, wagon, etc., for me, and on the whole I think I cleared, by those two months' work, about six thousand dollars. I then returned to headquarters at Sonoma, in time to attend my fellow aide-de-camp Gibbs through a long and dangerous sickness, during which he was on board a store-ship, guarded by Captain George Johnson, who now resides in San Francisco. General Smith had agreed that on the first good opportunity he would send me to the United States as a bearer of dispatches, but this he could not do until he had made the examination of Oregon, which was also in his command. During the summer of 1849 there continued to pour into California a perfect stream of people. Steamers came, and a line was established from San Francisco to Sacramento, of which the Senator was the pioneer, charging sixteen dollars a passage, and actually coining money. Other boats were built out of materials which had either come around Cape Horn or were brought from the Sandwich Islands. Wharves were built, houses were springing up as if by magic, and the Bay of San Francisco presented as busy a scene of life as any part of the world. Major Allen, of the Quartermaster's Department, who had come out as chief-quartermaster of the division, was building a large warehouse at Benicia, with a row of quarters, out of lumber at one hundred dollars per thousand feet, and the work was done by men at sixteen dollars a day. I have seen a detailed soldier, who got only his monthly pay of eight dollars a month, and twenty cents a day for extra duty, nailing on weather-boards and shingles, alongside a citizen who was paid sixteen dollars a day. This was a real injustice, made the soldiers discontented, and it was hardly to be wondered at that so many deserted.

While the mass of people were busy at gold and in mammoth speculations, a set of busy politicians were at work to secure the prizes of civil government. Gwin and Fremont were there, and T. Butler King, of Georgia, had come out from the East, scheming for office. He staid with us at Sonoma, and was generally regarded as the Government candidate

46

for United States Senator. General Riley as Governor, and Captain Halleck as Secretary of State, had issued a proclamation for the election of a convention to frame a State constitution. In due time the elections were held, and the convention was assembled at Monterey. Dr. Semple was elected president; and Gwin, Sutter, Halleck, Butler King, Sherwood, Gilbert, Shannon, and others, were members. General Smith took no part in this convention, but sent me down to watch the proceedings, and report to him. The only subject of interest was the slavery question. There were no slaves then in California, save a few who had come out as servants, but the Southern people at that time claimed their share of territory, out of that acquired by the common labors of all sections of the Union in the war with Mexico. Still, in California there was little feeling on the subject. I never heard General Smith, who was a Louisianian, express any opinion about it. Nor did Butler King, of Georgia, ever manifest any particular interest in the matter. A committee was named to draft a constitution, which in due time was reported, with the usual clause, then known as the Wilmot Proviso, excluding slavery; and during the debate which ensued very little opposition was made to this clause, which was finally adopted by a large majority, although the convention was made up in large part of men from our Southern States. This matter of California being a free State, afterward, in the national Congress, gave rise to angry debates, which at one time threatened civil war. The result of the convention was the election of State officers, and of the Legislature which sat in San Jose in October and November, 1849, and which elected Fremont and Gwin as the first United States Senators in Congress from the Pacific coast.

Shortly after returning from Monterey, I was sent by General Smith up to Sacramento City to instruct Lieutenants Warner and Williamson, of the Engineers, to push their surveys of the Sierra Nevada Mountains, for the purpose of ascertaining the possibility of passing that range by a railroad, a subject that then elicited universal interest. It was generally assumed that such a road could not be made along any of the immigrant roads then in use, and Warner's orders were to look farther north up the Feather River, or some one of its tributaries. Warner was engaged in this survey during the summer and fall of 1849, and had explored, to the very end of Goose Lake, the source of Feather River. Then, leaving Williamson with the baggage and part of the men, he took about ten men and a first-rate guide, crossed the summit to the east, and had turned south, having the range of mountains on his right hand, with the intention of regaining his camp by another pass in the mountain. The party was strung out, single file, with wide spaces between, Warner ahead. He had just crossed a small valley and ascended one of the spurs covered with sage-brush and rocks, when a band of Indians rose up and poured in a shower of arrows. The mule turned and ran back to the valley, where Warner fell off dead, punctured by five arrows. The mule also died. The guide, who was near to Warner, was mortally wounded; and one or two men had arrows in their bodies, but recovered. The party gathered about Warner's body, in sight of the Indians, who whooped and yelled, but did not venture away from their cover of rocks. This party of men remained there all day without burying the bodies, and at night, by a wide circuit, passed the mountain, and reached Williamson's camp. The news of Warner's death cast a gloom over all the old Californians, who knew him well. He was a careful, prudent, and honest officer, well qualified for his business, and extremely accurate in all his work. He and I had been intimately associated during our four years together in California, and I felt his loss deeply. The season was then too far advanced to attempt to avenge his death, and it was not until the next spring that a party was sent out to gather up and bury his scattered bones.

As winter approached, the immigrants overland came pouring into California, dusty and worn with their two thousand miles of weary travel across the plains and mountains. Those who arrived in October and November reported thousands still behind them, with oxen perishing, and short of food. Appeals were made for help, and General Smith resolved to attempt relief. Major Rucker, who had come across with Pike. Graham's Battalion of Dragoons, had exchanged with Major Fitzgerald, of the Quartermaster's Department, and was detailed to conduct this relief. General Smith ordered him to be supplied with one hundred thousand dollars out of the civil fund, subject to his control, and with this to purchase at Sacramento flour, bacon, etc., and to hire men and mules to send out and meet the immigrants. Major Rucker fulfilled this duty perfectly, sending out pack-trains loaded with food by the many routes by which the immigrants were known to be approaching, went out himself with one of these trains, and remained in the mountains until the last immigrant had got in. No doubt this expedition saved many a life which has since been most useful to the country. I remained at Sacramento a good part of the fall of 1849, recognizing among the immigrants many of my old personal friends—John C. Fall, William King, Sam Stambaugh, Hugh Ewing, Hampton Denman, etc. I got Rucker to give these last two employment along with the train for the relief of the immigrants. They had proposed to begin a ranch on my land on the Cosumnes, but afterward changed their minds, and went out with Rucker.

While I was at Sacramento General Smith had gone on his contemplated trip to Oregon, and promised that he would be back in December, when he would send me home with dispatches. Accordingly, as the winter and rainy season was at hand, I went to San Francisco, and spent some time at the Presidio, waiting patiently for General Smith's return. About Christmas a vessel arrived from Oregon with the dispatches, and an order for me to deliver them in person to General Winfield Scott, in New York City. General Smith had sent them down, remaining in Oregon for a time. Of course I was all ready, and others of our set were going home by the same conveyance, viz., Rucker, Ord, A. J. Smith—some under orders, and the others on leave. Wanting to see my old friends in Monterey, I arranged for my passage in the steamer of January 1, 1850, paying six hundred dollars for passage to New York, and went down to Monterey by land, Rucker accompanying me. The weather was unusually rainy, and all the plain about Santa Clara was under water; but we reached Monterey in time. I again was welcomed by my friends, Dona Augustias, Manuelita, and the family, and it was resolved that I should take two of the boys home with me and put them at Georgetown College for education, viz., Antonio and Porfirio, thirteen and eleven years old. The dona gave me a bag of gold-dust to pay for their passage and to deposit at the college. On the 2d day of January punctually appeared the steamer Oregon.

We were all soon on board and off for home. At that time the steamers touched at San Diego, Acapulco, and Panama. Our passage down the coast was unusually pleasant. Arrived at Panama, we hired mules and rode across to Gorgona, on the Cruces River, where we hired a boat and paddled down to the mouth of the river, off which lay the steamer Crescent City. It usually took four days to cross the isthmus, every passenger taking care of himself, and it was really funny to watch the efforts of women and men unaccustomed to mules. It was an old song to us, and the trip across was easy and interesting. In due time we were rowed off to the Crescent City, rolling back and forth in the swell, and we scrambled aboard by a "Jacob's ladder" from the stern. Some of the women had to be hoisted aboard by lowering a tub from the end of a boom; fun to us who looked on, but awkward enough to the poor women, especially to a very fat one, who attracted much notice. General Fremont, wife and child (Lillie) were passengers with us down from San Francisco; but Mrs. Fremont not being well, they remained over one trip at Panama.

Senator Gwin was one of our passengers, and went through to New York. We reached New York about the close of January, after a safe and pleasant trip. Our party, composed of Ord, A. J. Smith, and Rucker, with the two boys, Antonio and Porfirio, put up at Delmonico's, on Bowling Green; and, as soon as we had cleaned up somewhat, I took a carriage, went to General Scott's office in Ninth Street, delivered my dispatches, was ordered to dine with him next day, and then went forth to hunt up my old friends and relations, the Scotts, Hoyts, etc., etc.

On reaching New York, most of us had rough soldier's clothing, but we soon got a new outfit, and I dined with General Scott's family, Mrs. Scott being present, and also their son-in-law and daughter (Colonel and Mrs. H. L. Scott). The general questioned me pretty closely in regard to things on the Pacific coast, especially the politics, and startled me with the assertion that "our country was on the eve of a terrible civil war." He interested me by anecdotes of my old army comrades in his recent battles around the city of Mexico, and I felt deeply the fact that our country had passed through a foreign war, that my comrades had fought great battles, and yet I had not heard a hostile shot. Of course, I thought it the last and only chance in my day, and that my career as a soldier was at an end. After some four or five days spent in New York, I was, by an order of General Scott, sent to Washington, to lay before the Secretary of War (Crawford, of Georgia) the dispatches which I had brought from California. On reaching Washington, I found that Mr. Ewing was Secretary of the Interior, and I at once became a member of his family. The family occupied the house of Mr. Blair, on Pennsylvania Avenue, directly in front of the War Department. I immediately repaired to the War Department, and placed my dispatches in the hands of Mr. Crawford, who questioned me somewhat about California, but seemed little interested in the subject, except so far as it related to slavery and the routes through Texas. I then went to call on the President at the White House. I found Major Bliss, who had been my teacher in mathematics at West Point, and was then General Taylor's son-in-law and private secretary. He took me into the room, now used by the President's private secretaries, where President Taylor was. I had never seen him before, though I had served under him in Florida in 1840-'41, and was most agreeably surprised at his fine personal appearance, and his pleasant, easy manners. He received me with great kindness, told me that Colonel Mason had mentioned my name with praise, and that he would be pleased to do me any act of favor. We were with him nearly an hour, talking about California generally, and of his personal friends, Persifer Smith, Riley, Canby, and others: Although General Scott was generally regarded by the army as the most accomplished soldier of the Mexican War, yet General Taylor had that blunt, honest, and stern character, that endeared him to the masses of the people, and made him President. Bliss, too, had gained a large fame by his marked skill and intelligence as an adjutant-general and military adviser. His manner was very unmilitary, and in his talk he stammered and hesitated, so as to make an unfavorable impression on a stranger; but he was wonderfully accurate and skillful with his pen, and his orders and letters form a model of military precision and clearness.

CHAPTER IV.
MISSOURI, LOUISIANA, AND CALIFORNIA

1850-1855.

Having returned from California in January, 1850, with dispatches for the War Department, and having delivered them in person first to General Scott in New York City, and afterward to the Secretary of War (Crawford) in Washington City, I applied for and received a leave of absence for six months. I first visited my mother, then living at Mansfield, Ohio, and returned to Washington, where, on the 1st day of May, 1850, I was married to Miss Ellen Boyle Ewing, daughter of the Hon. Thomas Ewing, Secretary of the Interior. The marriage ceremony was attended by a large and distinguished company, embracing Daniel Webster, Henry Clay, T. H. Benton, President Taylor, and all his cabinet. This occurred at the house of Mr. Ewing, the same now owned and occupied by Mr. F. P. Blair, senior, on Pennsylvania Avenue, opposite the War Department. We made a wedding tour to Baltimore, New York, Niagara, and Ohio, and returned to Washington by the 1st of July. General Taylor participated in the celebration of the Fourth of July, a very hot day, by hearing a long speech from the Hon. Henry S. Foote, at the base of the Washington Monument. Returning from the celebration much heated and fatigued, he partook too freely of his favorite iced milk with cherries, and during that night was seized with a severe colic, which by morning had quite prostrated him. It was said that he sent for his son-in-law, Surgeon Wood, United States Army, stationed in Baltimore, and declined medical assistance from anybody else. Mr. Ewing visited him several times, and was manifestly uneasy and anxious, as was also his son-in-law, Major Bliss, then of the army, and his confidential secretary. He rapidly grew worse, and died in about four days.

At that time there was a high state of political feeling pervading the country, on account of the questions growing out of the new Territories just acquired from Mexico by the war. Congress was in session, and General Taylor's sudden death evidently created great alarm. I was present in the Senate-gallery, and saw the oath of office administered to the Vice-President, Mr. Fillmore, a man of splendid physical proportions and commanding appearance; but on the faces of Senators and people could easily be read the feelings of doubt and uncertainty that prevailed. All knew that a change in the cabinet and general policy was likely to result, but at the time it was supposed that Mr. Fillmore, whose home was in Buffalo, would be less liberal than General Taylor to the politicians of the South, who feared, or pretended to fear, a crusade against slavery; or, as was the political cry of the day, that slavery would be prohibited in the Territories and in the places exclusively under the jurisdiction of the United States. Events, however, proved the contrary.

I attended General Taylor's funeral as a sort of aide-decamp, at the request of the Adjutant-General of the army, Roger Jones, whose brother, a militia-general, commanded the escort, composed of militia and some regulars. Among the regulars I recall the names of Captains John Sedgwick and W. F. Barry.

Hardly was General Taylor decently buried in the Congressional Cemetery when the political struggle recommenced, and it became manifest that Mr. Fillmore favored the general compromise then known as Henry Clay's "Omnibus Bill," and that a general change of cabinet would at once occur: Webster was to succeed Mr. Clayton as Secretary of State, Corwin to succeed Mr. Meredith as Secretary of the Treasury, and A. H. H. Stuart to succeed Mr. Ewing as Secretary of the Interior. Mr. Ewing, however, was immediately appointed by the Governor of the State to succeed Corwin in the Senate. These changes made it necessary for Mr. Ewing to discontinue house-keeping, and Mr. Corwin took his home and furniture off his hands. I escorted the family out to their home in Lancaster, Ohio; but, before this had occurred, some most interesting debates took place in the Senate, which I regularly attended, and heard Clay, Benton, Foots, King of Alabama, Dayton, and the many real orators of that day. Mr. Calhoun was in his seat, but he was evidently approaching his end, for he was pale and feeble in the extreme. I heard Mr. Webster's last speech on the floor of the Senate, under circumstances that warrant a description. It was publicly known that he was to leave the Senate, and enter the new cabinet of Mr. Fillmore, as his Secretary of State, and that prior to leaving he was to make a great speech on the "Omnibus Bill." Resolved to hear it, I went up to the Capitol on the day named, an hour or so earlier than usual. The speech was to be delivered in the old Senate-chamber, now used by the Supreme Court. The galleries were much smaller than at present, and I found them full to overflowing, with a dense crowd about the door, struggling to reach the stairs. I could not get near, and then tried the reporters' gallery, but found it equally crowded; so I feared I should lose the only possible opportunity to hear Mr. Webster.

I had only a limited personal acquaintance with any of the Senators, but had met Mr. Corwin quite often at Mr. Ewing's house, and I also knew that he had been extremely friendly to my father in his lifetime; so I ventured to send in to him my card, "W. T. S., First-Lieutenant, Third Artillery." He came to the door promptly, when I said, "Mr. Corwin, I believe Mr. Webster is to speak to-day." His answer was, "Yes, he has the floor at one o'clock." I then added that I was extremely anxious to hear him. "Well," said he, "why don't you go into the gallery?" I explained that it was full, and I had tried every access, but found all jammed with people. "Well," said he, "what do you want of me?" I explained that I would like him to take me on the floor of the Senate; that I had often seen from the gallery persons on the floor, no better entitled to it than I. He then asked in his quizzical way, "Are you a foreign embassador?" "No." "Are you the Governor of a State?" "No." "Are you a member of the other House?" "Certainly not!" "Have you ever had a vote of thanks by name?" "No!" "Well, these are the only privileged members." I then told him he knew well enough who I was, and that if he chose he could take me in. He then said, "Have you any impudence?" I told him, "A reasonable amount if occasion called for it." "Do you think you could become so interested in my conversation as not to notice the door-keeper?" (pointing to him). I told him that there was not the least doubt of it, if he would tell me one of his funny stories. He then took my arm, and led me a turn in the vestibule, talking about some indifferent matter, but all the time directing my looks to his left hand, toward which he was gesticulating with his right; and thus we approached the door-keeper, who began asking me, "Foreign ambassador? Governor of a State? Member of Congress?" etc.; but I caught Corwin's eye, which said plainly, "Don't mind him, pay attention to me," and in this way we entered the Senate-chamber by a side-door. Once in, Corwin said, "Now you can take care of yourself," and I thanked him cordially.

I found a seat close behind Mr. Webster, and near General Scott, and heard the whole of the speech. It was heavy in the extreme, and I confess that I was disappointed and tired long before it was finished. No doubt the speech was full of fact and argument, but it had none of the fire of oratory, or intensity of feeling, that marked all of Mr. Clay's efforts.

Toward the end of July, as before stated, all the family went home to Lancaster. Congress was still in session, and the bill adding four captains to the Commissary Department had not passed, but was reasonably certain to, and I was equally sure of being one of them. At that time my name was on the muster-roll of (Light) Company C, Third Artillery (Bragg's), stationed at Jefferson Barracks, near St. Louis. But, as there was cholera at St. Louis, on application, I was permitted to delay joining my company until September. Early in that month, I proceeded to Cincinnati, and thence by steamboat to St. Louis, and then to Jefferson Barracks, where I reported for duty to Captain and Brevet-Colonel Braxton Bragg, commanding (Light) Company C, Third Artillery. The other officers of the company were First-Lieutenant James A. Hardie, and afterward Haekaliah Brown. New horses had just been purchased for the battery, and we were preparing for work, when the mail brought the orders announcing the passage of the bill increasing the Commissary Department by four captains, to which were promoted Captains Shiras, Blair, Sherman, and Bowen. I was ordered to take post at St. Louis, and to relieve Captain A. J. Smith, First Dragoons, who had been acting in that capacity for some months. My commission bore date September 27,1850. I proceeded forthwith to the city, relieved Captain Smith, and entered on the discharge of the duties of the office.

Colonel N. S. Clarke, Sixth Infantry, commanded the department; Major D. C. Buell was adjutant-general, and Captain W. S. Hancock was regimental quartermaster; Colonel Thomas Swords was the depot quartermaster, and we had our offices in the same building, on the corner of Washington Avenue and Second. Subsequently Major S. Van Vliet relieved Colonel Swords. I remained at the Planters' House until my family arrived, when we occupied a house on Chouteau Avenue, near Twelfth.

During the spring and summer of 1851, Mr. Ewing and Mr. Henry Stoddard, of Dayton, Ohio, a cousin of my father, were much in St. Louis, on business connected with the estate of Major Amos Stoddard, who was of the old army, as early as the beginning of this century. He was stationed at the village of St. Louis at the time of the Louisiana purchase, and when Lewis and Clarke made their famous expedition across the continent to the Columbia River. Major Stoddard at that early day had purchased a small farm back of the village, of some Spaniard or Frenchman but, as he was a bachelor, and was killed at Fort Meigs, Ohio, during the War of 1812, the title was for many years lost sight of, and the farm was covered over by other claims and by occupants. As St. Louis began to grow, his brothers and sisters, and their descendants, concluded to look up the property. After much and fruitless litigation, they at last retained Mr. Stoddard, of Dayton, who in turn employed Mr. Ewing, and these, after many years of labor, established the title, and in the summer of 1851 they were put in possession by the United States marshal. The ground was laid off, the city survey extended over it, and the whole was sold in partition. I made some purchases, and acquired an interest, which I have retained more or less ever since.

We continued to reside in St. Louis throughout the year 1851, and in the spring of 1852 I had occasion to visit Fort Leavenworth on duty, partly to inspect a lot of cattle which a Mr. Gordon, of Cass County, had contracted to deliver in New Mexico, to enable Colonel Sumner to attempt his scheme of making the soldiers in New Mexico self-supporting, by raising their own meat, and in a measure their own vegetables. I found Fort Leavenworth then, as now, a most beautiful spot, but in the midst of a wild Indian country. There were no whites settled in what is now the State of Kansas. Weston, in Missouri, was the great town, and speculation in town-lots there and thereabout burnt the fingers of some of the army-officers, who wanted to plant their scanty dollars in a fruitful soil. I rode on horseback over to Gordon's farm, saw the cattle, concluded the bargain, and returned by way of Independence, Missouri. At Independence I found F. X. Aubrey, a noted man of that day, who had just made a celebrated ride of six hundred miles in six days. That spring the United States quartermaster, Major L. C. Easton, at Fort Union, New Mexico, had occasion to send some message east by a certain date, and contracted with Aubrey to carry it to the nearest post-office (then Independence, Missouri), making his compensation conditional on the time consumed. He was supplied with a good horse, and an order on the outgoing trains for an exchange. Though the whole route was infested with hostile Indians, and not a house on it, Aubrey started alone with his rifle. He was fortunate in meeting several outward-bound trains, and there, by made frequent changes of horses, some four or five, and reached Independence in six days, having hardly rested or slept the whole way. Of course, he was extremely fatigued, and said there was an opinion among the wild Indians that if a man "sleeps out his sleep," after such extreme exhaustion, he will never awake; and, accordingly, he instructed his landlord to wake him up after eight hours of sleep. When aroused at last, he saw by the clock that he had been asleep twenty hours, and he was dreadfully angry, threatened to murder his landlord, who protested he had tried in every way to get him up, but found it impossible, and had let him "sleep it out" Aubrey, in describing his sensations to me, said he took it for granted he was a dead man; but in fact he sustained no ill effects, and was off again in a few days. I met him afterward often in California, and always esteemed him one of the best samples of that bold race of men who had grown up on the Plains, along with the Indians, in the service of the fur companies. He was afterward, in 1856, killed by R. C. Weightman, in a bar-room row, at Santa Fe, New Mexico, where he had just arrived from California.

In going from Independence to Fort Leavenworth, I had to swim Milk Creek, and sleep all night in a Shawnee camp. The next day I crossed the Kaw or Kansas River in a ferry boat, maintained by the blacksmith of the tribe, and reached the fort in the evening. At that day the whole region was unsettled, where now exist many rich counties, highly cultivated, embracing several cities of from ten to forty thousand inhabitants. From Fort Leavenworth I returned by steamboat to St. Louis.

In the summer of 1852, my family went to Lancaster, Ohio; but I remained at my post. Late in the season, it was rumored that I was to be transferred to New Orleans, and in due time I learned the cause. During a part of the Mexican War, Major Seawell, of the Seventh Infantry, had been acting commissary of subsistence at New Orleans, then the great depot of supplies for the troops in Texas, and of those operating beyond the Rio Grande. Commissaries at that time were allowed to purchase in open market, and were not restricted to advertising and awarding contracts to the lowest bidders. It was reported that Major Seawell had purchased largely of the house of Perry Seawell & Co., Mr. Seawell being a relative of his. When he was relieved in his duties by Major Waggman, of the regular Commissary Department, the latter found Perry Seawell & Co. so prompt and satisfactory that he continued the patronage; for which there was a good reason, because stores for the use of the troops at remote posts had to be packed in a particular way, to bear transportation in wagons, or even on pack-mules; and this firm had made extraordinary preparations for this exclusive purpose. Some time about 1849, a brother of Major Waggaman, who had been clerk to Captain Casey, commissary of subsistence, at Tampa Bay, Florida, was thrown out of office by the death of the captain, and he naturally applied to his brother in New Orleans for employment; and he, in turn, referred him to his friends, Messrs. Perry Seawell & Co. These first employed him as a clerk, and afterward admitted him as a partner. Thus it resulted, in fact, that Major Waggaman was dealing largely, if not exclusively, with a firm of which his brother was a partner.

One day, as General Twiggs was coming across Lake Pontchartrain, he fell in with one of his old cronies, who was an extensive grocer. This gentleman gradually led the conversation to the downward tendency of the times since he and Twiggs were young, saying that, in former years, all the merchants of New Orleans had a chance at government patronage; but now, in order to sell to the army commissary, one had to take a brother in as a partner. General Twiggs resented this, but the merchant again affirmed it, and gave names. As soon as General Twiggs reached his office, he instructed his adjutant-general, Colonel Bliss—who told me this—to address a categorical note of inquiry to Major Waggaman. The major very frankly stated the facts as they had arisen, and insisted that the firm of Perry

Seawell & Co. had enjoyed a large patronage, but deserved it richly by reason of their promptness, fairness, and fidelity. The correspondence was sent to Washington, and the result was, that Major Waggaman was ordered to St. Louis, and I was ordered to New Orleans.

I went down to New Orleans in a steamboat in the month of September, 1852, taking with me a clerk, and, on arrival, assumed the office, in a bank-building facing Lafayette Square, in which were the offices of all the army departments. General D. Twiggs was in command of the department, with Colonel W. W. S. Bliss (son-in-law of General Taylor) as his adjutant-general. Colonel A. C. Myers was quartermaster, Captain John F. Reynolds aide-de-camp, and Colonel A. J. Coffee paymaster. I took rooms at the St. Louis Hotel, kept by a most excellent gentleman, Colonel Mudge.

Mr. Perry Seawell came to me in person, soliciting a continuance of the custom which he had theretofore enjoyed; but I told him frankly that a change was necessary, and I never saw or heard of him afterward. I simply purchased in open market, arranged for the proper packing of the stores, and had not the least difficulty in supplying the troops and satisfying the head of the department in Washington.

About Christmas, I had notice that my family, consisting of Mrs. Sherman, two children, and nurse, with my sister Fanny (now Mrs. Moulton, of Cincinnati, Ohio), were en route for New Orleans by steam-packet; so I hired a house on Magazine Street, and furnished it. Almost at the moment of their arrival, also came from St. Louis my personal friend Major Turner, with a parcel of documents, which, on examination, proved to be articles of copartnership for a bank in California under the title of "Lucas, Turner & Co.," in which my name was embraced as a partner. Major Turner was, at the time, actually en route for New York, to embark for San Francisco, to inaugurate the bank, in the nature of a branch of the firm already existing at St. Louis under the name of "Lucas & Symonds." We discussed the matter very fully, and he left with me the papers for reflection, and went on to New York and California.

Shortly after arrived James H. Lucas, Esq., the principal of the banking-firm in St. Louis, a most honorable and wealthy gentleman. He further explained the full programme of the branch in California; that my name had been included at the insistence of Major Turner, who was a man of family and property in St. Louis, unwilling to remain long in San Francisco, and who wanted me to succeed him there. He offered me a very tempting income, with an interest that would accumulate and grow. He also disclosed to me that, in establishing a branch in California, he was influenced by the apparent prosperity of Page, Bacon & Co., and further that he had received the principal data, on which he had founded the scheme, from B. R. Nisbet, who was then a teller in the firm of Page, Bacon & Co., of San Francisco; that he also was to be taken in as a partner, and was fully competent to manage all the details of the business; but, as Nisbet was comparatively young, Mr. Lucas wanted me to reside in San Francisco permanently, as the head of the firm. All these matters were fully discussed, and I agreed to apply for a six months' leave of absence, go to San Francisco, see for myself, and be governed by appearances there. I accordingly, with General Twiggs's approval, applied to the adjutant-general for a six months' leave, which was granted; and Captain John F. Reynolds was named to perform my duties during my absence.

During the stay of my family in New Orleans, we enjoyed the society of the families of General Twiggs, Colonel Myers, and Colonel Bliss, as also of many citizens, among whom was the wife of Mr. Day, sister to my brother-in-law, Judge Bartley. General Twiggs was then one of the oldest officers of the army. His history extended back to the War of 1812, and he had served in early days with General Jackson in Florida and in the Creek campaigns. He had fine powers of description, and often entertained us, at his office, with accounts of his experiences in the earlier settlements of the Southwest. Colonel Bliss had been General Taylor's adjutant in the Mexican War, and was universally regarded as one of the most finished and accomplished scholars in the army, and his wife was a most agreeable and accomplished lady.

Late in February, I dispatched my family up to Ohio in the steamboat Tecumseh (Captain Pearce); disposed of my house and furniture; turned over to Major Reynolds the funds, property, and records of the office; and took passage in a small steamer for

Nicaragua, en route for California. We embarked early in March, and in seven days reached Greytown, where we united with the passengers from New York, and proceeded, by the Nicaragua River and Lake, for the Pacific Ocean. The river was low, and the little steam canal-boats, four in number, grounded often, so that the passengers had to get into the water, to help them over the bare. In all there were about six hundred passengers, of whom about sixty were women and children. In four days we reached Castillo, where there is a decided fall, passed by a short railway, and above this fall we were transferred to a larger boat, which carried us up the rest of the river, and across the beautiful lake Nicaragua, studded with volcanic islands. Landing at Virgin Bay, we rode on mules across to San Juan del Sur, where lay at anchor the propeller S. S. Lewis (Captain Partridge, I think). Passengers were carried through the surf by natives to small boats, and rowed off to the Lewis. The weather was very hot, and quite a scramble followed for state-rooms, especially for those on deck. I succeeded in reaching the purser's office, got my ticket for a berth in one of the best state-rooms on deck, and, just as I was turning from the window, a lady who was a fellow-passenger from New Orleans, a Mrs. D-, called to me to secure her and her lady friend berths on deck, saying that those below were unendurable. I spoke to the purser, who, at the moment perplexed by the crowd and clamor, answered: "I must put their names down for the other two berths of your state-room; but, as soon as the confusion is over, I will make some change whereby you shall not suffer." As soon as these two women were assigned to a state-room, they took possession, and I was left out. Their names were recorded as "Captain Sherman and ladies." As soon as things were quieted down I remonstrated with the purser, who at last gave me a lower berth in another and larger state-room on deck, with five others, so that my two ladies had the state-room all to themselves. At every meal the steward would come to me, and say, "Captain Sherman, will you bring your ladies to the table?" and we had the best seats in the ship.

This continued throughout the voyage, and I assert that "my ladies" were of the most modest and best-behaved in the ship; but some time after we had reached San Francisco one of our fellow-passengers came to me and inquired if I personally knew Mrs. D—, with flaxen tresses, who sang so sweetly for us, and who had come out under my especial escort. I replied I did not, more than the chance acquaintance of the voyage, and what she herself had told me, viz., that she expected to meet her husband, who lived about Mokelumne Hill. He then informed me that she was a woman of the town. Society in California was then decidedly mixed. In due season the steamship Lewis got under weigh. She was a wooden ship, long and narrow, bark-rigged, and a propeller; very slow, moving not over eight miles an hour. We stopped at Acapulco, and, in eighteen days, passed in sight of Point Pinoa at Monterey, and at the speed we were traveling expected to reach San Francisco at 4 A. M. the next day. The cabin passengers, as was usual, bought of the steward some champagne and cigars, and we had a sort of ovation for the captain, purser, and surgeon of the ship, who were all very clever fellows, though they had a slow and poor ship. Late at night all the passengers went to bed, expecting to enter the port at daylight. I did not undress, as I thought the captain could and would run in at night, and I lay down with my clothes on. About 4 A. M. I was awakened by a bump and sort of grating of the vessel, which I thought was our arrival at the wharf in San Francisco; but instantly the ship struck heavily; the engines stopped, and the running to and fro on deck showed that something was wrong. In a moment I was out of my state-room, at the bulwark, holding fast to a stanchion, and looking over the side at the white and seething water caused by her sudden and violent stoppage. The sea was comparatively smooth, the night pitch-dark, and the fog deep and impenetrable; the ship would rise with the swell, and come down with a bump and quiver that was decidedly unpleasant. Soon the passengers were out of their rooms, undressed, calling for help, and praying as though the ship were going to sink immediately. Of course she could not sink, being already on the bottom, and the only question was as to the strength of hull to stand the bumping and straining. Great confusion for a time prevailed, but soon I realized that the captain had taken all proper precautions to secure his boats, of which there were six at the davits. These are the first things that steerage-passengers make for in case of shipwreck, and right over my head I heard the captain's voice say in a low tone, but quite decided: "Let go that falls, or, damn you, I'll blow your head off!" This seemingly harsh language gave me great comfort at the time, and on saying so to the captain afterward, he explained that it was addressed to a passenger who attempted to lower one of the boats. Guards, composed of the crew, were soon posted to prevent any interference with the boats, and the officers circulated among the passengers the report that there was no immediate danger; that, fortunately, the sea was smooth; that we were simply aground, and must quietly await daylight.

They advised the passengers to keep quiet, and the ladies and children to dress and sit at the doors of their state-rooms, there to await the advice and action of the officers of the ship, who were perfectly cool and self-possessed. Meantime the ship was working over a reef-for a time I feared she would break in two; but, as the water gradually rose inside to a level with the sea outside, the ship swung broadside to the swell, and all her keel seemed to rest on the rock or sand. At no time did the sea break over the deck—but the water below drove all the people up to the main-deck and to the promenade-deck, and thus we remained for about three hours, when daylight came; but there was a fog so thick that nothing but water could be seen. The captain caused a boat to be carefully lowered, put in her a trustworthy officer with a boat-compass, and we saw her depart into the fog. During her absence the ship's bell was kept tolling. Then the fires were all out, the ship full of water, and gradually breaking up, wriggling with every swell like a willow basket—the sea all round us full of the floating fragments of her sheeting, twisted and torn into a spongy condition. In less than an hour the boat returned, saying that the beach was quite near, not more than a mile away, and had a good place for landing. All the boats were then carefully lowered, and manned by crews belonging to the ship; a piece of the gangway, on the leeward side, was cut away, and all the women, and a few of the worst-scared men, were lowered into the boats, which pulled for shore. In a comparatively short time the boats returned, took new loads, and the debarkation was afterward carried on quietly and systematically. No baggage was allowed to go on shore except bags or parcels carried in the hands of passengers. At times the fog lifted so that we could see from the wreck the tops of the hills, and the outline of the shore; and I remember sitting on, the upper or hurricane deck with the captain, who had his maps and compass before him, and was trying to make out where the ship was. I thought I recognized the outline of the hills below the mission of Dolores, and so stated to him; but he called my attention to the fact that the general line of hills bore northwest, whereas the coast south of San Francisco bears due north and south. He therefore concluded that the ship had overrun her reckoning, and was then to the north of San Francisco. He also explained that, the passage up being longer than usual, viz., eighteen days, the coal was short; that at the time the firemen were using some cut-up spars along with the slack of coal, and that this fuel had made more than usual steam, so that the ship must have glided along faster than reckoned. This proved to be the actual case, for, in fact, the steamship Lewis was wrecked April 9, 1853, on "Duckworth Reef," Baulinas Bay, about eighteen miles above the entrance to San Francisco.

The captain had sent ashore the purser in the first boat, with orders to work his way to the city as soon as possible, to report the loss of his vessel, and to bring back help. I remained on the wreck till among the last of the passengers, managing to get a can of crackers and some sardines out of the submerged pantry, a thing the rest of the passengers did not have, and then I went quietly ashore in one of the boats. The passengers were all on the beach, under a steep bluff; had built fires to dry their clothes, but had seen no human being, and had no idea where they were. Taking along with me a fellow-passenger, a young chap about eighteen years old, I scrambled up the bluff, and walked back toward the hills, in hopes to get a good view of some known object. It was then the month of April, and the hills were covered with the beautiful grasses and flowers of that season of the year. We soon found horse paths and tracks, and following them we came upon a drove of horses grazing at large, some of which had saddle-marks. At about two miles from the beach we found a corral; and thence, following one of the strongest-marked paths, in about a mile more we descended into a valley, and, on turning a sharp point, reached a board shanty, with a horse picketed near by. Four men were inside eating a meal. I inquired if any of the Lewis's people had been there; they did not seem to understand what I meant when I explained to them that about three miles from them, and beyond the old corral, the steamer Lewis was wrecked, and her passengers were on the beach. I inquired where we were, and they answered, "At Baulinas Creek;" that they were employed at a saw-mill just above, and were engaged in shipping lumber to San Francisco; that a schooner loaded with lumber was then about two miles down the creek, waiting for the tide to get out, and doubtless if we would walk down they would take us on board.

I wrote a few words back to the captain, telling him where he was, and that I would hurry to the city to send him help. My companion and I then went on down the creek, and soon descried the schooner anchored out in the stream. On being hailed, a small boat came in and took us on board. The "captain" willingly agreed for a small sum to carry us down to San Francisco; and, as his whole crew consisted of a small boy about twelve years old, we helped him to get up his anchor and pole the schooner down the creek and out over the bar on a high tide. This must have been about 2 P.M. Once over the bar, the sails were hoisted, and we glided along rapidly with a strong, fair, northwest wind. The fog had lifted, so we could see the shores plainly, and the entrance to the bay. In a couple of hours we were entering the bay, and running "wing-and-wing." Outside the wind was simply the usual strong breeze; but, as it passes through the head of the Golden Gate, it increases, and there, too, we met a strong ebb-tide.

The schooner was loaded with lumber, much of which was on deck, lashed down to ring bolts with raw-hide thongs. The captain was steering, and I was reclining on the lumber, looking at the familiar shore, as we approached Fort Point, when I heard a sort of cry, and felt the schooner going over. As we got into the throat of the "Heads," the force of the wind, meeting a strong ebb-tide, drove the nose of the schooner under water; she dove like a duck, went over on her side, and began, to drift out with the tide. I found myself in the water, mixed up with pieces of plank and ropes; struck out, swam round to the stern, got on the keel, and clambered up on the side. Satisfied that she could not sink, by reason of her cargo, I was not in the least alarmed, but thought two shipwrecks in one day not a good beginning for a new, peaceful career. Nobody was drowned, however; the captain and crew were busy in securing such articles as were liable to float off, and I looked out for some passing boat or vessel to pick us up. We were drifting steadily out to sea, while I was signaling to a boat about three miles off, toward Saucelito, and saw her tack and stand toward us. I was busy watching this sail-boat, when I heard a Yankee's voice, close behind, saying, "This is a nice mess you've got yourselves into," and looking about I saw a man in a small boat, who had seen us upset, and had rowed out to us from a schooner anchored close under the fort. Some explanations were made, and when the sail-boat coming from Saucelito was near enough to be spoken to, and the captain had engaged her to help his schooner, we bade him good by, and got the man in the small boat-to carry us ashore, and land us at the foot of the bluff, just below the fort. Once there, I was at home, and we footed it up to the Presidio. Of the sentinel I inquired who was in command of the post, and was answered, "Major Merchant." He was not then in, but his adjutant, Lieutenant Gardner, was. I sent my card to him; he came out, and was much surprised to find me covered with sand, and dripping with water, a good specimen of a shipwrecked mariner. A few words of explanation sufficed; horses were provided, and we rode hastily into the city, reaching the office of the Nicaragua Steamship Company (C. K. Garrison, agent) about dark, just as the purser had arrived; by a totally different route. It was too late to send relief that night, but by daylight next morning two steamers were en route for and reached the place of wreck in time to relieve the passengers and bring them, and most of the baggage. I lost my carpet-bag, but saved my trunk. The Lewis went to pieces the night after we got off, and, had there been an average sea during the night of our shipwreck, none of us probably would have escaped. That evening in San Francisco I hunted up Major Turner, whom I found boarding, in company with General E. A. Hitchcock, at a Mrs. Ross's, on Clay Street, near Powell. I took quarters with them, and began to make my studies, with a view to a decision whether it was best to undertake this new and untried scheme of banking, or to return to New Orleans and hold on to what I then had, a good army commission.

At the time of my arrival, San Francisco was an the top wave of speculation and prosperity. Major Turner had rented at six hundred dollars a month the office formerly used and then owned by Adams & Co., on the east side of Montgomery Street, between

Sacramento and California Streets. B. R. Nisbet was the active partner, and James Reilly the teller. Already the bank of Lucas, Turner & Co. was established, and was engaged in selling bills of exchange, receiving deposits, and loaning money at three per cent. a month.

Page, Bacon & Co., and Adams & Co., were in full blast across the street, in Parrott's new granite building, and other bankers were doing seemingly a prosperous business, among them Wells, Fargo & Co.; Drexel, Sather & Church; Burgoyne & Co.; James King of Win.; Sanders & Brenham; Davidson & Co.; Palmer, Cook & Co., and others. Turner and I had rooms at Mrs. Ross's, and took our meals at restaurants down-town, mostly at a Frenchman's named Martin, on the southwest corner of Montgomery and California Streets. General Hitchcock, of the army, commanding the Department of California, usually messed with us; also a Captain Mason, and Lieutenant Whiting, of the Engineer Corps. We soon secured a small share of business, and became satisfied there was room for profit. Everybody seemed to be making money fast; the city was being rapidly extended and improved; people paid their three per cent. a month interest without fail, and without deeming it excessive. Turner, Nisbet, and I, daily discussed the prospects, and gradually settled down to the conviction that with two hundred thousand dollars capital, and a credit of fifty thousand dollars in New York, we could build up a business that would help the St. Louis house, and at the same time pay expenses in California, with a reasonable profit. Of course, Turner never designed to remain long in California, and I consented to go back to St. Louis, confer with Mr. Lucas and Captain Simonds, agree upon further details, and then return permanently.

I have no memoranda by me now by which to determine the fact, but think I returned to New York in July, 1853, by the Nicaragua route, and thence to St. Louis by way of Lancaster, Ohio, where my family still was. Mr. Lucas promptly agreed to the terms proposed, and further consented, on the expiration of the lease of the Adams & Co. office, to erect a new banking-house in San Francisco, to cost fifty thousand dollars. I then returned to Lancaster, explained to Mr. Ewing and Mrs. Sherman all the details of our agreement, and, meeting their approval, I sent to the Adjutant-General of the army my letter of resignation, to take effect at the end of the six months' leave, and the resignation was accepted, to take effect September 6, 1853. Being then a citizen, I engaged a passage out to California by the Nicaragua route, in the steamer leaving New York September 20th, for myself and family, and accordingly proceeded to New York, where I had a conference with Mr. Meigs, cashier of the American Exchange Bank, and with Messrs. Wadsworth & Sheldon, bankers, who were our New York correspondents; and on the 20th embarked for San Juan del Norte, with the family, composed of Mrs. Sherman, Lizzie, then less than a year old, and her nurse, Mary Lynch. Our passage down was uneventful, and, on the boats up the Nicaragua River, pretty much the same as before. On reaching Virgin Bay, I engaged a native with three mules to carry us across to the Pacific, and as usual the trip partook of the ludicrous—Mrs. Sherman mounted on a donkey about as large as a Newfoundland dog; Mary Lynch on another, trying to carry Lizzie on a pillow before her, but her mule had a fashion of lying down, which scared her, till I exchanged mules, and my California spurs kept that mule on his legs. I carried Lizzie some time till she was fast asleep, when I got our native man to carry her awhile. The child woke up, and, finding herself in the hands of a dark-visaged man, she yelled most lustily till I got her away. At the summit of the pass, there was a clear-running brook, where we rested an hour, and bathed Lizzie in its sweet waters. We then continued to the end of our journey, and, without going to the tavern at San Juan del Sur, we passed directly to the vessel, then at anchor about two miles out. To reach her we engaged a native boat, which had to be kept outside the surf. Mrs. Sherman was first taken in the arms of two stout natives; Mary Lynch, carrying Lizzie, was carried by two others; and I followed, mounted on the back of a strapping fellow, while fifty or a hundred others were running to and fro, cackling like geese.

Mary Lynch got scared at the surf, and began screaming like a fool, when Lizzie became convulsed with fear, and one of the natives rushed to her, caught her out of Mary's arms, and carried her swiftly to Mrs. Sherman, who, by that time, was in the boat, but Lizzie had fainted with fear, and for a long time sobbed as though permanently injured. For years she showed symptoms that made us believe she had never entirely recovered from the effects of the scare. In due time we reached the steamer Sierra Nevada, and got a good state-room. Our passage up the coast was pleasant enough; we reached San Francisco; on the 15th of October, and took quarters at an hotel on Stockton Street, near Broadway.

Major Turner remained till some time in November, when he also departed for the East, leaving me and Nisbet to manage the bank. I endeavored to make myself familiar with the business, but of course Nisbet kept the books, and gave his personal attention to the loans, discounts, and drafts, which yielded the profits. I soon saw, however, that the three per cent. charged as premium on bills of exchange was not all profit, but out of this had to come one and a fourth to one and a half for freight, one and a third for insurance, with some indefinite promise of a return premium; then, the, cost of blanks, boxing of the bullion, etc., etc. Indeed, I saw no margin for profit at all. Nisbet, however, who had long been familiar with the business, insisted there was a profit, in the fact that the gold-dust or bullion shipped was more valuable than its cost to us. We, of course, had to remit bullion to meet our bills on New York, and bought crude gold-dust, or bars refined by Kellogg & Humbert or E. Justh & Co., for at that time the United States Mint was not in operation. But, as the reports of our shipments came back from New York, I discovered that I was right, and Nisbet was wrong; and, although we could not help selling our checks on New York and St. Louis at the same price as other bankers, I discovered that, at all events, the exchange business in San Francisco was rather a losing business than profitable. The same as to loans. We could loan, at three per cent. a month, all our own money, say two hundred and fifty thousand dollars, and a part of our deposit account. This latter account in California was decidedly uncertain. The balance due depositors would run down to a mere nominal sum on steamer-days, which were the 1st and 15th of each month, and then would increase till the next steamer-day, so that we could not make use of any reasonable part of this balance for loans beyond the next steamer-day; or, in other words, we had an expensive bank, with expensive clerks, and all the machinery for taking care of other people's money for their benefit, without corresponding profit. I also saw that loans were attended with risk commensurate with the rate; nevertheless, I could not attempt to reform the rules and customs established by others before me, and had to drift along with the rest toward that Niagara that none foresaw at the time.

Shortly after arriving out in 1853, we looked around for a site for the new bank, and the only place then available on Montgomery Street, the Wall Street of San Francisco, was a lot at the corner of Jackson Street, facing Montgomery, with an alley on the north, belonging to James Lick. The ground was sixty by sixty-two feet, and I had to pay for it thirty-two thousand dollars. I then made a contract with the builders, Keyser, & Brown, to erect a three-story brick building, with finished basement, for about fifty thousand dollars. This made eighty-two thousand instead of fifty thousand dollars, but I thought Mr. Lucas could stand it and would approve, which he did, though it resulted in loss to him. After the civil war, he told me he had sold the building for forty thousand dollars, about half its cost, but luckily gold was then at 250, so that he could use the forty thousand dollars gold as the equivalent of one hundred thousand dollars currency. The building was erected; I gave it my personal supervision, and it was strongly and thoroughly built, for I saw it two years ago, when several earthquakes had made no impression on it; still, the choice of site was unfortunate, for the city drifted in the opposite direction, viz., toward Market Street. I then thought that all the heavy business would remain toward the foot of Broadway and Jackson Street, because there were the deepest water and best wharves, but in this I made a mistake. Nevertheless, in the spring of 1854, the new bank was finished, and we removed to it, paying rents thereafter to our Mr. Lucas instead of to Adams & Co. A man named Wright, during the same season, built a still finer building just across the street from us; Pioche, Bayerque & Co. were already established on another corner of Jackson Street, and the new Metropolitan Theatre was in progress diagonally opposite us. During the whole of 1854 our business steadily grew, our average deposits going up to half a million, and our sales of exchange and consequent shipment of bullion averaging two hundred thousand dollars per steamer. I signed all bills of exchange, and insisted on Nisbet consulting me on loans and discounts. Spite of every caution, however, we lost occasionally by bad loans, and worse by the steady depreciation of real estate. The city of San Francisco was then extending her streets, sewering them, and planking them, with three-inch lumber. In payment for the lumber and the work of contractors, the city authorities paid scrip in even sums of one hundred, five hundred, one thousand, and five thousand dollars. These formed a favorite collateral for loans at from fifty to sixty cents on the dollar, and no one doubted their ultimate value, either by redemption or by being converted into city bonds. The notes also of H. Meiggs, Neeley Thompson & Co., etc., lumber-dealers, were favorite notes, for they paid their interest promptly, and lodged large margins of these street-improvement warrants as collateral. At that time, Meiggs was a prominent man, lived in style in a large house on Broadway, was a member of the City Council, and owned large saw-mills up the coast about Mendocino. In him Nisbet had unbounded faith, but, for some reason, I feared or mistrusted him, and remember that I cautioned Nisbet not to extend his credit, but to gradually contract his loans. On looking over our bills receivable, then about six hundred thousand dollars, I found Meiggs, as principal or indorser, owed us about eighty thousand dollars—all, however, secured by city warrants; still, he kept bank accounts elsewhere, and was generally a borrower. I instructed Nisbet to insist on his reducing his line as the notes matured, and, as he found it indelicate to speak to Meiggs, I instructed him to refer him to me; accordingly, when, on the next steamer-day, Meiggs appealed at the counter for a draft on Philadelphia, of about twenty thousand dollars, for which he offered his note and collateral, he was referred to me, and I explained to him that our draft was the same as money; that he could have it for cash, but that we were already in advance to him some seventy-five or eighty thousand dollars, and that instead of increasing the amount I must insist on its reduction. He inquired if I mistrusted his ability, etc. I explained, certainly not, but that our duty was to assist those who did all their business with us, and, as our means were necessarily limited, I must restrict him to some reasonable sum, say, twenty-five thousand dollars. Meiggs invited me to go with him to a rich mercantile house on Clay Street, whose partners belonged in Hamburg, and there, in the presence of the principals of the house, he demonstrated, as clearly as a proposition in mathematics, that his business at Mendocino was based on calculations that could not fail. The bill of exchange which he wanted, he said would make the last payment on a propeller already built in Philadelphia, which would be sent to San Francisco, to tow into and out of port the schooners and brigs that were bringing his lumber down the coast. I admitted all he said, but renewed my determination to limit his credit to twenty-five thousand dollars. The Hamburg firm then agreed to accept for him the payment of all his debt to us, except the twenty-five thousand dollars, payable in equal parts for the next three steamer-days. Accordingly, Meiggs went back with me to our bank, wrote his note for twenty-five thousand dollars, and secured it by mortgage on real estate and city warrants, and substituted the three acceptances of the Hamburg firm for the overplus. I surrendered to him all his former notes, except one for which he was indorser. The three acceptances duly matured and were paid; one morning Meiggs and family were missing, and it was discovered they had embarked in a sailing-vessel for South America. This was the beginning of a series of failures in San Francisco, that extended through the next two years. As soon as it was known that Meiggs had fled, the town was full of rumors, and everybody was running to and fro to secure his money. His debts amounted to nearly a million dollars. The Hamburg house which, had been humbugged, were heavy losers and failed, I think. I took possession of Meiggs's dwelling-house and other property for which I held his mortgage, and in the city warrants thought I had an overplus; but it transpired that Meiggs, being in the City Council, had issued various quantities of street scrip, which was adjudged a forgery, though, beyond doubt, most of it, if not all, was properly signed, but fraudulently issued. On this city scrip our bank must have lost about ten thousand dollars. Meiggs subsequently turned up in Chili, where again he rose to wealth and has paid much of his San Francisco debts, but none to us. He is now in Peru, living like a prince. With Meiggs fell all the lumber-dealers, and many persons dealing in city scrip. Compared with others, our loss was a trifle. In a short time things in San Francisco resumed their wonted course, and we generally laughed at the escapade of Meiggs, and the cursing of his deluded creditors.

Shortly after our arrival in San Francisco, I rented of a Mr. Marryat, son of the English Captain Marryat, the author, a small frame-house on Stockton Street, near Green, buying of him his furniture, and we removed to it about December 1,1853. Close by, around on Green Street, a man named Dickey was building two small brick-houses, on ground which he had leased of Nicholson. I bought one of these houses, subject to the ground-rent, and moved into it as soon as finished. Lieutenant T. H. Stevens, of the United States Navy, with his family, rented the other; we lived in this house throughout the year 1854, and up to April 17, 1855.

CHAPTER V.
CALIFORNIA

1855-1857.

During the winter of 1854-'55, I received frequent intimations in my letters from the St. Louis house, that the bank of Page, Bacon & Co. was in trouble, growing out of their relations to the Ohio & Mississippi Railroad, to the contractors for building which they had made large advances, to secure which they had been compelled to take, as it were, an assignment of the contract itself, and finally to assume all the liabilities of the contractors. Then they had to borrow money in New York, and raise other money from time to time, in the purchase of iron and materials for the road, and to pay the hands. The firm in St. Louis and that in San Francisco were different, having different partners, and the St. Louis house naturally pressed the San Francisco firm to ship largely of "gold-dust," which gave them a great name; also to keep as large a balance as possible in New York to sustain their credit. Mr. Page was a very wealthy man, but his wealth consisted mostly of land and property in St. Louis. He was an old man, and a good one; had been a baker, and knew little of banking as a business. This part of his general business was managed exclusively by his son-in-law, Henry D. Bacon, who was young, handsome, and generally popular. How he was drawn into that affair of the Ohio & Mississippi road I have no means of knowing, except by hearsay. Their business in New York was done through the American Exchange Bank, and through Duncan, Sherman & Co. As we were rival houses, the St. Louis partners removed our account from the American Exchange Bank to the Metropolitan Bank; and, as Wadsworth & Sheldon had failed, I was instructed to deal in time bills, and in European exchange, with Schnchardt & Gebhard, bankers in Nassau Street.

In California the house of Page, Bacon & Co. was composed of the same partners as in St. Louis, with the addition of Henry Haight, Judge Chambers, and young Frank Page. The latter had charge of the "branch" in Sacramento. Haight was the real head-man, but he was too fond of lager-beer to be in trusted with so large a business. Beyond all comparison, Page, Bacon & Co. were the most prominent bankers in California in 1853-'55. Though I had notice of danger in that quarter, from our partners in St. Louis, nobody in California doubted their wealth and stability. They must have had, during that winter, an average deposit account of nearly two million dollars, of which seven hundred thousand dollars was in "certificates of deposit," the most stable of all accounts in a bank. Thousands of miners invested their earnings in such certificates, which they converted into drafts on New York, when they were ready to go home or wanted to send their "pile" to their families. Adams & Co. were next in order, because of their numerous offices scattered throughout the mining country. A gentleman named Haskell had been in charge of Adams & Co. in San Francisco, but in the winter of 1854-'55 some changes were made, and the banking department had been transferred to a magnificent office in Halleck's new Metropolitan Block. James King of Wm. had discontinued business on his own account, and been employed by Adams & Co. as their cashier and banker, and Isaiah C. Wood had succeeded Haskell in chief control of the express department. Wells, Fargo & Co. were also bankers as well as expressmen, and William J. Pardee was the resident partner.

As the mail-steamer came in on February 17, 1855, according to her custom, she ran close to the Long Wharf (Meiggs's) on North Beach, to throw ashore the express-parcels of news for speedy delivery. Some passenger on deck called to a man of his acquaintance standing on the wharf, that Page & Bacon had failed in New York. The news spread like wild-fire, but soon it was met by the newspaper accounts to the effect that some particular acceptances of Page & Bacon, of St. Louis, in the hands of Duncan, Sherman & Co., in New York, had gone to protest. All who had balances at Page, Bacon & Co.'s, or held certificates of deposit, were more or less alarmed, wanted to secure their money, and a general excitement pervaded the whole community. Word was soon passed round that the matter admitted of explanation, viz., that the two houses were distinct and separate concerns, that every draft of the California house had been paid in New York, and would continue to be paid. It was expected that this assertion would quiet the fears of the California creditors, but for the next three days there was a steady "run" on that bank. Page, Bacon & Co. stood the first day's run very well, and, as I afterward learned, paid out about six hundred thousand dollars in gold coin. On the 20th of February Henry Height came to our bank, to see what help we were willing to give him; but I was out, and Nisbet could not answer positively for the firm. Our condition was then very strong. The deposit account was about six hundred thousand dollars, and we had in our vault about five hundred thousand dollars in coin and bullion, besides an equal amount of good bills receivable. Still I did not like to weaken ourselves to help others; but in a most friendly spirit, that night after bank-hours, I went down to Page, Bacon & Co., and entered their office from the rear. I found in the cashier's room Folsom, Parrott, Dewey and Payne, Captain Ritchie, Donohue, and others, citizens and friends of the house, who had been called in for consultation. Passing into the main office, where all the book-keepers, tellers, etc., with gas-lights, were busy writing up the day's work, I found Mr. Page, Henry Height, and Judge Chambers. I spoke to Height, saying that I was sorry I had been out when he called at our bank, and had now come to see him in the most friendly spirit. Height had evidently been drinking, and said abruptly that "all the banks would break," that "no bank could instantly pay all its obligations," etc. I answered he could speak for himself, but not for me; that I had come to offer to buy with cash a fair proportion of his bullion, notes, and bills; but, if they were going to fail, I would not be drawn in. Height's manner was extremely offensive, but Mr. Page tried to smooth it over, saying they had had a bad day's run, and could not answer for the result till their books were written up.

I passed back again into the room where the before-named gentlemen were discussing some paper which lay before them, and was going to pass out, when Captain Folsom, who was an officer of the army, a class-mate and intimate friend of mine, handed me the paper the contents of which they were discussing. It was very short, and in Henry Haight's handwriting, pretty much in these terms: "We, the undersigned property-holders of San Francisco, having personally examined the books, papers, etc., of Page, Bacon & Co., do hereby certify that the house is solvent and able to pay all its debts," etc. Height had drawn up and asked them to sign this paper, with the intention to publish it in the next morning's papers, for effect. While I was talking with Captain Folsom, Height came into the room to listen. I admitted that the effect of such a publication would surely be good, and would probably stave off immediate demand till their assets could be in part converted or realized; but I naturally inquired of Folsom, "Have you personally examined the accounts, as herein recited, and the assets, enough to warrant your signature to this paper?" for, "thereby you in effect become indorsers." Folsom said they had not, when Height turned on me rudely and said, "Do you think the affairs of such a house as Page, Bacon & Co. can be critically examined in an hour?" I answered: "These gentlemen can do what they please, but they have twelve hours before the bank will open on the morrow, and if the ledger is written up" (as I believed it was or could be by midnight), "they can (by counting the coin, bullion on hand, and notes or stocks of immediate realization) approximate near enough for them to indorse for the remainder." But Height pooh-poohed me, and I left. Folsom followed me out, told me he could not afford to imperil all he had, and asked my advice. I explained to him that my partner Nisbet had been educated and trained in that very house of Page, Bacon & Co.; that we kept our books exactly as they did; that every day the ledger was written up, so that from it one could see exactly how much actual money was due the depositors and certificates; and then by counting the money in the vault, estimating the bullion on hand, which, though not actual money, could easily be converted into coin, and supplementing these amounts by "bills receivable," they ought to arrive at an approximate-result. After Folsom had left me, John Parrott also stopped and talked with me to the same effect. Next morning I looked out for the notice, but no such notice appeared in the morning papers, and I afterward learned that, on Parrott and Folsom demanding an actual count of the money in the vault, Haight angrily refused unless they would accept his word for it, when one after the other declined to sign his paper.

The run on Page, Bacon & Co. therefore continued throughout the 21st, and I expected all day to get an invitation to close our bank for the next day, February 22, which we could have made a holiday by concerted action; but each banker waited for Page, Bacon & Co. to ask for it, and, no such circular coming, in the then state of feeling no other banker was willing to take the initiative. On the morning of February 22, 1855, everybody was startled by receiving a small slip of paper, delivered at all the houses, on which was printed a short notice that, for "want of coin," Page, Bacon & Co. found it necessary to close their bank for a short time. Of course, we all knew the consequences, and that every other bank in San Francisco would be tried. During the 22d we all kept open, and watched our depositors closely; but the day was generally observed by the people as a holiday, and the firemen paraded the streets of San Francisco in unusual strength. But, on writing up our books that night, we found that our deposit account had diminished about sixty-five thousand dollars. Still, there was no run on us, or any other of the banks, that day; yet, observing little knots of men on the street, discussing the state of the banks generally, and overhearing Haight's expression quoted, that, in case of the failure of Page, Bacon & Co., "all the other banks would break," I deemed it prudent to make ready. For some days we had refused all loans and renewals, and we tried, without, success, some of our call-loans; but, like Hotspur's spirits, they would not come.

Our financial condition on that day (February 22, 1855) was: Due depositors and demand certificates, five hundred and twenty thousand dollars; to meet which, we had in the vault: coin, three hundred and eighty thousand dollars; bullion, seventy-five thousand dollars; and bills receivable, about six hundred thousand dollars. Of these, at least one hundred thousand dollars were on demand, with stock collaterals. Therefore, for the extent of our business, we were stronger than the Bank of England, or any bank in New York City.

Before daylight next morning, our door-bell was rung, and I was called down-stairs by E. Casserly, Esq. (an eminent lawyer of the day, since United States Senator), who informed me he had just come up from the office of Adams & Co., to tell me that their affairs were in such condition that they would not open that morning at all; and that this, added to the suspension of Page, Bacon & Co., announced the day before, would surely cause a general run on all the banks. I informed him that I expected as much, and was prepared for it.

In going down to the bank that morning, I found Montgomery Street full; but, punctually to the minute, the bank opened, and in rushed the crowd. As usual, the most noisy and clamorous were men and women who held small certificates; still, others with larger accounts were in the crowd, pushing forward for their balances. All were promptly met and paid. Several gentlemen of my personal acquaintance merely asked my word of honor that their money was safe, and went away; others, who had large balances, and no immediate use for coin, gladly accepted gold-bars, whereby we paid out the seventy-five thousand dollars of bullion, relieving the coin to that amount.

Meantime, rumors from the street came pouring in that Wright & Co. had failed; then Wells, Fargo & Co.; then Palmer, Cook & Co., and indeed all, or nearly all, the banks of the city; and I was told that parties on the street were betting high, first, that we would close our doors at eleven o'clock; then twelve, and so on; but we did not, till the usual hour that night. We had paid every demand, and still had a respectable amount left.

This run on the bank (the only one I ever experienced) presented all the features, serious and comical, usual to such occasions. At our counter happened that identical case, narrated of others, of the Frenchman, who was nearly squeezed to death in getting to the counter, and, when he received his money, did not know what to do with it. "If you got the money, I no want him; but if you no got him, I want it like the devil!"

Toward the close of the day, some of our customers deposited, rather ostentatiously, small amounts, not aggregating more than eight or ten thousand dollars. Book-keepers and tellers were kept at work to write up the books; and these showed:

Due depositors and certificates, about one hundred and twenty thousand dollars, for which remained of coin about fifty thousand dollars. I resolved not to sleep until I had collected from those owing the bank a part of their debts; for I was angry with them that they had stood back and allowed the panic to fall on the banks alone. Among these were Captain Folsom, who owed us twenty-five thousand dollars, secured by a mortgage on the American Theatre and Tehama Hotel; James Smiley, contractor for building the Custom-House, who owed us two notes of twenty thousand and sixteen thousand dollars, for which we held, as collateral, two acceptances of the collector of the port, Major R. P. Hammond, for twenty thousand dollars each; besides other private parties that I need not name. The acceptances given to Smiley were for work done on the Custom-House, but could not be paid until the work was actually laid in the walls, and certified by Major Tower, United States Engineers; but Smiley had an immense amount of granite, brick, iron, etc., on the ground, in advance of construction, and these acceptances were given him expressly that he might raise money thereon for the payment of such materials.

Therefore, as soon as I got my dinner, I took my saddle-horse, and rode to Captain Folsom's house, where I found him in great pain and distress, mental and physical. He was sitting in a chair, and bathing his head with a sponge. I explained to him the object of my visit, and he said he had expected it, and had already sent his agent, Van Winkle, down-town, with instructions to raise what money he could at any cost; but he did not succeed in raising a cent. So great was the shock to public confidence, that men slept on their money, and would not loan it for ten per cent. a week, on any security whatever—even on mint certificates, which were as good as gold, and only required about ten days to be paid in coin by the United States Mint. I then rode up to Hammond's house, on Rincon Hill, and found him there. I explained to him exactly Smiley's affairs, and only asked him to pay one of his acceptances. He inquired, "Why not both?" I answered that was so much the better; it would put me under still greater obligations. He then agreed to meet me at our bank at 10 P.M. I sent word to others that I demanded them to pay what they could on their paper, and then returned to the bank, to meet Hammond. In due time, he came down with Palmer (of Palmer, Cook & Co.), and there he met Smiley, who was, of course, very anxious to retire his notes. We there discussed the matter fully, when Hammond said, "Sherman, give me up my two acceptances, and I will substitute therefor my check of forty thousand dollars," with "the distinct understanding that, if the money is not needed by you, it shall be returned to me, and the transaction then to remain statu quo." To this there was a general assent. Nisbet handed him his two acceptances, and he handed me his check, signed as collector of the port, on Major J. R. Snyder, United States Treasurer, for forty thousand dollars. I afterward rode out, that night, to Major Snyder's house on North Beach, saw him, and he agreed to meet me at 8 a.m. next day, at the United States Mint, and to pay the check, so that I could have the money before the bank opened. The next morning, as agreed on, we met, and he paid me the check in two sealed bags of gold-coin, each marked twenty thousand dollars, which I had carried to the bank, but never opened them, or even broke the seals.

That morning our bank opened as usual, but there was no appearance of a continuation of the "run;" on the contrary, money began to come back on deposit, so that by night we had a considerable increase, and this went on from day to day, till nearly the old condition of things returned. After about three days, finding I had no use for the money obtained on Hammond's check, I took the identical two bags back to the cashier of the Custom-House, and recovered the two acceptances which had been surrendered as described; and Smiley's two notes were afterward paid in their due course, out of the cash received on those identical acceptances. But, years afterward, on settling with Hammond for the Custom-House contract when completed, there was a difference, and Smiley sued Lucas, Turner & Co. for money had and received for his benefit, being the identical forty thousand dollars herein explained, but he lost his case. Hammond, too, was afterward removed from office, and indicted in part for this transaction. He was tried before the United States Circuit Court, Judge McAlister presiding, for a violation of the sub-Treasury Act, but was acquitted.

Our bank, having thus passed so well through the crisis, took at once a first rank; but these bank failures had caused so many mercantile losses, and had led to such an utter downfall in the value of real estate, that everybody lost more or less money by bad debts, by depreciation of stocks and collaterals, that became unsalable, if not worthless.

About this time (viz., February, 1855) I had exchanged my house on Green, street, with Mr. Sloat, for the half of a fifty-vara lot on Harrison Street, between Fremont and First, on which there was a small cottage, and I had contracted for the building of a new frame-house thereon, at six thousand dollars. This house was finished on the 9th of April, and my family moved into it at once.

For some time Mrs. Sherman had been anxious to go home to Lancaster, Ohio, where we had left our daughter Minnie, with her grandparents, and we arranged that S. M. Bowman, Esq., and wife, should move into our new house and board us, viz., Lizzie, Willie with the nurse Biddy, and myself, for a fair consideration. It so happened that two of my personal friends, Messrs. Winters and Cunningham of Marysville, and a young fellow named Eagan, now a captain in the Commissary Department, were going East in the steamer of the middle of April, and that Mr.. William H. Aspinwall, of New York, and Mr. Chauncey, of Philadelphia, were also going back; and they all offered to look to the personal comfort of Mrs. Sherman on the voyage. They took passage in the steamer Golden Age (Commodore Watkins), which sailed on April 17, 1855. Their passage down the coast was very pleasant till within a day's distance of Panama, when one bright moonlit night, April 29th, the ship, running at full speed, between the Islands Quibo and Quicara, struck on a sunken reef, tore out a streak in her bottom, and at once began to fill with water. Fortunately she did not sink fast, but swung off into deep water, and Commodore Watkins happening to be on deck at the moment, walking with Mr. Aspinwall, learning that the water was rushing in with great rapidity, gave orders for a full head of steam, and turned the vessel's bow straight for the Island Quicara. The water rose rapidly in the hold, the passengers were all assembled, fearful of going down, the fires were out, and the last revolution of the wheels made, when her bow touched gently on the beach, and the vessel's stern sank in deep water. Lines were got out, and the ship held in an upright position, so that the passengers were safe, and but little incommoded. I have often heard Mrs. Sherman tell of the boy Eagan, then about fourteen years old, coming to her state-room, and telling to her not to be afraid, as he was a good swimmer; but on coming out into the cabin, partially dressed, she felt more confidence in the cool manner, bearing, and greater strength of Mr. Winters. There must have been nearly a thousand souls on board at the time, few of whom could have been saved had the steamer gone down in mid-channel, which surely would have resulted, had not Commodore Watkins been on deck, or had he been less prompt in his determination to beach his ship. A sailboat was dispatched toward Panama, which luckily met the steamer John T. Stephens, just coming out of the bay, loaded with about a thousand passengers bound for San Francisco, and she at once proceeded to the relief of the Golden Age. Her passengers were transferred in small boats to the Stephens, which vessel, with her two thousand people crowded together with hardly standing-room, returned to Panama, whence the passengers for the East proceeded to their destination without further delay. Luckily for Mrs. Sherman, Purser Goddard, an old Ohio friend of ours, was on the Stephens, and most kindly gave up his own room to her, and such lady friends as she included in her party. The Golden Age was afterward partially repaired at Quicara, pumped out, and steamed to Panama, when, after further repairs, she resumed her place in the line. I think she is still in existence, but Commodore Watkins afterward lost his life in China, by falling down a hatchway.

Mrs. Sherman returned in the latter part of November of the same year, when Mr. and Mrs. Bowman, who meantime had bought a lot next to us and erected a house thereon, removed to it, and we thus continued close neighbors and friends until we left the country for good in 1857.

During the summer of 1856, in San Francisco, occurred one of those unhappy events, too common to new countries, in which I became involved in spite of myself.

William Neely Johnson was Governor of California, and resided at Sacramento City; General John E. Wool commanded the Department of California, having succeeded General Hitchcock, and had his headquarters at Benicia; and a Mr. Van Ness was mayor of the city.

Politics had become a regular and profitable business, and politicians were more than suspected of being corrupt. It was reported and currently believed that the sheriff (Scannell) had been required to pay the Democratic Central Committee a hundred thousand dollars for his nomination, which was equivalent to an election, for an office of the nominal salary of twelve thousand dollars a year for four years. In the election all sorts of dishonesty were charged and believed, especially of "ballot-box stuffing," and too generally the better classes avoided the elections and dodged jury-duty, so that the affairs of the city government necessarily passed into the hands of a low set of professional politicians. Among them was a man named James Casey, who edited a small paper, the printing office of which was in a room on the third floor of our banking office. I hardly knew him by sight, and rarely if ever saw his paper; but one day Mr. Sather, of the excellent banking firm of Drexel, Sather & Church, came to me, and called my attention to an article in Casey's paper so full of falsehood and malice, that we construed it as an effort to black-mail the banks generally. At that time we were all laboring to restore confidence, which had been so rudely shaken by the panic, and I went up-stairs, found Casey, and pointed out to him the objectionable nature of his article, told him plainly that I could not tolerate his attempt to print and circulate slanders in our building, and, if he repeated it, I would cause him and his press to be thrown out of the windows. He took the hint and moved to more friendly quarters. I mention this fact, to show my estimate of the man, who became a figure in the drama I am about to describe. James King of Wm., as before explained, was in 1853 a banker on his own account, but some time in 1854 he had closed out his business, and engaged with Adams & Co. as cashier. When this firm failed, he, in common with all the employees, was thrown out of employment, and had to look around for something else. He settled down to the publication of an evening paper, called the Bulletin, and, being a man of fine manners and address, he at once constituted himself the champion of society against the public and private characters whom he saw fit to arraign.

As might have been expected, this soon brought him into the usual newspaper war with other editors, and especially with Casey, and epithets a la "Eatanswill" were soon bandying back and forth between them. One evening of May, 1856, King published, in the Bulletin, copies of papers procured from New York, to show that Casey had once been sentenced to the State penitentiary at Sing Sing. Casey took mortal offense, and called at the Bulletin office, on the corner of Montgomery and Merchant Streets, where he found King, and violent words passed between them, resulting in Casey giving King notice that he would shoot him on sight. King remained in his office till about 5 or 6 p.m., when he started toward his home on Stockton Street, and, as he neared the corner of Washington, Casey approached him from the opposite direction, called to him, and began firing. King had on a short cloak, and in his breast-pocket a small pistol, which he did not use. One of Casey's shots struck him high up in the breast, from which he reeled, was caught by some passing friend, and carried into the express-office on the corner, where he was laid on the counter; and a surgeon sent for. Casey escaped up Washington Street, went to the City Hall, and delivered himself to the sheriff (Scannell), who conveyed him to jail and locked him in a cell. Meantime, the news spread like wildfire, and all the city was in commotion, for grog was very popular. Nisbet, who boarded with us on Harrison Street, had been delayed at the bank later than usual, so that he happened to be near at the time, and, when he came out to dinner, he brought me the news of this affair, and said that there was every appearance of a riot downtown that night. This occurred toward the evening of May 14, 1856.

It so happened that, on the urgent solicitation of Van Winkle and of Governor Johnson; I had only a few days before agreed to accept the commission of major-general of the Second Division of Militia, embracing San Francisco. I had received the commission, but had not as yet formally accepted it, or even put myself in communication with the volunteer companies of the city. Of these, at that moment of time, there was a company of artillery with four guns, commanded by a Captain Johns, formerly of the army, and two or three uniformed companies of infantry. After dinner I went down town to see what was going on; found that King had been removed to a room in the Metropolitan Block; that his life was in great peril; that Casey was safe in jail, and the sheriff had called to his assistance a posse of the city police, some citizens, and one of the militia companies. The people were gathered in groups on the streets, and the words "Vigilance Committee" were freely spoken, but I saw no signs of immediate violence. The next morning, I again went to the jail, and found all things quiet, but the militia had withdrawn. I then went to the City Hall, saw the mayor, Van Ness, and some of the city officials, agreed to do what I could to maintain order with such militia as were on hand, and then formally accepted the commission, and took the "oath."

In 1851 (when I was not in California) there had been a Vigilance Committee, and it was understood that its organization still existed. All the newspapers took ground in favor of the Vigilance Committee, except the Herald (John Nugent, editor), and nearly all the best people favored that means of redress. I could see they were organizing, hiring rendezvous, collecting arms, etc., without concealment. It was soon manifest that the companies of volunteers would go with the "committee," and that the public authorities could not rely on them for aid or defense. Still, there were a good many citizens who contended that, if the civil authorities were properly sustained by the people at large, they could and would execute the law. But the papers inflamed the public mind, and the controversy spread to the country. About the third day after the shooting of King, Governor Johnson telegraphed me that he would be down in the evening boat, and asked me to meet him on arrival for consultation. I got C. H. Garrison to go with me, and we met the Governor and his brother on the wharf, and walked up to the International Hotel on Jackson Street, above Montgomery. We discussed the state of affairs fully; and Johnson, on learning that his particular friend, William T. Coleman, was the president of the Vigilance Committee, proposed to go and see him. En route we stopped at King's room, ascertained that he was slowly sinking, and could not live long; and then near midnight we walked to the Turnverein Hall, where the committee was known to be sitting in consultation. This hall was on Bush Street, at about the intersection of Stockton. It was all lighted up within, but the door was locked. The Governor knocked at the door, and on inquiry from inside "Who's there?"—gave his name. After some delay we were admitted into a sort of vestibule, beyond which was a large hall, and we could hear the suppressed voices of a multitude. We were shown into a bar-room to the right, when the Governor asked to see Coleman. The man left us, went into the main hall, and soon returned with Coleman, who was pale and agitated. After shaking hands all round, the Governor said, "Coleman, what the devil is the matter here?" Coleman said, "Governor, it is time this shooting on our streets should stop." The Governor replied, "I agree with you perfectly, and have come down, from Sacramento to assist." Coleman rejoined that "the people were tired of it, and had no faith in the officers of the law." A general conversation then followed, in which it was admitted that King would die, and that Casey must be executed; but the manner of execution was the thing to be settled, Coleman contending that the people would do it without trusting the courts or the sheriff. It so happened that at that time Judge Norton was on the bench of the court having jurisdiction, and he was universally recognized as an able and upright man, whom no one could or did mistrust; and it also happened that a grand-jury was then in session. Johnson argued that the time had passed in California for mobs and vigilance committees, and said if Coleman and associates would use their influence to support the law, he (the Governor) would undertake that, as soon as King died, the grand-jury should indict, that Judge Norton would try the murderer, and the whole proceeding should be as speedy as decency would allow. Then Coleman said "the people had no confidence in Scannell, the sheriff," who was, he said, in collusion with the rowdy element of San Francisco. Johnson then offered to be personally responsible that Casey should be safely guarded, and should be forthcoming for trial and execution at the proper time. I remember very well Johnson's assertion that he had no right to make these stipulations, and maybe no power to fulfill them; but he did it to save the city and state from the disgrace of a mob. Coleman disclaimed that the vigilance organization was a "mob," admitted that the proposition of the Governor was fair, and all he or any one should ask; and added, if we would wait awhile, he would submit it to the council, and bring back an answer.

We waited nearly an hour, and could hear the hum of voices in the hall, but no words, when Coleman came back, accompanied by a committee, of which I think the two brothers Arrington, Thomas Smiley the auctioneer, Seymour, Truett, and others, were members. The whole conversation was gone over again, and the Governor's proposition was positively agreed to, with this further condition, that the Vigilance Committee should send into the jail a small force of their own men, to make certain that Casey should not be carried off or allowed to escape.

The Governor, his brother William, Garrison, and I, then went up to the jail, where we found the sheriff and his posse comitatus of police and citizens. These were styled the "Law-and-Order party," and some of them took offense that the Governor should have held communication with the "damned rebels," and several of them left the jail; but the sheriff seemed to agree with the Governor that what he had done was right and best; and, while we were there, some eight or ten armed men arrived from the Vigilance Committee, and were received by the sheriff (Scannell) as a part of his regular posse.

The Governor then, near daylight, went to his hotel, and I to my house for a short sleep. Next day I was at the bank, as usual, when, about noon the Governor called, and asked me to walk with him down-street He said he had just received a message from the Vigilance Committee to the effect that they were not bound by Coleman's promise not to do any thing till the regular trial by jury should be had, etc. He was with reason furious, and asked me to go with him to Truett's store, over which the Executive Committee was said to be in session. We were admitted to a front-room up-stairs, and heard voices in the back-room. The Governor inquired for Coleman, but he was not forthcoming. Another of the committee, Seymour, met us, denied in toto the promise of the night before, and the Governor openly accused him of treachery and falsehood.

The quarrel became public, and the newspapers took it up, both parties turning on the Governor; one, the Vigilantes, denying the promise made by Coleman, their president; and the other, the "Law-and-Order party," refusing any farther assistance, because Johnson had stooped to make terms with rebels. At all events, he was powerless, and had to let matters drift to a conclusion.

King died about Friday, May 20th, and the funeral was appointed for the next Sunday. Early on that day the Governor sent for me at my house. I found him on the roof of the International, from which we looked down on the whole city, and more especially the face of Telegraph Hill, which was already covered with a crowd of people, while others were moving toward the jail on Broadway. Parties of armed men, in good order, were marching by platoons in the same direction; and formed in line along Broadway, facing the jail-door. Soon a small party was seen to advance to this door, and knock; a parley ensued, the doors were opened, and Casey was led out. In a few minutes another prisoner was brought out, who, proved to be Cora, a man who had once been tried for killing Richardson, the United States Marshal, when the jury disagreed, and he was awaiting a new trial. These prisoners were placed in carriages, and escorted by the armed force down to the rooms of the Vigilance Committee, through the principal streets of the city. The day was exceedingly beautiful, and the whole proceeding was orderly in the extreme. I was under the impression that Casey and Cora were hanged that same Sunday, but was probably in error; but in a very few days they were hanged by the neck—dead—suspended from beams projecting from the windows of the committee's rooms, without other trial than could be given in secret, and by night.

We all thought the matter had ended there, and accordingly the Governor returned to Sacramento in disgust, and I went about my business. But it soon became manifest that the Vigilance Committee had no intention to surrender the power thus usurped. They took a building on Clay Street, near Front, fortified it, employed guards and armed sentinels, sat in midnight council, issued writs of arrest and banishment, and utterly ignored all authority but their own. A good many men were banished and forced to leave the country, but they were of that class we could well spare. Yankee Sullivan, a prisoner in their custody, committed suicide, and a feeling of general insecurity pervaded the city. Business was deranged; and the Bulletin, then under control of Tom King, a brother of James, poured out its abuse on some of our best men, as well as the worst. Governor Johnson, being again appealed to, concluded to go to work regularly, and telegraphed me about the 1st of June to meet him at General Wool's headquarters at Benicia that night. I went up, and we met at the hotel where General Wool was boarding. Johnson had with him his Secretary of State. We discussed the state of the country generally, and I had agreed that if Wool would give us arms and ammunition out of the United States Arsenal at Benicia, and if Commodore Farragat, of the navy, commanding the navy-yard on Mare Island, would give us a ship, I would call out volunteers, and, when a sufficient number had responded, I would have the arms come down from Benicia in the ship, arm my men, take possession of a thirty-two-pound-gun battery at the Marine Hospital on Rincon Point, thence command a dispersion of the unlawfully-armed force of the Vigilance Committee, and arrest some of the leaders.

We played cards that night, carrying on a conversation, in which Wool insisted on a proclamation commanding the Vigilance Committee to disperse, etc., and he told us how he had on some occasion, as far back as 1814, suppressed a mutiny on the Northern frontier. I did not understand him to make any distinct promise of assistance that night, but he invited us to accompany him on an inspection of the arsenal the next day, which we did. On handling some rifled muskets in the arsenal storehouse he asked me how they would answer our purpose. I said they were the very things, and that we did not want cartridge boxes or belts, but that I would have the cartridges carried in the breeches-pockets, and the caps in the vestpockets. I knew that there were stored in that arsenal four thousand muskets, for I recognized the boxes which we had carried out in the Lexington around Cape Horn in 1846. Afterward we all met at the quarters of Captain D. R. Jones of the army, and I saw the Secretary of State, D. F. Douglass, Esq., walk out with General Wool in earnest conversation, and this Secretary of State afterward asserted that Wool there and then promised us the arms and ammunition, provided the Governor would make his proclamation for the committee to disperse, and that I should afterward call out the militia, etc. On the way back to the hotel at Benicia, General Wool, Captain Callendar of the arsenal, and I, were walking side by side, and I was telling him (General Wool) that I would also need some ammunition for the thirty-two-pound guns then in position at Rincon Point, when Wool turned to Callendar and inquired, "Did I not order those guns to be brought away?" Callendar said "Yes, general. I made a requisition on the quartermaster for transportation, but his schooner has been so busy that the guns are still there." Then said Wool: "Let them remain; we may have use for them." I therefrom inferred, of course, that it was all agreed to so far as he was concerned.

Soon after we had reached the hotel, we ordered a buggy, and Governor Johnson and I drove to Vallejo, six miles, crossed over to Mare Island, and walked up to the commandant's house, where we found Commodore Farragut and his family. We stated our business fairly, but the commodore answered very frankly that he had no authority, without orders from his department, to take any part in civil broils; he doubted the wisdom of the attempt; said he had no ship available except the John Adams, Captain Boutwell, and that she needed repairs. But he assented at last, to the proposition to let the sloop John Adams drop down abreast of the city after certain repairs, to lie off there for moral effect, which afterward actually occurred.

We then returned to Benicia, and Wool's first question was, "What luck?" We answered, "Not much," and explained what Commodore Farragut could and would do, and that, instead of having a naval vessel, we would seize and use one of the Pacific Mail Company's steamers, lying at their dock in Benicia, to carry down to San Francisco the arms and munitions when the time came.

As the time was then near at hand for the arrival of the evening boats, we all walked down to the wharf together, where I told Johnson that he could not be too careful; that I had not heard General Wool make a positive promise of assistance.

Upon this, Johnson called General Wool to one side, and we three drew together. Johnson said: "General Wool, General Sherman is very particular, and wants to know exactly what you propose to do." Wool answered: "I understand, Governor, that in the first place a writ of Habeas corpus will be issued commanding the jailers of the Vigilance Committee to produce the body of some one of the prisoners held by them (which, of course, will be refused); that you then issue your proclamation commanding them to disperse, and, failing this, you will call out the militia, and command General Sherman with it to suppress the Vigilance Committee as an unlawful body;" to which the Governor responded, "Yes." "Then," said Wool, "on General Sherman's making his requisition, approved by you, I will order the issue of the necessary arms and ammunition." I remember well that I said, emphatically: "That is all I want. —Now, Governor, you may go ahead." We soon parted; Johnson and Douglas taking the boat to Sacramento, and I to San Francisco.

The Chief-Justice, Terry, came to San Francisco the next day, issued a writ of habeas corpus for the body of one Maloney, which writ was resisted, as we expected. The Governor then issued his proclamation, and I published my orders, dated June 4, 1855. The Quartermaster-General of the State, General Kibbe, also came to San Francisco, took an office in the City Hall, engaged several rooms for armories, and soon the men began to enroll into companies. In my general orders calling out the militia, I used the expression, "When a sufficient number of men are enrolled, arms and ammunition will be supplied." Some of the best men of the "Vigilantes" came to me and remonstrated, saying that collision would surely result; that it would be terrible, etc. All I could say in reply was, that it was for them to get out of the way. "Remove your fort; cease your midnight councils; and prevent your armed bodies from patrolling the streets." They inquired where I was to get arms, and I answered that I had them certain. But personally I went right along with my business at the bank, conscious that at any moment we might have trouble. Another committee of citizens, a conciliatory body, was formed to prevent collision if possible, and the newspapers boiled over with vehement vituperation. This second committee was composed of such men as Crockett, Ritchie, Thornton, Bailey Peyton, Foote, Donohue, Kelly, and others, a class of the most intelligent and wealthy men of the city, who earnestly and honestly desired to prevent bloodshed. They also came to me, and I told them that our men were enrolling very fast, and that, when I deemed the right moment had come, the Vigilance Committee must disperse, else bloodshed and destruction of property would inevitably follow. They also had discovered that the better men of the Vigilance Committee itself were getting tired of the business, and thought that in the execution of Casey and Cora, and the banishment of a dozen or more rowdies, they had done enough, and were then willing to stop. It was suggested that, if our Law-and-Order party would not arm, by a certain day near at hand the committee would disperse, and some of their leaders would submit to an indictment and trial by a jury of citizens, which they knew would acquit them of crime. One day in the bank a man called me to the counter and said, "If you expect to get arms of General Wool, you will be mistaken, for I was at Benicia yesterday, and heard him say he would not give them." This person was known to me to be a man of truth, and I immediately wrote to General Wool a letter telling him what I had heard, and how any hesitation on his part would compromise me as a man of truth and honor; adding that I did not believe we should ever need the arms, but only the promise of them, for "the committee was letting down, and would soon disperse and submit to the law," etc. I further asked him to answer me categorically that very night, by the Stockton boat, which would pass Benicia on its way down about midnight, and I would sit up and wait for his answer. I did wait for his letter, but it did not come, and the next day I got a telegraphic dispatch from Governor Johnson, who, at Sacramento, had also heard of General Wool's "back-down," asking me to meet him again at Benicia that night.

I went up in the evening boat, and found General Wool's aide-de-camp, Captain Arnold, of the army, on the wharf, with a letter in his hand, which he said was for me. I asked for it, but he said he knew its importance, and preferred we should go to General Wool's room together, and the general could hand it to me in person. We did go right up to General Wool's, who took the sealed parcel and laid it aside, saying that it was literally a copy of one he had sent to Governor Johnson, who would doubtless give me a copy; but I insisted that I had made a written communication, and was entitled to a written answer.

At that moment several gentlemen of the "Conciliation party," who had come up in the same steamer with me, asked for admission and came in. I recall the names of Crockett, Foote, Bailey Peyton, Judge Thornton, Donohue, etc., and the conversation became general, Wool trying to explain away the effect of our misunderstanding, taking good pains not to deny his promise made to me personally on the wharf. I renewed my application for the letter addressed to me, then lying on his table. On my statement of the case, Bailey Peyton said, "General Wool, I think General Sherman has a right to a written answer from you, for he is surely compromised." Upon this Wool handed me the letter. I opened and read it, and it denied any promise of arms, but otherwise was extremely evasive and non-committal. I had heard of the arrival at the wharf of the Governor and party, and was expecting them at

Wool's room, but, instead of stopping at the hotel where we were, they passed to another hotel on the block above. I went up and found there, in a room on the second floor over the bar-room, Governor Johnson, Chief-Justice Terry, Jones, of Palmer, Cooke & Co., E. D. Baker, Volney E. Howard, and one or two others. All were talking furiously against Wool, denouncing him as a d——d liar, and not sparing the severest terms. I showed the Governor General Wool's letter to me, which he said was in effect the same as the one addressed to and received by him at Sacramento. He was so offended that he would not even call on General Wool, and said he would never again recognize him as an officer or gentleman. We discussed matters generally, and Judge Terry said that the Vigilance Committee were a set of d——d pork-merchants; that they were getting scared, and that General Wool was in collusion with them to bring the State into contempt, etc. I explained that there were no arms in the State except what General Wool had, or what were in the hands of the Vigilance Committee of San Francisco, and that the part of wisdom for us was to be patient and cautious. About that time Crockett and his associates sent up their cards, but Terry and the more violent of the Governor's followers denounced them as no better than "Vigilantes," and wanted the Governor to refuse even to receive them. I explained that they were not "Vigilantes," that Judge Thornton was a "Law-and-Order" man, was one of the first to respond to the call of the the sheriff, and that he went actually to the jail with his one arm the night we expected the first attempt at rescue, etc. Johnson then sent word for them to reduce their business to writing. They simply sent in a written request for an audience, and they were then promptly admitted. After some general conversation, the Governor said he was prepared to hear them, when Mr. Crockett rose and made a prepared speech embracing a clear and fair statement of the condition of things in San Francisco, concluding with the assertion of the willingness of the committee to disband and submit to trial after a certain date not very remote. All the time Crockett was speaking, Terry sat with his hat on, drawn over his eyes, and with his feet on a table. As soon as Crockett was through, they were dismissed, and Johnson began to prepare a written answer. This was scratched, altered, and amended, to suit the notions of his counselors, and at last was copied and sent. This answer amounted to little or nothing. Seeing that we were powerless for good, and that violent counsels would prevail under the influence of Terry and others, I sat down at the table, and wrote my resignation, which Johnson accepted in a complimentary note on the spot, and at the same time he appointed to my place General Volney E. Howard, then present, a lawyer who had once been a member of Congress from Texas, and who was expected to drive the d——d pork-merchants into the bay at short notice. I went soon after to General Wool's room, where I found Crockett and the rest of his party; told them that I was out of the fight, having resigned my commission; that I had neglected business that had been intrusted to me by my St. Louis partners; and that I would thenceforward mind my own business, and leave public affairs severely alone. We all returned to San Francisco that night by the Stockton boat, and I never after-ward had any thing to do with politics in California, perfectly satisfied with that short experience. Johnson and Wool fought out their quarrel of veracity in the newspapers and on paper. But, in my opinion, there is not a shadow of doubt that General Wool did deliberately deceive us; that he had authority to issue arms, and that, had he adhered to his promise, we could have checked the committee before it became a fixed institution, and a part of the common law of California. Major-General Volney E. Howard came to San Francisco soon after; continued the organization of militia which I had begun; succeeded in getting a few arms from the country; but one day the Vigilance Committee sallied from their armories, captured the arms of the "Law-and-Order party," put some of their men into prison, while General Howard, with others, escaped to the country; after which the Vigilance Committee had it all their own way. Subsequently, in July, 1856, they arrested Chief-Justice Terry, and tried him for stabbing one of their constables, but he managed to escape at night, and took refuge on the John Adams. In August, they hanged Hetherington and Brace in broad daylight, without any jury-trial; and, soon after, they quietly disbanded. As they controlled the press, they wrote their own history, and the world generally gives them the credit of having purged San Francisco of rowdies and roughs; but their success has given great stimulus to a dangerous principle, that would at any time justify the mob in seizing all the power of government; and who is to say that the Vigilance Committee may not be composed of the worst, instead of the best, elements of a community? Indeed, in San Francisco, as soon as it was demonstrated that the real power had passed from the City Hall to the committee room, the same set of bailiffs, constables, and rowdies that had infested the City Hall were found in the employment of the "Vigilantes;" and, after three months experience, the better class of people became tired of the midnight sessions and left the business and power of the committee in the hands of a court, of which a Sydney man was reported to be the head or chief-justice.

During the winter of 1855-'56, and indeed throughout the year 1856, all kinds of business became unsettled in California. The mines continued to yield about fifty millions of gold a year; but little attention was paid to agriculture or to any business other than that of "mining," and, as the placer-gold was becoming worked out, the miners were restless and uneasy, and were shifting about from place to place, impelled by rumors put afloat for speculative purposes. A great many extensive enterprises by joint-stock companies had been begun, in the way of water-ditches, to bring water from the head of the mountain-streams down to the richer alluvial deposits, and nearly all of these companies became embarrassed or bankrupt. Foreign capital, also, which had been attracted to California by reason of the high rates of interest, was being withdrawn, or was tied up in property which could not be sold; and, although our bank's having withstood the panic gave us great credit, still the community itself was shaken, and loans of money were risky in the extreme. A great many merchants, of the highest name, availed themselves of the extremely liberal bankrupt law to get discharged of their old debts, without sacrificing much, if any, of their stocks of goods on hand, except a lawyer's fee; thus realizing Martin Burke's saying that "many a clever fellow had been ruined by paying his debts." The merchants and business-men of San Francisco did not intend to be ruined by such a course. I raised the rate of exchange from three to three and a half, while others kept on at the old rate; and I labored hard to collect old debts, and strove, in making new loans, to be on the safe side. The State and city both denied much of their public debt; in fact, repudiated it; and real estate, which the year before had been first-class security, became utterly unsalable.

The office labor and confinement, and the anxiety attending the business, aggravated my asthma to such an extent that at times it deprived me of sleep, and threatened to become chronic and serious; and I was also conscious that the first and original cause which had induced Mr. Lucas to establish the bank in California had ceased. I so reported to him, and that I really believed that he could use his money more safely and to better advantage in St. Louis. This met his prompt approval, and he instructed me gradually to draw out, preparatory to a removal to New York City. Accordingly, early in April, 1857, I published an advertisement in the San Francisco papers, notifying our customers that, on the 1st day of May, we would discontinue business and remove East, requiring all to withdraw their accounts, and declaring that, if any remained on that day of May, their balances would be transferred to the banking-house of Parrott & Co. Punctually to the day, this was done, and the business of Lucas, Turner & Co., of San Francisco, was discontinued, except the more difficult and disagreeable part of collecting their own moneys and selling the real estate, to which the firm had succeeded by purchase or foreclosure. One of the partners, B. R. Nisbet, assisted by our attorney, S. M. Bowman, Esq., remained behind to close up the business of the bank.

CHAPTER VI.
CALIFORNIA, NEW YORK, AND KANSAS.

1857-1859.

Having closed the bank at San Francisco on the 1st day of May, 1857, accompanied by my family I embarked in the steamer Sonora for Panama, crossed the isthmus, and sailed to New York, whence we proceeded to Lancaster, Ohio, where Mrs. Sherman and the family stopped, and I went on to St. Louis. I found there that some changes had been made in the parent, house, that Mr. Lucas had bought out his partner, Captain Symonds, and that the firm's name had been changed to that of James H. Lucas & Co.

It had also been arranged that an office or branch was to be established in New York City, of which I was to have charge, on pretty much the same terms and conditions as in the previous San Francisco firm.

Mr. Lucas, Major Turner, and I, agreed to meet in New York, soon after the 4th of July. We met accordingly at the Metropolitan Hotel, selected an office, No. 12 Pall Street, purchased the necessary furniture, and engaged a teller, bookkeeper, and porter. The new firm was to bear the same title of Lucas, Turner & Co., with about the same partners in interest, but the nature of the business was totally different. We opened our office on the 21st of July, 1857, and at once began to receive accounts from the West and from California, but our chief business was as the resident agents of the St. Louis firm of James H. Lucas & Co. Personally I took rooms at No. 100 Prince Street, in which house were also quartered Major J. G. Barnard, and Lieutenant J. B. McPherson, United States Engineers, both of whom afterward attained great fame in the civil war.

My business relations in New York were with the Metropolitan Bank and Bank of America; and with the very wealthy and most respectable firm of Schuchhardt & Gebhard, of Nassau Street. Every thing went along swimmingly till the 21st of August, when all Wall Street was thrown into a spasm by the failure of the Ohio Life and Trust Company, and the panic so resembled that in San Francisco, that, having nothing seemingly at stake, I felt amused. But it soon became a serious matter even to me. Western stocks and securities tumbled to such a figure, that all Western banks that held such securities, and had procured advances thereon, were compelled to pay up or substitute increased collaterals. Our own house was not a borrower in New York at all, but many of our Western correspondents were, and it taxed my tune to watch their interests. In September, the panic extended so as to threaten the safety of even some of the New York banks not connected with the West; and the alarm became general, and at last universal.

In the very midst of this panic came the news that the steamer Central America, formerly the George Law, with six hundred passengers and about sixteen hundred thousand dollars of treasure, coming from Aspinwall, had foundered at sea, off the coast of Georgia, and that about sixty of the passengers had been providentially picked up by a Swedish bark, and brought into Savannah. The absolute loss of this treasure went to swell the confusion and panic of the day.

A few days after, I was standing in the vestibule of the Metropolitan Hotel, and heard the captain of the Swedish bark tell his singular story of the rescue of these passengers. He was a short, sailor-like-looking man, with a strong German or Swedish accent. He said that he was sailing from some port in Honduras for Sweden, running down the Gulf Stream off Savannah. The weather had been heavy for some days, and, about nightfall, as he paced his deck, he observed a man-of-war hawk circle about his vessel, gradually lowering, until the bird was as it aiming at him. He jerked out a belaying-pin, struck at the bird, missed it, when the hawk again rose high in the air, and a second time began to descend, contract his circle, and make at him again. The second time he hit the bird, and struck it to the deck.... This strange fact made him uneasy, and he thought it betokened danger; he went to the binnacle, saw the course he was steering, and without any particular reason he ordered the steersman to alter the course one point to the east.

After this it became quite dark, and he continued to promenade the deck, and had settled into a drowsy state, when as in a dream he thought he heard voices all round his ship. Waking up, he ran to the side of the ship, saw something struggling in the water, and heard clearly cries for help. Instantly heaving his ship to, and lowering all his boats, he managed to pick up sixty or more persons who were floating about on skylights, doors, spare, and whatever fragments remained of the Central America. Had he not changed the course of his vessel by reason of the mysterious conduct of that man-of-war hawk, not a soul would probably have survived the night. It was stated by the rescued passengers, among whom was Billy Birch, that the Central America had sailed from Aspinwall with the passengers and freight which left San Francisco on the 1st of September, and encountered the gale in the Gulf Stream somewhere off Savannah, in which she sprung a leak, filled rapidly, and went down. The passengers who were saved had clung to doors, skylights, and such floating objects as they could reach, and were thus rescued; all the rest, some five hundred in number, had gone down with the ship.

The panic grew worse and worse, and about the end of September there was a general suspension of the banks of New York, and a money crisis extended all over the country. In New York, Lucas, Turner & Co. had nothing at risk. We had large cash balances in the Metropolitan Bank and in the Bank of America, all safe, and we held, for the account of the St. Louis house, at least two hundred thousand dollars, of St. Louis city and county bonds, and of acceptances falling due right along, none extending beyond ninety days. I was advised from St. Louis that money matters were extremely tight; but I did not dream of any danger in that quarter. I knew well that Mr. Lucas was worth two or three million dollars in the best real estate, and inferred from the large balances to their credit with me that no mere panic could shake his credit; but, early on the morning of October 7th, my cousin, James M. Hoyt, came to me in bed, and read me a paragraph in the morning paper, to the effect that James H. Lucas & Co., of St. Louis, had suspended. I was, of course, surprised, but not sorry; for I had always contended that a man of so much visible wealth as Mr. Lucas should not be engaged in a business subject to such vicissitudes. I hurried down to the office, where I received the same information officially, by telegraph, with instructions to make proper disposition of the affairs of the bank, and to come out to St. Louis, with such assets as would be available there. I transferred the funds belonging to all our correspondents, with lists of outstanding checks, to one or other of our bankers, and with the cash balance of the St. Louis house and their available assets started for St. Louis. I may say with confidence that no man lost a cent by either of the banking firms of Lucas, Turner & Co., of San Francisco or New York; but, as usual, those who owed us were not always as just. I reached St. Louis October 17th, and found the partners engaged in liquidating the balances due depositors as fast as collections could be forced; and, as the panic began to subside, this process became quite rapid, and Mr. Lucas, by making a loan in Philadelphia, was enabled to close out all accounts without having made any serious sacrifices, Of course, no person ever lost a cent by him: he has recently died, leaving an estate of eight million dollars. During his lifetime, I had opportunities to know him well, and take much pleasure in bearing testimony to his great worth and personal kindness. On the failure of his bank, he assumed personally all the liabilities, released his partners of all responsibility, and offered to assist me to engage in business, which he supposed was due to me because I had resigned my army commission. I remained in St. Louis till the 17th of December, 1857, assisting in collecting for the bank, and in controlling all matters which came from the New York and San Francisco branches. B. R. Nisbet was still in San Francisco, but had married a Miss Thornton, and was coming home. There still remained in California a good deal of real estate, and notes, valued at about two hundred thousand dollars in the aggregate; so that, at Mr. Lucas's request, I agreed to go out again, to bring matters, if possible, nearer a final settlement. I accordingly left St. Louis, reached Lancaster, where my family was, on the 10th, staid there till after Christmas, and then went to New York, where I remained till January 5th, when I embarked on the steamer Moles Taylor (Captain McGowan) for Aspinwall; caught the Golden Gate (Captain Whiting) at Panama, January 15, 1858; and reached San Francisco on the 28th of January. I found that Nisbet and wife had gone to St. Louis, and that we had passed each other at sea. He had carried the ledger and books to St. Louis, but left a schedule, notes, etc., in the hands of S. M. Bowman, Esq., who passed them over to me.

On the 30th of January I published a notice of the dissolution of the partnership, and called on all who were still indebted to the firm of Lucas, Turner & Co. to pay up, or the notes would be sold at auction. I also advertised that all the real property, was for sale.

Business had somewhat changed since 1857. Parrott & Co.; Garrison, Fritz & Ralston; Wells, Fargo & Co.; Drexel, Sather & Church, and Tallant & Wilde, were the principal bankers. Property continued almost unsalable, and prices were less than a half of what they had been in 1853-'54. William Blending, Esq., had rented my house on Harrison Street; so I occupied a room in the bank, No. 11, and boarded at the Meiggs House, corner of Broadway and Montgomery, which we owned. Having reduced expenses to a minimum, I proceeded, with all possible dispatch, to collect outstanding debts, in some instances making sacrifices and compromises. I made some few sales, and generally aimed to put matters in such a shape that time would bring the best result. Some of our heaviest creditors were John M. Rhodes & Co., of Sacramento and Shasta; Langton & Co., of Downieville; and E. M. Stranger of Murphy's. In trying to put these debts in course of settlement, I made some arrangement in Downieville with the law-firm of Spears & Thornton, to collect, by suit, a certain note of Green & Purdy for twelve thousand dollars. Early in April, I learned that Spears had collected three thousand seven hundred dollars in money, had appropriated it to his own use, and had pledged another good note taken in part payment of three thousand and fifty-three dollars. He pretended to be insane. I had to make two visits to Downieville on this business, and there, made the acquaintance of Mr. Stewart, now a Senator from Nevada. He was married to a daughter of Governor Foote; was living in a small frame house on the bar just below the town; and his little daughter was playing about the door in the sand. Stewart was then a lawyer in Downieville, in good practice; afterward, by some lucky stroke, became part owner of a valuable silver-mine in Nevada, and is now accounted a millionaire. I managed to save something out of Spears, and more out of his partner Thornton. This affair of Spears ruined him, because his insanity was manifestly feigned.

I remained in San Francisco till July 3d, when, having collected and remitted every cent that I could raise, and got all the property in the best shape possible, hearing from St. Louis that business had revived, and that there was no need of further sacrifice; I put all the papers, with a full letter of instructions, and power of attorney, in the hands of William Blending, Esq., and took passage on the good steamer Golden Gate, Captain Whiting, for Panama and home. I reached Lancaster on July 28, 1858, and found all the family well. I was then perfectly unhampered, but the serious and greater question remained, what was I to do to support my family, consisting of a wife and four children, all accustomed to more than the average comforts of life?

I remained at Lancaster all of August, 1858, during which time I was discussing with Mr. Ewing and others what to do next. Major Turner and Mr. Lucas, in St. Louis, were willing to do any thing to aid me, but I thought best to keep independent. Mr. Ewing had property at Chauncey, consisting of salt-wells and coal-mines, but for that part of Ohio I had no fancy. Two of his sons, Hugh and T. E., Jr., had established themselves at Leavenworth, Kansas, where they and their father had bought a good deal of land, some near the town, and some back in the country. Mr. Ewing offered to confide to me the general management of his share of interest, and Hugh and T. E., Jr., offered me an equal copartnership in their law-firm.

Accordingly, about the 1st of September, I started for Kansas, stopping a couple of weeks in St. Louis, and reached Leavenworth. I found about two miles below the fort, on the river-bank, where in 1851 was a tangled thicket, quite a handsome and thriving city, growing rapidly in rivalry with Kansas City, and St. Joseph, Missouri. After looking about and consulting with friends, among them my classmate Major Stewart Van Vliet, quartermaster at the fort, I concluded to accept the proposition of Mr. Ewing, and accordingly the firm of Sherman & Ewing was duly announced, and our services to the public offered as attorneys-at-law. We had an office on Main Street, between Shawnee and Delaware, on the second floor, over the office of Hampton Denman, Esq., mayor of the city. This building was a mere shell, and our office was reached by a stairway on the outside. Although in the course of my military reading I had studied a few of the ordinary law-books, such as Blackstone, Kent, Starkie, etc., I did not presume to be a lawyer; but our agreement was that Thomas Ewing, Jr., a good and thorough lawyer, should manage all business in the courts, while I gave attention to collections, agencies for houses and lands, and such business as my experience in banking had qualified me for. Yet, as my name was embraced in a law-firm, it seemed to me proper to take out a license. Accordingly, one day when United States Judge Lecompte was in our office, I mentioned the matter to him; he told me to go down to the clerk of his court, and he would give me the license. I inquired what examination I would have to submit to, and he replied, "None at all;" he would admit me on the ground of general intelligence.

During that summer we got our share of the business of the profession, then represented by several eminent law-firms, embracing names that have since flourished in the Senate, and in the higher courts of the country. But the most lucrative single case was given me by my friend Major Van Vliet, who employed me to go to Fort Riley, one hundred and thirty-six miles west of Fort Leavenworth, to superintend the repairs to the military road. For this purpose he supplied me with a four-mule ambulance and driver. The country was then sparsely settled, and quite as many Indians were along the road as white people; still there were embryo towns all along the route, and a few farms sprinkled over the beautiful prairies. On reaching Indianola, near Topeka, I found everybody down with the chills and fever. My own driver became so shaky that I had to act as driver and cook. But in due season I reconnoitred the road, and made contracts for repairing some bridges, and for cutting such parts of the road as needed it. I then returned to Fort Leavenworth, and reported, receiving a fair compensation. On my way up I met Colonel Sumner's column, returning from their summer scout on the plains, and spent the night with the officers, among whom were Captains Sackett, Sturgis, etc. Also at Fort Riley I was cordially received and entertained by some old army-friends, among them Major Sedgwick, Captains Totted, Eli Long, etc.

Mrs. Sherman and children arrived out in November, and we spent the winter very comfortably in the house of Thomas Ewing, Jr., on the corner of Third and Pottawottamie Streets. On the 1st of January, 1859, Daniel McCook, Esq., was admitted to membership in our firm, which became Sherman, Ewing & McCook. Our business continued to grow, but, as the income hardly sufficed for three such expensive personages, I continued to look about for something more certain and profitable, and during that spring undertook for the Hon. Thomas Ewing, of Ohio, to open a farm on a large tract of land he owned on Indian Creek, forty miles west of Leavenworth, for the benefit of his grand-nephew, Henry Clark, and his grand-niece, Mrs. Walker. These arrived out in the spring, by which time I had caused to be erected a small frame dwelling-house, a barn, and fencing for a hundred acres. This helped to pass away time, but afforded little profit; and on the 11th of June, 1859, I wrote to Major D. C. Buel, assistant adjutant-general, on duty in the War Department with Secretary of War Floyd, inquiring if there was a vacancy among the army paymasters, or any thing in his line that I could obtain. He replied promptly, and sent me the printed programme for a military college about to be organized in Louisiana, and advised me to apply for the superintendent's place, saying that General G. Mason Graham, the half-brother of my old commanding-general, R. B. Mason, was very influential in this matter, and would doubtless befriend me on account of the relations that had existed between General Mason and myself in California. Accordingly, I addressed a letter of application to the Hon. R. C. Wickliffe, Baton Rouge, Louisiana, asking the answer to be sent to me at Lancaster, Ohio, where I proposed to leave my family. But, before leaving this branch of the subject, I must explain a little matter of which I have seen an account in print, complimentary or otherwise of the firm of Sherman, Ewing & McCook, more especially of the senior partner.

One day, as I sat in our office, an Irishman came in and said he had a case and wanted a lawyer. I asked him to sit down and give me the points of his case, all the other members of the firm being out. Our client stated that he had rented a lot of an Irish landlord for five dollars a month; that he had erected thereon a small frame shanty, which was occupied by his family; that he had, paid his rent regularly up to a recent period, but to his house he had appended a shed which extended over a part of an adjoining vacant lot belonging to the same landlord, for which he was charged two and a half dollars a month, which he refused to pay. The consequence was, that his landlord had for a few months declined even his five dollars monthly rent until the arrears amounted to about seventeen dollars, for which he was sued. I told him we would undertake his case, of which I took notes, and a fee of five dollars in advance, and in due order I placed the notes in the hands of McCook, and thought no more of it.

A month or so after, our client rushed into the office and said his case had been called at Judge Gardner's (I think), and he wanted his lawyer right away. I sent him up to the

Circuit Court, Judge Pettit's, for McCook, but he soon returned, saying he could not find McCook, and accordingly I hurried with him up to Judge Gardner's office, intending to ask a continuance, but I found our antagonist there, with his lawyer and witnesses, and Judge Gardner would not grant a continuance, so of necessity I had to act, hoping that at every minute McCook would come. But the trial proceeded regularly to its end; we were beaten, and judgment was entered against our client for the amount claimed, and costs. As soon as the matter was explained to McCook, he said "execution" could not be taken for ten days, and, as our client was poor, and had nothing on which the landlord could levy but his house, McCook advised him to get his neighbors together, to pick up the house, and carry it on to another vacant lot, belonging to a non-resident, so that even the house could not be taken in execution. Thus the grasping landlord, though successful in his judgment, failed in the execution, and our client was abundantly satisfied.

In due time I closed up my business at Leavenworth, and went to Lancaster, Ohio, where, in July, 1859, I received notice from Governor Wickliffe that I had been elected superintendent of the proposed college, and inviting me to come down to Louisiana as early as possible, because they were anxious to put the college into operation by the 1st of January following. For this honorable position I was indebted to Major D. C. Buell and General G. Mason Graham, to whom I have made full and due acknowledgment. During the civil war, it was reported and charged that I owed my position to the personal friendship of Generals Bragg and Beauregard, and that, in taking up arms against the South, I had been guilty of a breach of hospitality and friendship. I was not indebted to General Bragg, because he himself told me that he was not even aware that I was an applicant, and had favored the selection of Major Jenkins, another West Point graduate. General Beauregard had nothing whatever to do with the matter. .

CHAPTER VII.
LOUISIANA

1859-1861.

In the autumn of 1859, having made arrangements for my family to remain in Lancaster, I proceeded, via Columbus, Cincinnati, and Louisville, to Baton Rouge, Louisiana, where I reported for duty to Governor Wickliffe, who, by virtue of his office, was the president of the Board of Supervisors of the new institution over which I was called to preside. He explained to me the act of the Legislature under which the institution was founded; told me that the building was situated near Alexandria, in the parish of Rapides, and was substantially finished; that the future management would rest with a Board of Supervisors, mostly citizens of Rapides Parish, where also resided the Governor-elect, T. O. Moore, who would soon succeed him in his office as Governor and president ex officio; and advised me to go at once to Alexandria, and put myself in communication with Moore and the supervisors. Accordingly I took a boat at Baton Rouge, for the mouth of Red River.

The river being low, and its navigation precarious, I there took the regular mail-coach, as the more certain conveyance, and continued on toward Alexandria. I found, as a fellow-passenger in the coach, Judge Henry Boyce, of the United States District Court, with whom I had made acquaintance years before, at St. Louis, and, as we neared Alexandria, he proposed that we should stop at Governor Moore's and spend the night. Moore's house and plantation were on Bayou Robert, about eight miles from Alexandria. We found him at home, with his wife and a married daughter, and spent the night there. He sent us forward to Alexandria the next morning, in his own carriage. On arriving at Alexandria, I put up at an inn, or boarding-house, and almost immediately thereafter went about ten miles farther up Bayou Rapides, to the plantation and house of General G. Mason Graham, to whom I looked as the principal man with whom I had to deal. He was a high-toned gentleman, and his whole heart was in the enterprise. He at once put me at ease. We acted together most cordially from that time forth, and it was at his house that all the details of the seminary were arranged. We first visited the college-building together. It was located on an old country place of four hundred acres of pineland, with numerous springs, and the building was very large and handsome. A carpenter, named James, resided there, and had the general charge of the property; but, as there was not a table, chair, black-board, or any thing on hand, necessary for a beginning, I concluded to quarter myself in one of the rooms of the seminary, and board with an old black woman who cooked for James, so that I might personally push forward the necessary preparations. There was an old rail-fence about the place, and a large pile of boards in front. I immediately engaged four carpenters, and set them at work to make out of these boards mess-tables, benches, black-boards, etc. I also opened a correspondence with the professors-elect, and with all parties of influence in the State, who were interested in our work: At the meeting of the Board of Supervisors, held at Alexandria, August 2, 1859, five professors had been elected: 1. W. T. Sherman, Superintendent, and Professor of Engineering, etc.; 2. Anthony Vallas, Professor of Mathematics, Philosophy, etc.; 3. Francis W. Smith, Professor of Chemistry, etc.; 4. David F. Boyd, Professor of Languages, English and Ancient; 5. E. Berti St. Ange, Professor of French and Modern Languages.

These constituted the Academic Board, while the general supervision remained in the Board of Supervisors, composed of the Governor of the State, the Superintendent of Public Education, and twelve members, nominated by the Governor, and confirmed by the Senate. The institution was bound to educate sixteen beneficiary students, free of any charge for tuition. These had only to pay for their clothing and books, while all others had to pay their entire expenses, including tuition.

Early in November, Profs. Smith, Yallas, St. Ange, and I, met a committee of the Board of Supervisors, composed of T. C. Manning, G. Mason Graham, and W. W. Whittington, at General Graham's house, and resolved to open the institution to pupils on the 1st day of January, 1860. We adopted a series of bylaws for the government of the institution, which was styled the "Louisiana Seminary of Learning and Military Academy." This title grew out of the original grant, by the Congress of the United States, of a certain township of public land, to be sold by the State, and dedicated to the use of a "seminary of learning." I do not suppose that Congress designed thereby to fix the name or title; but the subject had so long been debated in Louisiana that the name, though awkward, had become familiar. We appended to it "Military Academy," as explanatory of its general design.

On the 17th of November, 1859, the Governor of the State, Wickliffe, issued officially a general circular, prepared by us, giving public notice that the "Seminary of Learning" would open on the 1st day of January, 1860; containing a description of the locality, and the general regulations for the proposed institution; and authorizing parties to apply for further information to the "Superintendent," at Alexandria, Louisiana.

The Legislature had appropriated for the sixteen beneficiaries at the rate of two hundred and eighty-three dollars per annum, to which we added sixty dollars as tuition for pay cadets; and, though the price was low, we undertook to manage for the first year on that basis.

Promptly to the day, we opened, with about sixty cadets present. Major Smith was the commandant of cadets, and I the superintendent. I had been to New Orleans, where I had bought a supply of mattresses, books, and every thing requisite, and we started very much on the basis of West Point and of the Virginia Military Institute, but without uniforms or muskets; yet with roll-calls, sections, and recitations, we kept as near the standard of West Point as possible. I kept all the money accounts, and gave general directions to the steward, professors, and cadets. The other professors had their regular classes and recitations. We all lived in rooms in the college building, except Vallas, who had a family, and rented a house near by. A Creole gentleman, B. Jarrean, Esq., had been elected steward, and he also had his family in a house not far off. The other professors had a mess in a room adjoining the mess-hall. A few more cadets joined in the course of the winter, so that we had in all, during the first term, seventy-three cadets, of whom fifty-nine passed the examination on the 30th of

July, 1860. During our first term many defects in the original act of the Legislature were demonstrated, and, by the advice of the Board of Supervisors, I went down to Baton Rouge during the session of the Legislature, to advocate and urge the passage of a new bill, putting the institution on a better footing. Thomas O. Moors was then Governor, Bragg was a member of the Board of Public Works, and Richard Taylor was a Senator. I got well acquainted with all of these, and with some of the leading men of the State, and was always treated with the greatest courtesy and kindness. In conjunction with the proper committee of the Legislature, we prepared a new bill, which was passed and approved on the 7th of March, 1860, by which we were to have a beneficiary cadet for each parish, in all fifty-six, and fifteen thousand dollars annually for their maintenance; also twenty thousand dollars for the general use of the college. During that session we got an appropriation of fifteen thousand dollars for building two professors' houses, for the purchase of philosophical and chemical apparatus, and for the beginning of a college library. The seminary was made a State Arsenal, under the title of State Central Arsenal, and I was allowed five hundred dollars a year as its superintendent. These matters took me several times to Baton Rouge that winter, and I recall an event of some interest, which most have happened in February. At that time my brother, John Sherman, was a candidate, in the national House of Representatives, for Speaker, against Bocock, of Virginia. In the South he was regarded as an "abolitionist," the most horrible of all monsters; and many people of Louisiana looked at me with suspicion, as the brother of the abolitionist, John Sherman, and doubted the propriety of having me at the head of an important State institution. By this time I was pretty well acquainted with many of their prominent men, was generally esteemed by all in authority, and by the people of Rapides Parish especially, who saw that I was devoted to my particular business, and that I gave no heed to the political excitement of the day. But the members of the State Senate and House did not know me so well, and it was natural that they should be suspicions of a Northern man, and the brother of him who was the "abolition" candidate for Speaker of the House.

One evening, at a large dinner-party at Governor Moore's, at which were present several members of the Louisiana Legislature, Taylor, Bragg, and the Attorney-General Hyams, after the ladies had left the table, I noticed at Governor Moore's end quite a lively discussion going on, in which my name was frequently used; at length the Governor called to me, saying: "Colonel Sherman, you can readily understand that, with your brother the abolitionist candidate for Speaker, some of our people wonder that you should be here at the head of an important State institution. Now, you are at my table, and I assure you of my confidence. Won't you speak your mind freely on this question of slavery, that so agitates the land? You are under my roof, and, whatever you say, you have my protection."

I answered: "Governor Moors, you mistake in calling my brother, John Sherman, an abolitionist. We have been separated since childhood—I in the army, and he pursuing his profession of law in Northern Ohio; and it is possible we may differ in general sentiment, but I deny that he is considered at home an abolitionist; and, although he prefers the free institutions under which he lives to those of slavery which prevail here, he would not of himself take from you by law or force any property whatever, even slaves."

Then said Moore: "Give us your own views of slavery as you see it here and throughout the South."

I answered in effect that "the people of Louisiana were hardly responsible for slavery, as they had inherited it; that I found two distinct conditions of slavery, domestic and field hands. The domestic slaves, employed by the families, were probably better treated than any slaves on earth; but the condition of the field-hands was different, depending more on the temper and disposition of their masters and overseers than were those employed about the house;" and I went on to say that, "were I a citizen of Louisiana, and a member of the Legislature, I would deem it wise to bring the legal condition of the slaves more near the status of human beings under all Christian and civilized governments. In the first place, I argued that, in sales of slaves made by the State, I would forbid the separation of families, letting the father, mother, and children, be sold together to one person, instead of each to the highest bidder. And, again, I would advise the repeal of the statute which enacted a severe penalty for even the owner to teach his slave to read and write, because that actually qualified property and took away a part of its value; illustrating the assertion by the case of Henry Sampson, who had been the slave of Colonel Chambers, of Rapides Parish, who had gone to California as the servant of an officer of the army, and who was afterward employed by me in the bank at San Francisco. At first he could not write or read, and I could only afford to pay him one hundred dollars a month; but he was taught to read and write by Reilley, our bank-teller, when his services became worth two hundred and fifty dollars a month, which enabled him to buy his own freedom and that of his brother and his family."

What I said was listened to by all with the most profound attention; and, when I was through, some one (I think it was Mr. Hyams) struck the table with his fist, making the glasses jingle, and said, "By God, he is right!" and at once he took up the debate, which went on, for an hour or more, on both sides with ability and fairness. Of course, I was glad to be thus relieved, because at the time all men in Louisiana were dreadfully excited on questions affecting their slaves, who constituted the bulk of their wealth, and without whom they honestly believed that sugar, cotton, and rice, could not possibly be cultivated.

On the 30th and 31st of July, 1860, we had an examination at the seminary, winding up with a ball, and as much publicity as possible to attract general notice; and immediately thereafter we all scattered—the cadets to their homes, and the professors wherever they pleased—all to meet again on the 1st day of the next November. Major Smith and I agreed to meet in New York on a certain day in August, to purchase books, models, etc. I went directly to my family in Lancaster, and after a few days proceeded to Washington, to endeavor to procure from the General Government the necessary muskets and equipments for our cadets by the beginning of the next term. I was in Washington on the 17th day of August, and hunted up my friend Major Buell, of the Adjutant-General's Department, who was on duty with the Secretary of War, Floyd. I had with me a letter of Governor Moore's, authorizing me to act in his name. Major Buell took me into Floyd's room at the War Department, to whom I explained my business, and I was agreeably surprised to meet with such easy success. Although the State of Louisiana had already drawn her full quota of arms, Floyd promptly promised to order my requisition to be filled, and I procured the necessary blanks at the Ordnance-Office, filled them with two hundred cadet muskets, and all equipments complete, and was assured that all these articles would be shipped to Louisiana in season for our use that fall. These assurances were faithfully carried out.

I then went on to New York, there met Major Smith according to appointment, and together we selected and purchased a good supply of uniforms, clothing, and text books, as well as a fair number of books of history and fiction, to commence a library.

When this business was completed, I returned to Lancaster, and remained with my family till the time approached for me to return to Louisiana. I again left my family at Lancaster, until assured of the completion of the two buildings designed for the married professors for which I had contracted that spring with Mr. Mills, of Alexandria, and which were well under progress when I left in August. One of these was designed for me and the other for Vallas. Mr. Ewing presented me with a horse, which I took down the river with me, and en route I ordered from Grimsley & Co. a full equipment of saddle, bridle, etc., the same that I used in the war, and which I lost with my horse, shot under me at Shiloh.

Reaching Alexandria early in October, I pushed forward the construction of the two buildings, some fences, gates, and all other work, with the object of a more perfect start at the opening of the regular term November 1, 1860.

About this time Dr. Powhatan Clark was elected Assistant Professor of Chemistry, etc., and acted as secretary of the Board of Supervisors, but no other changes were made in our small circle of professors.

November came, and with it nearly if not quite all our first set of cadets, and others, to the number of about one hundred and thirty. We divided them into two companies, issued arms and clothing, and began a regular system of drills and instruction, as well as the regular recitations. I had moved into my new house, but prudently had not sent for my family, nominally on the ground of waiting until the season was further advanced, but really because of the storm that was lowering heavy on the political horizon. The presidential election was to occur in November, and the nominations had already been made in stormy debates by the usual conventions. Lincoln and Hamlin (to the South utterly unknown) were the nominees of the Republican party, and for the first time both these candidates were from Northern States. The Democratic party divided—one set nominating a ticket at Charleston, and the other at Baltimore. Breckenridge and Lane were the nominees of the Southern or Democratic party; and Bell and Everett, a kind of compromise, mostly in favor in Louisiana. Political excitement was at its very height, and it was constantly asserted that Mr. Lincoln's election would imperil the Union. I purposely kept aloof from politics, would take no part, and remember that on the day of the election in November I was notified that it would be advisable for me to vote for Bell and Everett, but I openly said I would not, and I did not. The election of Mr. Lincoln fell upon us all like a clap of thunder. People saw and felt that the South had threatened so long that, if she quietly submitted, the question of slavery in the Territories was at an end forever. I mingled freely with the members of the Board of Supervisors, and with the people of Rapides Parish generally, keeping aloof from all cliques and parties, and I certainly hoped that the threatened storm would blow over, as had so often occurred before, after similar threats. At our seminary the order of exercises went along with the regularity of the seasons. Once a week, I had the older cadets to practise reading, reciting, and elocution, and noticed that their selections were from Calhoun, Yancey, and other Southern speakers, all treating of the defense of their slaves and their home institutions as the very highest duty of the patriot. Among boys this was to be expected; and among the members of our board, though most of them declaimed against politicians generally, and especially abolitionists, as pests, yet there was a growing feeling that danger was in the wind. I recall the visit of a young gentleman who had been sent from Jackson, by the Governor of Mississippi, to confer with Governor Moore, then on his plantation at Bayou Robert, and who had come over to see our college. He spoke to me openly of secession as a fixed fact, and that its details were only left open for discussion. I also recall the visit of some man who was said to be a high officer in the order of "Knights of the Golden Circle," of the existence of which order I was even ignorant, until explained to me by Major Smith and Dr. Clark. But in November, 1860, no man ever approached me offensively, to ascertain my views, or my proposed course of action in case of secession, and no man in or out of authority ever tried to induce me to take part in steps designed to lead toward disunion. I think my general opinions were well known and understood, viz., that "secession was treason, was war;" and that in no event would the North and West permit the Mississippi River to pass out of their control. But some men at the South actually supposed at the time that the Northwestern States, in case of a disruption of the General Government, would be drawn in self-interest to an alliance with the South. What I now write I do not offer as any thing like a history of the important events of that time, but rather as my memory of them, the effect they had on me personally, and to what extent they influenced my personal conduct.

South Carolina seceded December 20, 1860, and Mississippi soon after. Emissaries came to Louisiana to influence the Governor, Legislature, and people, and it was the common assertion that, if all the Cotton States would follow the lead of South Carolina, it would diminish the chances of civil war, because a bold and determined front would deter the General Government from any measures of coercion. About this time also, viz., early in December, we received Mr. Buchanan's annual message to Congress, in which he publicly announced that the General Government had no constitutional power to "coerce a State." I confess this staggered me, and I feared that the prophecies and assertions of Alison and other European commentators on our form of government were right, and that our Constitution was a mere rope of sand, that would break with the first pressure.

The Legislature of Louisiana met on the 10th of December, and passed an act calling a convention of delegates from the people, to meet at Baton Rouge, on the 8th of January, to take into consideration the state of the Union; and, although it was universally admitted that a large majority of the voters of the State were opposed to secession, disunion, and all the steps of the South Carolinians, yet we saw that they were powerless, and that the politicians would sweep them along rapidly to the end, prearranged by their leaders in Washington. Before the ordinance of secession was passed, or the convention had assembled, on the faith of a telegraphic dispatch sent by the two Senators, Benjamin and Slidell, from their seats in the United States Senate at Washington, Governor Moore ordered the seizure of all the United States forts at the mouth of the Mississippi and Lake Pontchartrain, and of the United States arsenal at Baton Rouge. The forts had no garrisons, but the arsenal was held by a small company of artillery, commanded by Major Haskins, a most worthy and excellent officer, who had lost an arm in Mexico. I remember well that I was strongly and bitterly impressed by the seizure of the arsenal, which occurred on January 10, 1861.

When I went first to Baton Rouge, in 1859, en route to Alexandria, I found Captain Rickett's company of artillery stationed in the arsenal, but soon after there was somewhat of a clamor on the Texas frontier about Brownsville, which induced the War Department to order Rickett's company to that frontier. I remember that Governor Moore remonstrated with the Secretary of War because so much dangerous property, composed of muskets, powder, etc., had been left by the United States unguarded, in a parish where the slave population was as five or six to one of whites; and it was on his official demand that the United States Government ordered Haskinss company to replace Rickett's. This company did not number forty men. In the night of January 9th, about five hundred New Orleans militia, under command of a Colonel Wheat, went up from New Orleans by boat, landed, surrounded the arsenal, and demanded its surrender. Haskins was of course unprepared for such a step, yet he at first resolved to defend the post as he best could with his small force. But Bragg, who was an old army acquaintance of his, had a parley with him, exhibited to him the vastly superior force of his assailants, embracing two field-batteries, and offered to procure for him honorable terms, to march out with drums and colors, and to take unmolested passage in a boat up to St. Louis; alleging, further, that the old Union was at an end, and that a just settlement would be made between the two new fragments for all the property stored in the arsenal. Of course it was Haskins's duty to have defended his post to the death; but up to that time the national authorities in Washington had shown such pusillanimity, that the officers of the army knew not what to do. The result, anyhow, was that Haskins surrendered his post, and at once embarked for St. Louis. The arms and munitions stored in the arsenal were scattered—some to Mississippi, some to New Orleans, some to Shreveport; and to me, at the Central Arsenal, were consigned two thousand muskets, three hundred Jager rifles, and a large amount of cartridges and ammunition. The invoices were signed by the former ordnance-sergeant, Olodowski, as a captain of ordnance, and I think he continued such on General Bragg's staff through the whole of the subsequent civil war. These arms, etc., came up to me at Alexandria, with orders from Governor Moore to receipt for and account for them. Thus I was made the receiver of stolen goods, and these goods the property of the United States. This grated hard on my feelings as an ex-army-officer, and on counting the arms I noticed that they were packed in the old familiar boxes, with the "U. S." simply scratched off. General G. Mason Graham had resigned as the chairman of the Executive Committee, and Dr. S. A. Smith, of Alexandria, then a member of the State Senate, had succeeded him as chairman, and acted as head of the Board of Supervisors. At the time I was in most intimate correspondence with all of these parties, and our letters must have been full of politics, but I have only retained copies of a few of the letters, which I will embody in this connection, as they will show, better than by any thing I can now recall, the feelings of parties at that critical period. The seizure of the arsenal at Baton Rouge occurred January 10, 1861, and the secession ordinance was not passed until about the 25th or 26th of the same month. At all events, after the seizure of the arsenal, and before the passage of the ordinance of secession, viz., on the 18th of January, I wrote as follows:

Louisiana State Seminary of Learning and Military Academy
January 18, 1861

Governor THOMAS O. MOORE, Baton, Rouge, Louisiana.

Sir: As I occupy a quasi-military position under the laws of the State, I deem it proper to acquaint you that I accepted such position when Louisiana was a State in the Union, and when the motto of this seminary was inserted in marble over the main door: "By the liberality of the General Government of the United States.

The Union—esto perpetua."

Recent events foreshadow a great change, and it becomes all men to choose. If Louisiana withdraw from the Federal Union, I prefer to maintain my allegiance to the Constitution as long as a fragment of it survives; and my longer stay here would be wrong in every sense of the word.

In that event, I beg you will send or appoint some authorized agent to take charge of the arms and munitions of war belonging to the State, or advise me what disposition to make of them.

And furthermore, as president of the Board of Supervisors, I beg you to take immediate steps to relieve me as superintendent, the moment the State determines to secede, for on no earthly account will I do any act or think any thought hostile to or in defiance of the old Government of the United States.

With great respect, your obedient servant,

W. T. SHERMAN, Superintendent.

[PRIVATE.]

January 18, 1861.

To Governor Moore:

My Dear Sir: I take it for granted that you have been expecting for some days the accompanying paper from me (the above official letter). I have repeatedly and again made known to General Graham and Dr. Smith that, in the event of a severance of the relations hitherto existing between the Confederated States of this Union, I would be forced to choose the old Union. It is barely possible all the States may secede, South and North, that new combinations may result, but this process will be one of time and uncertainty, and I cannot with my opinions await the subsequent development.

I have never been a politician, and therefore undervalue the excited feelings and opinions of present rulers, but I do think, if this people cannot execute a form of government like the present, that a worse one will result.

I will keep the cadets as quiet as possible. They are nervous, but I think the interest of the State requires them here, guarding this property, and acquiring a knowledge which will be useful to your State in after-times.

When I leave, which I now regard as certain, the present professors can manage well enough, to afford you leisure time to find a suitable successor to me. You might order Major Smith to receipt for the arms, and to exercise military command, while the academic exercises could go on under the board. In time, some gentleman will turn up, better qualified than I am, to carry on the seminary to its ultimate point of success. I entertain the kindest feelings toward all, and would leave the State with much regret; only in great events we must choose, one way or the other.

Truly, your friend,

W. T. SHERMAN

January 19, 1881—Saturday.

Dr. S. A. Smith, President Board of Supervisors, Baton Rouge, Louisiana.

Dear Sir: I have just finished my quarterly reports to the parents of all the cadets here, or who have been here.

All my books of account are written up to date. All bills for the houses, fences, etc., are settled, and nothing now remains but the daily tontine of recitations and drills. I have written officially and unofficially to Governor Moore, that with my opinions of the claimed right of accession, of the seizure of public forts, arsenals, etc., and the ignominious capture of a United States garrison, stationed in your midst, as a guard to the arsenal and for the protection of your own people, it would be highly improper for me longer to remain. No great inconvenience can result to the seminary. I will be the chief loser. I came down two months before my pay commenced. I made sacrifices in Kansas to enable me thus to obey the call of Governor Wickliffe, and you know that last winter I declined a most advantageous offer of employment abroad; and thus far I have received nothing as superintendent of the arsenal, though I went to Washington and New York (at my own expense) on the faith of the five hundred dollars salary promised.

These are all small matters in comparison with those involved in the present state of the country, which will cause sacrifices by millions, instead of by hundreds. The more I think of it, the more I think I should be away, the sooner the better; and therefore I hope you will join with Governor Moors in authorizing me to turn over to Major Smith the military command here, and to the academic board the control of the daily exercises and recitations.

There will be no necessity of your coming up. You can let Major Smith receive the few hundreds of cash I have on hand, and I can meet you on a day certain in New Orleans, when we can settle the bank account. Before I leave, I can pay the steward Jarrean his account for the month, and there would be no necessity for other payments till about the close of March, by which time the board can meet, and elect a treasurer and superintendent also.

At present I have no class, and there will be none ready till about the month of May, when there will be a class in "surveying." Even if you do not elect a superintendent in the mean time, Major Smith could easily teach this class, as he is very familiar with the subject-matter. Indeed, I think you will do well to leave the subject of a new superintendent until one perfectly satisfactory turns up.

There is only one favor I would ask. The seminary has plenty of money in bank. The Legislature will surely appropriate for my salary as superintendent of this arsenal. Would you not let me make my drafts on the State Treasury, send them to you, let the Treasurer note them for payment when the appropriation is made, and then pay them out of the seminary fund? The drafts will be paid in March, and the seminary will lose nothing. This would be just to me; for I actually spent two hundred dollars and more in going to Washington and New York, thereby securing from the United States, in advance, three thousand dollars' worth of the very best arms; and clothing and books, at a clear profit to the seminary of over eight hundred dollars. I may be some time in finding new employment, and will stand in need of this money (five hundred dollars); otherwise I would abandon it.

I will not ask you to put the Board of Supervisors to the trouble of meeting, unless you can get a quorum at Baton Rouge.

With great respect, your friend,

W. T. SHERMAN.

By course of mail, I received the following answer from Governor Moore, the original of which I still possess. It is all in General Braggs handwriting, with which I am familiar.

Executive Office,

BATON ROUGE, LOUISIANA, January 23, 1861

MY DEAR SIR: It is with the deepest regret I acknowledge receipt of your communication of the 18th inst. In the pressure of official business, I can now only request you to transfer to Prof. Smith the arms, munitions, and funds in your hands, whenever you conclude to withdraw from the position you have filled with so much distinction. You cannot regret more than I do the necessity which deprives us of your services, and you will bear with you the respect, confidence, and admiration, of all who have been associated with you. Very truly, your friend,

Thomas O. Moore.

Colonel W. T. SHERMAN, Superintendent Military Academy, Alexandria.

I must have received several letters from Bragg, about this time, which have not been preserved; for I find that, on the 1st of February, 1861, I wrote him thus:

Seminary of Learning Alexandria, LOUISIANA, February 1, 1881.

Colonel Braxton BRAGG, Baton, Rouge, Louisiana.

Dear Sir: Yours of January 23d and 27th are received. I thank you most kindly, and Governor Moors through you, for the kind manner in which you have met my wishes.

Now that I cannot be compromised by political events, I will so shape my course as best to serve the institution, which has a strong hold on my affections and respect.

The Board of Supervisors will be called for the 9th instant, and I will cooperate with them in their measures to place matters here on a safe and secure basis. I expect to be here two weeks, and will make you full returns of money and property belonging to the State Central Arsenal. All the arms and ammunition are safely stored here. Then I will write you more at length. With sincere respect, your friend,

W. T. SHERMAN.

Major Smith's receipt to me, for the arms and property belonging both to the seminary and to the arsenal, is dated February 19, 1861. I subjoin also, in this connection, copies of one or two papers that may prove of interest

BATON ROUGE, January 28, 1881.
To Major SHERMAN, Superintendent, Alexandria.

My DEAR SIR: Your letter was duly receive, and would have been answered ere this time could I have arranged sooner the matter of the five hundred dollars. I shall go from here to New Orleans to-day or tomorrow, and will remain there till Saturday after next, perhaps. I shall expect to meet you there, as indicated in your note to me.

I need not tell you that it is with no ordinary regret that I view your determination to leave us, for really I believe that the success of our institution, now almost assured, is jeopardized thereby. I am sore that we will never have a superintendent with whom I shall have more pleasant relations than those which have existed between yourself and me.

I fully appreciate the motives which have induced you to give up a position presenting so many advantages to yourself, and sincerely hope that you may, in any future enterprise, enjoy the success which your character and ability merit and deserve.

Should you come down on the Rapides (steamer), please look after my wife, who will, I hope, accompany you on said boat, or some other good one.

Colonel Bragg informs me that the necessary orders have been given for the transfer and receipt by Major Smith of the public property.

I herewith transmit a request to the secretary to convene the Board of Supervisors, that they may act as seems best to them in the premises.

In the mean time, Major Smith will command by seniority the cadets, and the Academic Board will be able to conduct the scientific exercises of the institution until the Board of Supervisors can have time to act. Hoping to meet you soon at the St. Charles, I am,

Most truly, your friend and servant, S. A. Smith

P. S. Governor Moors desires me to express his profound regret that the State is about to lose one who we all fondly hoped had cast his destinies for weal or for woe among us; and that he is sensible that we lose thereby an officer whom it will be difficult, if not impossible, to replace.

S. A. S.

BATON ROUGE, February 11, 1881.
To Major Sherman, Alexandria.

Dear Sir: I have been in New Orleans for ten days, and on returning here find two letters from you, also your prompt answer to the resolution of the House of Representatives, for which I am much obliged.

The resolution passed the last day before adjournment. I was purposing to respond, when your welcome reports came to hand. I have arranged to pay you your five hundred dollars.

I will say nothing of general politics, except to give my opinion that there is not to be any war.

In that event, would it not be possible for you to become a citizen of our State? Everyone deplores your determination to leave us. At the same time, your friends feel that you are abandoning a position that might become an object of desire to any one.

I will try to meet you in New Orleans at any time you may indicate; but it would be best for you to stop here, when, if possible, I will accompany you. Should you do so, you will find me just above the State-House, and facing it.

Bring with you a few copies of the "Rules of the Seminary."

Yours truly,

S. A. Smith

Colonel W. T. SHERMAN.

Sir: I am instructed by the Board of Supervisors of this institution to present a copy of the resolutions adopted by them at their last meeting.

"Resolved, That the thanks of the Board of Supervisors are due, and are hereby tendered, to Colonel William T. Sherman for the able and efficient manner in which he has conducted the affairs of the seminary during the time the institution has been under his control—a period attended with unusual difficulties, requiring on the part of the superintendent to successfully overcome them a high order of administrative talent. And the board further bear willing testimony to the valuable services that Colonel Sherman has rendered them in their efforts to establish an institution of learning in accordance with the beneficent design of the State and Federal Governments; evincing at all times a readiness to adapt himself to the ever-varying requirements of an institution of learning in its infancy, struggling to attain a position of honor and usefulness.

"Resolved, further, That, in accepting the resignation of Colonel Sherman as Superintendent of the State Seminary of Learning and Military Academy, we tender to him assurances of our high personal regard, and our sincere regret at the occurrence of causes that render it necessary to part with so esteemed and valued a friend, as well as co-laborer in the cause of education."

Powhatan Clarke, Secretary of the Board.

A copy of the resolution of the Academic Board, passed at their session of April 1,1861:

"Resolved, That in the resignation of the late superintendent, Colonel W. T. Sherman, the Academic Board deem it not improper to express their deep conviction of the loss the institution has sustained in being thus deprived of an able head. They cannot fail to appreciate the manliness of character which has always marked the actions of Colonel Sherman. While he is personally endeared to many of them as a friend, they consider it their high pleasure to tender to him in this resolution their regret on his separation, and their sincere wish for his future welfare."

I have given the above at some length, because, during the civil war, it was in Southern circles asserted that I was guilty of a breach of hospitality in taking up arms against the South. They were manifestly the aggressors, and we could only defend our own by assailing them. Yet, without any knowledge of what the future had in store for me, I took unusual precautions that the institution should not be damaged by my withdrawal. About the 20th of February, having turned over all property, records, and money, on hand, to Major Smith, and taking with me the necessary documents to make the final settlement with Dr. S. A. Smith, at the bank in New Orleans, where the funds of the institution were deposited to my credit, I took passage from Alexandria for that city, and arrived there, I think, on the 23d. Dr. Smith met me, and we went to the bank, where I turned over to him the balance, got him to audit all my accounts, certify that they were correct and just, and that there remained not one cent of balance in my hands. I charged in my account current for my salary up to the end of February, at the rate of four thousand dollars a year, and for the five hundred dollars due me as superintendent of the Central Arsenal, all of which was due and had been fairly earned, and then I stood free and discharged of any and every obligation, honorary or business, that was due by me to the State of Louisiana, or to any corporation or individual in that State.

This business occupied two or three days, during which I staid at the St. Louis Hotel. I usually sat at table with Colonel and Mrs. Bragg, and an officer who wore the uniform of the State of Louisiana, and was addressed as captain. Bragg wore a colonel's uniform, and explained to me that he was a colonel in the State service, a colonel of artillery, and that some companies of his regiment garrisoned Forts Jackson and St. Philip, and the arsenal at Baton Rouge.

Beauregard at the time had two sons at the Seminary of Learning. I had given them some of my personal care at the father's request, and, wanting to tell him of their condition and progress, I went to his usual office in the Custom-House Building, and found him in the act of starting for Montgomery, Alabama. Bragg said afterward that Beauregard had been sent for by Jefferson Davis, and that it was rumored that he had been made a brigadier-general, of which fact he seemed jealous, because in the old army Bragg was the senior.

Davis and Stephens had been inaugurated President and Vice-President of the Confederate States of America, February 18, 1860, at Montgomery, and those States only embraced the seven cotton States. I recall a conversation at the tea-table, one evening, at the St. Louis Hotel. When Bragg was speaking of Beauregard's promotion, Mrs. Bragg, turning to me, said, "You know that my husband is not a favorite with the new President." My mind was resting on Mr. Lincoln as the new President, and I said I did not know that Bragg had ever met Mr. Lincoln, when Mrs. Bragg said, quite pointedly, "I didn't mean your President, but our President." I knew that Bragg hated Davis bitterly, and that he had resigned from the army in 1855, or 1856, because Davis, as Secretary of War, had ordered him, with his battery, from Jefferson Barracks, Missouri, to Fort Smith or Fort Washita, in the Indian country, as Bragg expressed it, "to chase Indians with six-pounders."

I visited the quartermaster, Colonel A. C. Myers, who had resigned from the army, January 28, 1861, and had accepted service under the new regime. His office was in the same old room in the Lafayette Square building, which he had in 1853, when I was there a commissary, with the same pictures on the wall, and the letters "U. S." on every thing, including his desk, papers, etc. I asked him if he did not feel funny. "No, not at all. The thing was inevitable, secession was a complete success; there would be no war, but the two Governments would settle all matters of business in a friendly spirit, and each would go on in its allotted sphere, without further confusion." About this date, February 16th, General Twiggs, Myers's father-in-law, had surrendered his entire command, in the Department of Texas, to some State troops, with all the Government property, thus consummating the first serious step in the drama of the conspiracy, which was to form a confederacy of the cotton States, before working upon the other slave or border States, and before the 4th of March, the day for the inauguration of President Lincoln.

I walked the streets of New Orleans, and found business going along as usual. Ships were strung for miles along the lower levee, and steamboats above, all discharging or receiving cargo. The Pelican flag of Louisiana was flying over the Custom House, Mint, City Hall, and everywhere. At the levee ships carried every flag on earth except that of the United States, and I was told that during a procession on the 22d of February, celebrating their emancipation from the despotism of the United States Government, only one national flag was shown from a house, and that the houses of Cuthbert Bullitt, on Lafayette Square. He was commanded to take it down, but he refused, and defended it with his pistol.

The only officer of the army that I can recall, as being there at the time, who was faithful, was Colonel C. L. Kilburn, of the Commissary Department, and he was preparing to escape North.

Everybody regarded the change of Government as final; that Louisiana, by a mere declaration, was a free and independent State, and could enter into any new alliance or combination she chose.

Men were being enlisted and armed, to defend the State, and there was not the least evidence that the national Administration designed to make any effort, by force, to vindicate the national authority. I therefore bade adieu to all my friends, and about the 25th of February took my departure by railroad, for Lancaster, via Cairo and Cincinnati.

Before leaving this subject, I will simply record the fate of some of my associates. The seminary was dispersed by the war, and all the professors and cadets took service in the Confederacy, except Yallas, St. Ange, and Cadet Taliaferro. The latter joined a Union regiment, as a lieutenant, after New Orleans was retaken by the United States fleet under Farragut. I think that both Yallas and St. Ange have died in poverty since the war. Major Smith joined the rebel army in Virginia, and was killed in April, 1865, as he was withdrawing his garrison, by night, from the batteries at Drury's Bluff, at the time General Lee began his final retreat from Richmond. Boyd became a captain of engineers on the staff of General Richard Taylor, was captured, and was in jail at Natchez, Mississippi, when I was on my Meridian expedition. He succeeded in getting a letter to me on my arrival at Vicksburg, and, on my way down to New Orleans, I stopped at Natchez, took him along, and enabled him to effect an exchange through General Banks. As soon as the war was over, he returned to Alexandria, and reorganized the old institution, where I visited him in 1867; but, the next winter, the building took fire end burned to the ground. The students, library, apparatus, etc., were transferred to Baton Rouge, where the same institution now is, under the title of the Louisiana University. I have been able to do them many acts of kindness, and am still in correspondence, with Colonel Boyd, its president.

General G. Mason Graham is still living on his plantation, on Bayou Rapides, old and much respected.

Dr. S. A. Smith became a surgeon in the rebel army, and at the close of the war was medical director of the trans-Mississippi Department, with General Kirby Smith. I have seen him since the war, at New Orleans, where he died about a year ago.

Dr. Clark was in Washington recently, applying for a place as United States consul abroad. I assisted him, but with no success, and he is now at Baltimore, Maryland.

After the battle of Shiloh, I found among the prisoners Cadet Barrow, fitted him out with some clean clothing, of which he was in need, and from him learned that Cadet Workman was killed in that battle.

Governor Moore's plantation was devastated by General Banks's troops. After the war he appealed to me, and through the Attorney-General, Henry Stanbery, I aided in having his land restored to him, and I think he is now living there.

Bragg, Beauregard, and Taylor, enacted high parts in the succeeding war, and now reside in Louisiana or Texas.

CHAPTER VIII.
MISSOURI

APRIL AND MAY, 1861.

During the time of these events in Louisiana, I was in constant correspondence with my brother, John Sherman, at Washington; Mr. Ewing, at Lancaster, Ohio; and Major H. S. Turner, at St. Louis. I had managed to maintain my family comfortably at Lancaster, but was extremely anxious about the future. It looked like the end of my career, for I did not suppose that "civil war" could give me an employment that would provide for the family. I thought, and may have said, that the national crisis had been brought about by the politicians, and, as it was upon us, they "might fight it out" Therefore, when I turned North from New Orleans, I felt more disposed to look to St. Louis for a home, and to Major. Turner to find me employment, than to the public service.

I left New Orleans about the 1st of March, 1861, by rail to Jackson and Clinton, Mississippi, Jackson, Tennessee, and Columbus, Kentucky, where we took a boat to Cairo, and thence, by rail, to Cincinnati and Lancaster. All the way, I heard, in the cars and boats, warm discussions about politics; to the effect that, if Mr. Lincoln should attempt coercion of the seceded States, the other slave or border States would make common cause, when, it was believed, it would be madness to attempt to reduce them to subjection. In the South, the people were earnest, fierce and angry, and were evidently organizing for action; whereas, in Illinois, Indiana, and Ohio, I saw not the least sign of preparation. It certainly looked to me as though the people of the North would tamely submit to a disruption of the Union, and the orators of the South used, openly and constantly, the expressions that there would be no war, and that a lady's thimble would hold all the blood to be shed. On reaching Lancaster, I found letters from my brother John, inviting me to come to Washington, as he wanted to see me; and from Major Tamer, at St. Louis, that he was trying to secure for me the office of president of the Fifth Street Railroad, with a salary of twenty-five hundred dollars; that Mr. Lucas and D. A. January held a controlling interest of stock, would vote for me, and the election would occur in March. This suited me exactly, and I answered Turner that I would accept, with thanks. But I also thought it right and proper that I should first go to Washington, to talk with my brother, Senator Sherman.

Mr. Lincoln had just been installed, and the newspapers were filled with rumors of every kind indicative of war; the chief act of interest was that Major Robert Anderson had taken by night into Fort Sumter all the troops garrisoning Charleston Harbor, and that he was determined to defend it against the demands of the State of South Carolina and of the Confederate States. I must have reached Washington about the 10th of March. I found my brother there, just appointed Senator, in place of Mr. Chase, who was in the cabinet, and I have no doubt my opinions, thoughts, and feelings, wrought up by the events in Louisiana; seemed to him gloomy and extravagant. About Washington I saw but few signs of preparation, though the Southern Senators and Representatives were daily sounding their threats on the floors of Congress, and were publicly withdrawing to join the Confederate Congress at Montgomery. Even in the War Department and about the public offices there was open, unconcealed talk, amounting to high-treason.

One day, John Sherman took me with him to see Mr. Lincoln. He walked into the room where the secretary to the President now sits, we found the room full of people, and Mr. Lincoln sat at the end of the table, talking with three or four gentlemen, who soon left. John walked up, shook hands, and took a chair near him, holding in his hand some papers referring to, minor appointments in the State of Ohio, which formed the subject of conversation. Mr. Lincoln took the papers, said he would refer them to the proper heads of departments, and would be glad to make the appointments asked for, if not already promised. John then turned to me, and said, "Mr. President, this is my brother, Colonel Sherman, who is just up from Louisiana, he may give you some information you want." "Ah!" said Mr. Lincoln, "how are they getting along down there?" I said, "They think they are getting along swimmingly—they are preparing for war." "Oh, well!" said he, "I guess we'll manage to keep house." I was silenced, said no more to him, and we soon left. I was sadly disappointed, and remember that I broke out on John, d—ning the politicians generally, saying, "You have got things in a hell of a fig, and you may get them out as you best can," adding that the country was sleeping on a volcano that might burst forth at any minute, but that I was going to St. Louis to take care of my family, and would have no more to do with it. John begged me to be more patient, but I said I would not; that I had no time to wait, that I was off for St. Louis; and off I went. At Lancaster I found letters from Major Turner, inviting me to St. Louis, as the place in the Fifth Street Railroad was a sure thing, and that Mr. Lucas would rent me a good house on Locust Street, suitable for my family, for six hundred dollars a year.

Mrs. Sherman and I gathered our family and effects together, started for St. Louis March 27th, where we rented of Mr. Lucas the house on Locust Street, between Tenth and Eleventh, and occupied it on the 1st of April. Charles Ewing and John Hunter had formed a law-partnership in St. Louis, and agreed to board with us, taking rooms on the third floor In the latter part of March, I was duly elected president of the Fifth Street Railroad, and entered on the discharge of my duties April 1, 1861. We had a central office on the corner of Fifth and Locust, and also another up at the stables in Bremen. The road was well stocked and in full operation, and all I had to do was to watch the economical administration of existing affairs, which I endeavored to do with fidelity and zeal. But the whole air was full of wars and rumors of wars. The struggle was going on politically for the border States. Even in Missouri, which was a slave State, it was manifest that the Governor of the State, Claiborne Jackson, and all the leading politicians, were for the South in case of a war. The house on the northwest corner of Fifth and Pine was the rebel headquarters, where the rebel flag was hung publicly, and the crowds about the Planters' House were all more or less rebel. There was also a camp in Lindell's Grove, at the end of Olive, Street, under command of General

D. M. Frost, a Northern man, a graduate of West Point, in open sympathy with the Southern leaders. This camp was nominally a State camp of instruction, but, beyond doubt, was in the interest of the Southern cause, designed to be used against the national authority in the event of the General Government's attempting to coerce the Southern Confederacy. General William S. Harvey was in command of the Department of Missouri, and resided in his own house, on Fourth Street, below Market; and there were five or six companies of United States troops in the arsenal, commanded by Captain N. Lyon; throughout the city, there had been organized, almost exclusively out of the German part of the population, four or five regiments of "Home Guards," with which movement Frank Blair, B. Gratz Brown, John M. Schofield, Clinton B. Fisk, and others, were most active on the part of the national authorities. Frank Blair's brother Montgomery was in the cabinet of Mr. Lincoln at Washington, and to him seemed committed the general management of affairs in Missouri.

The newspapers fanned the public excitement to the highest pitch, and threats of attacking the arsenal on the one hand, and the mob of d—d rebels in Camp Jackson on the other, were bandied about. I tried my best to keep out of the current, and only talked freely with a few men; among them Colonel John O'Fallon, a wealthy gentleman who resided above St. Louis. He daily came down to my office in Bremen, and we walked up and down the pavement by the hour, deploring the sad condition of our country, and the seeming drift toward dissolution and anarchy. I used also to go down to the arsenal occasionally to see Lyon, Totten, and other of my army acquaintance, and was glad to see them making preparations to defend their post, if not to assume the offensive.

The bombardment of Fort Sumter, which was announced by telegraph, began April 12th, and ended on the 14th. We then knew that the war was actually begun, and though the South was openly, manifestly the aggressor, yet her friends and apologists insisted that she was simply acting on a justifiable defensive, and that in the forcible seizure of, the public forts within her limits the people were acting with reasonable prudence and foresight. Yet neither party seemed willing to invade, or cross the border. Davis, who ordered the bombardment of Sumter, knew the temper of his people well, and foresaw that it would precipitate the action of the border States; for almost immediately Virginia, North Carolina, Arkansas, and Tennessee, followed the lead of the cotton States, and conventions were deliberating in Kentucky and Missouri.

On the night of Saturday, April 6th, I received the following, dispatch:

Washington, April 6, 1861.

Major W. T. Sherman:

Will you accept the chief clerkship of the War Department? We will make you assistant Secretary of War when Congress meets.

M. Blair, Postmaster-General.

To which I replied by telegraph, Monday morning; "I cannot accept;" and by mail as follows:

Monday, April 8, 1861.
Office of the St. Louis Railroad Company.

Hon. M. Blair, Washington, D. C.

I received, about nine o'clock Saturday night, your telegraph dispatch, which I have this moment answered, "I cannot accept."

I have quite a large family, and when I resigned my place in Louisiana, on account of secession, I had no time to lose; and, therefore, after my hasty visit to Washington, where I saw no chance of employment, I came to St. Louis, have accepted a place in this company, have rented a house, and incurred other obligations, so that I am not at liberty to change.

I thank you for the compliment contained in your offer, and assure you that I wish the Administration all success in its almost impossible task of governing this distracted and anarchical people.

Yours truly,

W.T. SHERMAN

I was afterward told that this letter gave offense, and that some of Mr. Lincoln's cabinet concluded that I too would prove false to the country.

Later in that month, after the capture of Fort Sumter by the Confederate authorities, a Dr. Cornyn came to our house on Locust Street, one night after I had gone to bed, and told me he had been sent by Frank Blair, who was not well, and wanted to see me that night at his house. I dressed and walked over to his house on Washington Avenue, near Fourteenth, and found there, in the front-room, several gentlemen, among whom I recall Henry T. Blow. Blair was in the back-room, closeted with some gentleman, who soon left, and I was called in. He there told me that the Government was mistrustful of General Harvey, that a change in the command of the department was to be made; that he held it in his power to appoint a brigadier-general, and put him in command of the department, and he offered me the place. I told him I had once offered my services, and they were declined; that I had made business engagements in St. Louis, which I could not throw off at pleasure; that I had long deliberated on my course of action, and must decline his offer, however tempting and complimentary. He reasoned with me, but I persisted. He told me, in that event, he should appoint Lyon, and he did so.

Finding that even my best friends were uneasy as to my political status, on the 8th of May I addressed the following official letter to the Secretary of War:

Office of the St. Louis Railroad Company,
May 8,1881.

Hon. S. Cameron, Secretary of War, Washington, D. C.

Dear Sir: I hold myself now, as always, prepared to serve my country in the capacity for which I was trained. I did not and will not volunteer for three months, because I cannot throw my family on the cold charity of the world. But for the three-years call, made by the President, an officer can prepare his command and do good service.

I will not volunteer as a soldier, because rightfully or wrongfully I feel unwilling to take a mere private's place, and, having for many years lived in California and Louisiana, the men are not well enough acquainted with me to elect me to my appropriate place.

Should my services be needed, the records of the War Department will enable you to designate the station in which I can render most service.

Yours truly, W. T. SHERMAN.

To this I do not think I received a direct answer; but, on the 10th of the same month, I was appointed colonel of the Thirteenth Regular Infantry.

I remember going to the arsenal on the 9th of May, taking my children with me in the street-cars. Within the arsenal wall were drawn up in parallel lines four regiments of the "Home Guards," and I saw men distributing cartridges to the boxes. I also saw General Lyon running about with his hair in the wind, his pockets full of papers, wild and irregular, but I knew him to be a man of vehement purpose and of determined action. I saw of course that it meant business, but whether for defense or offense I did not know. The next morning I went up to the railroad-office in Bremen, as usual, and heard at every corner of the streets that the "Dutch" were moving on Camp Jackson. People were barricading their houses, and men were running in that direction. I hurried through my business as quickly as I could, and got back to my house on Locust Street by twelve o'clock. Charles Ewing and Hunter were there, and insisted on going out to the camp to see "the fun." I tried to dissuade them, saying that in case of conflict the bystanders were more likely to be killed than the men engaged, but they would go. I felt as much interest as anybody else, but staid at home, took my little son Willie, who was about seven years old, and walked up and down the pavement in front of our house, listening for the sound of musketry or cannon in the direction of Camp Jackson. While so engaged Miss Eliza Dean, who lived opposite us, called me across the street, told me that her brother-in-law, Dr. Scott, was a surgeon in Frost's camp, and she was dreadfully afraid he would be killed. I reasoned with her that General Lyon was a regular officer; that if he had gone out, as reported, to Camp Jackson, he would take with him such a force as would make resistance impossible; but she would not be comforted, saying that the camp was made up of the young men from the first and best families of St. Louis, and that they were proud, and would fight. I explained that young men of the best families did not like to be killed better than ordinary people. Edging gradually up the street, I was in Olive Street just about Twelfth, when I saw a man running from the direction of Camp Jackson at full speed, calling, as he went, "They've surrendered, they've surrendered!" So I turned back and rang the bell at Mrs. Dean's. Eliza came to the door, and I explained what I had heard; but she angrily slammed the door in my face! Evidently she was disappointed to find she was mistaken in her estimate of the rash courage of the best families.

I again turned in the direction of Camp Jackson, my boy Willie with me still. At the head of Olive Street, abreast of Lindell's Grove, I found Frank Blair's regiment in the street, with ranks opened, and the Camp Jackson prisoners inside. A crowd of people was gathered around, calling to the prisoners by name, some hurrahing for Jeff Davis, and others encouraging the troops. Men, women, and children, were in the crowd. I passed along till I found myself inside the grove, where I met Charles Ewing and John Hunter, and we stood looking at the troops on the road, heading toward the city. A band of music was playing at the head, and the column made one or two ineffectual starts, but for some reason was halted. The battalion of regulars was abreast of me, of which Major Rufus Saxton was in command, and I gave him an evening paper, which I had bought of the newsboy on my way out. He was reading from it some piece of news, sitting on his horse, when the column again began to move forward, and he resumed his place at the head of his command. At that part of the road, or street, was an embankment about eight feet high, and a drunken fellow tried to pass over it to the people opposite.

One of the regular sergeant file-closers ordered him back, but he attempted to pass through the ranks, when the sergeant barred his progress with his musket "a-port." The drunken man seized his musket, when the sergeant threw him off with violence, and he rolled over and over down the bank. By the time this man had picked himself up and got his hat, which had fallen off, and had again mounted the embankment, the regulars had passed, and the head of Osterhaus's regiment of Home Guards had come up. The man had in his hand a small pistol, which he fired off, and I heard that the ball had struck the leg of one of Osterhaus's staff; the regiment stopped; there was a moment of confusion, when the soldiers of that regiment began to fire over our heads in the grove. I heard the balls cutting the leaves above our heads, and saw several men and women running in all directions, some of whom were wounded. Of course there was a general stampede. Charles Ewing threw Willie on the ground and covered him with his body. Hunter ran behind the hill, and I also threw myself on the ground. The fire ran back from the head of the regiment toward its rear, and as I saw the men reloading their pieces, I jerked Willie up, ran back with him into a gully which covered us, lay there until I saw that the fire had ceased, and that the column was again moving on, when I took up Willie and started back for home round by way of Market Street. A woman and child were killed outright; two or three men were also killed, and several others were wounded. The great mass of the people on that occasion were simply curious spectators, though men were sprinkled through the crowd calling out, "Hurrah for Jeff Davis!" and others were particularly abusive of the "damned Dutch" Lyon posted a guard in charge of the vacant camp, and marched his prisoners down to the arsenal; some were paroled, and others held, till afterward they were regularly exchanged.

A very few days after this event, May 14th, I received a dispatch from my brother Charles in Washington, telling me to come on at once; that I had been appointed a colonel of the Thirteenth Regular Infantry, and that I was wanted at Washington immediately.

Of course I could no longer defer action. I saw Mr. Lucas, Major Turner, and other friends and parties connected with the road, who agreed that I should go on. I left my family, because I was under the impression that I would be allowed to enlist my own regiment, which would take some time, and I expected to raise the regiment and organize it at Jefferson Barracks. I repaired to Washington, and there found that the Government was trying to rise to a level with the occasion. Mr. Lincoln had, without the sanction of law, authorized the raising of ten new regiments of regulars, each infantry regiment to be composed of three battalions of eight companies each; and had called for seventy-five thousand State volunteers. Even this call seemed to me utterly inadequate; still it was none of my business. I took the oath of office, and was furnished with a list of officers, appointed to my regiment, which was still, incomplete. I reported in person to General Scott, at his office on Seventeenth Street, opposite the War Department, and applied for authority to return West, and raise my regiment at Jefferson Barracks, but the general said my lieutenant-colonel, Burbank, was fully qualified to superintend the enlistment, and that he wanted me there; and he at once dictated an order for me to report to him in person for inspection duty.

Satisfied that I would not be permitted to return to St. Louis, I instructed Mrs. Sherman to pack up, return to Lancaster, and trust to the fate of war.

I also resigned my place as president of the Fifth Street Railroad, to take effect at the end of May, so that in fact I received pay from that road for only two months' service, and then began my new army career.

CHAPTER IX.
FROM THE BATTLE OF BULL RUN TO PADUCAH KENTUCKY AND MISSOURI

1861-1862.

And now that, in these notes, I have fairly reached the period of the civil war, which ravaged our country from 1861 to 1865—an event involving a conflict of passion, of prejudice, and of arms, that has developed results which, for better or worse, have left their mark on the world's history—I feel that I tread on delicate ground.

I have again and again been invited to write a history of the war, or to record for publication my personal recollections of it, with large offers of money therefor; all of which I have heretofore declined, because the truth is not always palatable, and should not always be told. Many of the actors in the grand drama still live, and they and their friends are quick to controversy, which should be avoided. The great end of peace has been attained, with little or no change in our form of government, and the duty of all good men is to allow the passions of that period to subside, that we may direct our physical and mental labor to repair the waste of war, and to engage in the greater task of continuing our hitherto wonderful national development.

What I now propose to do is merely to group some of my personal recollections about the historic persons and events of the day, prepared not with any view to their publication, but rather for preservation till I am gone; and then to be allowed to follow into oblivion the cords of similar papers, or to be used by some historian who may need them by way of illustration.

I have heretofore recorded how I again came into the military service of the United States as a colonel of the Thirteenth Regular Infantry, a regiment that had no existence at the time, and that, instead of being allowed to enlist the men and instruct them, as expected, I was assigned in Washington City, by an order of Lieutenant-General Winfield Scott, to inspection duty near him on the 20th of June, 1861.

At that time Lieutenant-General Scott commanded the army in chief, with Colonel E. D. Townsend as his adjutant-general,

Major G. W. Cullum, United States Engineers, and Major Schuyler Hamilton, as aides.-de-camp. The general had an office up stairs on Seventeenth Street, opposite the War Department, and resided in a house close by, on Pennsylvania Avenue. All fears for the immediate safety of the capital had ceased, and quite a large force of regulars and volunteers had been collected in and about Washington. Brigadier-General J. K. Mansfield commanded in the city, and Brigadier-General Irvin McDowell on the other side of the Potomac, with his headquarters at Arlington House. His troops extended in a semicircle from Alexandria to above Georgetown. Several forts and redoubts were either built or in progress, and the people were already clamorous for a general forward movement. Another considerable army had also been collected in Pennsylvania under General Patterson, and, at the time I speak of, had moved forward to Hagerstown and Williamsport, on the Potomac River. My brother, John Sherman, was a volunteer aide-de-camp to General Patterson, and, toward the end of June, I went up to Hagerstown to see him. I found that army in the very act of moving, and we rode down to Williamsport in a buggy, and were present when the leading division crossed the Potomac River by fording it waist-deep. My friend and classmate, George H. Thomas, was there, in command of a brigade in the leading division. I talked with him a good deal, also with General Cadwalader, and with the staff-officers of General Patterson, viz., Fitz-John Porter, Belger, Beckwith, and others, all of whom seemed encouraged to think that the war was to be short and decisive, and that, as soon as it was demonstrated that the General Government meant in earnest to defend its rights and property, some general compromise would result.

Patterson's army crossed the Potomac River on the 1st or 2d of July, and, as John Sherman was to take his seat as a Senator in the called session of Congress, to meet July 4th, he resigned his place as aide-de-camp, presented me his two horses and equipment, and we returned to Washington together.

The Congress assembled punctually on the 4th of July, and the message of Mr. Lincoln was strong and good: it recognized the fact that civil war was upon us, that compromise of any kind was at an end; and he asked for four hundred thousand men, and four hundred million dollars, wherewith to vindicate the national authority, and to regain possession of the captured forts and other property of the United States.

It was also immediately demonstrated that the tone and temper of Congress had changed since the Southern Senators and members had withdrawn, and that we, the military, could now go to work with some definite plans and ideas.

The appearance of the troops about Washington was good, but it was manifest they were far from being soldiers. Their uniforms were as various as the States and cities from which they came; their arms were also of every pattern and calibre; and they were so loaded down with overcoats, haversacks, knapsacks, tents, and baggage, that it took from twenty-five to fifty wagons to move the camp of a regiment from one place to another, and some of the camps had bakeries and cooking establishments that would have done credit to Delmonico.

While I was on duty with General Scott, viz., from June 20th to about June 30th, the general frequently communicated to those about him his opinions and proposed plans. He seemed vexed with the clamors of the press for immediate action, and the continued interference in details by the President, Secretary of War, and Congress. He spoke of organizing a grand army of invasion, of which the regulars were to constitute the "iron column," and seemed to intimate that he himself would take the field in person, though he was at the time very old, very heavy, and very unwieldy. His age must have been about seventy-five years.

At that date, July 4, 1861, the rebels had two armies in front of Washington; the one at Manassas Junction, commanded by General Beauregard, with his advance guard at Fairfax Court House, and indeed almost in sight of Washington. The other, commanded by General Joe Johnston, was at Winchester, with its advance at Martinsburg and Harper's Ferry; but the advance had fallen back before Patterson, who then occupied Martinsburg and the line of the Baltimore & Ohio Railroad.

The temper of Congress and the people would not permit the slow and methodical preparation desired by General Scott; and the cry of "On to Richmond!" which was shared by the volunteers, most of whom had only engaged for ninety days, forced General Scott to hasten his preparations, and to order a general advance about the middle of July. McDowell was to move from the defenses of Washington, and Patterson from Martinsburg. In the organization of McDowell's army into divisions and brigades, Colonel David Hunter was assigned to command the Second Division, and I was ordered to take command of his former brigade, which was composed of five regiments in position in and about Fort Corcoran, and on the ground opposite Georgetown. I assumed command on the 30th of June, and proceeded at once to prepare it for the general advance. My command constituted the Third Brigade of the First Division, which division was commanded by Brigadier-General Daniel Tyler, a graduate of West Point, but who had seen little or no actual service. I applied to General McDowell for home staff-officers, and he gave me, as adjutant-general, Lieutenant Piper, of the Third Artillery, and, as aide-de-camp, Lieutenant McQuesten, a fine young cavalry-officer, fresh from West Point.

I selected for the field the Thirteenth New York, Colonel Quinby; the Sixty-ninth New York, Colonel Corcoran; the Seventy-ninth New York, Colonel Cameron; and the Second Wisconsin, Lieutenant—Colonel Peck. These were all good, strong, volunteer regiments, pretty well commanded; and I had reason to believe that I had one of the best brigades in the whole army. Captain Ayres's battery of the Third Regular Artillery was also attached to my brigade. The other regiment, the Twenty-ninth New York, Colonel Bennett, was destined to be left behind in charge of the forts and camps during our absence, which was expected to be short. Soon after I had assumed the command, a difficulty arose in the Sixty-ninth, an Irish regiment. This regiment had volunteered in New York, early in April, for ninety days; but, by reason of the difficulty of passing through Baltimore, they had come via Annapolis, had been held for duty on the railroad as a guard for nearly a month before they actually reached Washington, and were then mustered in about a month after enrollment. Some of the men claimed that they were entitled to their discharge in ninety days from the time of enrollment, whereas the muster-roll read ninety days from the date of muster-in. One day, Colonel Corcoran explained this matter to me. I advised him to reduce the facts to writing, and that I would submit it to the War Department for an authoritative decision. He did so, and the War Department decided that the muster-roll was the only contract of service, that it would be construed literally; and that the regiment would be held till the expiration of three months from the date of muster-in, viz., to about August 1, 1861. General Scott at the same time wrote one of his characteristic letters to Corcoran, telling him that we were about to engage in battle, and he knew his Irish friends would not leave him in such a crisis. Corcoran and the officers generally wanted to go to the expected battle, but a good many of the men were not so anxious. In the Second Wisconsin, also, was developed a personal difficulty. The actual colonel was S. P. Coon, a good-hearted gentleman, who knew no more of the military art than a child; whereas his lieutenant-colonel, Peck, had been to West Point, and knew the drill. Preferring that the latter should remain in command of the regiment, I put Colonel Coon on my personal staff, which reconciled the difficulty.

In due season, about July 15th, our division moved forward leaving our camps standing; Keyes's brigade in the lead, then Schenck's, then mine, and Richardson's last. We marched via Vienna, Germantown, and Centreville, where all the army, composed of five divisions, seemed to converge. The march demonstrated little save the general laxity of discipline; for with all my personal efforts I could not prevent the men from straggling for water, blackberries, or any thing on the way they fancied.

At Centreville, on the 18th, Richardson's brigade was sent by General Tyler to reconnoitre Blackburn's Ford across Bull Run, and he found it strongly guarded. From our camp, at Centreville, we heard the cannonading, and then a sharp musketry-fire. I received orders from General Tyler to send forward Ayres's battery, and very soon after another order came for me to advance with my whole brigade. We marched the three miles at the double-quick, arrived in time to relieve Richardson's brigade, which was just drawing back from the ford, worsted, and stood for half an hour or so under a fire of artillery, which killed four or five of my men. General Tyler was there in person, giving directions, and soon after he ordered us all back to our camp in Centreville. This reconnoissance had developed a strong force, and had been made without the orders of General McDowell; however, it satisfied us that the enemy was in force on the other side of Bull Run, and had no intention to leave without a serious battle. We lay in camp at Centreville all of the 19th and 20th, and during that night began the movement which resulted in the battle of Bull Run, on July 21st. Of this so much has been written that more would be superfluous; and the reports of the opposing commanders, McDowell and Johnston, are fair and correct. It is now generally admitted that it was one of the best-planned battles of the war, but one of the worst-fought. Our men had been told so often at home that all they had to do was to make a bold appearance, and the rebels would run; and nearly all of us for the first time then heard the sound of cannon and muskets in anger, and saw the bloody scenes common to all battles, with which we were soon to be familiar. We had good organization, good men, but no cohesion, no real discipline, no respect for authority, no real knowledge of war. Both armies were fairly defeated, and, whichever had stood fast, the other would have run. Though the North was overwhelmed with mortification and shame, the South really had not much to boast of, for in the three or four hours of fighting their organization was so broken up that they did not and could not follow our army, when it was known to be in a state of disgraceful and causeless flight. It is easy to criticise a battle after it is over, but all now admit that none others, equally raw in war, could have done better than we did at Bull Run; and the lesson of that battle should not be lost on a people like ours.

I insert my official report, as a condensed statement of my share in the battle:

HEADQUARTERS THIRD BRIGADE, FIRST DIVISION
FORT CORCORAN, July 25, 1861

To Captain A. BAIRD, Assistant Adjutant-General, First Division (General Tyler's).

Sir: I have the honor to submit this my report of the operations of my brigade during the action of the 21st instant. The brigade is composed of the Thirteenth New York Volunteers, Colonel Quinby's Sixty-ninth New York, Colonel Corcoran; Seventy-ninth New York, Colonel Cameron; Second Wisconsin, Lieutenant-Colonel Peck; and Company E, Third Artillery, under command of Captain R. B. Ayres, Fifth Artillery.

We left our camp near Centreville, pursuant to orders, at half-past 2 A. M., taking place in your column, next to the brigade of General Schenck, and proceeded as far as the halt, before the enemy's position, near the stone bridge across Bull Run. Here the brigade was deployed in line along the skirt of timber to the right of the Warrenton road, and remained quietly in position till after 10 a.m. The enemy remained very quiet, but about that time we saw a rebel regiment leave its cover in our front, and proceed in double-quick time on the road toward Sudley Springs, by which we knew the columns of Colonels Hunter and Heintzelman were approaching. About the same time we observed in motion a large mass of the enemy, below and on the other side of the stone bridge. I directed Captain Ayres to take position with his battery near our right, and to open fire on this mass; but you had previously detached the two rifle-guns belonging to this battery, and, finding that the smooth-bore guns did not reach the enemy's position, we ceased firing, and I sent a request that you would send to me the thirty-pounder rifle-gun attached to Captain Carlisle's battery. At the same time I shifted the New York Sixty-ninth to the extreme right of the brigade. Thus we remained till we heard the musketry-fire across Bull Run, showing that the head of Colonel Hunter's column was engaged. This firing was brisk, and showed that Hunter was driving before him the enemy, till about noon, when it became certain the enemy had come to a stand, and that our forces on the other side of Bull Run were all engaged, artillery and infantry.

Here you sent me the order to cross over with the whole brigade, to the assistance of Colonel Hunter. Early in the day, when reconnoitring the ground, I had seen a horseman descend from a bluff in our front, cross the stream, and show himself in the open field on this side; and, inferring that we could cross over at the same point, I sent forward a company as skirmishers, and followed with the whole brigade, the New York Sixty-ninth leading.

We found no difficulty in crossing over, and met with no opposition in ascending the steep bluff opposite with our infantry, but it was impassable to the artillery, and I sent word back to Captain Ayres to follow if possible, otherwise to use his discretion. Captain Ayres did not cross Bull Run, but remained on that side, with the rest of your division. His report herewith describes his operations during the remainder of the day. Advancing slowly and cautiously with the head of the column, to give time for the regiments in succession to close up their ranks, we first encountered a party of the enemy retreating along a cluster of pines; Lieutenant-Colonel Haggerty, of the Sixty-ninth, without orders, rode out alone, and endeavored to intercept their retreat. One of the enemy, in full view, at short range, shot Haggerty, and he fell dead from his horse. The Sixty-ninth opened fire on this party, which was returned; but, determined to effect our junction with Hunter's division, I ordered this fire to cease, and we proceeded with caution toward the field where we then plainly saw our forces engaged. Displaying our colors conspicuously at the head of our column, we succeeded in attracting the attention of our friends, and soon formed the brigade in rear of Colonel Porter's. Here I learned that Colonel Hunter was disabled by a severe wound, and that General McDowell was on the field. I sought him out, and received his orders to join in pursuit of the enemy, who was falling back to the left of the road by which the army had approached from Sudley Springs. Placing Colonel Quinby's regiment of rifles in front, in column, by division, I directed the other regiments to follow in line of battle, in the order of the Wisconsin Second, New York Seventy-ninth, and New York Sixty-ninth. Quinby's regiment advanced steadily down the hill and up the ridge, from which he opened fire upon the enemy, who had made another stand on ground very favorable to him, and the regiment continued advancing as the enemy gave way, till the head of the column reached the point near which Rickett's battery was so severely cut up. The other regiments descended the hill in line of battle, under a severe cannonade; and, the ground affording comparative shelter from the enemy's artillery, they changed direction, by the right flank, and followed the road before mentioned. At the point where this road crosses the ridge to our left front, the ground was swept by a most severe fire of artillery, rifles, and musketry, and we saw, in succession, several regiments driven from it; among them the Zouaves and battalion of marines. Before reaching the crest of this hill, the roadway was worn deep enough to afford shelter, and I kept the several regiments in it as long as possible; but when the Wisconsin Second was abreast of the enemy, by order of Major Wadsworth, of General McDowell's staff, I ordered it to leave the roadway, by the left flank, and to attack the enemy.

This regiment ascended to the brow of the hill steadily, received the severe fire of the enemy, returned it with spirit, and advanced, delivering its fire. This regiment is uniformed in gray cloth, almost identical with that of the great bulk of the secession army; and, when the regiment fell into confusion and retreated toward the road, there was a universal cry that they were being fired on by our own men. The regiment rallied again, passed the brow of the hill a second time, but was again repulsed in disorder. By this time the New York Seventy-ninth had closed up, and in like manner it was ordered to cross the brow of, the hill, and drive the enemy from cover. It was impossible to get a good view of this ground. In it there was one battery of artillery, which poured an incessant fire upon our advancing column, and the ground was very irregular with small clusters of pines, affording shelter, of which the enemy took good advantage. The fire of rifles and musketry was very severe. The Seventy-ninth, headed by its colonel, Cameron, charged across the hill, and for a short time the contest was severe; they rallied several times under fire, but finally broke, and gained the cover of the hill.

This left the field open to the New York Sixty-ninth, Colonel Corcoran, who, in his turn, led his regiment *over the crest; and had in full, open view the ground so severely contested; the fire was very severe, and the roar of cannon, musketry, and rifles, incessant; it was manifest the enemy was here in great force, far superior to us at that point. The Sixty-ninth held the ground for some time, but finally fell back in disorder.*

All this time Quinby's regiment occupied another ridge, to our left, overlooking the same field of action, and similarly engaged. Here, about half-past 3 p.m., began the scene of confusion and disorder that characterized the remainder of the day. Up to that time, all had kept their places, and seemed perfectly cool, and used to the shell and shot that fell, comparatively harmless, all around us; but the short exposure to an intense fire of small-arms, at close range, had killed many, wounded more, and had produced disorder in all of the battalions that had attempted to encounter it. Men fell away from their ranks, talking, and in great confusion. Colonel Cameron had been mortally wounded, was carried to an ambulance, and reported dying. Many other officers were reported dead or missing, and many of the wounded were making their way, with more or less assistance, to the buildings used as hospitals, on the ridge to the west. We succeeded in partially reforming the regiments, but it was manifest that they would not stand, and I directed Colonel Corcoran to move along the ridge to the rear, near the position where we had first formed the brigade. General McDowell was there in person, and need all possible efforts to reassure the men. By the active exertions of Colonel Corcoran, we formed an irregular square against the cavalry which were then seen to issue from the position from which we had been driven, and we began our retreat toward the same ford of Bull Run by which we had approached the field of battle. There was no positive order to retreat, although for an hour it had been going on by the operation of the men themselves. The ranks were thin and irregular, and we found a stream of people strung from the hospital across Bull Run, and far toward Centreville. After putting in motion the irregular square in person, I pushed forward to find Captain Ayres's battery at the crossing of Bull Run. I sought it at its last position, before the brigade had crossed over, but it was not there; then passing through the woods, where, in the morning, we had first formed line, we approached the blacksmith's shop, but there found a detachment of the secession cavalry and thence made a circuit, avoiding Cub Run Bridge, into Centreville, where I found General McDowell, and from him understood that it was his purpose to rally the forces, and make a stand at Centreville.

But, about nine o'clock at night, I received from General Tyler, in person, the order to continue the retreat to the Potomac. This retreat was by night, and disorderly in the extreme. The men of different regiments mingled together, and some reached the river at Arlington, some at Long Bridge, and the greater part returned to their former camp, at or near Fort Corcoran. I reached this point at noon the next day, and found a miscellaneous crowd crossing over the aqueduct and ferries.. Conceiving this to be demoralizing, I at once commanded the guard to be increased, and all persons attempting to pass over to be stopped. This soon produced its effect; men sought their proper companies and regiments. Comparative order was restored, and all were posted to the best advantage.

I herewith inclose the official report of Captain Belly, commanding officer of the New York Sixty-ninth; also, full lists of the killed, wounded, and missing.

Our loss was heavy, and occurred chiefly at the point near where Rickett's battery was destroyed. Lieutenant-Colonel Haggerty was killed about noon, before we had effected a junction with Colonel Hunter's division. Colonel Cameron was mortally wounded leading his regiment in the charge, and Colonel Corcoran has been missing since the cavalry-charge near the building used as a hospital.

For names, rank, etc., of the above, I refer to the lists herewith.

Lieutenants Piper and McQuesten, of my personal staff, were under fire all day, and carried orders to and fro with as much coolness as on parade. Lieutenant Bagley, of the New York Sixty-ninth, a volunteer aide, asked leave to serve with his company, during the action, and is among those reported missing. I have intelligence that he is a prisoner, and slightly wounded.

Colonel Coon, of Wisconsin, a volunteer aide, also rendered good service during the day.

W. T. SHERMAN, Colonel commanding Brigade.

This report, which I had not read probably since its date till now, recalls to me vividly the whole scene of the affair at Blackburn's Ford, when for the first time in my life I saw cannonballs strike men and crash through the trees and saplings above and around us, and realized the always sickening confusion as one approaches a fight from the rear; then the night-march from Centreville, on the Warrenton road, standing for hours wondering what was meant; the deployment along the edge of the field that sloped down to Bull-Run, and waiting for Hunter's approach on the other aide from the direction of Sudley Springs, away off to our right; the terrible scare of a poor negro who was caught between our lines; the crossing of Bull Run, and the fear lest we should be fired on by our own men; the killing of Lieutenant-Colonel Haggerty, which occurred in plain sight; and the first scenes of a field strewed with dead men and horses. Yet, at that period of the battle, we were the victors and felt jubilant. At that moment, also, my brigade passed Hunter's division; but Heintzelman's was still ahead of us, and we followed its lead along the road toward Manassas Junction, crossing a small stream and ascending a long hill, at the summit of which the battle was going on. Here my regiments came into action well, but successively, and were driven back, each in its turn. For two hours we continued to dash at the woods on our left front, which were full of rebels; but I was convinced their organization was broken, and that they had simply halted there and taken advantage of these woods as a cover, to reach which we had to pass over the intervening fields about the Henry House, which were clear, open, and gave them a decided advantage. After I had put in each of my regiments, and had them driven back to the cover of the road, I had no idea that we were beaten, but reformed the regiments in line in their proper order, and only wanted a little rest, when I found that my brigade was almost alone, except Syke's regulars, who had formed square against cavalry and were coming back. I then realized that the whole army was "in retreat," and that my own men were individually making back for the stone bridge. Corcoran and I formed the brigade into an irregular square, but it fell to pieces; and, along with a crowd, disorganized but not much scared, the brigade got back to Centreville to our former camps. Corcoran was captured, and held a prisoner for some time; but I got safe to Centreville. I saw General McDowell in Centreville, and understood that several of his divisions had not been engaged at all, that he would reorganize them at Centreville, and there await the enemy. I got my four regiments in parallel lines in a field, the same in which we had camped before the battle, and had lain down to sleep under a tree, when I heard some one asking for me. I called out where I was, when General Tyler in person gave me orders to march back to our camps at Fort Corcoran. I aroused my aides, gave them orders to call up the sleeping men, have each regiment to leave the field by a flank and to take the same road back by which we had come. It was near midnight, and the road was full of troops, wagons, and batteries. We tried to keep our regiments separate, but all became inextricably mixed. Toward morning we reached Vienna, where I slept some hours, and the next day, about noon, we reached Fort Corcoran.

A slow, mizzling rain had set in, and probably a more gloomy day never presented itself. All organization seemed to be at an end; but I and my staff labored hard to collect our men into their proper companies and camps, and, on the 23d of July, I moved the Second Wisconsin and Seventy-ninth New York closer in to Fort Corcoran, and got things in better order than I had expected. Of course, we took it for granted that the rebels would be on our heels, and we accordingly prepared to defend our posts. By the 25th I had collected all the materials, made my report, and had my brigade about as well governed as any in that army; although most of the ninety-day men, especially the Sixty-ninth, had become extremely tired of the war, and wanted to go home. Some of them were so mutinous, at one time, that I had the battery to unlimber, threatening, if they dared to leave camp without orders, I would open fire on them. Drills and the daily exercises were resumed, and I ordered that at the three principal roll-calls the men should form ranks with belts and muskets, and that they should keep their ranks until I in person had received the reports and had dismissed them. The Sixty-ninth still occupied Fort Corcoran, and one morning, after reveille, when I had just received the report, had dismissed the regiment, and was leaving, I found myself in a crowd of men crossing the drawbridge on their way to a barn close by, where they had their sinks; among them was an officer, who said: "Colonel, I am going to New York today. What can I do for you?" I answered: "How can you go to New York? I do not remember to have signed a leave for you." He said, "No; he did not want a leave. He had engaged to serve three months, and had already served more than that time. If the Government did not intend to pay him, he could afford to lose the money; that he was a lawyer, and had neglected his business long enough, and was then going home." I noticed that a good many of the soldiers had paused about us to listen, and knew that, if this officer could defy me, they also would. So I turned on him sharp, and said: "Captain, this question of your term of service has been submitted to the rightful authority, and the decision has been published in orders. You are a soldier, and must submit to orders till you are properly discharged. If you attempt to leave without orders, it will be mutiny, and I will shoot you like a dog! Go back into the fort now, instantly, and don't dare to leave without my consent." I had on an overcoat, and may have had my hand about the breast, for he looked at me hard, paused a moment, and then turned back into the fort. The men scattered, and I returned to the house where I was quartered, close by.

That same day, which must have been about July 26th, I was near the river-bank, looking at a block-house which had been built for the defense of the aqueduct, when I saw a carriage coming by the road that crossed the Potomac River at Georgetown by a ferry. I thought I recognized in the carriage the person of President Lincoln. I hurried across a bend, so as to stand by the road-side as the carriage passed. I was in uniform, with a sword on, and was recognized by Mr. Lincoln and Mr. Seward, who rode side by side in an open hack. I inquired if they were going to my camps, and Mr. Lincoln said: "Yes; we heard that you had got over the big scare, and we thought we would come over and see the 'boys.'" The roads had been much changed and were rough. I asked if I might give directions to his coachman, he promptly invited me to jump in and to tell the coachman which way to drive. Intending to begin on the right and follow round to the left, I turned the driver into a side-road which led up a very steep hill, and, seeing a soldier, called to him and sent him up hurriedly to announce to the colonel (Bennett, I think) that the President was coming: As we slowly ascended the hill, I discovered that Mr. Lincoln was full of feeling, and wanted to encourage our men. I asked if he intended to speak to them, and he said he would like to. I asked him then to please discourage all cheering, noise, or any sort of confusion; that we had had enough of it before Bull Run to ruin any set of men, and that what we needed were cool, thoughtful, hard-fighting soldiers—no more hurrahing, no more humbug. He took my remarks in the most perfect good-nature. Before we had reached the first camp, I heard the drum beating the "assembly," saw the men running for their tents, and in a few minutes the regiment was in line, arms presented, and then brought to an order and "parade rest!"

Mr. Lincoln stood up in the carriage, and made one of the neatest, best, and most feeling addresses I ever listened to, referring to our late disaster at Bull Run, the high duties that still devolved on us, and the brighter days yet to come. At one or two points the soldiers began to cheer, but he promptly checked them, saying: "Don't cheer, boys. I confess I rather like it myself, but Colonel Sherman here says it is not military; and I guess we had better defer to his opinion." In winding up, he explained that, as President, he was commander-in-chief; that he was resolved that the soldiers should have every thing that the law allowed; and he called on one and all to appeal to him personally in case they were wronged. The effect of this speech was excellent.

We passed along in the same manner to all the camps of my brigade; and Mr. Lincoln complimented me highly for the order, cleanliness, and discipline, that he observed. Indeed, he and Mr. Seward both assured me that it was the first bright moment they had experienced since the battle.

At last we reached Fort Corcoran. The carriage could not enter, so I ordered the regiment, without arms, to come outside, and gather about Mr. Lincoln, who would speak to them. He made to them the same feeling address, with more personal allusions, because of their special gallantry in the battle under Corcoran, who was still a prisoner in the hands of the enemy; and he concluded with the same general offer of redress in case of grievances. In the crowd I saw the officer with whom I had had the passage at reveille that morning. His face was pale, and lips compressed. I foresaw a scene, but sat on the front seat of the carriage as quiet as a lamb. This officer forced his way through the crowd to the carriage, and said: "Mr. President, I have a cause of grievance. This morning I went to speak to Colonel Sherman, and he threatened to shoot me." Mr. Lincoln, who was still standing, said, "Threatened to shoot you?" "Yes, sir, he threatened to shoot me." Mr. Lincoln looked at him, then at me, and stooping his tall, spare form toward the officer, said to him in a loud stage-whisper, easily heard for some yards around: "Well, if I were you, and he threatened to shoot, I would not trust him, for I believe he would do it." The officer turned about and disappeared, and the men laughed at him. Soon the carriage drove on, and, as we descended the hill, I explained the facts to the President, who answered, "Of course I didn't know any thing about it, but I thought you knew your own business best." I thanked him for his confidence, and assured him that what he had done would go far to enable me to maintain good discipline, and it did.

By this time the day was well spent. I asked to take my leave, and the President and Mr. Seward drove back to Washington. This spirit of mutiny was common to the whole army, and was not subdued till several regiments or parts of regiments had been ordered to Fort Jefferson, Florida, as punishment.

General McDowell had resumed his headquarters at the Arlington House, and was busily engaged in restoring order to his army, sending off the ninety-days men, and replacing them by regiments which had come under the three-years call. We were all trembling lest we should be held personally accountable for the disastrous result of the battle. General McClellan had been summoned from the West to Washington, and changes in the subordinate commands were announced almost daily. I remember, as a group of officers were talking in the large room of the Arlington House, used as the adjutant-general's office, one evening, some young officer came in with a list of the new brigadiers just announced at the War Department, which-embraced the names of Heintzehvan, Keyes, Franklin, Andrew Porter, W. T. Sherman, and others, who had been colonels in the battle, and all of whom had shared the common stampede. Of course, we discredited the truth of the list; and Heintzehvan broke out in his nasal voice, "Boys, it's all a lie! every mother's son of you will be cashiered." We all felt he was right, but, nevertheless, it was true; and we were all announced in general orders as brigadier-generals of volunteers.

General McClellan arrived, and, on assuming command, confirmed McDowell's organization. Instead of coming over the river, as we expected, he took a house in Washington, and only came over from time to time to have a review or inspection.

I had received several new regiments, and had begun two new forts on the hill or plateau, above and farther out than Fort Corcoran; and I organized a system of drills, embracing the evolutions of the line, all of which was new to me, and I had to learn the tactics from books; but I was convinced that we had a long, hard war before us, and made up my mind to begin at the very beginning to prepare for it.

August was passing, and troops were pouring in from all quarters; General McClellan told me he intended to organize an army of a hundred thousand men, with one hundred field-batteries, and I still hoped he would come on our side of the Potomac, pitch his tent, and prepare for real hard work, but his headquarters still remained in a house in Washington City. I then thought, and still think, that was a fatal mistake. His choice as general-in-chief at the time was fully justified by his high reputation in the army and country, and, if he then had any political views or ambition, I surely did not suspect it.

About the middle of August I got a note from Brigadier-General Robert Anderson, asking me to come and see him at his room at Willard's Hotel. I rode over and found him in conversation with several gentlemen, and he explained to me that events in Kentucky were approaching a crisis; that the Legislature was in session, and ready, as soon as properly backed by the General Government, to take open sides for the Union cause; that he was offered the command of the Department of the Cumberland, to embrace Kentucky, Tennessee, etc., and that he wanted help, and that the President had offered to allow him to select out of the new brigadiers four of his own choice. I had been a lieutenant in Captain Anderson's company, at Fort Moultrie, from 1843 to 1846, and he explained that he wanted me as his right hand. He also indicated George H. Thomas, D. C. Buell, and Burnside, as the other three. Of course, I always wanted to go West, and was perfectly willing to go with Anderson, especially in a subordinate capacity: We agreed to call on the President on a subsequent day, to talk with him about it, and we did. It hardly seems probable that Mr. Lincoln should have come to Willard's Hotel to meet us, but my impression is that he did, and that General Anderson had some difficulty in prevailing on him to appoint George H. Thomas, a native of Virginia, to be brigadier-general, because so many Southern officers, had already played false; but I was still more emphatic in my indorsement of him by reason of my talk with him at the time he crossed the Potomac with Patterson's army, when Mr. Lincoln promised to appoint him and to assign him to duty with General Anderson. In this interview with Mr. Lincoln, I also explained to him my extreme desire to serve in a subordinate capacity, and in no event to be left in a superior command. He promised me this with promptness, making the jocular remark that his chief trouble was to find places for the too many generals who wanted to be at the head of affairs, to command armies, etc.

The official order is dated:

[Special Order No. 114.]
HEADQUARTERS OF THE ARMY
Washington, August 24, 1881.

The following assignment is made of the general officers of the volunteer service, whose appointment was announced in General Orders No. 82, from the War Department

To the Department of the Cumberland, Brigadier-General Robert Anderson commanding:

Brigadier-General W. T. Sherman,
Brigadier-General George H. Thomas.

By command of Lieutenant-General Scott:
E. D. TOWNSEND, Assistant adjutant-General.

After some days, I was relieved in command of my brigade and post by Brigadier General Fitz-John Porter, and at once took my departure for Cincinnati, Ohio, via Cresson, Pennsylvania, where General Anderson was with his family; and he, Thomas, and I, met by appointment at the house of his brother, Larz Anderson, Esq., in Cincinnati. We were there on the 1st and 2d of September, when several prominent gentlemen of Kentucky met us, to discuss the situation, among whom were Jackson, Harlan, Speed, and others. At that time, William Nelson, an officer of the navy, had been commissioned a brigadier-general of volunteers, and had his camp at Dick Robinson, a few miles beyond the Kentucky River, south of Nicholasville; and Brigadier-General L. H. Rousseau had another camp at Jeffersonville, opposite Louisville. The State Legislature was in session at Frankfort, and was ready to take definite action as soon as General Anderson was prepared, for the State was threatened with invasion from Tennessee, by two forces: one from the direction of Nashville, commanded by Generals Albert Sidney Johnston and Buckner; and the other from the direction of Cumberland Gap, commanded by Generals Crittenden and Zollicoffer. General Anderson saw that he had not force enough to resist these two columns, and concluded to send me in person for help to Indianapolis and Springfield, to confer with the Governors of Indiana, and Illinois, and to General Fremont, who commanded in St. Louis.

McClellan and Fremont were the two men toward whom the country looked as the great Union leaders, and toward them were streaming the newly-raised regiments of infantry and cavalry, and batteries of artillery; nobody seeming to think of the intervening link covered by Kentucky. While I was to make this tour, Generals Anderson and Thomas were to go to Louisville and initiate the department. None of us had a staff, or any of the machinery for organizing an army, and, indeed, we had no army to organize. Anderson was empowered to raise regiments in Kentucky, and to commission a few brigadier-generals.

At Indianapolis I found Governor Morton and all the State officials busy in equipping and providing for the new regiments, and my object was to divert some of them toward Kentucky; but they were called for as fast as they were mustered in, either for the army of McClellan or Fremont. At Springfield also I found the same general activity and zeal, Governor Yates busy in providing for his men; but these men also had been promised to Fremont. I then went on to St. Louis, where all was seeming activity, bustle, and preparation. Meeting R. M. Renick at the Planters' House (where I stopped), I inquired where I could find General Fremont. Renick said, "What do you want with General Fremont?" I said I had come to see him on business; and he added, "You don't suppose that he will see such as you?" and went on to retail all the scandal of the day: that Fremont was a great potentate, surrounded by sentries and guards; that he had a more showy court than any real king; that he kept senators, governors, and the first citizens, dancing attendance for days and weeks before granting an audience, etc.; that if I expected to see him on business, I would have to make my application in writing, and submit to a close scrutiny by his chief of staff and by his civil surroundings. Of course I laughed at all this, and renewed my simple inquiry as to where was his office, and was informed that he resided and had his office at Major Brant's new house on Chouteau Avenue. It was then late in the afternoon, and I concluded to wait till the next morning; but that night I received a dispatch from General Anderson in Louisville to hurry back, as events were pressing, and he needed me.

Accordingly, I rose early next morning before daybreak, got breakfast with the early railroad-passengers, and about sunrise was at the gate of General Fremont's headquarters. A sentinel with drawn sabre paraded up and down in front of the house. I had on my undress uniform indicating my rank, and inquired of the sentinel, "Is General Fremont up?" He answered, "I don't know." Seeing that he was a soldier by his bearing, I spoke in a sharp, emphatic voice, "Then find out." He called for the corporal of the guard, and soon a fine-looking German sergeant came, to whom I addressed the same inquiry. He in turn did not know, and I bade him find out, as I had immediate and important business with the general. The sergeant entered the house by the front-basement door, and after ten or fifteen minutes the main front-door above was slowly opened from the inside, and who should appear but my old San Francisco acquaintance Isaiah C. Woods, whom I had not seen or heard of since his flight to Australia, at the time of the failure of Adams & Co. in 1851! He ushered me in hastily, closed the door, and conducted me into the office on the right of the hall. We were glad to meet, after so long and eventful an interval, and mutually inquired after our respective families and special acquaintances. I found that he was a commissioned officer, a major on duty with Fremont, and Major Eaton, now of the paymaster's Department, was in the same office with him. I explained to them that I had come from General Anderson, and wanted to confer with General Fremont in person. Woods left me, but soon returned, said the general would see me in a very few minutes, and within ten minutes I was shown across the hall into the large parlor, where General Fremont received me very politely. We had met before, as early as 1847, in California, and I had also seen him several times when he was senator. I then in a rapid manner ran over all the points of interest in General Anderson's new sphere of action, hoped he would spare us from the new levies what troops he could, and generally act in concert with us. He told me that his first business would be to drive the rebel General Price and his army out of Missouri, when he would turn his attention down the Mississippi. He asked my opinion about the various kinds of field-artillery which manufacturers were thrusting on him, especially the then newly-invented James gun, and afterward our conversation took a wide turn about the character of the principal citizens of St. Louis, with whom I was well acquainted.

Telling General Fremont that I had been summoned to Louisville and that I should leave in the first train, viz., at 3 p.m., I took my leave of him. Returning to Wood's office, I found there two more Californians, viz., Messrs. Palmer and Haskell, so I felt that, while Fremont might be suspicious of others, he allowed free ingress to his old California acquaintances.

Returning to the Planters' House, I heard of Beard, another Californian, a Mormon, who had the contract for the line of redoubts which Fremont had ordered to be constructed around the city, before he would take his departure for the interior of the State; and while I stood near the office-counter, I saw old Baron Steinberger, a prince among our early California adventurers, come in and look over the register. I avoided him on purpose, but his presence in St. Louis recalled the maxim, "Where the vultures are, there is a carcass close by;" and I suspected that the profitable contracts of the quartermaster, McKinstry, had drawn to St. Louis some of the most enterprising men of California. I suspect they can account for the fact that, in a very short time, Fremont fell from his high estate in Missouri, by reason of frauds, or supposed frauds, in the administration of the affairs of his command.

I left St. Louis that afternoon and reached Louisville the next morning. I found General Anderson quartered at the Louisville Hotel, and he had taken a dwelling homes on _____ Street as an office. Captain O. D. Greens was his adjutant-general, Lieutenant Throckmorton his aide, and Captain Prime, of the Engineer Corps, was on duty with him. General George H. Thomas had been dispatched to camp Dick Robinson, to relieve Nelson.

The city was full of all sorts of rumors. The Legislature, moved by considerations purely of a political nature, had taken the step, whatever it was, that amounted to an adherence to the Union, instead of joining the already-seceded States. This was universally known to be the signal for action. For it we were utterly unprepared, whereas the rebels were fully prepared. General Sidney Johnston immediately crossed into Kentucky, and advanced as far as Bowling Green, which he began to fortify, and thence dispatched General Buckner with a division forward toward Louisville; General Zollicoffer, in like manner, entered the State and advanced as far as Somerset. On the day I reached Louisville the excitement ran high. It was known that Columbus, Kentucky, had been occupied, September 7th, by a strong rebel force, under Generals Pillow and Polk, and that General Grant had moved from Cairo and occupied Paducah in force on the 6th. Many of the rebel families expected Buckner to reach Louisville at any moment. That night, General Anderson sent for me, and I found with him Mr. Guthrie, president of the Louisville & Nashville Railroad, who had in his hands a dispatch to the effect that the bridge across the Rolling Fork of Salt Creek, less than thirty miles out, had been burned, and that Buckner's force, en route for Louisville, had been detained beyond Green River by a train thrown from the track. We learned afterward that a man named Bird had displaced a rail on purpose to throw the train off the track, and thereby give us time.

Mr. Guthrie explained that in the ravine just beyond Salt Creek were several high and important trestles which, if destroyed, would take months to replace, and General Anderson thought it well. worth the effort to save them. Also, on Muldraugh's Hill beyond, was a strong position, which had in former years been used as the site for the State "Camp of Instruction," and we all supposed that General Buckner, who was familiar with the ground, was aiming for a position there, from which to operate on Louisville.

All the troops we had to counteract Buckner were Rousseau's Legion, and a few Home Guards in Louisville. The former were still encamped across the river at Jeffersonville; so General Anderson ordered me to go over, and with them, and such Home Guards as we could collect, make the effort to secure possession of Muldraugh's Hill before Buckner could reach it. I took Captain Prime with me; and crossed over to Rousseau's camp. The long-roll was beaten, and within an hour the men, to the number of about one thousand, were marching for the ferry-boat and for the Nashville depot. Meantime General Anderson had sent to collect some Home Guards, and Mr. Guthrie to get the trains ready. It was after midnight before we began to move. The trains proceeded slowly, and it was daybreak when we reached Lebanon Junction, twenty-six miles out, where we disembarked, and marched to the bridge over Salt River, which we found had been burnt; whether to prevent Buckner coming into Louisville, or us from going out, was not clear. Rousseau's Legion forded the stream and marched up to the State Camp of Instruction, finding the high trestles all secure. The railroad hands went to work at once to rebuild the bridge. I remained a couple of days at Lebanon Junction, during which General Anderson forwarded two regiments of volunteers that had come to him. Before the bridge was done we advanced the whole camp to the summit of Muldraugh's Hill, just back of Elizabethtown. There I learned definitely that General Buckner had not crossed Green River at all, that General Sidney Johnston was fortifying Bowling Green, and preparing for a systematic advance into Kentucky, of which he was a native, and with whose people and geography he must have been familiar. As fast as fresh troops reached Louisville, they were sent out to me at Muldraugh's Hill, where I was endeavoring to put them into shape for service, and by the 1st of October I had the equivalent of a division of two brigades preparing to move forward toward Green River. The daily correspondence between General Anderson and myself satisfied me that the worry and harassment at Louisville were exhausting his strength and health, and that he would soon leave. On a telegraphic summons from him, about the 5th of October, I went down to Louisville, when General Anderson said he could not stand the mental torture of his command any longer, and that he must go away, or it would kill him. On the 8th of October he actually published an order relinquishing the command, and, by reason of my seniority, I had no alternative but to assume command, though much against the grain, and in direct violation of Mr. Lincoln's promise to me. I am certain that, in my earliest communication to the War Department, I renewed the expression of my wish to remain in a subordinate position, and that I received the assurance that Brigadier-General Buell would soon arrive from California, and would be sent to relieve me. By that time I had become pretty familiar with the geography and the general resources of Kentucky. We had parties all over the State raising regiments and companies; but it was manifest that the young men were generally inclined to the cause of the South, while the older men of property wanted to be let alone—i.e., to remain neutral. As to a forward movement that fall, it was simply impracticable; for we were forced to use divergent lines, leading our columns farther and farther apart; and all I could attempt was to go on and collect force and material at the two points already chosen, viz., Dick Robinson and Elizabethtown. General George H. Thomas still continued to command the former, and on the 12th of October I dispatched Brigadier-General A. McD. McCook to command the latter, which had been moved forward to Nolin Creek, fifty-two miles out of Louisville, toward Bowling Green. Staff-officers began to arrive to relieve us of the constant drudgery which, up to that time, had been forced on General Anderson and myself; and these were all good men. Colonel Thomas Swords, quartermaster, arrived on the 13th; Paymaster Larned on the 14th; and Lieutenant Smyzer, Fifth Artillery, acting ordnance-officer, on the 20th; Captain Symonds was already on duty as the commissary of subsistence; Captain O. D. Greene was the adjutant-general, and completed a good working staff.

The everlasting worry of citizens complaining of every petty delinquency of a soldier, and forcing themselves forward to discuss politics, made the position of a commanding general no sinecure. I continued to strengthen the two corps forward and their routes of supply; all the time expecting that Sidney Johnston, who was a real general, and who had as correct information of our situation as I had, would unite his force with Zollicoffer, and fall on Thomas at Dick Robinson, or McCook at Nolin: Had he done so in October, 1861, he could have walked into Louisville, and the vital part of the population would have hailed him as a deliverer. Why he did not, was to me a mystery then and is now; for I know that he saw the move; and had his wagons loaded up at one time for a start toward Frankfort, passing between our two camps. Conscious of our weakness, I was unnecessarily unhappy, and doubtless exhibited it too much to those near me; but it did seem to me that the Government at Washington, intent on the larger preparations of Fremont in Missouri and McClellan in Washington, actually ignored us in Kentucky.

About this time, say the middle of October, I received notice, by telegraph, that the Secretary of War, Mr. Cameron (then in St. Louis), would visit me at Louisville, on his way back to Washington. I was delighted to have an opportunity to properly represent the actual state of affairs, and got Mr. Guthrie to go with me across to Jeffersonville, to meet the Secretary of War and escort him to Louisville. The train was behind time, but Mr. Guthrie and I waited till it actually arrived. Mr. Cameron was attended by Adjutant-General Lorenzo Thomas, and six or seven gentlemen who turned out to be newspaper reporters. Mr. Cameron's first inquiry was, when he could start for Cincinnati, saying that, as he had been detained at St. Louis so long, it was important he should hurry on to Washington. I explained that the regular mail-boat would leave very soon—viz., at 12 M.—but I begged him to come over to Louisville; that I wanted to see him on business as important as any in Washington, and hoped he would come and spend at least a day with us. He asked if every thing was not well with us, and I told him far from it; that things were actually bad, as bad as bad could be. This seemed to surprise him, and Mr. Guthrie added his persuasion to mine; when Mr. Cameron, learning that he could leave Louisville by rail via Frankfort next morning early, and make the same connections at Cincinnati, consented to go with us to Louisville, with the distinct understanding that he must leave early the next morning for Washington.

We accordingly all took hacks, crossed the river by the ferry, and drove to the Galt House, where I was then staying. Brigadier-General T. J. Wood had come down from Indianapolis by the same train, and was one of the party. We all proceeded to my room on the first floor of the Galt House, where our excellent landlord, Silas Miller, Esq., sent us a good lunch and something to drink. Mr. Cameron was not well, and lay on my bed, but joined in the general conversation. He and his party seemed to be full of the particulars of the developments in St. Louis of some of Fremont's extravagant contracts and expenses, which were the occasion of Cameron's trip to St. Louis, and which finally resulted in Fremont's being relieved, first by General Hunter, and after by General H. W. Halleck.

After some general conversation, Mr. Cameron called to me, "Now, General Sherman, tell us of your troubles." I said I preferred not to discuss business with so many strangers present. He said, "They are all friends, all members of my family, and you may speak your mind freely and without restraint." I am sure I stepped to the door, locked it to prevent intrusion, and then fully and fairly represented the state of affairs in Kentucky, especially the situation and numbers of my troops. I complained that the new levies of Ohio and Indiana were diverted East and West, and we got scarcely any thing; that our forces at Nolin and Dick Robinson were powerless for invasion, and only tempting to a general such as we believed Sidney Johnston to be; that, if Johnston chose, he could march to Louisville any day. Cameron exclaimed: "You astonish me! Our informants, the Kentucky Senators and members of Congress, claim that they have in Kentucky plenty of men, and all they want are arms and money." I then said it was not true; for the young men were arming and going out openly in broad daylight to the rebel camps, provided with good horses and guns by their fathers, who were at best "neutral;" and as to arms, he had, in Washington, promised General Anderson forty thousand of the best Springfield muskets, instead of which we had received only about twelve thousand Belgian muskets, which the Governor of Pennsylvania had refused, as had also the Governor of Ohio, but which had been adjudged good enough for Kentucky. I asserted that volunteer colonels raising regiments in various parts of the State had come to Louisville for arms, and when they saw what I had to offer had scorned to receive them—to confirm the truth of which I appealed to Mr. Guthrie, who said that every word I had spoken was true, and he repeated what I had often heard him say, that no man who owned a slave or a mule in Kentucky could be trusted.

Mr. Cameron appeared alarmed at what was said, and turned to Adjutant-General L. Thomas, to inquire if he knew of any troops available, that had not been already assigned. He mentioned Negley's Pennsylvania Brigade, at Pittsburg, and a couple of other regiments that were then en route for St. Louis. Mr. Cameron ordered him to divert these to Louisville, and Thomas made the telegraphic orders on the spot. He further promised, on reaching Washington, to give us more of his time and assistance.

In the general conversation which followed, I remember taking a large map of the United States, and assuming the people of the whole South to be in rebellion, that our task was to subdue them, showed that McClellan was on the left, having a frontage of less than a hundred miles, and Fremont the right, about the same; whereas I, the centre, had from the Big Sandy to Paducah, over three hundred miles of frontier; that McClellan had a hundred thousand men, Fremont sixty thousand, whereas to me had only been allotted about eighteen thousand. I argued that, for the purpose of defense we should have sixty thousand men at once, and for offense, would need two hundred thousand, before we were done. Mr. Cameron, who still lay on the bed, threw up his hands and exclaimed, "Great God! where are they to come from?" I asserted that there were plenty of men at the North, ready and willing to come, if he would only accept their services; for it was notorious that regiments had been formed in all the Northwestern States, whose services had been refused by the War Department, on the ground that they would not be needed. We discussed all these matters fully, in the most friendly spirit, and I thought I had aroused Mr. Cameron to a realization of the great war that was before us, and was in fact upon us. I heard him tell General Thomas to make a note of our conversation, that he might attend to my requests on reaching Washington. We all spent the evening together agreeably in conversation, many Union citizens calling to pay their respects, and the next morning early we took the train for Frankfort; Mr. Cameron and party going on to Cincinnati and Washington, and I to Camp Dick Robinson to see General Thomas and the troops there.

I found General Thomas in a tavern, with most of his regiments camped about him. He had sent a small force some miles in advance toward Cumberland Gap, under Brigadier-General Schoepf. Remaining there a couple of days, I returned to Louisville; on the 22d of October, General Negley's brigade arrived in boats from Pittsburg, was sent out to Camp Nolin; and the Thirty-seventh Indiana., Colonel Hazzard, and Second Minnesota, Colonel Van Cleve, also reached Louisville by rail, and were posted at Elizabethtown and Lebanon Junction. These were the same troops which had been ordered by Mr. Cameron when at Louisville, and they were all that I received thereafter, prior to my leaving Kentucky. On reaching Washington, Mr. Cameron called on General Thomas, as he himself afterward told me, to submit his memorandum of events during his absence, and in that memorandum was mentioned my insane request for two hundred thousand men. By some newspaper man this was seen and published, and, before I had the least conception of it, I was universally published throughout the country as "insane, crazy," etc. Without any knowledge, however, of this fact, I had previously addressed to the Adjutant-General of the army at Washington this letter:

HEADQUARTERS DEPARTMENT OP THE CUMBERLAND, LOUISVILLE, KENTUCKY,
October 22, 1881.

To General L. THOMAS, Adjutant-General, Washington, D. C.

Sir: On my arrival at Camp Dick Robinson, I found General Thomas had stationed a Kentucky regiment at Rock Castle Hill, beyond a river of the same name, and had sent an Ohio and an Indiana regiment forward in support. He was embarrassed for transportation, and I authorized him to hire teams, and to move his whole force nearer to his advance-guard, so as to support it, as he had information of the approach of Zollicoffer toward London. I have just heard from him, that he had sent forward General Schoepf with Colonel Wolford's cavalry, Colonel Steadman's Ohio regiment, and a battery of artillery, followed on a succeeding day by a Tennessee brigade. He had still two Kentucky regiments, the Thirty-eighth Ohio and another battery of artillery, with which he was to follow yesterday. This force, if concentrated, should be strong enough for the purpose; at all events, it is all he had or I could give him.

I explained to you fully, when here, the supposed position of our adversaries, among which was a force in the valley of Big Sandy, supposed to be advancing on Paris, Kentucky. General Nelson at Maysville was instructed to collect all the men he could, and Colonel Gill's regiment of Ohio Volunteers. Colonel Harris was already in position at Olympian Springs, and a regiment lay at Lexington, which I ordered to his support. This leaves the line of Thomas's operations exposed, but I cannot help it. I explained so fully to yourself and the Secretary of War the condition of things, that I can add nothing new until further developments, You know my views that this great centre of our field is too weak, far too weak, and I have begged and implored till I dare not say more.

Buckner still is beyond Green River. He sent a detachment of his men, variously estimated at from two to four thousand toward Greensburg. General Ward, with about one thousand men, retreated to Campbellsburg, where he called to his assistance some partially-formed regiments to the number of about two thousand. The enemy did not advance, and General Ward was at last dates at Campbellsburg. The officers charged with raising regiments must of necessity be near their homes to collect men, and for this reason are out of position; but at or near Greensburg and Lebanon, I desire to assemble as large a force of the Kentucky Volunteers as possible. This organization is necessarily irregular, but the necessity is so great that I must have them, and therefore have issued to them arms and clothing during the process of formation. This has facilitated their enlistment; but inasmuch as the Legislature has provided money for organizing the Kentucky Volunteers, and intrusted its disbursement to a board of loyal gentlemen, I have endeavored to cooperate with them to hasten the formation of these corps.

The great difficulty is, and has been, that as volunteers offer, we have not arms and clothing to give them. The arms sent us are, as you already know, European muskets of uncouth pattern, which the volunteers will not touch.

General McCook has now three brigades—Johnson's, Wood's, and Rousseau's. Negley's brigade arrived to-day, and will be sent out at once. The Minnesota regiment has also arrived, and will be sent forward. Hazzard's regiment of Indiana troops I have ordered to the month of Salt Creek, an important point on the turnpike-road leading to Elizabethtown.

I again repeat that our force here is out of all proportion to the importance of the position. Our defeat would be disastrous to the nation; and to expect of new men, who never bore arms, to do miracles, is not right.

I am, with much respect, yours truly,

W. T. SHERMAN, Brigadier-General commanding.

About this time my attention was drawn to the publication in all the Eastern papers, which of course was copied at the West, of the report that I was "crazy, insane, and mad," that "I had demanded two hundred thousand men for the defense of Kentucky;" and the authority given for this report was stated to be the Secretary of War himself, Mr. Cameron, who never, to my knowledge, took pains to affirm or deny it. My position was therefore simply unbearable, and it is probable I resented the cruel insult with language of intense feeling. Still I received no orders, no reenforcements, not a word of encouragement or relief. About November 1st, General McClellan was appointed commander-in-chief of all the armies in the field, and by telegraph called for a report from me. It is herewith given:

HEADQUARTERS THE DEPARTMENT OF THE CUMBERLAND, Louisville, Kentucky, November 4, 1861

General L. THOMAS, Adjutant-General, Washington, D. C.

Sir: In compliance with the telegraphic orders of General McClellan, received late last night, I submit this report of the forces in Kentucky, and of their condition.

The tabular statement shows the position of the several regiments. The camp at Nolin is at the present extremity of the Nashville Railroad. This force was thrown forward to meet the advance of Buckner's army, which then fell back to Green River, twenty-three miles beyond. These regiments were substantially without means of transportation, other than the railroad, which is guarded at all dangerous points, yet is liable to interruption at any moment, by the tearing up of a rail by the disaffected inhabitants or a hired enemy. These regiments are composed of good materials, but devoid of company officers of experience, and have been put under thorough drill since being in camp. They are generally well clad, and provided for. Beyond Green River, the enemy has masked his forces, and it is very difficult to ascertain even the approximate numbers. No pains have been spared to ascertain them, but without success, and it is well known that they far outnumber us. Depending, however, on the railroads to their rear for transportation, they have not thus far advanced this side of Green River, except in marauding parties. This is the proper line of advance, but will require a very large force, certainly fifty thousand men, as their railroad facilities south enable them to concentrate at

Munfordsville the entire strength of the South. General McCook's command is divided into four brigades, under Generals Wood, R. W. Johnson, Rousseau, and Negley.

General Thomas's line of operations is from Lexington, toward Cumberland Gap and Ford, which are occupied by a force of rebel Tennesseeans, under the command of Zollicoffer. Thomas occupies the position at London, in front of two roads which lead to the fertile part of Kentucky, the one by Richmond, and the other by Crab Orchard, with his reserve at Camp Dick Robinson, eight miles south of the Kentucky River. His provisions and stores go by railroad from Cincinnati to Nicholasville, and thence in wagons to his several regiments. He is forced to hire transportation.

Brigadier-General Nelson is operating by the line from Olympian Springs, east of Paris, on the Covington & Lexington Railroad, toward Prestonburg, in the valley of the Big Sandy where is assembled a force of from twenty-five to thirty-five hundred rebel Kentuckians waiting reenforcements from Virginia. My last report from him was to October 28th, at which time he had Colonel Harris's Ohio Second, nine hundred strong; Colonel Norton's Twenty-first Ohio, one thousand; and Colonel Sill's Thirty-third Ohio, seven hundred and fifty strong; with two irregular Kentucky regiments, Colonels Marshall and Metcalf. These troops were on the road near Hazel Green and West Liberty, advancing toward Prestonburg.

Upon an inspection of the map, you will observe these are all divergent lines, but rendered necessary, from the fact that our enemies choose them as places of refuge from pursuit, where they can receive assistance from neighboring States. Our lines are all too weak, probably with the exception of that to Prestonburg. To strengthen these, I am thrown on the raw levies of Ohio and Indiana, who arrive in detachments, perfectly fresh from the country, and loaded down with baggage, also upon the Kentuckians, who are slowly forming regiments all over the State, at points remote from danger, and whom it will be almost impossible to assemble together. The organization of this latter force is, by the laws of Kentucky, under the control of a military board of citizens, at the capital, Frankfort, and they think they will be enabled to have fifteen regiments toward the middle of this month, but I doubt it, and deem it unsafe to rely on them: There are four regiments forming in the neighborhood of Owensboro, near the mouth of Green River, who are doing good service, also in the neighborhood of Campbellsville, but it is unsafe to rely on troops so suddenly armed and equipped. They are not yet clothed or uniformed. I know well you will think our force too widely distributed, but we are forced to it by the attitude of our enemies, whose force and numbers the country never has and probably never will comprehend.

I am told that my estimate of troops needed for this line, viz., two hundred thousand, has been construed to my prejudice, and therefore leave it for the future. This is the great centre on which our enemies can concentrate whatever force is not employed elsewhere. Detailed statement of present force inclosed with this.

With great respect, your obedient servant,

W. T. SHERMAN, Brigadier-General commanding.

BRIGADIER-GENERAL McCOOK'S CAMP, AT NOLIN, FIFTY-TWO MILES FROM LOUISVILLE, KENTUCKY, NOVEMBER 4, 1861.

First Brigade (General ROUSSEAU).-Third Kentucky, Colonel Bulkley; Fourth Kentucky, Colonel Whittaker; First Cavalry, Colonel Board; Stone's battery; two companies Nineteenth United States Infantry, and two companies Fifteenth United States Infantry, Captain Gilman.

Second Brigade (General T. J. WOOD).-Thirty-eighth Indiana, Colonel Scribner; Thirty-ninth Indiana, Colonel Harrison; Thirtieth Indiana, Colonel Bass; Twenty-ninth Indiana, Colonel Miller.

Third Brigade (General JOHNSON).-Forty-ninth Ohio, Colonel Gibson; Fifteenth Ohio, Colonel Dickey; Thirty-fourth Illinois, Colonel King; Thirty-second Indiana, Colonel Willach.

Fourth Brigade (General NEGLEY).-Seventy-seventh Pennsylvania, Colonel Hambright; Seventy-eighth Pennsylvania, Colonel Sinnell; Seventy-ninth Pennsylvania, Colonel Stambaugh; Battery, Captain Mueller.

Camp Dick Robinson (General G. H. THOMAS).—-Kentucky, Colonel Bramlette;—Kentucky, Colonel Fry;—Kentucky Cavalry, Colonel Woolford; Fourteenth Ohio, Colonel Steadman; First Artillery, Colonel Barnett; Third Ohio, Colonel Carter;—East Tennessee, Colonel Byrd.

Bardstown, Kentucky.-Tenth Indiana, Colonel Manson.

Crab Orchard.-Thirty-third Indiana, Colonel Coburn.

Jeffersonville, Indiana.-Thirty-fourth Indiana, Colonel Steele; Thirty-sixth Indiana, Colonel Gross; First Wisconsin, Colonel Starkweather.

Mouth of Salt River.-Ninth Michigan, Colonel Duffield; Thirty-seventh Indiana, Colonel Hazzard.

Lebanon Junction..-Second Minnesota, Colonel Van Cleve.

Olympian Springs.-Second Ohio, Colonel Harris.

Cynthiana, Kentucky.-Thirty-fifth Ohio, Colonel Vandever.

Nicholasville, Kentucky.-Twenty-first Ohio, Colonel Norton; Thirty-eighth Ohio, Colonel Bradley.

Big Hill.-Seventeenth Ohio, Colonel Connell.

Colesburg.-Twenty-fourth Illinois, Colonel Hecker.

Elizabethtown, Kentucky.-Nineteenth Illinois, Colonel Turchin.

Owensboro' or Henderson.-Thirty-first Indiana, Colonel Cruft; Colonel Edwards, forming Rock Castle; Colonel Boyle, Harrodsburg; Colonel Barney, Irvine; Colonel Hazzard, Burksville; Colonel Haskins, Somerset.
    And, in order to conclude this subject, I also add copies of two telegraphic dispatches, sent for General McClellan's use about the same time, which are all the official letters received at his headquarters, as certified by the Adjutant-General, L. Thomas, in a letter of February 1, 1862; in answer to an application of my brother, Senator John Sherman, and on which I was adjudged insane:

Louisville, November 3, 10 p.m.

To General McLELLAN, Washington, D. C.:

Dispatch just received. We are forced to operate on three lines, all dependent on railroads of doubtful safety, requiring strong guards. From Paris to Prestonbnrg, three Ohio regiments and some militia—enemy variously reported from thirty-five hundred to seven thousand. From Lexington toward Cumberland Gap, Brigadier-General Thomas, one Indiana and five Ohio regiments, two Kentucky and two Tennessee; hired wagons and badly clad. Zollicoffer, at Cumberland Ford, about seven thousand. Lee reported on the way with Virginia reenforcements. In front of Louisville, fifty-two miles, McCook, with four brigades of about thirteen thousand, with four regiments to guard the railroad, at all times in danger. Enemy along the railroad from Green River to Bowling Green, Nashville, and Clarksville. Buckner, Hardee, Sidney Johnston, Folk, and Pillow, the two former in immediate command, the force as large as they want or can subsist, from twenty-five to thirty thousand. Bowling Green strongly fortified. Our forces too small to do good, and too large to sacrifice.

W. T. SHERMAN, Brigadier-General.

HEADQUARTERS THE DEPARTMENT OF THE CUMBERLAND, Louisville, Kentucky, November 6, 1861

General L. THOMAS, Adjutant-General.

Sir: General McClellan telegraphs me to report to him daily the situation of affairs here. The country is so large that it is impossible to give clear and definite views. Our enemies have a terrible advantage in the fact that in our midst, in our camps, and along our avenues of travel, they have active partisans, farmers and business-men, who seemingly pursue their usual calling, but are in fact spies. They report all our movements and strength, while we can procure information only by circuitous and unreliable means. I inclose you the copy of an intercepted letter, which is but the type of others. Many men from every part of the State are now enrolled under Buckner—have gone to him—while ours have to be raised in neighborhoods, and cannot be called together except at long notice. These volunteers are being organized under the laws of the State, and the 10th of November is fixed for the time of consolidating them into companies and regiments. Many of them are armed by the United States as home guards, and many by General Anderson and myself, because of the necessity of being armed to guard their camps against internal enemies. Should we be overwhelmed, they would scatter, and their arms and clothing will go to the enemy, furnishing the very material they so much need. We should have here a very large force, sufficient to give confidence to the Union men of the ability to do what should be done—possess ourselves of all the State. But all see and feel we are brought to a stand-still, and this produces doubt and alarm. With our present force it would be simple madness to cross Green River, and yet hesitation may be as fatal. In like manner the other columns are in peril, not so much in front as rear, the railroads over which our stores must pass being much exposed. I have the Nashville Railroad guarded by three regiments, yet it is far from being safe; and, the moment actual hostilities commence, these roads will be interrupted, and we will be in a dilemma. To meet this in part I have put a cargo of provisions at the mouth of Salt River, guarded by two regiments. All these detachments weaken the main force, and endanger the whole. Do not conclude, as before, that I exaggerate the facts. They are as stated, and the future looks as dark as possible. It would be better if some man of sanguine mind were here, for I am forced to order according to my convictions.

Yours truly,
W. T. SHERMAN, Brigadier-General commanding.

After the war was over, General Thomas J. Wood, then in command of the district of Vicksburg, prepared a statement addressed to the public, describing the interview with the Secretary of War, which he calls a "Council of War." I did not then deem it necessary to renew a matter which had been swept into oblivion by the war itself; but, as it is evidence by an eyewitness, it is worthy of insertion here.

STATEMENT.

On the 11th of October, 1861, the writer, who had been personally on mustering duty in Indiana, was appointed a brigadier-general of volunteers, and ordered to report to General Sherman, then in command of the Department of the Cumberland, with his headquarters at Louisville, having succeeded General Robert Anderson. When the writer was about leaving Indianapolis to proceed to Louisville, Mr. Cameron, returning from his famous visit of inspection to General Fremont's department, at St. Louis, Missouri, arrived at Indianapolis, and announced his intention to visit General Sherman.

The writer was invited to accompany the party to Louisville. Taking the early morning train from Indianapolis to Louisville on the 16th of October, 1861, the party arrived in Jeffersonville shortly after mid-

day. General Sherman met the party in Jeffersonville, and accompanied it to the Galt House, in Louisville, the hotel at which he was stopping.

During the afternoon General Sherman informed the writer that a council of war was to be held immediately in his private room in the hotel, and desired him to be present at the council. General Sherman and the writer proceeded directly to the room. The writer entered the room first, and observed in it Mr. Cameron, Adjutant-General L. Thomas, and some other persons, all of whose names he did not know, but whom he recognized as being of Mr. Cameron's party. The name of one of the party the writer had learned, which he remembers as Wilkinson, or Wilkerson, and who he understood was a writer for the New York Tribune newspaper. The Hon. James Guthrie was also in the room, having been invited, on account of his eminent position as a citizen of Kentucky, his high civic reputation, and his well-known devotion to the Union, to meet the Secretary of War in the council. When General Sherman entered the room he closed the door, and turned the key in the lock.

Before entering on the business of the meeting, General Sherman remarked substantially: "Mr. Cameron, we have met here to discuss matters and interchange views which should be known only by persons high in the confidence of the Government. There are persons present whom I do not know, and I desire to know, before opening the business of the council, whether they are persons who may be properly allowed to hear the views which I have to submit to you." Mr. Cameron replied, with some little testiness of manner, that the persons referred to belonged to his party, and there was no objection to their knowing whatever might be communicated to him.

Certainly the legitimate and natural conclusion from this remark of Mr. Cameron's was that whatever views might be submitted by General Sherman would be considered under the protection of the seal of secrecy, and would not be divulged to the public till all apprehension of injurious consequences from such disclosure had passed. And it may be remarked, further, that justice to General Sherman required that if, at any future time, his conclusions as to the amount of force necessary to conduct the operations committed to his charge should be made public, the grounds on which his conclusions were based should be made public at the same time.

Mr. Cameron then asked General Sherman what his plans were. To this General Sherman replied that he had no plans; that no sufficient force had been placed at his disposition with which to devise any plan of operations; that, before a commanding general could project a plan of campaign, he must know what amount of force he would have to operate with.

The general added that he had views which he would be happy to submit for the consideration of the Secretary. Mr. Cameron desired to hear General Sherman's views.

General Sherman began by giving his opinion of the people of Kentucky, and the then condition of the State. He remarked that he believed a very large majority of the people of Kentucky were thoroughly devoted to the Union, and loyal to the Government, and that the Unionists embraced almost all the older and more substantial men in the State; but, unfortunately, there was no organization nor arms among the Union men; that the rebel minority, thoroughly vindictive in its sentiments, was organized and armed (this having been done in advance by their leaders), and, beyond the reach of the Federal forces, overawed and prevented the Union men from organizing; that, in his opinion, if Federal protection were extended throughout the State to the Union men, a large force could be raised for the service of the Government.

General Sherman next presented a resume of the information in his possession as to the number of the rebel troops in Kentucky. Commencing with the force at Columbus, Kentucky, the reports varied, giving the strength from ten to twenty thousand. It was commanded by Lieutenant-General Polk. General Sherman fixed it at the lowest estimate; say, ten thousand. The force at Bowling Green, commanded by General. A. S. Johnston, supported by Hardee, Buckner, and others, was variously estimated at from eighteen to thirty thousand. General Sherman estimated this force at the lowest figures given to it by his information—eighteen thousand.

He explained that, for purposes of defense, these two forces ought, owing to the facility with which troops might be transported from one to the other, by the net-work of railroads in Middle and West Tennessee, to be considered almost as one. General Sherman remarked, also, on the facility with which reinforcements could be transported by railroad to Bowling Green, from the other rebellious States.

The third organized body of rebel troops was in Eastern Kentucky, under General Zollicoffer, estimated, according to the most reliable information, at six thousand men. This force threatened a descent, if unrestrained, on the blue-grass region of Kentucky, including the cities of Lexington, and Frankfort, the capital of the State; and if successful in its primary movements, as it would gather head as it advanced, might endanger the safety of Cincinnati.

General Sherman said that the information in his possession indicated an intention, on the part of the rebels, of a general and grand advance toward the Ohio River. He further expressed the opinion that, if such advance should be made, and not checked, the rebel force would be swollen by at least twenty thousand recruits from the disloyalists in Kentucky. His low computation of the organized rebel soldiers then in Kentucky fixed the strength at about thirty-five thousand. Add twenty thousand for reenforcements gained in Kentucky, to say nothing of troops drawn from other rebel States, and the effective rebel force in the State, at a low estimate, would be fifty-five thousand men.

General Sherman explained forcibly how largely the difficulties of suppressing the rebellion would be enhanced, if the rebels should be allowed to plant themselves firmly, with strong fortifications, at commanding points on the Ohio River. It would be facile for them to carry the war thence into the loyal States north of the river.

To resist an advance of the rebels, General Sherman stated that he did not have at that time in Kentucky more than some twelve to fourteen thousand effective men. The bulk of this force was posted at camp Nolin, on the Louisville & Nashville Railway, fifty miles south of Louisville. A part of it was in Eastern Kentucky, under General George H. Thomas, and a very small force was in the lower valley of Green River.

This disposition of the force had been made for the double purpose of watching and checking the rebels, and protecting the raising and organization of troops among the Union men of Kentucky.

Having explained the situation from the defensive point of view, General Sherman proceeded to consider it from the offensive stand-point. The Government had undertaken to suppress the rebellion; the onus faciendi, therefore, rested on the Government. The rebellion could never be put down, the authority of the paramount Government asserted, and the union of the States declared perpetual, by force of arms, by maintaining the defensive; to accomplish these grand desiderata, it was absolutely necessary the Government should adopt, and maintain until the rebellion was crushed, the offensive.

For the purpose of expelling the rebels from Kentucky, General Sherman said that at least sixty thousand soldiers were necessary. Considering that the means of accomplishment must always be proportioned to the end to be achieved, and bearing in mind the array of rebel force then in Kentucky, every sensible man must admit that the estimate of the force given by General Sherman, for driving the rebels out of the State, and reestablishing and maintaining the authority of the Government, was a very low one. The truth is that, before the rebels were driven from Kentucky, many more than sixty thousand soldiers were sent into the State.

Ascending from the consideration of the narrow question of the political and military situation in Kentucky, and the extent of force necessary to redeem the State from rebel thraldom, forecasting in his sagacious intellect the grand and daring operations which, three years afterward, he realized in a campaign, taken in its entirety, without a parallel in modern times, General Sherman expressed the opinion that, to carry the war to the Gulf of Mexico, and destroy all armed opposition to the Goverment, in the entire Mississippi Valley, at least two hundred thousand troops were absolutely requisite.

So soon as General Sherman had concluded the expression of his views, Mr. Cameron asked, with much warmth and apparent irritation, "Where do you suppose, General Sherman, all this force is to come from." General Sherman replied that he did not know; that it was not his duty to raise, organize, and put the necessary military force into the field; that duty pertained to the War Department. His duty was to organize *campaigns and command the troops after they had been put into the field.*

At this point of the proceedings, General Sherman suggested that it might be agreeable to the Secretary to hear the views of Mr. Guthrie. Thus appealed to, Mr. Guthrie said he did not consider himself, being a civilian, competent to give an opinion as to the extent of force necessary to parry the war to the Gulf of Mexico; but, being well informed of the condition of things in Kentucky, he indorsed fully General Sherman's opinion of the force required to drive the rebels out of the State.

The foregoing is a circumstantial account of the deliberations of the council that were of any importance.

A good deal of desultory conversation followed, on immaterial matters; and some orders were issued by telegraph, by the Secretary of War, for some small reenforcements to be sent to Kentucky immediately, from Pennsylvania and Indiana.

A short time after the council was held—the exact time is not now remembered by the writer—an imperfect narrative of it appeared in the New York Tribune. This account announced to the public the conclusions uttered by General Sherman in the council, without giving the reasons on which his conclusions were based. The unfairness of this course to General Sherman needs no comment. All military men were shocked by the gross breach of faith which had been committed.

TH. J. WOOD, Major-General Volunteers

Vicksburg, Mississippi, August 24, 1886.

Brigadier-General Don Carlos Buell arrived at Louisville about the middle of November, with orders to relieve me, and I was transferred for duty to the Department of the Missouri, and ordered to report in person to Major-General H. W. Halleck at St. Louis. I accompanied General Buell to the camp at Nolin, where he reviewed and inspected the camp and troops under the command of General A. McD. McCook, and on our way back General Buell inspected the regiment of Hazzard at Elizabethtown. I then turned over my command to him, and took my departure for St. Louis.

At the time I was so relieved I thought, of course, it was done in fulfillment of Mr. Lincoln's promise to me, and as a necessary result of my repeated demand for the fulfillment of that promise; but I saw and felt, and was of course deeply moved to observe, the manifest belief that there was more or less of truth in the rumor that the cares, perplexities, and anxiety of the situation had unbalanced my judgment and mind. It was, doubtless, an incident common to all civil wars, to which I could only submit with the best grace possible, trusting to the future for an opportunity to redeem my fortune and good name. Of course I could not deny the fact, and had to submit to all its painful consequences for months; and, moreover, I could not hide from myself that many of the officers and soldiers subsequently placed under my command looked at me askance and with suspicion. Indeed, it was not until the following April that the battle of Shiloh gave me personally the chance to redeem my good name.

On reaching St. Louis and reporting to General Halleck, I was received kindly, and was shortly afterward (viz., November 23d) sent up to Sedalia to inspect the camp there, and the troops located along the road back to Jefferson City, and I was ordered to assume command in a certain contingency. I found General Steels at Sedalia with his regiments scattered about loosely; and General Pope at Otterville, twenty miles back, with no concert between them. The rebel general, Sterling Price, had his forces down about Osceola and Warsaw. I advised General Halleck to collect the whole of his men into one camp on the La Mine River, near Georgetown, to put them into brigades and divisions, so as to be ready to be handled, and I gave some preliminary orders looking to that end. But the newspapers kept harping on my insanity and paralyzed my efforts. In spite of myself, they tortured from me some words and acts of imprudence. General Halleck telegraphed me on November

26th: "Unless telegraph-lines are interrupted, make no movement of troops without orders;" and on November 29th: "No forward movement of troops on Osceola will be made; only strong reconnoitring-parties will be sent out in the supposed direction of the enemy; the bulk of the troops being held in position till more reliable information is obtained."

About the same time I received the following dispatch:

HEADQUARTERS, ST. LOUIS, MISSOURI
November 28, 1881. Brigadier General SHERMAN, Sedalia:

Mrs. Sherman is here. General Halleck is satisfied, from reports of scouts received here, that no attack on Sedalia is intended. You will therefore return to this city, and report your observations on the condition of the troops you have examined. Please telegraph when you will leave.

SCHUYLER HAMILTON, Brigadier-General and Aide-de-Camp.

I accordingly returned to St. Louis, where I found Mrs. Sherman, naturally and properly distressed at the continued and reiterated reports of the newspapers of my insanity, and she had come from Lancaster to see me. This recall from Sedalia simply swelled the cry. It was alleged that I was recalled by reason of something foolish I had done at Sedalia, though in fact I had done absolutely nothing, except to recommend what was done immediately thereafter on the advice of Colonel McPherson, on a subsequent inspection. Seeing and realizing that my efforts were useless, I concluded to ask for a twenty days' leave of absence, to accompany Mrs. Sherman to our home in Lancaster, and to allow the storm to blow over somewhat. It also happened to be mid-winter, when, nothing was doing; so Mrs. Sherman and I returned to Lancaster, where I was born, and where I supposed I was better known and appreciated.

The newspapers kept up their game as though instigated by malice, and chief among them was the Cincinnati Commercial, whose editor, Halsted, was generally believed to be an honorable man. P. B. Ewing, Esq., being in Cincinnati, saw him and asked him why he, who certainly knew better, would reiterate such a damaging slander. He answered, quite cavalierly, that it was one of the news-items of the day, and he had to keep up with the time; but he would be most happy to publish any correction I might make, as though I could deny such a malicious piece of scandal affecting myself. On the 12th of November I had occasion to write to General Halleck, and I have a copy of his letter in answer:

ST. Louis, December 18, 1881.
Brigadier-General W. T. SHERMAN, Lancaster, Ohio.

My DEAR GENERAL: Yours of the 12th was received a day or two ago, but was mislaid for the moment among private papers, or I should have answered it sooner. The newspaper attacks are certainly shameless and scandalous, but I cannot agree with you, that they have us in their power "to destroy us as they please." I certainly get my share of abuse, but it will not disturb me.

Your movement of the troops was not countermanded by me because I thought it an unwise one in itself, but because I was not then ready for it. I had better information of Price's movements than you had, and I had no apprehension of an attack. I intended to concentrate the forces on that line, but I wished the movement delayed until I could determine on a better position.

After receiving Lieutenant-Colonel McPherson's report, I made precisely the location you had ordered. I was desirous at the time not to prevent the advance of Price by any movement on our part, hoping that he would move on Lexington; but finding that he had determined to remain at Osceola for some time at least, I made the movement you proposed. As you could not know my plans, you and others may have misconstrued the reason of my countermanding your orders....

I hope to see you well enough for duty soon. Our organization goes on slowly, but we will effect it in time. Yours truly,

H. W. HALLECK.

And subsequently, in a letter to Hon. Thomas Ewing, in answer to some inquiries involving the same general subject, General Halleck wrote as follows:

Hon. THOMAS EWING, Lancaster, Ohio.

DEAR SIR: Your note of the 13th, and one of this date, from Mr. Sherman, in relation to Brigadier-General Sherman's having being relieved from command in Sedalia, in November last, are just received. General Sherman was not put in command at Sedalia; he was authorized to assume it, and did so for a day or two. He did not know my plans, and his movement of troops did not accord with them. I therefore directed him to leave them as they were, and report here the result of his inspection, for which purpose he had been ordered there.

No telegram or dispatch of any kind was sent by me, or by any one with my knowledge or authority, in relation to it. After his return here, I gave him a leave of absence of twenty days, for the benefit of his health. As I was then pressing General McClellan for more officers, I deemed it necessary to explain why I did so. I used these words: "I am satisfied that General Sherman's physical and mental system is so completely broken by labor and care as to render him, for the present, unfit for duty; perhaps a few weeks' rest may restore him." This was the only communication I made on the subject. On no occasion have I ever expressed an opinion that his mind was affected otherwise than by over-exertion; to have said so would have done him the greatest injustice.

After General Sherman returned from his short leave, I found that his health was nearly restored, and I placed him temporarily in command of the camp of instruction, numbering over fifteen thousand men. I then wrote to General McClellan that he would soon be able to again take the field. I gave General Sherman a copy of my letter. This is the total of my correspondence on the subject. As evidence that I have every confidence in General Sherman, I have placed him in command of Western Kentucky—a command only second in importance in this department. As soon as divisions and columns can be organized, I propose to send him into the field where he can render most efficient service. I have seen newspaper squibs, charging him with being "crazy," etc. This is the grossest injustice; I do not, however, consider such attacks worthy of notice. The best answer is General Sherman's present position, and the valuable services he is rendering to the country. I have the fullest confidence in him.

Very respectfully, your obedient servant,

H. W. HALLECK, Major-General.

On returning to St. Louis, on the expiration of my leave of absence, I found that General Halleck was beginning to move his troops: one part, under General U. S. Grant, up the Tennessee River; and another part, under General S. R. Curtis, in the direction of Springfield, Missouri. General Grant was then at Paducah, and General Curtis was under orders for Rolls. I was ordered to take Curtis's place in command of the camp of instruction, at Benton Barracks, on the ground back of North St. Louis, now used as the Fair Grounds, by the following order: >

HEADQUARTERS DEPARTMENT OF THE MISSOURI
St. Louis, December 23, 1861

[EXTRACT.]

Brigadier-General W. T. Sherman, United States Volunteers, is hereby assigned to the command of the camp of instruction and post of Benton Barracks. He will have every armed regiment and company in his command ready for service at a moment's warning, and will notify all concerned that, when marching orders are received, it is expected that they will be instantly obeyed; no excuses for delay will be admitted. General Sherman will immediately report to these headquarters what regiments and companies, at Benton Barracks, are ready for the field.

By order of Major-General Halleck,

J. C. KELTEN, Assistant Adjutant-General.

I immediately assumed command, and found, in the building constructed for the commanding officer, Brigadier-General Strong, and the family of a captain of Iowa cavalry, with whom we boarded. Major Curtis, son of General Curtis, was the adjutant-general, but was soon relieved by Captain J. H. Hammond, who was appointed assistant adjutant-general, and assigned to duty with me.

Brigadier-General Hurlbut was also there, and about a dozen regiments of infantry and cavalry. I at once gave all matters pertaining to the post my personal attention, got the regiments in as good order as possible, kept up communication with General Halleck's headquarters by telegraph, and, when orders came for the movement of any regiment or detachment, it moved instantly. The winter was very wet, and the ground badly drained. The quarters had been erected by General Fremont, under contract; they were mere shells, but well arranged for a camp, embracing the Fair Grounds, and some forty acres of flat ground west of it. I instituted drills, and was specially ordered by General Halleck to watch Generals Hurlbut and Strong, and report as to their fitness for their commissions as brigadier-generals. I had known Hurlbut as a young lawyer, in Charleston, South Carolina, before the Mexican War, at which time he took a special interest in military matters, and I found him far above the average in the knowledge of regimental and brigade drill, and so reported. General Strong had been a merchant, and he told me that he never professed to be a soldier, but had been urged on the Secretary of War for the commission of a brigadier-general, with the expectation of be coming quartermaster or commissary-general. He was a good, kind-hearted gentleman, boiling over with patriotism and zeal. I advised him what to read and study, was considerably amused at his receiving instruction from a young lieutenant who knew the company and battalion drill, and could hear him practise in his room the words of command, and tone of voice, "Break from the right, to march to the left!" "Battalion, halt!" "Forward into line!" etc. Of course I made a favorable report in his case. Among the infantry and cavalry colonels were some who afterward rose to distinction—David Stuart, Gordon Granger, Bussey, etc., etc.

Though it was mid-winter, General Halleck was pushing his preparations most vigorously, and surely he brought order out of chaos in St. Louis with commendable energy. I remember, one night, sitting in his room, on the second floor of the Planters' House, with him and General Cullum, his chief of staff, talking of things generally, and the subject then was of the much-talked-of "advance," as soon as the season would permit. Most people urged the movement down the Mississippi River; but Generals Polk and Pillow had a large rebel force, with heavy guns in a very strong position, at Columbus, Kentucky, about eighteen miles below Cairo. Commodore Foote had his gunboat fleet at Cairo; and General U. S. Grant, who commanded the district, was collecting a large force at Paducah, Cairo, and Bird's Point. General Halleck had a map on his table, with a large pencil in his hand, and asked, "where is the rebel line?" Cullum drew the pencil through Bowling Green, Forts Donelson and Henry, and Columbus, Kentucky. "That is their line," said Halleck. "Now, where is the proper place to break it?" And either Cullum or I said, "Naturally the centre." Halleck drew a line perpendicular to the other, near its middle, and it coincided nearly with the general course of the Tennessee River; and he said, "That's the true line of operations." This occurred more than a month before General Grant began the movement, and, as he was subject to General Halleck's orders, I have always given Halleck the full credit for that movement, which was skillful, successful, and extremely rich in military results; indeed, it was the first real success on our side in the civil war. The movement up the Tennessee began about the 1st of February, and Fort Henry was captured by the joint action of the navy under Commodore Foote, and the land forces under General Grant, on the 6th of February, 1862. About the same time, General S. R. Curtis had moved forward from Rolls, and, on the 8th of March, defeated the rebels under McCulloch, Van Dom, and Price, at Pea Ridge.

As soon as Fort Henry fell, General Grant marched straight across to Fort Donelson, on the Cumberland River, invested the place, and, as soon as the gunboats had come round from the Tennessee, and had bombarded the water-front, he assaulted; whereupon Buckner surrendered the garrison of twelve thousand men; Pillow and ex-Secretary of War General Floyd having personally escaped across the river at night, occasioning a good deal of fun and criticism at their expense.

Before the fall of Donelson, but after that of Henry, I received, at Benton Barracks, the following orders:

HEADQUARTERS THE DEPARTMENT OF MISSOURI
St. Louis, February 13, 1862

Brigadier-General SHERMAN, Benton Barracks:

You will immediately repair to Paducah, Kentucky, and assume command of that post. Brigadier-General Hurlbut will accompany you. The command of Benton Barracks will be turned over to General Strong.

H. W. HALLECK, Major-General.

I started for Paducah the same day, and think that General Cullum went with me to Cairo; General Halleck's purpose being to push forward the operations up the Tennessee River with unusual vigor. On reaching Paducah, I found this dispatch:

HEADQUARTERS THE DEPARTMENT OF MISSOURI
St. Louis, February 15, 1862

Brigadier-General SHERMAN, Paducah, Kentucky:

Send General Grant every thing you can spare from Paducah and Smith and also General Hurlbut.

Bowling Green has been evacuated entirely.

H. W. HALLECK, Major-General.

118

The next day brought us news of the surrender of Buckner, and probably at no time during the war did we all feel so heavy a weight raised from our breasts, or so thankful for a most fruitful series of victories. They at once gave Generals Halleck, Grant, and C. F. Smith, great fame. Of course, the rebels let go their whole line, and fell back on Nashville and Island No. Ten, and to the Memphis & Charleston Railroad. Everybody was anxious to help. Boats passed up and down constantly, and very soon arrived the rebel prisoners from Donelson. I saw General Buckner on the boat, he seemed self-sufficient, and thought their loss was not really so serious to their cause as we did.

About this time another force of twenty or twenty-five thousand men was collected on the west bank of the Mississippi, above Cairo, under the command of Major-General John Pope, designed to become the "Army of the Mississippi," and to operate, in conjunction with the navy, down the river against the enemy's left flank, which had held the strong post of Columbus, Kentucky, but which, on the fall of Fort Donelson, had fallen back to New Madrid and Island No. 10.

CHAPTER X.
BATTLE of SHILOH.

MARCH AND APRIL, 1862.

By the end of February, 1862, Major-General Halleck commanded all the armies in the valley of the Mississippi, from his headquarters in St: Louis. These were, the Army of the Ohio, Major-General Buell, in Kentucky; the Army of the Tennessee, Major-General Grant, at Forts Henry and Donelson; the Army of the Mississippi, Major-General Pope; and that of General S. R. Curtis, in Southwest Missouri. He posted his chief of staff, General Cullum, at Cairo, and me at Paducah, chiefly to expedite and facilitate the important operations then in progress up the Tennessee, and Cumberland Rivers.

Fort Donelson had surrendered to General Grant on the 16th of February, and there must have been a good deal of confusion resulting from the necessary care of the wounded, and disposition of prisoners, common to all such occasions, and there was a real difficulty in communicating between St. Louis and Fort Donelson.

General Buell had also followed up the rebel army, which had retreated hastily from Bowling Green to and through Nashville, a city of so much importance to the South, that it was at one time proposed as its capital. Both Generals Grant and Buell looked to its capture as an event of great importance. On the 21st General Grant sent General Smith with his division to Clarksville, fifty miles above Donelson, toward Nashville, and on the 27th went himself to Nashville to meet and confer with General Buell, but returned to Donelson the next day.

Meantime, General Halleck at St. Louis must have felt that his armies were getting away from him, and began to send dispatches to me at Paducah, to be forwarded by boat, or by a rickety telegraph-line up to Fort Henry, which lay entirely in a hostile country, and was consequently always out of repair. On the 1st of March I received the following dispatch, and forwarded it to General Grant, both by the telegraph and boat:

To General GRANT, Fort Henry

Transports will be sent you as soon as possible, to move your column up the Tennessee River. The main object of this expedition will be to destroy the railroad-bridge over Bear Creek, near Eastport, Mississippi; and also the railroad connections at Corinth, Jackson, and Humboldt. It is thought best that these objects be attempted in the order named. Strong detachments of cavalry and light artillery, supported by infantry, may by rapid movements reach these points from the river, without any serious opposition.

Avoid any general engagements with strong forces. It will be better to retreat than to risk a general battle. This should be strongly impressed on the officers sent with expeditions from the river. General C. F. Smith or some very discreet officer should be selected for such commands. Having accomplished these objects, or such of them as may be practicable, you will return to Danville, and move on Paris.

Perhaps the troops sent to Jackson and Humbolt can reach Paris by land as easily as to return to the transports. This must depend on the character of the roads and the position of the enemy. All telegraphic lines which can be reached must be cut. The gunboats will accompany the transports for their protection. Any loyal Tennesseeans who desire it, may be enlisted and supplied with arms. Competent officers should be left to command Forts Henry and Donelson in your absence. I have indicated in general terms the object of this.

H. W. HALLECK, Major-General.

Again on the 2d:

Cairo, March 1, 1862

To General GRANT:

General Halleck, February 25th, telegraphs me: "General Grant will send no more forces to Clarksville. General Smith's division will come to Fort Henry, or a point higher up on the Tennessee River; transports will also be collected at Paducah. Two gunboats in Tennessee River with Grant. General Grant will immediately have small garrisons detailed for Forts Henry and Donelson, and all other forces made ready for the field."

From your letter of the 28th, I learn you were at Fort Donelson, and General Smith at Nashville, from which I infer you could not have received orders. Halleck's telegram of last night says: "Who sent Smith's division to Nashville? I ordered it across to the Tennessee, where they are wanted immediately. Order them back. Send all spare transports up Tennessee to General Grant." Evidently the general supposes you to be on the Tennessee. I am sending all the transports I can find for you, reporting to General Sherman for orders to go up the Cumberland for you, or, if you march across to Fort Henry, then to send them up the Tennessee.
    G. W. CULLUM, Brigadier-General.

On the 4th came this dispatch:

To Major-General U. S. GRANT

You will place Major-General C. F. Smith in command of expedition, and remain yourself at Fort Henry. Why do you not obey my orders to report strength and positions of your command?

H. W. HALLECK, Major-General.

Halleck was evidently working himself into a passion, but he was too far from the seat of war to make due allowance for the actual state of facts. General Grant had done so much, that General Halleck should have been patient. Meantime, at Paducah, I was busy sending boats in every direction—some under the orders of General Halleck, others of General Cullum; others for General Grant, and still others for General Buell at Nashville; and at the same time I was organizing out of the new troops that were arriving at Paducah a division for myself when allowed to take the field, which I had been promised by General Halleck. His purpose was evidently to operate up the Tennessee River, to break up Bear Creek Bridge and the railroad communications between the Mississippi and Tennessee Rivers, and no doubt he was provoked that Generals Grant and Smith had turned aside to Nashville. In the mean time several of the gunboats, under Captain Phelps, United States Navy, had gone up the Tennessee as far as Florence, and on their return had reported a strong Union feeling among the people along the river. On the 10th of March, having received the necessary orders from General Halleck, I embarked my division at Paducah. It was composed of four brigades. The First, commanded by Colonel S. G. Hicks, was composed of the Fortieth Illinois, Forty-sixth Ohio, and Morton's Indiana Battery, on the boats Sallie List, Golden Gate, J. B. Adams, and Lancaster.

The Second Brigade, Colonel D. Stuart, was composed of the Fifty-fifth Illinois, Seventy-first Ohio, and Fifty-fourth Ohio; embarked on the Hannibal, Universe, Hazel Dell, Cheeseman, and Prairie Rose.

The Third Brigade, Colonel Hildebrand, was composed of the Seventy-seventh Ohio, Fifty-seventh Ohio, and Fifty-third Ohio; embarked on the Poland, Anglo-Saxon, Ohio No. Three, and Continental.

The Fourth Brigade, Colonel Buckland, was composed of the Seventy-second Ohio, Forty-eighth Ohio, and Seventieth Ohio; embarked on the Empress, Baltic, Shenango, and Marrengo.

We steamed up to Fort Henry, the river being high and in splendid order. There I reported in person to General C. F. Smith, and by him was ordered a few miles above, to the remains of the burned railroad bridge, to await the rendezvous of the rest of his army. I had my headquarters on the Continental.

Among my colonels I had a strange character—Thomas Worthington, colonel of the Forty-sixth Ohio. He was a graduate of West Point, of the class of 1827; was, therefore, older than General Halleck, General Grant, or myself, and claimed to know more of war than all of us put together. In ascending the river he did not keep his place in the column, but pushed on and reached Savannah a day before the rest of my division. When I reached that place, I found that Worthington had landed his regiment, and was flying about giving orders, as though he were commander-in-chief. I made him get back to his boat, and gave him to understand that he must thereafter keep his place. General C. F. Smith arrived about the 13th of March, with a large fleet of boats, containing Hurlbut's division, Lew. Wallace's division, and that of himself, then commanded by Brigadier-General W. H. L. Wallace.

General Smith sent for me to meet him on his boat, and ordered me to push on under escort of the two gunboats, Lexington and Tyler, commanded by Captains Gwin and Shirk, United States Navy. I was to land at some point below Eastport, and make a break of the Memphis & Charleston Railroad, between Tuscumbia and Corinth. General Smith was quite unwell, and was suffering from his leg, which was swollen and very sore, from a mere abrasion in stepping into a small boat. This actually mortified, and resulted in his death about a month after, viz., April 25, 1862. He was adjutant of the Military Academy during the early part of my career there, and afterward commandant of cadets. He was a very handsome and soldierly man, of great experience, and at Donelson had acted with so much personal bravery that to him many attributed the success of the assault.

I immediately steamed up the Tennessee River, following the two gunboats, and, in passing Pittsburg Landing, was told by Captain Gwin that, on his former trip up the river, he had found a rebel regiment of cavalry posted there, and that it was the usual landing-place for the people about Corinth, distant thirty miles. I sent word back to General Smith that, if we were detained up the river, he ought to post some troops at Pittsburg Landing. We went on up the river cautiously, till we saw Eastport and Chickasaw, both of which were occupied by rebel batteries and a small rebel force of infantry.

We then dropped back quietly to the mouth of Yellow River, a few miles below, whence led a road to Burnsville, a place on the Memphis & Charleston road, where were the company's repair-shops. We at once commenced disembarking the command: first the cavalry, which started at once for Burnsville, with orders to tear up the railroad-track, and burn the depots, shops, etc; and I followed with the infantry and artillery as fast as they were disembarked. It was raining very hard at the time. Daylight found us about six miles out, where we met the cavalry returning. They had made numerous attempts to cross the streams, which had become so swollen that mere brooks covered the whole bottom; and my aide-de-camp, Sanger, whom I had dispatched with the cavalry, reported the loss, by drowning, of several of the men. The rain was pouring in torrents, and reports from the rear came that the river was rising very fast, and that, unless we got back to our boats soon, the bottom would be simply impassable. There was no alternative but to regain our boats; and even this was so difficult, that we had to unharness the artillery-horses, and drag the guns under water through the bayous, to reach the bank of the river. Once more embarked, I concluded to drop down to Pittsburg Landing, and to make the attempt from there. During the night of the 14th, we dropped down to Pittsburg Landing, where I found Hurlbut's division in boats. Leaving my command there, I steamed down to Savannah, and reported to General Smith in person, who saw in the flooded Tennessee the full truth of my report; and he then instructed me to disembark my own division, and that of General Hurlbut, at Pittsburg Landing; to take positions well back, and to leave room for his whole army; telling me that he would soon come up in person, and move out in force to make the lodgment on the railroad, contemplated by General Halleck's orders.

Lieutenant-Colonel McPherson, of General C. F. Smith's, or rather General Halleck's, staff, returned with me, and on the 16th of March we disembarked and marched out about ten miles toward Corinth, to a place called Monterey or Pea Ridge, where the rebels had a cavalry regiment, which of course decamped on our approach, but from the people we learned that trains were bringing large masses of men from every direction into Corinth. McPherson and I reconnoitred the ground well, and then returned to our boats. On the 18th, Hurlbut disembarked his division and took post about a mile and a half out, near where the roads branched, one leading to Corinth and the other toward Hamburg. On the 19th I disembarked my division, and took post about three miles back, three of the brigades covering the roads to Purdy and Corinth, and the other brigade (Stuart's) temporarily at a place on the Hamburg Road, near Lick Creek Ford, where the Bark Road came into the Hamburg Road. Within a few days, Prentiss's division arrived and camped on my left, and afterward McClernand's and W. H. L. Wallace's divisions, which formed a line to our rear. Lew Wallace's division remained on the north side of Snake Creek, on a road leading from Savannah or Cramp's Landing to Purdy.

General C. F. Smith remained back at Savannah, in chief command, and I was only responsible for my own division. I kept pickets well out on the roads, and made myself familiar with all the ground inside and outside my lines. My personal staff was composed of Captain J. H. Hammond, assistant adjutant-general; Surgeons Hartshorn and L'Hommedieu; Lieutenant Colonels Hascall and Sanger, inspector-generals; Lieutenants McCoy and John Taylor, aides-de-camp. We were all conscious that the enemy was collecting at Corinth, but in what force we could not know, nor did we know what was going on behind us. On the 17th of March, General U. S. Grant was restored to the command of all the troops up the Tennessee River, by reason of General Smith's extreme illness, and because he had explained to General Halleck satisfactorily his conduct after Donelson; and he too made his headquarters at Savannah, but frequently visited our camps. I always acted on the supposition that we were an invading army; that our purpose was to move forward in force, make a lodgment on the Memphis & Charleston road, and thus repeat the grand tactics of Fort Donelson, by separating the rebels in the interior from those at Memphis and on the Mississippi River. We did not fortify our camps against an attack, because we had no orders to do so, and because such a course would have made our raw men timid. The position was naturally strong, with Snake Creek on our right, a deep, bold stream, with a confluent (Owl Creek) to our right front; and Lick Creek, with a similar confluent, on our left, thus narrowing the space over which we could be attacked to about a mile and a half or two miles.

At a later period of the war, we could have rendered this position impregnable in one night, but at this time we did not do it, and it may be it is well we did not. From about the 1st of April we were conscious that the rebel cavalry in our front was getting bolder and more saucy; and on Friday, the 4th of April, it dashed down and carried off one of our picket-guards, composed of an officer and seven men, posted a couple of miles out on the Corinth road. Colonel Buckland sent a company to its relief, then followed himself with a regiment, and, fearing lest he might be worsted, I called out his whole brigade and followed some four or five miles, when the cavalry in advance encountered artillery. I then, after dark, drew back to our lines, and reported the fact by letter to General Grant, at Savannah; but thus far we had not positively detected the presence of infantry, for cavalry regiments generally had a couple of guns along, and I supposed the guns that opened on the on the evening of Friday, April 4th, belonged to the cavalry that was hovering along our whole front.

Saturday passed in our camps without any unusual event, the weather being wet and mild, and the roads back to the steamboat landing being heavy with mud; but on Sunday morning, the 6th, early, there was a good deal of picket-firing, and I got breakfast, rode out along my lines, and, about four hundred yards to the front of Appler's regiment, received from some bushes in a ravine to the left front a volley which killed my orderly, Holliday. About the same time I saw the rebel lines of battle in front coming down on us as far as the eye could reach. All my troops were in line of battle, ready, and the ground was favorable to us. I gave the necessary orders to the battery (Waterhouse's) attached to Hildebrand's brigade, and cautioned the men to reserve their fire till the rebels had crossed the ravine of Owl Creek, and had begun the ascent; also, sent staff-officers to notify Generals McClernand and Prentiss of the coming blow. Indeed, McClernand had already sent three regiments to the support of my left flank, and they were in position when the onset came.

In a few minutes the battle of "Shiloh" began with extreme fury, and lasted two days. Its history has been well given, and it has been made the subject of a great deal of controversy. Hildebrand's brigade was soon knocked to pieces, but Buckland's and McDowell's kept their organization throughout. Stuart's was driven back to the river, and did not join me in person till the second day of the battle. I think my several reports of that battle are condensed and good, made on the spot, when all the names and facts were fresh in my memory, and are herewith given entire:

HEADQUARTERS FIRST DIVISION
PITTSBURG LANDING, March 17, 1862

Captain Wm. McMICHAEL, Assistant Adjutant-General to General C. F SMITH, Savannah, Tennessee.

SIR: Last night I dispatched a party of cavalry, at 6 p.m., under the command of Lieutenant-Colonel Heath, Fifth Ohio Cavalry, for a strong reconnoissance, if possible, to be converted into an attack upon the Memphis road. The command got off punctually, followed at twelve o'clock at night by the First Brigade of my division, commanded by Colonel McDowell, the other brigades to follow in order.

About one at night the cavalry returned, reporting the road occupied in force by the enemy, with whose advance-guard they skirmished, driving them back—about a mile, taking two prisoners, and having their chief guide, Thomas Maxwell, Esq., and three men of the Fourth Illinois wounded.

Inclosed please find the report of Lieutenant-Colonel Heath; also a copy of his instructions, and the order of march. As soon as the cavalry returned, I saw that an attempt on the road was frustrated, and accordingly have placed McDowell's brigade to our right front, guarding the pass of Snake Creek; Stuart's brigade to the left front, to watch the pass of Lick Creek; and I shall this morning move directly out on the Corinth road, about eight miles to or toward Pea Ridge, which is a key-point to the southwest.

General Hurlbut's division will be landed to-day, and the artillery and infantry disposed so as to defend Pittsburg, leaving my division entire for any movement by land or water.

As near as I can learn, there are five regiments of rebel infantry at Purdy; at Corinth, and distributed along the railroad to Inca, are probably thirty thousand men; but my information from prisoners is very indistinct. Every road and path is occupied by the enemy's cavalry, whose orders seem to be to fire a volley, retire again, fire and retire. The force on the Purdy road attacked and driven by Major Bowman yesterday, was about sixty strong. That encountered last night on the Corinth road was about five companies of Tennessee cavalry, sent from Purdy about 2 p.m. yesterday.

I hear there is a force of two regiments on Pea Ridge, at the point where the Purdy and Corinth roads come together.

I am satisfied we cannot reach the Memphis & Charleston road without a considerable engagement, which is prohibited by General Halleck's instructions, so that I will be governed by your orders of yesterday, to occupy Pittsburg strongly, extend the pickets so as to include a semicircle of three miles, and push a strong reconnoissance as far out as Lick Creek and Pea Ridge.

I will send down a good many boats to-day, to be employed as you may direct; and would be obliged if you would send a couple of thousand sacks of corn, as much hay as you can possibly spare, and, if possible, a barge of coal.

I will send a steamboat under care of the gunboat, to collect corn from cribs on the river-bank.

I have the honor to be your obedient servant,

W. T. SHERMAN,
Brigadier-General, commanding First Division.

HEADQUARTERS, STEAMBOAT CONTINENTAL, Pittsburg, March 18, 1882.

Captain RAWLINS, Assistant Adjutant-General to General GRANT.

SIR: The division surgeon having placed some one hundred or more sick on board the Fanny Bullitt, I have permitted her to take them to Savannah. There is neither house nor building of any kind that can be used for a hospital here.

I hope to receive an order to establish floating hospitals, but in the mean time, by the advise of the surgeon, allow these sick men to leave. Let me hope that it will meet your approbation.

The order for debarkation came while General Sherman was absent with three brigades, and no men are left to move the effects of these brigades.

The landing, too, is small, with scarcely any chance to increase it; therefore there is a great accumulation of boats. Colonel McArthur has arrived, and is now cutting a landing for himself.

General Sherman will return this evening. I am obliged to transgress, and write myself in the mean time,

Respectfully your obedient servant,

J. H. HAMMOND, *Assistant Adjutant-General.*

P. S—4 p.m.—Just back; have been half-way to Corinth and to Purdy. All right. Have just read this letter, and approve all but floating hospitals; regimental surgeons can take care of all sick, except chronic cases, which can always be sent down to Paducah.

Magnificent plain for camping and drilling, and a military point of great strength. The enemy has felt us twice, at great loss and demoralization; will report at length this evening; am now much worn out.

W. T. SHERMAN, *Brigadier-General.*

HEADQUARTERS FIRST DIVISION
Pittsburg Landing, March 19, 1862.

Captain RAWLINS, Assistant Adjutant-General to General GRANT, Savannah, Tennessee.

SIR: *I have just returned from an extensive reconnoissance toward Corinth and Purdy, and am strongly impressed with the importance of this position, both for its land advantages and its strategic position. The ground itself admits of easy defense by a small command, and yet affords admirable camping-ground for a hundred thousand men. I will as soon as possible make or cause to be made a topographical sketch of the position. The only drawback is that, at this stage of water, the space for landing is contracted too much for the immense fleet now here discharging.*

I will push the loading and unloading of boats, but suggest that you send at once (Captain Dodd, if possible) the best quartermaster you can, that he may control and organize this whole matter. I have a good commissary, and will keep as few provisions afloat as possible. Yours, etc.,

W. T. SHERMAN, *Brigadier-General commanding.*

HEADQUARTERS SHERMAN'S DIVISION
Camp Shiloh, near Pittsburg Landing, Tennessee, April 2, 1862

Captain J. A. RAWLINS, Assistant Adjutant-General to General GRANT.

SIR: *In obedience to General Grant's instructions of March 31st, with one section of Captain Muench's Minnesota Battery, two twelve-pound howitzers, a detachment of Fifth Ohio Cavalry of one hundred and fifty men, under Major Ricker, and two battalions of infantry from the Fifty-seventh and Seventy-seventh Ohio, under the command of Colonels Hildebrand and Mungen, I marched to the river, and embarked on the steamers Empress and Tecumseh. The gunboat Cairo did not arrive at Pittsburg, until after midnight, and at 6 p.m. Captain Bryant, commanding the gunboat, notified me that he was ready to proceed up the river. I followed, keeping the transports within about three hundred yards of the gunboat. About 1 p.m., the Cairo commenced shelling the battery above the mouth of Indian Creek, but elicited no reply. She proceeded up the river steadily and cautiously, followed close by the Tyler and Lexington, all throwing shells at the points where, on former visits of the gunboats, enemy's batteries were found. In this order all followed, till it was demonstrated that all the enemy's batteries, including that at Chickasaw, were abandoned.*

I ordered the battalion of infantry under Colonel Hildebrand to disembark at Eastport, and with the other battalion proceeded to Chickasaw and landed. The battery at this point had evidently been abandoned some time, and consisted of the remains of an old Indian mound, partly washed away by the river, which had been fashioned into a two-gun battery, with a small magazine. The ground to its rear had evidently been overflowed during the late freshet, and led to the removal of the guns to Eastport, where the batteries were on high, elevated ground, accessible at all seasons from the country to the rear.

Upon personal inspection, I attach little importance to Chickasaw as a military position. The people, who had fled during the approach of the gunboats, returned to the village, and said the place had been occupied by one Tennessee regiment and a battery of artillery from Pensacola. After remaining at Chickasaw some hours, all the boats dropped back to Eastport, not more than a mile below, and landed there. Eastport Landing during the late freshet must have been about twelve feet under water, but at the present stage the landing is the best I have seen on the Tennessee River.

The levee is clear of trees or snags, and a hundred boats could land there without confusion.

The soil is of sand and gravel, and very firm. The road back is hard, and at a distance of about four hundred yards from the water begin the gravel hills of the country. The infantry scouts sent out by Colonel Hildebrand found the enemy's cavalry mounted, and watching the Inca road, about two miles back of Eastport. The distance to Inca is only eight miles, and Inca is the nearest point and has the best road by which the Charleston & Memphis Railroad can be reached. I could obtain no certain information as to the strength of the enemy there, but am satisfied that it would have been folly to have attempted it with my command. Our object being to dislodge the enemy from the batteries recently erected near Eastport, and this being attained, I have returned, and report the river to be clear to and beyond Chickasaw.

I have the honor to be, your obedient servant,

W. T. SHERMAN,
Brigadier-General commanding Division.

HEADQUARTERS FIFTH DIVISION
CAMP SHILOH, April 5, 1862.

Captain J. A. RAWLINS, Assistant Adjutant-General, District of Western Tennessee.

SIR: I have the honor to report that yesterday, about 3 p.m., the lieutenant commanding and seven men of the advance pickets imprudently advanced from their posts and were captured. I ordered Major Ricker, of the Fifth Ohio Cavalry, to proceed rapidly to the picket-station, ascertain the truth, and act according to circumstances. He reached the station, found the pickets had been captured as reported, and that a company of infantry sent by the brigade commander had gone forward in pursuit of some cavalry. He rapidly advanced some two miles, and found them engaged, charged the enemy, and drove them along the Ridge road, till he met and received three discharges of artillery, when he very properly wheeled under cover, and returned till he met me.

As soon as I heard artillery, I advanced with two regiments of infantry, and took position, and remained until the scattered companies of infantry and cavalry had returned. This was after night.

I infer that the enemy is in some considerable force at Pea Ridge, that yesterday morning they crossed a brigade of two regiments of infantry, one regiment of cavalry, and one battery of field-artillery, to the ridge on which the Corinth road lies. They halted the infantry and artillery at a point abort five miles in my front, sent a detachment to the lane of General Meeks, on the north of Owl Creek, and the cavalry down toward our camp. This cavalry captured a part of our advance pickets, and afterward engaged the two companies of Colonel Buckland's regiment, as described by him in his report herewith inclosed. Our cavalry drove them back upon their artillery and Infantry, killing many, and bringing off ten prisoners, all of the First Alabama Cavalry, whom I send to you.

We lost of the pickets one first-lieutenant and seven men of the Ohio Seventieth Infantry (list inclosed); one major, one lieutenant, and one private of the Seventy-second Ohio, taken prisoners; eight privates wounded (names in full, embraced in report of Colonel Buckland, inclosed herewith).

We took ten prisoners, and left two rebels wounded and many killed on the field.

I have the honor to be, your obedient servant,

W. T. SHERMAN,
Brigadier-General, commanding Division.

HEADQUARTERS FIFTH DIVISION
Camp Shiloh, April 10, 1862.

Captain J. A. RAWLINS, Assistant Adjutant-General to General GRANT.

SIR: I had the honor to report that, on Friday the 4th inst., the enemy's cavalry drove in our pickets, posted about a mile and a half in advance of my centre, on the main Corinth road, capturing one first-lieutenant and seven men; that I caused a pursuit by the cavalry of my division, driving them back about five miles, and killing many. On Saturday the enemy's cavalry was again very bold, coming well down to our front; yet I did not believe they designed any thing but a strong demonstration. On Sunday morning early, the 6th inst., the enemy drove our advance-guard back on the main body, when I ordered under arms all my division, and sent word to General McClernand, asking him to support my left; to General Prentiss, giving him notice that the enemy was in our front in force, and to General Hurlbut, asking him to support General Prentiss. At that time—7 a.m.—my division was arranged as follows:

First Brigade, composed of the Sixth Iowa, Colonel J. A. McDowell;

Fortieth Illinois, Colonel Hicks; Forty-sixth Ohio, Colonel Worthington; and the Morton battery, Captain Behr, on the extreme right, guarding the bridge on the Purdy road over Owl Creek.

Second Brigade, composed of the Fifty-fifth Illinois, Colonel D. Stuart; the Fifty-fourth Ohio, Colonel T. Kilby Smith; and the Seventy-first Ohio, Colonel Mason, on the extreme left, guarding the ford over Lick Creek.

Third Brigade, composed of the Seventy-seventh Ohio, Colonel Hildebrand; the Fifty-third Ohio, Colonel Appler; and the Fifty-seventh Ohio, Colonel Mungen, on the left of the Corinth road, its right resting on Shiloh meeting-house.

Fourth Brigade, composed of the Seventy-second Ohio, Colonel Buckland; the Forty-eighth Ohio, Colonel Sullivan; and the Seventieth Ohio, Colonel Cockerill, on the right of the Corinth road, its left resting on Shiloh meeting-house.

Two batteries of artillery—Taylor's and Waterhouse's—were posted, the former at Shiloh, and the latter on a ridge to the left, with a front-fire over open ground between Mungen's and Appler's regiments. The cavalry, eight companies of the Fourth Illinois, under Colonel Dickey, were posted in a large open field to the left and rear of Shiloh meeting-house, which I regarded as the centre of my position.

Shortly after 7 a.m., with my entire staff, I rode along a portion of our front, and when in the open field before Appler's regiment, the enemy's pickets opened a brisk fire upon my party, killing my orderly, Thomas D. Holliday, of Company H, Second Illinois Cavalry. The fire came from the bushes which line a small stream that rises in the field in front of Appler's camp, and flows to the north along my whole front.

This valley afforded the enemy partial cover; but our men were so posted as to have a good fire at them as they crossed the valley and ascended the rising ground on our side.

About 8 a.m. I saw the glistening bayonets of heavy masses of infantry to our left front in the woods beyond *the small stream alluded to, and became satisfied for the first time that the enemy designed a determined attack on our whole camp.*

All the regiments of my division were then in line of battle at their proper posts. I rode to Colonel Appler, and ordered him to hold his ground at all hazards, as he held the left flank of our first line of battle, and I informed him that he had a good battery on his right, and strong support to his rear. General McClernand had promptly and energetically responded to my request, and had sent me three regiments which were posted to protect Waterhouse's battery and the left flank of my line.

The battle opened by the enemy's battery, in the woods to our front, throwing shells into our camp. Taylor's and Waterhouse's batteries promptly responded, and I then observed heavy battalions of infantry passing obliquely to the left, across the open field in Appler's front; also, other columns advancing directly upon my division. Our infantry and artillery opened along the whole line, and the battle became general. Other heavy masses of the enemy's forces kept passing across the field to our left, and directing their course on General Prentiss. I saw at once that the enemy designed to pass my left flank, and fall upon Generals McClernand and Prentiss, whose line of camps was almost parallel with the Tennessee River, and about two miles back from it. Very soon the sound of artillery and musketry announced that General Prentiss was engaged; and about 9 A. M. I judged that he was falling back. About this time Appler's regiment broke in disorder, followed by Mungen's regiment, and the enemy pressed forward on Waterhouse's battery thereby exposed.

The three Illinois regiments in immediate support of this battery stood for some time; but the enemy's advance was so vigorous, and the fire so severe, that when Colonel Raith, of the Forty-third Illinois, received a severe wound and fell from his horse, his regiment and the others manifested disorder, and the enemy got possession of three guns of this (Waterhouse's) battery. Although our left was thus turned, and the enemy was pressing our whole line, I deemed Shiloh so important, that I remained by it and renewed my orders to Colonels McDowell and Buckland to hold their ground; and we did hold these positions until about 10 a.m., when the enemy had got his artillery to the rear of our left flank and some change became absolutely necessary. Two regiments of Hildebrand's brigade—Appler's and Mungen's—had already disappeared to the rear, and Hildebrand's own regiment was in disorder. I therefore gave orders for Taylor's battery—still at Shiloh—to fall back as far as the Purdy and Hamburg road, and for McDowell and Buckland to adopt that road as their new line. I rode across the angle and met Behr's battery at the cross-roads, and ordered it immediately to come into battery, action right. Captain Behr gave the order, but he was almost immediately shot from his horse, when drivers and gunners fled in disorder, carrying off the caissons, and abandoning five out of six guns, without firing a shot. The enemy pressed on, gaining this battery, and we were again forced to choose a new line of defense. Hildebrand's brigade had substantially disappeared from the field, though he himself bravely remained. McDowell's and Buckland's brigades maintained their organizations, and were conducted by my aides, so as to join on General McClernand's right, thus abandoning my original camps and line. This was about 10 1/2 a.m., at which time the enemy had made a furious attack on General McClernand's whole front. He struggled most determinedly, but, finding him pressed, I moved McDowell's brigade directly against the left flank of the enemy, forced him back some distance, and then directed the men to avail themselves of every cover-trees, fallen timber, and a wooded valley to our right. We held this position for four long hours, sometimes gaining and at others losing ground; General McClernand and myself acting in perfect concert, and struggling to maintain this line. While we were so hard pressed, two Iowa regiments approached from the rear, but could not be brought up to the severe fire that was raging in our front, and General Grant, who visited us on that ground, will remember our situation about 3 p.m.; but about 4 p.m. it was evident that Hurlbut's line had been driven back to the river; and knowing that General Lew Wallace was coming with reinforcements from Cramp's Landing, General McClernand and I, on consultation, selected a new line of defense, with its right covering a bridge by which General Wallace had to approach. We fell back as well as we could, gathering in addition to our own such scattered forces as we could find, and formed the new line.

During this change the enemy's cavalry charged us, but were handsomely repulsed by the Twenty-ninth Illinois Regiment. The Fifth Ohio Battery, which had come up, rendered good service in holding the enemy in check for some time, and Major Taylor also came up with another battery and got into position, just in time to get a good flank-fire upon the enemy's column, as he pressed on General McClernand's right, checking his advance; when General McClernand's division made a fine charge on the enemy and drove him back into the ravines to our front and right. I had a clear field, about two hundred yards wide, in my immediate front, and contented myself with keeping the enemy's infantry at that distance during the rest of the day. In this position we rested for the night.

My command had become decidedly of a mixed character. Buckland's brigade was the only one that retained its organization. Colonel Hildebrand was personally there, but his brigade was not. Colonel McDowell had been severely injured by a fall off his horse, and had gone to the river, and the three regiments of his brigade were not in line. The Thirteenth Missouri, Colonel Crafts J. Wright, had reported to me on the field, and fought well, retaining its regimental organization; and it formed a part of my line during Sunday night and all Monday. Other fragments of regiments and companies had also fallen into my division, and acted with it during the remainder of the battle. General Grant and Buell visited me in our bivouac that evening, and from them I learned the situation of affairs on other parts of the field. General Wallace arrived from Crump's Landing shortly after dark, and formed his line to my right rear. It rained hard during the night, but our men were in good spirits, lay on their arms, being satisfied with such bread and meat as could be gathered at the neighboring camps, and determined to redeem on Monday the losses of Sunday.

At daylight of Monday I received General Grant's orders to advance and recapture our original camps. I dispatched several members of my staff to bring up all the men they could find, especially the brigade of Colonel Stuart, which had been separated from the division all the day before; and at the appointed time the division, or rather what remained of it, with the Thirteenth Missouri and other fragments, moved forward and reoccupied the ground on the extreme right of General McClernand's camp, where we attracted the fire of a battery located near Colonel McDowell's former headquarters. Here I remained, patiently waiting for the sound of General Buell's advance upon the main Corinth road. About 10 a.m. the heavy firing in that direction, and its steady approach, satisfied me; and General Wallace being on our right flank with his well-conducted division, I led the head of my column to General McClernand's right, formed line of battle, facing south, with Buckland's brigade directly across the ridge, and Stuart's brigade on its right in the woods; and thus advanced, steadily and slowly, under a heavy fire of musketry and artillery. Taylor had just got to me from the rear, where he had gone for ammunition, and brought up three guns, which I ordered into position, to advance by hand firing. These guns belonged to Company A, Chicago Light Artillery, commanded by Lieutenant P. P. Wood, and did most excellent service. Under cover of their fire, we advanced till we reached the point where the Corinth road crosses the line of McClernand's camp, and here I saw for the first time the well-ordered and compact columns of General Buell's Kentucky forces, whose soldierly movements at once gave confidence to our newer and less disciplined men. Here I saw Willich's regiment advance upon a point of water-oaks and thicket, behind which I knew the enemy was in great strength, and enter it in beautiful style. Then arose the severest musketry-fire I ever heard, and lasted some twenty minutes, when this splendid regiment had to fall back. This green point of timber is about five hundred yards east of Shiloh meeting-home, and it was evident here was to be the struggle. The enemy could also be seen forming his lines to the south. General McClernand sending to me for artillery, I detached to him the three guns of Wood's battery, with which he speedily drove them back, and, seeing some others to the rear, I sent one of my staff to bring them forward, when, by almost providential decree, they proved to be two twenty-four pound howitzers belonging to McAlister's battery, and served as well as guns ever could be.

This was about 2 p.m. The enemy had one battery close by Shiloh, and another near the Hamburg road, both pouring grape and canister upon any column of troops that advanced upon the green point of water-oaks. Willich's regiment had been repulsed, but a whole brigade of McCook's division advanced beautifully, deployed, and entered this dreaded wood. I ordered my second brigade (then commanded by Colonel T. Kilby Smith, Colonel Smart being wounded) to form on its right, and my fourth brigade, Colonel Buckland, on its right; all to advance abreast with this Kentucky brigade before mentioned, which I afterward found to be Rousseau's brigade of McCook's division. I gave personal direction to the twenty-four pounder guns, whose well-directed fire first silenced the enemy's guns to the left, and afterward at the Shiloh meeting-house.

Rousseau's brigade moved in splendid order steadily to the front, sweeping every thing before it, and at 4 p.m. we stood upon the ground of our original front line; and the enemy was in full retreat. I directed my several brigades to resume at once their original camps.

Several times during the battle, cartridges gave out; but General Grant had thoughtfully kept a supply coming from the rear. When I appealed to regiments to stand fast, although out of cartridges, I did so because, to retire a regiment for any cause, has a bad effect on others. I commend the Fortieth Illinois and Thirteenth Missouri for thus holding their ground under heavy fire, although their cartridge-boxes were empty.

I am ordered by General Grant to give personal credit where I think it is due, and censure where I think it merited. I concede that General McCook's splendid division from Kentucky drove back the enemy along the Corinth road, which was the great centre of this field of battle, where Beauregard commanded in person, supported by Bragg's, Polk's, and Breckenridge's divisions. I think Johnston was killed by exposing himself in front of his troops, at the time of their attack on Buckland's brigade on Sunday morning; although in this I may be mistaken.

My division was made up of regiments perfectly new, nearly all having received their muskets for the first time at Paducah. None of them had ever been under fire or beheld heavy columns of an enemy bearing down on them as they did on last Sunday.

To expect of them the coolness and steadiness of older troops would be wrong. They knew not the value of combination and organization. When individual fears seized them, the first impulse was to get away. My third brigade did break much too soon, and I am not yet advised where they were during Sunday afternoon and Monday morning. Colonel Hildebrand, its commander, was as cool as any man I ever saw, and no one could have made stronger efforts to hold his men to their places than he did. He kept his own regiment with individual exceptions in hand, an hour after Appler's and Mungen's regiments had left their proper field of action. Colonel Buckland managed his brigade well. I commend him to your notice as a cool, intelligent, and judicious gentleman, needing only confidence and experience, to make a good commander. His subordinates, Colonels Sullivan and Cockerill, behaved with great gallantry; the former receiving a severe wound on Sunday, and yet commanding and holding his regiment well in hand all day, and on Monday, until his right arm was broken by a shot. Colonel Cookerill held a larger proportion of his men than any colonel in my division, and was with me from first to last.

Colonel J. A. McDowell, commanding the first brigade, held his ground on Sunday, till I ordered him to fall back, which he did in line of battle; and when ordered, he conducted the attack on the enemy's left in good style. In falling back to the next position, he was thrown from his horse and injured, and his brigade was not in position on Monday morning. His subordinates, Colonels Hicks and Worthington, displayed great personal courage. Colonel Hicks led his regiment in the attack on Sunday, and received a wound, which it is feared may prove mortal. He is a brave and gallant gentleman, and deserves well of his country. Lieutenant-Colonel Walcutt, of the Ohio Forty-sixth, was severely wounded on Sunday, and has been disabled ever since. My second brigade, Colonel Stuart, was detached nearly two miles from my headquarters. He had to fight his own battle on Sunday, against superior numbers, as the enemy interposed between him and General Prentiss early in the day. Colonel Stuart was wounded severely, and yet reported for duty on Monday morning, but was compelled to leave during the day, when the command devolved on Colonel T. Kilby Smith, who was always in the thickest of the fight, and led the brigade handsomely.

I have not yet received Colonel Stuart's report of the operations of his brigade during the time he was detached, and must therefore forbear to mention names. Lieutenant-Colonel Kyle, of the Seventy-first, was mortally wounded on Sunday, but the regiment itself I did not see, as only a small fragment of it was with the brigade when it joined the division on Monday morning. Great credit is due the fragments of men of the disordered regiments who kept in the advance. I observed and noticed them, but until the brigadiers and colonels make their reports, I cannot venture to name individuals, but will in due season notice all who kept in our front line, as well as those who preferred to keep back near the steamboat-landing. I will also send a full list of the killed, wounded, and missing, by name, rank, company, and regiment. At present I submit the result in figures:

[Summary of General Sherman's detailed table:]

Killed	18
Wounded	275

130

Missing 41

Aggregate loss in the
division: 034

The enemy captured seven of our guns on Sunday, but on Monday we recovered seven; not the identical guns we had lost, but enough in number to balance the account. At the time of recovering our camps our men were so fatigued that we could not follow the retreating masses of the enemy; but on the following day I followed up with Buckland's and Hildebrand's brigade for six miles, the result of which I have already reported.

Of my personal staff, I can only speak with praise and thanks. I think they smelled as much gunpowder and heard as many cannon-balls and bullets as must satisfy their ambition. Captain Hammond, my chief of staff, though in feeble health, was very active in rallying broken troops, encouraging the steadfast and aiding to form the lines of defense and attack. I recommend him to your notice. Major Sanger's intelligence, quick perception, and rapid execution, were of very great value to me, especially in bringing into line the batteries that cooperated so efficiently in our movements. Captains McCoy and Dayton, aides-de-camp, were with me all the time, carrying orders, and acting with coolness, spirit, and courage. To Surgeon Hartshorne and Dr. L'Hommedieu hundreds of wounded men are indebted for the kind and excellent treatment received on the field of battle and in the various temporary hospitals created along the line of our operations. They worked day and night, and did not rest till all the wounded of our own troops as well as of the enemy were in safe and comfortable shelter. To Major Taylor, chief of artillery, I feel under deep obligations, for his good sense and judgment in managing the batteries, on which so much depended. I inclose his report and indorse his recommendations. The cavalry of my command kept to the rear, and took little part in the action; but it would have been madness to have exposed horses to the musketry-fire under which we were compelled to remain from Sunday at 8 a.m. till Monday at 4 p.m. Captain Kossack, of the engineers, was with me all the time, and was of great assistance. I inclose his sketch of the battlefield, which is the best I have seen, and which will enable you to see the various positions occupied by my division, as well as of the others that participated in the battle. I will also send in, during the day, the detailed reports of my brigadiers and colonels, and will indorse them with such remarks as I deem proper.

I am, with much respect, your obedient servant,

W. T. SHERMAN,
Brigadier-General commanding Fifth Division.

HEADQUARTERS FIFTH DIVISION
Tuesday, April 8, 1862

Sir: With the cavalry placed at my command and two brigades of my fatigued troops, I went this morning out on the Corinth road. One after another of the abandoned camps of the enemy lined the roads, with hospital flags for their protection; at all we found more or less wounded and dead men. At the forks of the road I found the head of General T. J. Wood's division of Buell's Army. I ordered cavalry to examine both roads leading toward Corinth, and found the enemy on both. Colonel Dickey, of the Fourth Illinois Cavalry, asking for reenforcements, I ordered General Wood to advance the head of his column cautiously on the left-hand road, while I conducted the head of the third brigade of my division up the right-hand road. About half a mile from the forks was a clear field, through which the road passed, and, immediately beyond, a space of some two hundred yards of fallen timber, and beyond that an extensive rebel camp. The enemy's cavalry could be seen in this camp; after reconnoisance, I ordered the two advance companies of the Ohio Seventy-seventh, Colonel Hildebrand, to deploy forward as skirmishers, and the regiment itself forward into line, with an interval of one hundred yards. In this order we advanced cautiously until the skirmishers were engaged. Taking it for granted this disposition would clear the camp, I held Colonel Dickey's Fourth Illinois Cavalry ready for the charge. The enemy's cavalry came down boldly at a charge, led by General Forrest in person, breaking through our line of skirmishers; when the regiment of infantry, without cause, broke, threw away their muskets, and fled. The ground was admirably adapted for a defense of infantry against cavalry, being miry and covered with fallen timber.

As the regiment of infantry broke, Dickey's Cavalry began to discharge their carbines, and fell into disorder. I instantly sent orders to the rear for the brigade to form line of battle, which was promptly executed. The broken infantry and cavalry rallied on this line, and, as the enemy's cavalry came to it, our cavalry in turn charged and drove them from the field. I advanced the entire brigade over the same ground and sent Colonel Dickey's cavalry a mile farther on the road. On examining the ground which had been occupied by the Seventy-seventh Ohio, we found fifteen of our men dead and about twenty-five wounded. I sent for wagons and had all the wounded carried back to camp, and caused the dead to be buried, also the whole rebel camp to be destroyed.

Here we found much ammunition for field-pieces, which was destroyed; also two caissons, and a general hospital, with about two hundred and eighty Confederate wounded, and about fifty of our own wounded men. Not having the means of bringing them off, Colonel Dickey, by my orders, took a surrender, signed by the medical director (Lyle) and by all the attending surgeons, and a pledge to report themselves to you as prisoners of war; also a pledge that our wounded should be carefully attended to, and surrendered to us to-morrow as soon as ambulances could go out. I inclose this written document, and request that you cause wagons or ambulances for our wounded to be sent to-morrow, and that wagons' be sent to bring in the many tents belonging to us which are pitched along the road for four miles out. I did not destroy them, because I knew the enemy could not move them. The roads are very bad, and are strewed with abandoned wagons, ambulances, and limber-boxes. The enemy has succeeded in carrying off the guns, but has crippled his batteries by abandoning the hind limber-boxes of at least twenty caissons. I am satisfied the enemy's infantry and artillery passed Lick Creek this morning, traveling all of last night, and that he left to his rear all his cavalry, which has protected his retreat; but signs of confusion and disorder mark the whole road. The check sustained by us at the fallen timber delayed our advance, so that night came upon us before the wounded were provided for and the dead buried, and our troops being fagged out by three days' hard fighting, exposure, and privation, I ordered them back to their camps, where they now are.

I have the honor to be, your obedient servant,

W.T. SHERMAN Brigadier-General commanding Division.

General Grant did not make an official report of the battle of Shiloh, but all its incidents and events were covered by the reports of division commanders and Subordinates. Probably no single battle of the war gave rise to such wild and damaging reports. It was publicly asserted at the North that our army was taken completely by surprise; that the rebels caught us in our tents; bayoneted the men in their beds; that General Grant was drunk; that Buell's opportune arrival saved the Army of the Tennessee from utter annihilation, etc. These reports were in a measure sustained by the published opinions of Generals Buell, Nelson, and others, who had reached the steamboat-landing from the east, just before nightfall of the 6th, when there was a large crowd of frightened, stampeded men, who clamored and declared that our army was all destroyed and beaten. Personally I saw General Grant, who with his staff visited me about 10 a.m. of the 6th, when we were desperately engaged. But we had checked the headlong assault of our enemy, and then held our ground. This gave him great satisfaction, and he told me that things did not look as well over on the left. He also told me that on his way up from Savannah that morning he had stopped at Crump's Landing, and had ordered Lew Wallace's division to cross over Snake Creek, so as to come up on my right, telling me to look out for him. He came again just before dark, and described the last assault made by the rebels at the ravine, near the steamboat-landing, which he had repelled by a heavy battery collected under Colonel J. D. Webster and other officers, and he was convinced that the battle was over for that day. He ordered me to be ready to assume the offensive in the morning, saying that, as he had observed at Fort Donelson at the crisis of the battle, both sides seemed defeated, and whoever assumed the offensive was sure to win. General Grant also explained to me that General Buell had reached the bank of the Tennessee River opposite Pittsburg Landing, and was in the act of ferrying his troops across at the time he was speaking to me.

About half an hour afterward General Buell himself rode up to where I was, accompanied by Colonels Fry, Michler, and others of his staff. I was dismounted at the time, and General Buell made of me a good many significant inquiries about matters and things generally. By the aid of a manuscript map made by myself, I pointed out to him our positions as they had been in the morning, and our then positions; I also explained that my right then covered the bridge over Snake Creek by which we had all day been expecting Lew Wallace; that McClernand was on my left, Hurlbut on his left, and so on. But Buell said he had come up from the landing, and had not seen our men, of whose existence in fact he seemed to doubt. I insisted that I had five thousand good men still left in line, and thought that McClernand had as many more, and that with what was left of Hurlbut's, W. H. L. Wallace's, and Prentiss's divisions, we ought to have eighteen thousand men fit for battle. I reckoned that ten thousand of our men were dead, wounded, or prisoners, and that the enemy's loss could not be much less. Buell said that Nelson's, McCook's, and Crittendens divisions of his army, containing eighteen thousand men, had arrived and could cross over in the night, and be ready for the next day's battle. I argued that with these reenforcements we could sweep the field. Buell seemed to mistrust us, and repeatedly said that he did not like the looks of things, especially about the boat-landing,—and I really feared he would not cross over his army that night, lest he should become involved in our general disaster. He did not, of course, understand the shape of the ground, and asked me for the use of my map, which I lent him on the promise that he would return it. He handed it to Major Michler to have it copied, and the original returned to me, which Michler did two or three days after the battle. Buell did cross over that night, and the next day we assumed the offensive and swept the field, thus gaining the battle decisively. Nevertheless, the controversy was started and kept up, mostly to the personal prejudice of General Grant, who as usual maintained an imperturbable silence.

After the battle, a constant stream of civilian surgeons, and sanitary commission agents, men and women, came up the Tennessee to bring relief to the thousands of maimed and wounded soldiers for whom we had imperfect means of shelter and care. These people caught up the camp-stories, which on their return home they retailed through their local papers, usually elevating their own neighbors into heroes, but decrying all others: Among them was Lieutenant-Governor Stanton, of Ohio, who published in Belfontaine, Ohio, a most abusive article about General Grant and his subordinate generals. As General Grant did not and would not take up the cudgels, I did so. My letter in reply to Stanton, dated June 10, 1862, was published in the Cincinnati Commercial soon after its date. To this Lieutenant-Governor Stanton replied, and I further rejoined in a letter dated July 12, 1862. These letters are too personal to be revived. By this time the good people of the North had begun to have their eyes opened, and to give us in the field more faith and support. Stanton was never again elected to any public office, and was commonly spoken of as "the late Mr. Stanton." He is now dead, and I doubt not in life he often regretted his mistake in attempting to gain popular fame by abusing the army-leaders, then as now an easy and favorite mode of gaining notoriety, if not popularity. Of course, subsequent events gave General Grant and most of the other actors in that battle their appropriate place in history, but the danger of sudden popular clamors is well illustrated by this case.

The battle of Shiloh, or Pittsburg Landing, was one of the most fiercely contested of the war. On the morning of April 6, 1862, the five divisions of McClernand, Prentiss, Hurlbut, W. H. L. Wallace, and Sherman, aggregated about thirty-two thousand men. We had no intrenchments of any sort, on the theory that as soon as Buell arrived we would march to Corinth to attack the enemy. The rebel army, commanded by General Albert Sidney Johnston, was, according to their own reports and admissions, forty-five thousand strong, had the momentum of attack, and beyond all question fought skillfully from early morning till about 2 a.m., when their commander-in-chief was killed by a Mini-ball in the calf of his leg, which penetrated the boot and severed the main artery. There was then a perceptible lull for a couple of hours, when the attack was renewed, but with much less vehemence, and continued up to dark. Early at night the division of Lew Wallace arrived from the other side of Snake Creek, not having fired a shot. A very small part of General Buell's army was on our side of the Tennessee River that evening, and their loss was trivial.

During that night, the three divisions of McCook, Nelson, and Crittenden, were ferried across the Tennessee, and fought with us the next day (7th). During that night, also, the two wooden gunboats, Tyler, commanded by Lieutenant Groin, and Lexington, Lieutenant Shirk, both of the regular navy, caused shells to be thrown toward that part of the field of battle known to be occupied by the enemy. Beauregard afterward reported his entire loss as ten thousand six hundred and ninety-nine. Our aggregate loss, made up from official statements, shows seventeen hundred killed, seven thousand four hundred and ninety-five wounded, and three thousand and twenty-two prisoners; aggregate, twelve thousand two hundred and seventeen, of which twenty-one hundred and sixty-seven were in Buell's army, leaving for that of Grant ten thousand and fifty. This result is a fair measure of the amount of fighting done by each army.

CHAPTER XI.
SHILOH TO MEMPHIS.

APRIL TO JULY, 1862.

While, the "Army of the Tennessee," under Generals Grant and C. F. Smith, was operating up the Tennessee River, another force, styled the "Army of the Mississippi," commanded by Major-General John Pope, was moving directly down the Mississippi River, against that portion of the rebel line which, under Generals Polk and Pillow, had fallen back from Columbus, Kentucky, to Island Number Ten and New Madrid. This army had the full cooperation of the gunboat fleet, commanded by Admiral Foote, and was assisted by the high flood of that season, which enabled General Pope, by great skill and industry, to open a canal from a point above Island Number Ten to New Madrid below, by which he interposed between the rebel army and its available line of supply and retreat. At the very time that we were fighting the bloody battle on the Tennessee River, General Pope and Admiral Foote were bombarding the batteries on Island Number Ten, and the Kentucky shore abreast of it; and General Pope having crossed over by steamers a part of his army to the east bank, captured a large part of this rebel army, at and near Tiptonville.

General Halleck still remained at St. Louis, whence he gave general directions to the armies of General Curtis, Generals Grant, Buell, and Pope; and instead of following up his most important and brilliant successes directly down the Mississippi, he concluded to bring General Pope's army around to the Tennessee, and to come in person to command there. The gunboat fleet pushed on down the Mississippi, but was brought up again all standing by the heavy batteries at Fort Pillow, about fifty miles above Memphis. About this time Admiral Farragut, with another large sea-going fleet, and with the cooperating army of General Butler, was entering the Mississippi River by the Passes, and preparing to reduce Forts Jackson and St, Philip in order to reach New Orleans; so that all minds were turned to the conquest of the Mississippi River, and surely adequate means were provided for the undertaking.

The battle of Shiloh had been fought, as described, on the 6th and 7th of April; and when the movement of the 8th had revealed that our enemy was gone, in full retreat, leaving killed, wounded, and much property by the way, we all experienced a feeling of relief. The struggle had been so long, so desperate and bloody, that the survivors seemed exhausted and nerveless; we appreciated the value of the victory, but realized also its great cost of life. The close of the battle had left the Army of the Tennessee on the right, and the Army of the

Ohio on the left; but I believe neither General Grant nor Buell exercised command, the one over the other; each of them having his hands full in repairing damages. All the division, brigade, and regimental commanders were busy in collecting stragglers, regaining lost property, in burying dead men and horses, and in providing for their wounded. Some few new regiments came forward, and some changes of organization became necessary. Then, or very soon after, I consolidated my font brigades into three, which were commanded: First, Brigadier-General Morgan L: Smith; Second, Colonel John A. McDowell; Third, Brigadier-General J. W. Denver. About the same time I was promoted to major-general volunteers.

The Seventy-first Ohio was detached to Clarksville, Tennessee, and the Sixth and Eighth Missouri were transferred to my division.

In a few days after the battle, General Halleck arrived by steamboat from St. Louis, pitched his camp near the steamboat-landing, and assumed personal command of all the armies. He was attended by his staff, composed of General G. W. Cullum, U. S. Engineers, as his chief of staff; Colonel George Thom, U. S. Engineers; and Colonels Kelton and Kemper, adjutants-general. It soon became manifest that his mind had been prejudiced by the rumors which had gone forth to the detriment of General Grant; for in a few days he issued an order, reorganizing and rearranging the whole army. General Buell's Army of the Ohio constituted the centre; General Pope's army, then arriving at Hamburg Landing, was the left; the right was made up of mine and Hurlbut's divisions, belonging to the old Army of the Tennessee, and two new ones, made up from the fragments of the divisions of Prentiss and C. F. Smith, and of troops transferred thereto, commanded by Generals T. W. Sherman and Davies. General George H. Thomas was taken from Buell, to command the right. McClernand's and Lew Wallace's divisions were styled the reserve, to be commanded by McClernand. General Grant was substantially left out, and was named "second in command," according to some French notion, with no clear, well-defined command or authority. He still retained his old staff, composed of Rawlins, adjutant-general; Riggin, Lagow, and Hilyer, aides; and he had a small company of the Fourth Illinois Cavalry as an escort. For more than a month he thus remained, without any apparent authority, frequently visiting me and others, and rarely complaining; but I could see that he felt deeply the indignity, if not insult, heaped upon him.

General Thomas at once assumed command of the right wing, and, until we reached Corinth, I served immediately under his command. We were classmates, intimately acquainted, had served together before in the old army, and in Kentucky, and it made to us little difference who commanded the other, provided the good cause prevailed.

Corinth was about thirty miles distant, and we all knew that we should find there the same army with which we had so fiercely grappled at Shiloh, reorganized, reenforced, and commanded in chief by General Beauregard in place of Johnston, who had fallen at Shiloh. But we were also reenforced by Buell's and Pope's armies; so that before the end of April our army extended from Snake Creek on the right to the Tennessee River, at Hamburg, on the left, and must have numbered nearly one hundred thousand men.

Ample supplies of all kinds reached us by the Tennessee River, which had a good stage of water; but our wagon transportation was limited, and much confusion occurred in hauling supplies to the several camps. By the end of Aril, the several armies seemed to be ready, and the general forward movement on Corinth began. My division was on the extreme right of the right wing, and marched out by the "White House," leaving Monterey or Pea Ridge to the south. Crossing Lick Creek, we came into the main road about a mile south of Monterey, where we turned square to the right, and came into the Purdy road, near "Elams." Thence we followed the Purdy road to Corinth, my skirmishers reaching at all times the Mobile & Ohio Railroad. Of course our marches were governed by the main centre, which followed the direct road from Pittsburg Landing to Corinth; and this movement was provokingly slow. We fortified almost every camp at night, though we had encountered no serious opposition, except from cavalry, which gave ground easily as we advanced. The opposition increased as we neared Corinth, and at a place called Russell's we had a sharp affair of one brigade, under the immediate direction of Brigadier-General Morgan L. Smith, assisted by the brigade of General Denver. This affair occurred on the

19th of May, and our line was then within about two miles of the northern intrenchments of Corinth.

On the 27th I received orders from General Halleck "to send a force the next day to drive the rebels from the house in our front, on the Corinth road, to drive in their pickets as far as possible, and to make a strong demonstration on Corinth itself;" authorizing me to call on any adjacent division for assistance.

I reconnoitred the ground carefully, and found that the main road led forward along the fence of a large cotton-field to our right front, and ascended a wooded hill, occupied in some force by the enemy, on which was the farm-house referred to in General Halleck's orders. At the farther end of the field was a double log-house, whose chinking had been removed; so that it formed a good block house from which the enemy could fire on any person approaching from our quarter.

General Hurlbut's division was on my immediate left, and General McClernand's reserve on our right rear. I asked of each the assistance of a brigade. The former sent General Veatch's, and the latter General John A. Logan's brigade. I asked the former to support our left flank, and the latter our right flank. The next morning early, Morgan L. Smith's brigade was deployed under cover on the left, and Denver's on the right, ready to move forward rapidly at a signal. I had a battery of four twenty-pound Parrott guns, commanded by Captain Silversparre. Colonel Ezra Taylor, chief of artillery, had two of these guns moved up silently by hand behind a small knoll, from the crest of which the enemy's block-house and position could be distinctly seen; when all were ready, these guns were moved to the crest, and several quick rounds were fired at the house, followed after an interval by a single gum. This was the signal agreed on, and the troops responded beautifully, crossed the field in line of battle, preceded by their skirmishers who carried the position in good style, and pursued the enemy for half a mile beyond.

The main line halted on the crest of the ridge, from which we could look over the parapets of the rebel works at Corinth, and hear their drum and bugle calls. The rebel brigade had evidently been taken by surprise in our attack; it soon rallied and came back on us with the usual yell, driving in our skirmishers, but was quickly checked when it came within range of our guns and line of battle. Generals Grant and Thomas happened to be with me during this affair, and were well pleased at the handsome manner in which the troops behaved. That night we began the usual entrenchments, and the next day brought forward the artillery and the rest of the division, which then extended from the Mobile & Ohio Railroad, at Bowie Hill Out, to the Corinth & Purdy road, there connecting with Hurlbut's division. That night, viz., May 29th, we heard unusual sounds in Corinth, the constant whistling of locomotives, and soon after daylight occurred a series of explosions followed by a dense smoke rising high over the town. There was a telegraph line connecting my headquarters with those of General Halleck, about four miles off, on the Hamburg road. I inquired if he knew the cause of the explosions and of the smoke, and he answered to "advance with my division and feel the enemy if still in my front" I immediately dispatched two regiments from each of my three brigades to feel the immediate front, and in a very short time advanced with the whole division. Each brigade found the rebel parapets abandoned, and pushed straight for the town, which lies in the northeast angle of intersection of the Mobile & Ohio and Memphis & Charleston Railroads. Many buildings had been burned by the enemy on evacuation, which had begun the night before at 6 p.m., and continued through the night, the rear-guard burning their magazine at the time of withdrawing, about daybreak. Morgan L. Smith's brigade followed the retreating rear-guard some four miles to the Tuacumbia Bridge, which was found burned. I halted the other brigades at the college, about a mile to the southwest of the town, where I was overtaken by General Thomas in person.

The heads of all the columns had entered the rebel lines about the same time, and there was some rather foolish clamor for the first honors, but in fact there was no honor in the event. Beauregard had made a clean retreat to the south, and was only seriously pursued by cavalry from General Pope's flank. But he reached Tupelo, where he halted for reorganization; and there is no doubt that at the moment there was much disorganization in his ranks, for the woods were full of deserters whom we did not even take prisoners, but advised them to make their way home and stay there. We spent the day at and near the college, when General Thomas, who applied for orders at Halleck's headquarters, directed me to conduct my division back to the camp of the night before, where we had left our trains The advance on Corinth had occupied all of the month of May, the most beautiful and valuable month of the year for campaigning in this latitude. There had been little fighting, save on General Pope's left flank about Farmington; and on our right. I esteemed it a magnificent drill, as it served for the instruction of our men in guard and picket duty, and in habituating them to out-door life; and by the time we had reached Corinth I believe that army was the best then on this continent, and could have gone where it pleased. The four subdivisions were well commanded, as were the divisions and brigades of the whole army. General Halleck was a man of great capacity, of large acquirements, and at the time possessed the confidence of the country, and of most of the army. I held him in high estimation, and gave him credit for the combinations which had resulted in placing this magnificent army of a hundred thousand men, well equipped and provided, with a good base, at Corinth, from which he could move in any direction.

Had he held his force as a unit, he could have gone to Mobile, or Vicksburg, or anywhere in that region, which would by one move have solved the whole Mississippi problem; and, from what he then told me, I believe he intended such a campaign, but was overruled from Washington. Be that as it may, the army had no sooner settled down at Corinth before it was scattered: General Pope was called to the East, and his army distributed among the others; General Thomas was relieved from the command of the right wing, and reassigned to his division in the Army of the Ohio; and that whole army under General Buell was turned east along the Memphis & Charleston road, to march for Chattanooga. McClernand's "reserve" was turned west to Bolivar and Memphis. General Halleck took post himself at Corinth, assigned Lieutenant-Colonel McPherson to take charge of the railroads, with instructions to repair them as far as Columbus, Kentucky, and to collect cars and locomotives to operate them to Corinth and Grand Junction. I was soon dispatched with my own and Hurlbut's divisions northwest fourteen miles to Chewalla, to save what could be of any value out of six trains of cars belonging to the rebels which had been wrecked and partially burned at the time of the evacuation of Corinth.

A short time before leaving Corinth I rode from my camp to General Halleck's headquarters, then in tents just outside of the town, where we sat and gossiped for some time, when he mentioned to me casually that General Grant was going away the next morning. I inquired the cause, and he said that he did not know, but that Grant had applied for a thirty days' leave, which had been given him. Of course we all knew that he was chafing under the slights of his anomalous position, and I determined to see him on my way back. His camp was a short distance off the Monterey road, in the woods, and consisted of four or five tents, with a sapling railing around the front. As I rode up, Majors Rawlins, Lagow, and Hilyer, were in front of the camp, and piled up near them were the usual office and camp chests, all ready for a start in the morning. I inquired for the general, and was shown to his tent, where I found him seated on a camp-stool, with papers on a rude camp-table; he seemed to be employed in assorting letters, and tying them up with red tape into convenient bundles. After passing the usual compliments, I inquired if it were true that he was going away. He said, "Yes." I then inquired the reason, and he said "Sherman, you know. You know that I am in the way here. I have stood it as long as I can, and can endure it no longer." I inquired where he was going to, and he said, "St. Louis." I then asked if he had any business there, and he said, "Not a bit." I then begged him to stay, illustrating his case by my own.

Before the battle of Shiloh, I had been cast down by a mere newspaper assertion of "crazy;" but that single battle had given me new life, and now I was in high feather; and I argued with him that, if he went away, events would go right along, and he would be left out; whereas, if he remained, some happy accident might restore him to favor and his true place. He certainly appreciated my friendly advice, and promised to wait awhile; at all events, not to go without seeing me again, or communicating with me. Very soon after this, I was ordered to Chewalla, where, on the 6th of June, I received a note from him, saying that he had reconsidered his intention, and would remain. I cannot find the note, but my answer I have kept:

Chewalla, June 6, 1862.

Major-General GRANT.

My DEAR SIR: I have just received your note, and am rejoiced at your conclusion to remain; for you could not be quiet at home for a week when armies were moving, and rest could not relieve your mind of the gnawing sensation that injustice had been done you.

My orders at Chewalla were to rescue the wrecked trains there, to reconnoitre westward and estimate the amount of damage to the railroad as far as Grand Junction, about fifty miles. We camped our troops on high, healthy ground to the south of Chewalla, and after I had personally reconnoitred the country, details of men were made and volunteer locomotive engineers obtained to superintend the repairs. I found six locomotives and about sixty cars, thrown from the track, parts of the machinery detached and hidden in the surrounding swamp, and all damaged as much by fire as possible. It seems that these trains were inside of Corinth during the night of evacuation, loading up with all sorts of commissary stores, etc., and about daylight were started west; but the cavalry-picket stationed at the Tuscumbia bridge had, by mistake or panic, burned the bridge before the trains got to them. The trains, therefore, were caught, and the engineers and guards hastily scattered the stores into the swamp, and disabled the trains as far as they could, before our cavalry had discovered their critical situation. The weather was hot, and the swamp fairly stunk with the putrid flour and fermenting sugar and molasses; I was so much exposed there in the hot sun, pushing forward the work, that I got a touch of malarial fever, which hung on me for a month, and forced me to ride two days in an ambulance, the only time I ever did such a thing during the whole war. By the 7th I reported to General Halleck that the amount of work necessary to reestablish the railroad between Corinth and Grand Junction was so great, that he concluded not to attempt its repair, but to rely on the road back to Jackson (Tennessee), and forward to Grand Junction; and I was ordered to move to Grand Junction, to take up the repairs from there toward Memphis.

The evacuation of Corinth by Beauregard, and the movements of General McClernand's force toward Memphis, had necessitated the evacuation of Fort Pillow, which occurred about June 1st; soon followed by the further withdrawal of the Confederate army from Memphis, by reason of the destruction of the rebel gunboats in the bold and dashing attack by our gun-boats under command of Admiral Davis, who had succeeded Foote. This occurred June 7th. Admiral Farragut had also captured New Orleans after the terrible passage of Forts Jackson and St. Philip on May 24th, and had ascended the river as high as Vicksburg; so that it seemed as though, before the end of June, we should surely have full possession of the whole river. But it is now known that the progress of our Western armies had aroused the rebel government to the exercise of the most stupendous energy. Every man capable of bearing arms at the South was declared to be a soldier, and forced to act as such. All their armies were greatly reenforced, and the most despotic power was granted to enforce discipline and supplies. Beauregard was replaced by Bragg, a man of more ability— of greater powers of organization, of action, and discipline—but naturally exacting and severe, and not possessing the qualities to attract the love of his officers and men. He had a hard task to bring into order and discipline that mass of men to whose command he succeeded at Tupelo, with which he afterward fairly outmanoeuvred General Buell, and forced him back from Chattanooga to Louisville. It was a fatal mistake, however, that halted General Halleck at Corinth, and led him to disperse and scatter the best materials for a fighting army that, up to that date, had been assembled in the West.

During the latter part of June and first half of July, I had my own and Hurlbut's divisions about Grand Junction, Lagrange, Moscow, and Lafayette, building railroad-trestles and bridges, fighting off cavalry detachments coming from the south, and waging an everlasting quarrel with planters about their negroes and fences—they trying, in the midst of moving armies, to raise a crop of corn. On the 17th of June I sent a detachment of two brigades, under General M. L. Smith, to Holly Springs, in the belief that I could better protect the railroad from some point in front than by scattering our men along it; and, on the 23d, I was at Lafayette Station, when General Grant, with his staff and a very insignificant escort, arrived from Corinth en route for Memphis, to take command of that place and of the District of West Tennessee. He came very near falling into the hands of the enemy, who infested the whole country with small but bold detachments of cavalry. Up to that time I had received my orders direct from General Halleck at Corinth, but soon after I fell under the immediate command of General Grant and so continued to the end of the war; but, on the 29th, General Halleck notified me that "a division of troops under General C. S. Hamilton of 'Rosecrans's army corps,' had passed the Hatchie from Corinth," and was destined for Holly Springs, ordering me to "cooperate as far as advisable," but "not to neglect the protection of the road." I ordered General Hurlbut to leave detachments at Grand Junction and Lagrange, and to march for Holly Springs. I left detachments at Moscow and Lafayette, and, with about four thousand men, marched for the same point. Hurlbut and I met at Hudsonville, and thence marched to the Coldwater, within four miles of Holly Springs. We encountered only small detachments of rebel cavalry under Colonels Jackson and Pierson, and drove them into and through Holly Springs; but they hung about, and I kept an infantry brigade in Holly Springs to keep them out. I heard nothing from General Hamilton till the 5th of July, when I received a letter from him dated Rienzi, saying that he had been within nineteen miles of Holly Springs and had turned back for Corinth; and on the next day, July 6th, I got a telegraph order from General Halleck, of July 2d, sent me by courier from Moscow, "not to attempt to hold Holly Springs, but to fall back and protect the railroad." We accordingly marched back twenty-five miles—Hurlbut to Lagrange, and I to Moscow. The enemy had no infantry nearer than the Tallahatchee bridge, but their cavalry was saucy and active, superior to ours, and I despaired of ever protecting a railroad, preventing a broad front of one hundred miles, from their dashes.

About this time, we were taunted by the Confederate soldiers and citizens with the assertion that Lee had defeated McClellan at Richmond; that he would soon be in Washington; and that our turn would come next. The extreme caution of General Halleck also indicated that something had gone wrong, and, on the 16th of July, at Moscow, I received a dispatch from him, announcing that he had been summoned to Washington, which he seemed to regret, and which at that moment I most deeply deplored. He announced that his command would devolve on General Grant, who had been summoned around from Memphis to Corinth by way of Columbus, Kentucky, and that I was to go into Memphis to take command of the District of West Tennessee, vacated by General Grant. By this time, also, I was made aware that the great, army that had assembled at Corinth at the end of May had been scattered and dissipated, and that terrible disasters had befallen our other armies in Virginia and the East.

I soon received orders to move to Memphis, taking Hurlbut's division along. We reached Memphis on the 21st, and on the 22d I posted my three brigades mostly in and near Fort Dickering, and Hurlbut's division next below on the river-bank by reason of the scarcity of water, except in the Mississippi River itself. The weather was intensely hot. The same order that took us to Memphis required me to send the division of General Lew Wallace (then commanded by Brigadier-General A. P. Hovey) to Helena, Arkansas, to report to General Curtis, which was easily accomplished by steamboat. I made my own camp in a vacant lot, near Mr. Moon's house, and gave my chief attention to the construction of Fort Pickering, then in charge of Major Prime, United States Engineers; to perfecting the drill and discipline of the two divisions under my command; and to the administration of civil affairs.

At the time when General Halleck was summoned from Corinth to Washington, to succeed McClellan as commander-in-chief, I surely expected of him immediate and important results. The Army of the Ohio was at the time marching toward Chattanooga, and was strung from Eastport by Huntsville to Bridgeport, under the command of General Buell. In like manner, the Army of the Tennessee was strung along the same general line, from Memphis to Tuscumbia, and was commanded by General Grant, with no common commander for both these forces: so that the great army which General Halleck had so well assembled at Corinth, was put on the defensive, with a frontage of three hundred miles. Soon thereafter the rebels displayed peculiar energy and military skill. General Bragg had reorganized the army of Beauregard at Tupelo, carried it rapidly and skillfully toward Chattanooga, whence he boldly assumed the offensive, moving straight for Nashville and Louisville, and compelling General Buell to fall back to the Ohio River at Louisville.

The army of Van Dorn and Price had been brought from the trans-Mississippi Department to the east of the river, and was collected at and about Holly Springs, where, reenforced by Armstrong's and Forrests cavalry, it amounted to about forty thousand brave and hardy soldiers. These were General Grant's immediate antagonists, and so many and large detachments had been drawn from him, that for a time he was put on the defensive. In person he had his headquarters at Corinth, with the three divisions of Hamilton, Davies, and McKean, under the immediate orders of General Rosecrans. General Ord had succeeded to the division of McClernand (who had also gone to Washington), and held Bolivar and Grand Junction. I had in Memphis my own and Hurlbut's divisions, and other smaller detachments were strung along the Memphis & Charleston road. But the enemy's detachments could strike this road at so many points, that no use could be made of it, and General Grant had to employ the railroads, from Columbus, Kentucky, to Corinth and Grand Junction, by way of Jackson, Tennessee, a point common to both roads, and held in some force.

In the early part of September the enemy in our front manifested great activity, feeling with cavalry at all points, and on the 13th General Van Dorn threatened Corinth, while General Price seized the town of Iuka, which was promptly abandoned by a small garrison under Colonel Murphy. Price's force was about eight thousand men, and the general impression was that he was en route for Eastport, with the purpose to cross the Tennessee River in the direction of Nashville, in aid of General Bragg, then in full career for Kentucky. General Grant determined to attack him in force, prepared to regain Corinth before Van Dorn could reach it. He had drawn Ord to Corinth, and moved him, by Burnsville, on Iuka, by the main road, twenty-six miles. General Grant accompanied this column as far as Burnsville. At the same time he had dispatched Rosecrans by roads to the south, via Jacinto, with orders to approach Iuka by the two main roads, coming into Iuka from the south, viz., they Jacinto and Fulton roads.

On the 18th General Ord encountered the enemy about four miles out of Iuka. His orders contemplated that he should not make a serious attack, until Rosecrans had gained his position on the south; but, as usual, Rosecrans had encountered difficulties in the confusion of roads, his head of column did not reach the vicinity of Iuka till 4 p.m. of the 19th, and then his troops were long drawn out on the single Jacinto road, leaving the Fulton road clear for Price's use. Price perceived his advantage, and attacked with vehemence the head of Rosecrans's column, Hamilton's division, beating it back, capturing a battery, and killing and disabling seven hundred and thirty-six men, so that when night closed in Rosecrans was driven to the defensive, and Price, perceiving his danger, deliberately withdrew by the Fulton road, and the next morning was gone. Although General Ord must have been within four or six miles of this battle, he did not hear a sound; and he or General Grant did not know of it till advised the next morning by a courier who had made a wide circuit to reach them. General Grant was much offended with General Rosecrans because of this affair, but in my experience these concerted movements generally fail, unless with the very best kind of troops, and then in a country on whose roads some reliance can be placed, which is not the case in Northern Mississippi. If Price was aiming for Tennessee; he failed, and was therefore beaten. He made a wide circuit by the south, and again joined Van Dorn.

On the 6th of September, at Memphis, I received an order from General Grant dated the 2d, to send Hurlbut's division to Brownsville, in the direction of Bolivar, thence to report by letter to him at Jackson. The division started the same day, and, as our men and officers had been together side by side from the first landing at Shiloh, we felt the parting like the breaking up of a family. But General Grant was forced to use every man, for he knew well that Van Dorn could attack him at pleasure, at any point of his long line. To be the better prepared, on the 23d of September he took post himself at Jackson, Tennessee, with a small reserve force, and gave Rosecrans command of Corinth, with his three divisions and some detachments, aggregating about twenty thousand men. He posted General Ord with his own and Hurlbut'a divisions at Bolivar, with outposts toward Grand Junction and Lagrange. These amounted to nine or ten thousand men, and I held Memphis with my own division, amounting to about six thousand men. The whole of General Grant's men at that time may have aggregated fifty thousand, but he had to defend a frontage of a hundred and fifty miles, guard some two hundred miles of railway, and as much river. Van Dom had forty thousand men, united, at perfect liberty to move in any direction, and to choose his own point of attack, under cover of woods, and a superior body of cavalry, familiar with every foot of the ground. Therefore General Grant had good reason for telegraphing to General Halleck, on the 1st of October, that his position was precarious, "but I hope to get out of it all right." In Memphis my business was to hold fast that important flank, and by that date Fort Dickering had been made very strong, and capable of perfect defense by a single brigade. I therefore endeavored by excursions to threaten Van Dorn's detachments to the southeast and east. I repeatedly sent out strong detachments toward Holly Springs, which was his main depot of supply; and General Grierson, with his Sixth Illinois, the only cavalry I had, made some bold and successful dashes at the Coldwater, compelling Van Dorn to cover it by Armstrong's whole division of cavalry. Still, by the 1st of October, General Grant was satisfied that the enemy was meditating an attack in force on Bolivar or Corinth; and on the 2d Van Dorn made his appearance near Corinth, with his entire army. On the 3d he moved down on that place from the north and northwest, General Roseerana went out some four miles to meet him, but was worsted and compelled to fall back within the line of his forts. These had been began under General Halleck, but were much strengthened by General Grant, and consisted of several detached redoubts, bearing on each other, and inclosing the town and the depots of stores at the intersection of the two railroads. Van Dorn closed down on the forts by the evening of the 3d, and on the morning of the 4th assaulted with great vehemence. Our men, covered by good parapets, fought gallantly, and defended their posts well, inflicting terrible losses on the enemy, so that by noon the rebels were repulsed at all points, and drew off, leaving their dead and wounded in our hands. Their losses, were variously estimated, but the whole truth will probably never be known, for in that army reports and returns were not the fashion. General Rosecrans admitted his own loss to be three hundred and fifteen killed, eighteen hundred and twelve wounded, and two hundred and thirty-two missing or prisoners, and claimed on the part of the rebels fourteen hundred and twenty-three dead, two thousand and twenty-five prisoners and wounded. Of course, most of the wounded must have gone off or been carried off, so that, beyond doubt, the rebel army lost at Corinth fully six thousand men.

Meantime, General Grant, at Jackson, had dispatched Brigadier-General McPherson, with a brigade, directly for Corinth, which reached General Rosecrans after the battle; and, in anticipation of his victory, had ordered him to pursue instantly, notifying him that he had ordered Ord's and Hurlbut's divisions rapidly across to Pocahontas, so as to strike the rebels in flank. On the morning of the 5th, General Ord reached the Hatchie River, at Davies bridge, with four thousand men; crossed over and encountered the retreating army, captured a battery and several hundred prisoners, dispersing the rebel advance, and forcing the main column to make a wide circuit by the south in order to cross the Hatchie River. Had General Rosecrans pursued promptly, and been on the heels of this mass of confused and routed men, Van Dorn's army would surely have been utterly ruined; as it was, Van Dom regained Holly Springs somewhat demoralized.

General Rosecrans did not begin his pursuit till the next morning, the 5th, and it was then too late. General Grant was again displeased with him, and never became fully reconciled. General Rosecrans was soon after relieved, and transferred to the Army of the Cumberland, in Tennessee, of which he afterward obtained the command, in place of General Buell, who was removed.

The effect of the battle of Corinth was very great. It was, indeed, a decisive blow to the Confederate cause in our quarter, and changed the whole aspect of affairs in West

Tennessee. From the timid defensive we were at once enabled to assume the bold offensive. In Memphis I could see its effects upon the citizens, and they openly admitted that their cause had sustained a death-blow. But the rebel government was then at its maximum strength; Van Dorn was reenforced, and very soon Lieutenant-General J. C. Pemberton arrived and assumed the command, adopting for his line the Tallahatchie River, with an advance-guard along the Coldwater, and smaller detachments forward at Grand Junction and Hernando. General Grant, in like manner, was reenforced by new regiments.

Out of those which were assigned to Memphis, I organized two new brigades, and placed them under officers who had gained skill and experience during the previous campaign.

CHAPTER XII.
MEMPHIS TO ARKANSAS POST.

JULY, 1882 TO JANUARY, 1883

When we first entered Memphis, July 21,1862, I found the place dead; no business doing, the stores closed, churches, schools, and every thing shut up. The people were all more or less in sympathy with our enemies, and there was a strong prospect that the whole civil population would become a dead weight on our hands. Inasmuch as the Mississippi River was then in our possession northward, and steamboats were freely plying with passengers and freight, I caused all the stores to be opened, churches, schools, theatres, and places of amusement, to be reestablished, and very soon Memphis resumed its appearance of an active, busy, prosperous place. I also restored the mayor (whose name was Parks) and the city government to the performance of their public functions, and required them to maintain a good civil police.

Up to that date neither Congress nor the President had made any clear, well-defined rules touching the negro slaves, and the different generals had issued orders according to their own political sentiments. Both Generals Halleck and Grant regarded the slave as still a slave, only that the labor of the slave belonged to his owner, if faithful to the Union, or to the United States, if the master had taken up arms against the Government, or adhered to the fortunes of the rebellion. Therefore, in Memphis, we received all fugitives, put them to work on the fortifications, supplied them with food and clothing, and reserved the question of payment of wages for future decision. No force was allowed to be used to restore a fugitive slave to his master in any event; but if the master proved his loyalty, he was usually permitted to see his slave, and, if he could persuade him to return home, it was permitted. Cotton, also, was a fruitful subject of controversy. The Secretary of the Treasury; Mr. Chase, was extremely anxious at that particular time to promote the purchase of cotton, because each bale was worth, in gold, about three hundred dollars, and answered the purpose of coin in our foreign exchanges. He therefore encouraged the trade, so that hundreds of greedy speculators flocked down the Mississippi, and resorted to all sorts of measures to obtain cotton from the interior, often purchasing it from negroes who did not own it, but who knew where it was concealed. This whole business was taken from the jurisdiction of the military, and committed to Treasury agents appointed by Mr. Chase.

Other questions absorbed the attention of military commanders; and by way of illustration I here insert a few letters from my "letter-book," which contains hundreds on similar subjects:

HEADQUARTERS FIFTH DIVISION
Memphis, Tennessee, August 11, 1862

Hon. S. P. CHASE, Secretary of the Treasury.

Sir: Your letter of August 2d, just received, invites my discussion of the cotton question.

I will write plainly and slowly, because I know you have no time to listen to trifles. This is no trifle; when one nation is at war with another, all the people of the one are enemies of the other: then the rules are plain and easy of understanding. Most unfortunately, the war in which we are now engaged has been complicated with the belief on the one hand that all on the other are not enemies. It would have been better if, at the outset, this mistake had not been made, and it is wrong longer to be misled by it. The Government of the United States may now safely proceed on the proper rule that all in the South are enemies of all in the North; and not only are they unfriendly, but all who can procure arms now bear them as organized regiments, or as guerrillas. There is not a garrison in Tennessee where a man can go beyond the sight of the flag-staff without being shot or captured. It so happened that these people had cotton, and, whenever they apprehended our large armies would move, they destroyed the cotton in the belief that, of course, we world seize it, and convert it to our use. They did not and could not dream that we would pay money for it. It had been condemned to destruction by their own acknowledged government, and was therefore lost to their people; and could have been, without injustice, taken by us, and sent away, either as absolute prize of war, or for future compensation. But the commercial enterprise of the Jews soon discovered that ten cents would buy a pound of cotton behind our army; that four cents would take it to Boston, where they could receive thirty cents in gold. The bait was too tempting, and it spread like fire, when here they discovered that salt, bacon, powder, fire-arms, percussion-caps, etc., etc., were worth as much as gold; and, strange to say, this traffic was not only permitted, but encouraged. Before we in the interior could know it, hundreds, yea thousands of barrels of salt and millions of dollars had been disbursed; and I have no doubt that Bragg's army at Tupelo, and Van Dorn's at Vicksburg, received enough salt to make bacon, without which they could not have moved their armies in mass; and that from ten to twenty thousand fresh arms, and a due supply of cartridges, have also been got, I am equally satisfied. As soon as I got to Memphis, having seen the effect in the interior, I ordered (only as to my own command) that gold, silver, and Treasury notes, were contraband of war, and should not go into the interior, where all were hostile. It is idle to talk about Union men here: many want peace, and fear war and its results; but all prefer a Southern, independent government, and are fighting or working for it. Every gold dollar that was spent for cotton, was sent to the seaboard, to be exchanged for bank-notes and Confederate scrip, which will buy goods here, and are taken in ordinary transactions. I therefore required cotton to be paid for in such notes, by an obligation to pay at the end of the war, or by a deposit of the price in the hands of a trustee, viz., the United States Quartermaster. Under these rules cotton is being obtained about as fast as by any other process, and yet the enemy receives no "aid or comfort." Under the "gold" rule, the country people who had concealed their cotton from the burners, and who openly scorned our greenbacks, were willing enough to take Tennessee money, which will buy their groceries; but now that the trade is to be encouraged, and gold paid out, I admit that cotton will be sent in by our open enemies, who can make better use of gold than they can of their hidden bales of cotton.

I may not appreciate the foreign aspect of the question, but my views on this may be ventured. If England ever threatens war because we don't furnish her cotton, tell her plainly if she can't employ and feed her own people, to send them here, where they cannot only earn an honest living, but soon secure independence by moderate labor. We are not bound to furnish her cotton. She has more reason to fight the South for burning that cotton, than us for not shipping it. To aid the South on this ground would be hypocrisy which the world would detect at once. Let her make her ultimatum, and there are enough generous minds in Europe that will counteract her in the balance. Of course her motive is to cripple a power that rivals her in commerce and manufactures,

143

that threatens even to usurp her history. In twenty more years of prosperity, it will require a close calculation to determine whether England, her laws and history, claim for a home the Continent of America or the Isle of Britain. Therefore, finding us in a death-struggle for existence, she seems to seek a quarrel to destroy both parts in detail.

Southern people know this full well, and will only accept the alliance of England in order to get arms and manufactures in exchange for their cotton. The Southern Confederacy will accept no other mediation, because she knows full well that in Old England her slaves and slavery will receive no more encouragement than in New England.

France certainly does not need our cotton enough to disturb her equilibrium, and her mediation would be entitled to a more respect consideration than on the part of her present ally. But I feel assured the French will not encourage rebellion and secession anywhere as a political doctrine. Certainly all the German states must be our ardent friends; and, in case of European intervention; they could not be kept down.

With great respect, your obedient servant,

W. T. SHERMAN, Major-General.

HEADQUARTERS FIFTH DIVISION, ARMY OF THE TENNESSEE, Memphis, July 23, 1862

Dr. E. S. PLUMMER and others, Physician in Memphis, Signers to a Petition.

GENTLEMEN: I have this moment received your communication, and assure you that it grieves my heart thus to be the instrument of adding to the seeming cruelty and hardship of this unnatural war.

On my arrival here, I found my predecessor (General Hovey) had issued an order permitting the departure south of all persons subject to the conscript law of the Southern Confederacy. Many applications have been made to me to modify this order, but I regarded it as a condition precedent by which I was bound in honor, and therefore I have made no changes or modifications; nor shall I determine what action I shall adopt in relation to persons unfriendly to our cause who remain after the time limited by General Hovey's order had expired. It is now sunset, and all who have not availed themselves of General Hovey's authority, and who remain in Memphis, are supposed to be loyal and true men.

I will only say that I cannot allow the personal convenience of even a large class of ladies to influence me in my determination to make Memphis a safe place of operations for an army, and all people who are unfriendly should forthwith prepare to depart in such direction as I may hereafter indicate.

Surgeons are not liable to be made prisoners of war, but they should not reside within the lines of an army which they regard as hostile. The situation would be too delicate.

I am, with great respect, your obedient servant,

W. T. SHERMAN, Major-General.

HEADQUARTERS, MEMPHIS, July 24, 1862

SAMUEL SAWYER, Esq., Editor Union Appeal, Memphis.

DEAR SIR: It is well I should come to an understanding at once with the press as well as the people of

Memphis, which I am ordered to command; which means, to control for the interest, welfare; and glory of the whole Government of the United States.

Personalities in a newspaper are wrong and criminal. Thus, though you meant to be complimentary in your sketch of my career, you make more than a dozen mistakes of fact, which I need not correct, as I don't desire my biography to be written till I am dead. It is enough for the world to know that I live and am a soldier, bound to obey the orders of my superiors, the laws of my country, and to venerate its Constitution; and that, when discretion is given me, I shall exercise it wisely and account to my superiors.

I regard your article headed "City Council—General Sherman and Colonel Slack," as highly indiscreet. Of course, no person who can jeopardize the safety of Memphis can remain here, much less exercise public authority; but I must take time, and be satisfied that injustice be not done.

If the parties named be the men you describe, the fact should not be published, to put them on their guard and thus to encourage their escape. The evidence should be carefully collected, authenticated, and then placed in my hands. But your statement of facts is entirely qualified; in my mind, and loses its force by your negligence of the very simple facts within your reach as to myself: I had been in the army six years in 1846; am not related by blood to any member of Lucas, Turner & Co.; was associated with them in business six years (instead of two); am not colonel of the Fifteenth Infantry, but of the Thirteenth. Your correction, this morning, of the acknowledged error as to General Denver and others, is still erroneous. General Morgan L. Smith did not belong to my command at the battle of Shiloh at all, but he was transferred to my division just before reaching Corinth. I mention these facts in kindness, to show you how wrong it is to speak of persons.

I will attend to the judge, mayor, Boards of Aldermen, and policemen, all in good time.

Use your influence to reestablish system, order, government. You may rest easy that no military commander is going to neglect internal safety, or to guard against external danger; but to do right requires time, and more patience than I usually possess. If I find the press of Memphis actuated by high principle and a sole devotion to their country, I will be their best friend; but, if I find them personal, abusive, dealing in innuendoes and hints at a blind venture, and looking to their own selfish aggrandizement and fame, then they had better look out; for I regard such persons as greater enemies to their country and to mankind than the men who, from a mistaken sense of State pride, have taken up muskets, and fight us about as hard as we care about. In haste, but in kindness, yours, etc.,

W. T. SHERMAN, Major-General.

HEADQUARTERS FIFTH DIVISION,
MEMPHIS, TENNESSEE, July 27, 1882.

JOHN PARK, Mayor of Memphis, present.

Sir: Yours of July 24th is before me, and has received, as all similar papers ever will, my careful and most respectful consideration. I have the most unbounded respect for the civil law, courts, and authorities, and shall do all in my power to restore them to their proper use, viz., the protection of life, liberty, and property.

Unfortunately, at this time, civil war prevails in the land, and necessarily the military, for the time being, must be superior to the civil authority, but it does not therefore destroy it. Civil courts and executive officers should still exist and perform duties, without which civil or municipal bodies would soon pass into disrespect—an end to be avoided. I am glad to find in Memphis a mayor and municipal authorities not only in existence, but in the co-exercise of important functions, and I shall endeavor to restore one or more civil tribunals for the arbitration of contracts and punishment of crimes, which the military have neither time nor inclination to interfere with. Among these, first in importance is the maintenance of order, peace, and quiet, within the jurisdiction of Memphis. To insure this, I will keep a strong provost guard in the city, but will *limit their duty to guarding public property held or claimed by the United States, and for the arrest and confinement of State prisoners and soldiers who are disorderly or improperly away from their regiments. This guard ought not to arrest citizens for disorder or minor crimes. This should be done by the city police. I understand that the city police is too weak in numbers to accomplish this perfectly, and I therefore recommend that the City Council at once take steps to increase this force to a number which, in their judgment, day and night can enforce your ordinances as to peace, quiet, and order; so that any change in our military dispositions will not have a tendency to leave your people unguarded. I am willing to instruct the provost guard to assist the police force when any combination is made too strong for them to overcome; but the city police should be strong enough for any probable contingency. The cost of maintaining this police force must necessarily fall upon all citizens equitably. I am not willing, nor do I think it good policy, for the city authorities to collect the taxes belonging to the State and County, as you recommend; for these would have to be refunded. Better meet the expenses at once by a new tax on all interested. Therefore, if you, on consultation with the proper municipal body, will frame a good bill for the increase of your police force, and for raising the necessary means for their support and maintenance, I will approve it and aid you in the collection of the tax. Of course, I cannot suggest how this tax should be laid, but I think that it should be made uniform on all interests, real estate, and personal property, including money, and merchandise.*

All who are protected should share the expenses in proportion to the interests involved. I am, with respect, your obedient servant,

W. T. SHERMAN, Major-General commanding.

HEADQUARTERS FIFTH DIVISION,
MEMPHIS, August 7, 1862.

Captain FITCH, Assistant Quartermaster, Memphis, Tennessee.

SIR: The duties devolving on the quartermaster of this post, in addition to his legitimate functions, are very important and onerous, and I am fully aware that the task is more than should devolve on one man. I will endeavor to get you help in the person of some commissioned officer, and, if possible, one under bond, as he must handle large amounts of money in trust; but, for the present, we most execute the duties falling to our share as well as possible. On the subject of vacant houses, General Grant's orders are: "Take possession of all vacant stores and houses in the city, and have them rented at reasonable rates; rent to be paid monthly in advance. These buildings, with their tenants, can be turned over to proprietors on proof of loyalty; also take charge of such as have been leased out by disloyal owners."

I understand that General Grant takes the rents and profits of this class of real property under the rules and laws of war, and not under the confiscation act of Congress; therefore the question of title is not involved simply the possession, and the rents and profits of houses belonging to our enemies, which are not vacant, we hold in trust for them or the Government, according to the future decisions of the proper tribunals.

Mr. McDonald, your chief agent in renting and managing this business, called on me last evening and left with me written questions, which it would take a volume to answer and a Webster to elucidate; but as we can only attempt plain, substantial justice, I will answer these questions as well as I can, briefly and to the point.

First. When ground is owned by parties who have gone south, and have leased the ground to parties now in the city who own the improvements on the ground?

Answer. The United States takes the rents due the owner of the land; does not disturb the owner of the improvements.

Second. When parties owning houses have gone south, and the tenant has given his notes for the rent in advance?

146

Answer. Notes are mere evidence of the debt due landlord. The tenant pays the rent to the quartermaster, who gives a bond of indemnity against the notes representing the debt for the particular rent.

Third. When the tenant has expended several months' rent in repairs on the house?

Answer. Of course, allow all such credits on reasonable proof and showing.

Fourth. When the owner has gone south, and parties here hold liens on the property and are collecting the rents to satisfy their liens?

Answer. The rent of a house can only be mortgaged to a person in possession. If a loyal tenant be in possession and claim the rent from himself as due to himself on some other debt, allow it; but, if not in actual possession of the property, rents are not good liens for a debt, but must be paid to the quartermaster.

Fifth. Of parties claiming foreign protection?

Answer. Many claim foreign protection who are not entitled to it. If they are foreign subjects residing for business in this, country, they are entitled to consideration and protection so long as they obey the laws of the country. If they occupy houses belonging to absent rebels, they must pay rent to the quarter-master. If they own property, they must occupy it by themselves, tenants, or servants.

Eighth. When houses are occupied and the owner has gone south, leaving an agent to collect rent for his benefit?

Answer. Rent must be paid to the quartermaster. No agent can collect and remit money south without subjecting himself to arrest and trial for aiding and abetting the public enemy.

Ninth.. When houses are owned by loyal citizens, but are unoccupied?

Answer. Such should not be disturbed, but it would be well to advise them to have some servant at the house to occupy it.

Tenth. When parties who occupy the house are creditors of the owner, who has gone south? Answer. You only look to collection of rents. Any person who transmits money south is liable to arrest and trial for aiding and abetting the enemy; but I do not think it our business to collect debts other than rents.

Eleventh. When the parties who own the property have left the city under General Hovey's Order No. 1, but are in the immediate neighborhood, on their plantations?

Answer. It makes no difference where they are, so they are absent.

Twelfth. When movable property is found in stores that are closed?

Answer. The goods are security for the rent. If the owner of the goods prefers to remove the goods to paying rent, he can do so.

Thirteenth. When the owner lives in town, and refuses to take the oath of allegiance?

Answer. If the house be occupied, it does not fall under the order. If the house be vacant, it does. The owner can recover his property by taking the oath.

All persons in Memphis residing within our military lines are presumed to be loyal, good citizens, and may at any moment be called to serve on juries, posses comitatua, or other civil service required by the Constitution and laws of our country. Should they be called upon to do such duty, which would require them to acknowledge their allegiance and subordination to the Constitution of the United States, it would then be too late to refuse. So long as they remain quiet and conform to these laws, they are entitled to protection in their property and lives.

We have nothing to do with confiscation. We only deal with possession, and therefore the necessity of a strict accountability, because the United States assumes the place of trustee, and must account to the rightful owner for his property, rents, and profits. In due season courts will be established to execute the laws, the confiscation act included, when we will be relieved of this duty and trust. Until that time, every opportunity should be given to the wavering and disloyal to return to their allegiance to the Constitution of their birth or adoption. I am, etc.,

W. T. SHERMAN.

Major-General commanding.

*HEADQUARTERS FIFTH DIVISION
MEMPHIS, TENNESSEE, August 26,1862*

Major-General GRANT, Corinth, Mississippi.

Sir: In pursuance of your request that I should keep you advised of matters of interest here, in addition to the purely official matters, I now write.

I dispatched promptly the thirteen companies of cavalry, nine of Fourth Illinois, and four of Eleventh Illinois, to their respective destinations, punctually on the 23d instant, although the order was only received on the 22d. I received at the same time, from Colonel Dickey, the notice that the bridge over Hatchie was burned, and therefore I prescribed their order of march via Bolivar. They started at 12 m. of the 23d, and I have no news of them since. None of the cavalry ordered to me is yet heard from.

The guerrillas have destroyed several bridges over Wolf Creek; one at Raleigh, on the road by which I had prescribed trade and travel to and from the city. I have a strong guard at the lower bridge over Wolf River, by which we can reach the country to the north of that stream; but, as the Confederates have burned their own bridges, I will hold them to my order, and allow no trade over any other road than the one prescribed, using the lower or Randolph road for our own convenience. I am still satisfied there is no large force of rebels anywhere in the neighborhood. All the navy gunboats are below except the St. Louis, which lies off the city. When Commodore Davis passes down from Cairo, I will try to see him, and get him to exchange the St. Louis for a fleeter boat not iron-clad; one that can move up and down the river, to break up ferry-boats and canoes, and to prevent all passing across the river. Of course, in spite of all our efforts, smuggling is carried on. We occasionally make hauls of clothing, gold-lace, buttons, etc., but I am satisfied that salt and arms are got to the interior somehow. I have addressed the Board of Trade a letter on this point, which will enable us to control it better.

You may have been troubled at hearing reports of drunkenness here. There was some after pay-day, but generally all is as quiet and orderly as possible. I traverse the city every day and night, and assert that Memphis is and has been as orderly a city as St. Louis, Cincinnati, or New York.

Before the city authorities undertook to license saloons, there was as much whiskey here as now, and it would take all my command as customhouse inspectors, to break open all the parcels and packages containing liquor. I can destroy all groggeries and shops where soldiers get liquor just as we would in St. Louis.

The newspapers are accusing me of cruelty to the sick; as base a charge as was ever made. I would not let the Sanitary Committee carry off a boat-load of sick, because I have no right to. We have good hospitals here, and plenty of them. Our regimental hospitals are in the camps of the men, and the sick do much better there than in the general hospitals; so say my division surgeon and the regimental surgeons. The civilian doctors would, if permitted, take away our entire command. General Curtis sends his sick up here, but usually no nurses; and it is not right that nurses should be taken from my command for his sick. I think that, when we are endeavoring to raise soldiers and to instruct them, it is bad policy to keep them at hospitals as attendants and nurses.

I send you Dr. Derby's acknowledgment that he gave the leave of absence of which he was charged. I have placed him in arrest, in obedience to General Halleck's orders, but he remains in charge of the Overton Hospital, which is not full of patients.

The State Hospital also is not full, and I cannot imagine what Dr. Derby wants with the Female Academy on Vance Street. I will see him again, and now that he is the chief at Overton Hospital, I think he will not want the academy. Still, if he does, under your orders I will cause it to be vacated by the children and Sisters of Mercy. They have just advertised for more scholars, and will be sadly disappointed. If, however, this building or any other be needed for a hospital, it must be taken; but really, in my heart, I do not see what possible chance there is, under present circumstances, of filling with patients the two large hospitals now in use, besides the one asked for. I may, however, be mistaken in the particular building asked for by Dr. Derby, and will go myself to see.

The fort is progressing well, Captain Jenney having arrived. Sixteen heavy guns are received, with a large amount of shot and shell, but the platforms are not yet ready; still, if occasion should arise for dispatch, I can put a larger force to work. Captain Prime, when here, advised that the work should proceed regularly under the proper engineer officers and laborers. I am, etc.,

W. T. SHERMAN, Major-General commanding.

HEADQUARTERS FIFTH DIVISION
MEMPHIS, TENNESSEE, September 4, 1862

Colonel J. C, KELTON, Assistant Adjutant-General, Headquarters of the army, Washington, D. C.

DEAR COLONEL: Please acknowledge to the major-general commanding the receipt by me of his letter, and convey to him my assurances that I have promptly modified my first instructions about cotton, so as to conform to his orders. Trade in cotton is now free, but in all else I endeavor so to control it that the enemy shall receive no contraband goods, or any aid or comfort; still I feel sure that the officers of steamboats are sadly tempted by high prices to land salt and other prohibited articles at waypoints along the river. This, too, in time will be checked. All seems well here and hereabout; no large body of the enemy within striking distance. A force of about two thousand, cavalry passed through Grand Junction north last Friday, and fell on a detachment of the Bolivar army at Middleburg, the result of which is doubtless reported to you. As soon as I heard of the movement, I dispatched a force to the southeast by way of diversion, and am satisfied that the enemy's infantry and artillery fell back in consequence behind the Tallahatchie. The weather is very hot, country very dry, and dust as bad as possible. I hold my two divisions ready, with their original complement of transportation, for field service. Of course all things most now depend on events in front of Washington and in Kentucky. The gunboat Eastport and four transports loaded with prisoners of war destined for Vicksburg have been lying before Memphis for two days, but are now steaming up to resume their voyage. Our fort progresses well, but our guns are not yet mounted. The engineers are now shaping the banquette to receive platforms. I expect Captain Prime from Corinth in two or three days.

I am, with great respect, yours,

W. T. SHERMAN, Major-General commanding.

HEADQUARTERS FIFTH DIVISION
MEMPHIS, TENNESSEE, September 21, 1862

Editor Bulletin.

SIR: Your comments on the recent orders of Generals Halleck and McClellan afford the occasion appropriate for me to make public the fact that there is a law of Congress, as old as our Government itself, but reenacted on the 10th of April, 1806, and in force ever since. That law reads:

"All officers and soldiers are to behave themselves orderly in quarters and on the march; and whoever shall commit any waste or spoil, either in walks of trees, parks, warrens, fish-ponds, houses and gardens, cornfields, inclosures or meadows, or shall maliciously destroy any property whatever belonging to the inhabitants of the United States, unless by order of the commander-in-chief of the armies of said United States, shall (besides such penalties as they are liable to by law) be punished according to the nature and degree of the offense, by the judgment of a general or regimental court-martial."

Such is the law of Congress; and the orders of the commander-in-chief are, that officers or soldiers convicted of straggling and pillaging shall be punished with death. These orders have not come to me officially, but I have seen them in newspapers, and am satisfied that they express the determination of the commander-in-chief. Straggling and pillaging have ever been great military crimes; and every officer and soldier in my command knows what stress I have laid upon them, and that, so far as in my power lies, I will punish them to the full extent of the law and orders.

The law is one thing, the execution of the law another. God himself has commanded: "Thou shalt not kill," "thou shalt not steal," "thou shalt not covet thy neighbor's goods," etc. Will any one say these things are not done now as well as before these laws were announced at Sinai. I admit the law to be that "no officer or soldier of the United States shall commit waste or destruction of cornfields, orchards, potato-patches, or any kind of pillage on the property of friend or foe near Memphis," and that I stand prepared to execute the law as far as possible.

No officer or soldier should enter the house or premises of any peaceable citizen, no matter what his politics, unless on business; and no such officer or soldier can force an entrance unless he have a written order from a commanding officer or provost-marshal, which written authority must be exhibited if demanded. When property such as forage, building or other materials are needed by the United States, a receipt will be given by the officer taking them, which receipt should be presented to the quartermaster, who will substitute therefor a regular voucher, to be paid according to the circumstances of the case. If the officer refuse to give such receipt, the citizen may fairly infer that the property is wrongfully taken, and he should, for his own protection, ascertain the name, rank, and regiment of the officer, and report him in writing. If any soldier commits waste or destruction, the person whose property is thus wasted must find out the name, company, and regiment of the actual transgressor. In order to punish there must be a trial, and there must be testimony. It is not sufficient that a general accusation be made, that soldiers are doing this or that. I cannot punish my whole command, or a whole battalion, because one or two bad soldiers do wrong. The punishment must reach the perpetrators, and no one can identify them as well as the party who is interested. The State of Tennessee does not hold itself responsible for acts of larceny committed by her citizens, nor does the United Staten or any other nation. These are individual acts of wrong, and punishment can only be inflicted on the wrong-doer. I know the difficulty of identifying particular soldiers, but difficulties do not alter the importance of principles of justice. They should stimulate the parties to increase their efforts to find out the actual perpetrators of the crime.

Colonels of regiments and commanders of corps are liable to severe punishment for permitting their men to leave their camps to commit waste or destruction; but I know full well that many of the acts attributed to soldiers are committed by citizens and negroes, and are charged to soldiers because of a desire to find fault with them; but this only reacts upon the community and increases the mischief. While every officer would willingly follow up an accusation against any one or more of his men whose names or description were given immediately after the discovery of the act, he would naturally resent any general charge against his good men, for the criminal conduct of a few bad ones.

I have examined into many of the cases of complaint made in this general way, and have felt mortified that our soldiers should do acts which are nothing more or less than stealing, but I was powerless without some clew whereby to reach the rightful party. I know that the great mass of our soldiers would scorn to steal or commit crime, and I will not therefore entertain vague and general complaints, but stand, prepared always to follow up any reasonable complaint when the charge is definite and the names of witnesses furnished.

I know, moreover, in some instances when our soldiers are complained of, that they have been insulted by sneering remarks about "Yankees," "Northern barbarians," "Lincoln's hirelings," etc. People who use such language must seek redress through some one else, for I will not tolerate insults to our country or cause. When people forget their obligations to a Government that made them respected among the nations of the earth, and speak contemptuously of the flag which is the silent emblem of that country, I will not go out of my way to protect them or their property. I will punish the soldiers for trespass or waste if adjudged by a court-martial, because they disobey orders; but soldiers are men and citizens as well as soldiers, and should promptly resent any insult to their country, come from what quarter it may. I mention this phase because it is too common. Insult to a soldier does not justify pillage, but it takes from the officer the disposition he would otherwise feel to follow up the inquiry and punish the wrong-doers.

Again, armies in motion or stationary must commit some waste. Flankers must let down fences and cross fields; and, when an attack is contemplated or apprehended, a command will naturally clear the ground of houses, fences, and trees. This is waste, but is the natural consequence of war, chargeable on those who caused the war. So in fortifying a place, dwelling-houses must be taken, materials used, even wasted, and great damage done, which in the end may prove useless. This, too, is an expense not chargeable to us, but to those who made the war; and generally war is destruction and nothing else.

We must bear this in mind, that however peaceful things look, we are really at war; and much that looks like waste or destruction is only the removal of objects that obstruct our fire, or would afford cover to an enemy.

This class of waste must be distinguished from the wanton waste committed by army-stragglers, which is wrong, and can be punished by the death-penalty if proper testimony can be produced.

Yours, etc.,

W. T. SHERMAN, Major-General commanding.

Satisfied that, in the progress of the war, Memphis would become an important depot, I pushed forward the construction of Fort Pickering, kept most of the troops in camps back of the city, and my own headquarters remained in tents on the edge of the city, near Mr. Moon's house, until, on the approach of winter, Mrs. Sherman came down with the children to visit me, when I took a house nearer the fort.

All this time battalion and brigade drills were enforced, so that, when the season approached for active operations farther south, I had my division in the best possible order, and about the 1st of November it was composed as follows:

First Brigade, Brigadier-General M. L. SMITH—Eighth Missouri, Colonel G. A. Smith; Sixth Missouri, Colonel Peter E. Bland; One Hundred and Thirteenth Illinois, Colonel George B. Hoge; Fifty-fourth Ohio, Colonel T. Kilby Smith; One Hundred and Twentieth Illinois, Colonel G. W. McKeaig.

Second Brigade, Colonel JOHN ADAIR McDOWELL.—Sixth Iowa, Lieutenant-Colonel John M. Corse; Fortieth Illinois, Colonel J. W. Booth; Forty-sixth Ohio, Colonel O. C. Walcutt; Thirteenth United States Infantry, First Battalion, Major D. Chase.

Third Brigade, Brigadier-General J. W. DENVER.—Forty-eighth Ohio, Colonel P. J. Sullivan; Fifty-third Ohio, Colonel W. S. Jones; Seventieth Ohio, Colonel J. R. Cockerill.

Fourth Brigade, Colonel DAVID STUART.—Fifty-fifth Illinois, Colonel O. Malmburg; Fifty-seventh Ohio, Colonel W. Mungen; Eighty-third Indiana, Colonel B. Spooner; One Hundred and Sixteenth

Illinois, Colonel Tupper; One Hundred and Twenty-seventh Illinois, Lieutenant-Colonel Eldridge.

Fifth Brigade, Colonel R. P. BUCKLAND.—Seventy-second Ohio, Lieutenant-Colonel D. W. C. Loudon; Thirty-second Wisconsin, Colonel J. W. Howe; Ninety-third Indiana, Colonel Thomas; Ninety-third Illinois, Major J. M. Fisher.

Subsequently, Brigadier-General J. G. Lauman arrived at Memphis, and I made up a sixth brigade, and organized these six brigades into three divisions, under Brigadier-Generals M. L. Smith, J. W. Denver, and J. G. Lauman.

About the 17th of November I received an order from General Grant, dated:

LAGRANGE, November 16, 1862.
Meet me at Columbus, Kentucky, on Thursday next. If you have a good map of the country south of you, take it up with you.
U. S. GRANT, Major-General.

I started forthwith by boat, and met General Grant, who had reached Columbus by the railroad from Jackson, Tennessee. He explained to me that he proposed to move against Pemberton, then intrenched on a line behind the Tallahatchie River below Holly Springs; that he would move on Holly Springs and Abberville, from Grand Junction; that McPherson, with the troops at Corinth, would aim to make junction with him at Holly Springs; and that he wanted me to leave in Memphis a proper garrison, and to aim for the Tallahatchie, so as to come up on his right by a certain date. He further said that his ultimate object was to capture Vicksburg, to open the navigation of the Mississippi River, and that General Halleck had authorized him to call on the troops in the Department of Arkansas, then commanded by General S. R. Curtis, for cooperation. I suggested to him that if he would request General Curtis to send an expedition from some point on the Mississippi, near Helena, then held in force, toward Grenada, to the rear of Pemberton, it would alarm him for the safety of his communications, and would assist us materially in the proposed attack on his front. He authorized me to send to the commanding officer at Helena a request to that effect, and, as soon as I reached Memphis, I dispatched my aide, Major McCoy, to Helena, who returned, bringing me a letter from General Frederick Steele, who had just reached Helena with Osterhaus's division, and who was temporarily in command, General Curtis having gone to St. Louis. This letter contained the assurance that he "would send from Friar's Point a large force under Brigadier-General A. P. Hovey in the direction of Grenada, aiming to reach the Tallahatchie at Charleston, on the next Monday, Tuesday, or Wednesday (December 1st) at furthest." My command was appointed to start on Wednesday, November 24th, and meantime Major-General S. A. Hurlbut, having reported for duty, was assigned to the command of Memphis, with four regiments of infantry one battery of artillery, two companies of Thielman's cavalry and the certain prospect of soon receiving a number of new regiments, known to be en route.

I marched out of Memphis punctually with three small divisions, taking different roads till we approached the Tallahatchie, when we converged on Wyatt to cross the river, there a bold, deep stream, with a newly-constructed fort behind. I had Grierson's Sixth Illinois Cavalry with me, and with it opened communication with General Grant when we were abreast of Holly Springs. We reached Wyatt on the 2d day of December without the least opposition, and there learned that Pemberton's whole army had fallen back to the Yalabusha near Grenada, in a great measure by reason of the exaggerated reports concerning the Helena force, which had reached Charleston; and some of General Hovey's cavalry, under General Washburn, having struck the railroad in the neighborhood of Coffeeville, naturally alarmed General Pemberton for the safety of his communications, and made him

152

let go his Tallahatchie line with all the forts which he had built at great cost in labor. We had to build a bridge at Wyatt, which consumed a couple of days, and on the 5th of December my whole command was at College Hill, ten miles from Oxford, whence I reported to General Grant in Oxford.

On the 8th I received the following letter:

OXFORD MISSISSIPPI, December 8, 1862—Morning

General SHERMAN, College Hill.

DEAR GENERAL: The following is a copy of dispatch just received from Washington:

WASHINGTON, December 7, 1862—12M

General GRANT:

The capture of Grenada may change our plans in regard to Vicksburg. You will move your troops as you may deem best to accomplish the great object in view. You will retain, till further orders, all troops of General Curtis now in your department. Telegraph to General Allen in St. Louis for all steamboats you may require. Ask Porter to cooperate. Telegraph what are your present plans.

H. W. HALLECK, General-in.-Chief.

I wish you would come over this evening and stay to-night, or come in the morning. I would like to talk with you about this matter. My notion is to send two divisions back to Memphis, and fix upon a day when they should effect a landing, and press from here with this command at the proper time to cooperate. If I do not do this I will move our present force to Grenada, including Steele's, repairing road as we proceed, and establish a depot of provisions there. When a good ready is had, to move immediately on Jackson, Mississippi, cutting loose from the road. Of the two plans I look most favorably on the former.

Come over and we will talk this matter over. Yours truly,

U. S. GRANT, Major-General.

I repaired at once to Oxford, and found General Grant in a large house with all his staff, and we discussed every possible chance. He explained to me that large reenforcements had been promised, which would reach Memphis very soon, if not already there; that the entire gunboat fleet, then under the command of Admiral D. D. Porter, would cooperate; that we could count on a full division from the troops at Helena; and he believed that, by a prompt movement, I could make a lodgment up the Yazoo and capture Vicksburg from the rear; that its garrison was small, and he, at Oxford, would so handle his troops as to hold Pemberton away from Vicksburg. I also understood that, if Pemberton should retreat south, he would follow him up, and would expect to find me at the Yazoo River, if not inside of Vicksburg. I confess, at that moment I did not dream that General McClernand, or anybody else, was scheming for the mere honor of capturing Vicksburg. We knew at the time that General Butler had been reenforced by General Banks at New Orleans, and the latter was supposed to be working his way up-stream from New Orleans, while we were working down. That day General Grant dispatched to General Halleck, in Washington, as follows:

OXFORD, December 8, 1862.

Major-General H. W. HALLECK, Washington, D. C.:

General Sherman will command the expedition down the Mississippi. He will have a force of about forty thousand men; will land above Vicksburg (up the Yazoo, if practicable), and cut the Mississippi Central road and the road running east from Vicksburg, where they cross Black River. I will cooperate from here, my movements depending on those of the enemy. With the large cavalry force now at my command, I will be able to have them show themselves at different points on the Tallahatchie and Yalabusha; and, when an opportunity occurs, make a real attack. After cutting the two roads, General Sherman's movements to secure the end desired will necessarily be left to his judgment.

I will occupy this road to Coffeeville.

U. S. GRANT, Major-General.

I was shown this dispatch before it was sent, and afterward the general drew up for me the following letter of instructions in his own handwriting, which I now possess:

HEADQUARTERS THIRTEENTH ARMY CORPS DEPARTMENT OF THE TENNESSEE, OXFORD, Mississippi, December 8, 1862.

Major-General W. T. SHERMAN, commanding Right Wing Army In the Field, present.

GENERAL: You will proceed with as little delay as practicable to Memphis, Tennessee, taking with you one division of your present command. On your arrival at Memphis you will assume command of all the troops there, and that portion of General Curtis's forces at present east of the Mississippi River, and organize them into brigades and divisions in your own way.

As soon as possible move with them down the river to the vicinity of Vicksburg, and, with the cooperation of the gunboat fleet under command of Flag-Officer Porter, proceed to the reduction of that place in such manner as circumstances and your own judgment may dictate.

The amount of rations, forage, land transportation, etc., necessary to take, will be left entirely to yourself.

The quartermaster in St. Louis will be instructed to send you transportation for thirty thousand men. Should you still find yourself deficient, your quartermaster will be authorized to make up the deficiency from such transports as may come into the port of Memphis.

On arriving in Memphis put yourself in communication with Admiral Porter, and arrange with him for his cooperation.

Inform me at the earliest practicable day of the time when you will embark, and such plans as may then be matured. I will hold the forces here in readiness to cooperate with you in such manner as the movements of the enemy may make necessary.

Leave the District of Memphis in the command of an efficient officer and with a garrison of four regiments of infantry, the siege-guns, and what ever cavalry force may be there.

One regiment of infantry and at least a section of artillery will also be left at Friar's Point or Delta, to protect the stores of the cavalry post that will be left there. Yours truly,

U. S. GRANT, Major-General.

I also insert here another letter, dated the 14th instant, sent afterward to me at Memphis, which completes all instructions received by me governing the first movement against Vicksburg:

HEADQUARTERS DEPARTMENT OF THE TENNESSEE
OXFORD, MISSISSIPPI, December 14, 1862

Major-General SHERMAN, commanding, etc.,
Memphis, Tennessee.

I have not had one word from Grierson since he left, and am getting uneasy about him. I hope General Gorman will give you no difficulty about retaining the troops on this side the river, and Steele to command them. The twenty-one thousand men you have, with the twelve thousand from Helena, will make a good force. The enemy are as yet on the Yalabusha. I am pushing down on them slowly, but so as to keep up the impression of a continuous move. I feel particularly anxious to have the Helena cavalry on this side of the river; if not now, at least after you start. If Gorman will send them, instruct them where to go and how to communicate with me. My headquarters will probably be in Coffeeville one week hence.... In the mean time I will order transportation, etc.... It would be well if you could have two or three small boats suitable for navigating the Yazoo. It may become necessary for me to look to that base for supplies before we get through....

U. S. GRANT, Major-General.

When we rode to Oxford from College Hill, there happened a little circumstance which seems worthy of record. While General Van Dorn had his headquarters in Holly Springs, viz., in October, 1862, he was very short of the comforts and luxuries of life, and resorted to every possible device to draw from the abundant supplies in Memphis. He had no difficulty whatever in getting spies into the town for information, but he had trouble in getting bulky supplies out through our guards, though sometimes I connived at his supplies of cigars, liquors, boots, gloves, etc., for his individual use; but medicines and large supplies of all kinds were confiscated, if attempted to be passed out. As we rode that morning toward Oxford, I observed in a farmer's barn-yard a wagon that looked like a city furniture-wagon with springs. We were always short of wagons, so I called the attention of the quartermaster, Colonel J. Condit Smith, saying, "There is a good wagon; go for it." He dropped out of the retinue with an orderly, and after we had ridden a mile or so he overtook us, and I asked him, "What luck?" He answered, "All right; I have secured that wagon, and I also got another," and explained that he had gone to the farmer's house to inquire about the furniture-wagon, when the farmer said it did not belong to him, but to some party in Memphis, adding that in his barn was another belonging to the same party. They went to the barn, and there found a handsome city hearse, with pall and plumes. The farmer said they had had a big funeral out of Memphis, but when it reached his house, the coffin was found to contain a fine assortment of medicines for the use of Van Dorn's army. Thus under the pretense of a first-class funeral, they had carried through our guards the very things we had tried to prevent. It was a good trick, but diminished our respect for such pageants afterward.

As soon as I was in possession of General Grant's instructions of December 8th, with a further request that I should dispatch Colonel Grierson, with his cavalry, across by land to Helena, to notify General Steele of the general plan, I returned to College Hill, selected the division of Brigadier-General Morgan L. Smith to return with me to Memphis; started Grierson on his errand to Helena, and ordered Generals Denver and Lauman to report to General Grant for further orders. We started back by the most direct route, reached Memphis by noon of December 12th, and began immediately the preparations for the Vicksburg movement. There I found two irregular divisions which had arrived at Memphis in my absence, commanded respectively by Brigadier-General A. J. Smith and Brigadier-

General George W. Morgan. These were designated the First and Third Divisions, leaving the Second Division of Morgan Z. Smith to retain its original name and number.

I also sent orders, in the name of General Grant, to General Gorman, who meantime had replaced General Steele in command of Helena, in lieu of the troops which had been east of the Mississippi and had returned, to make up a strong division to report to me on my way down. This division was accordingly organized, and was commanded by Brigadier-General Frederick Steele, constituting my Fourth Division.

Meantime a large fleet of steamboats was assembling from St. Louis and Cairo, and Admiral Porter dropped down to Memphis with his whole gunboat fleet, ready to cooperate in the movement. The preparations were necessarily hasty in the extreme, but this was the essence of the whole plan, viz., to reach Vicksburg as it were by surprise, while General Grant held in check Pemberton's army about Grenada, leaving me to contend only with the smaller garrison of Vicksburg and its well-known strong batteries and defenses. On the 19th the Memphis troops were embarked, and steamed down to Helena, where on the 21st General Steele's division was also embarked; and on the 22d we were all rendezvoused at Friar's Point, in the following order, viz.:

Steamer Forest Queen, general headquarters, and battalion Thirteenth United States Infantry.

First Division, Brigadier-General A. J. SMITH.—Steamers Des Arc, division headquarters and escort; Metropolitan, Sixth Indiana; J. H. Dickey, Twenty-third Wisconsin; J. C. Snow, Sixteenth Indiana; Hiawatha, Ninety-sixth Ohio; J. S. Pringle, Sixty-seventh Indiana; J. W. Cheeseman, Ninth Kentucky; R. Campbell, Ninety-seventh Indiana; Duke of Argyle, Seventy-seventh Illinois; City of Alton, One Hundred and Eighth and Forty-eighth Ohio; City of Louisiana, Mercantile Battery; Ohio Belle, Seventeenth Ohio Battery; Citizen, Eighty-third Ohio; Champion, commissary-boat; General Anderson, Ordnance.

Second Division,, Brigadier-General M. L. SMITH.—Steamers Chancellor, headquarters, and Thielman's cavalry; Planet, One Hundred and Sixteenth Illinois; City of Memphis, Batteries A and B (Missouri Artillery), Eighth Missouri, and section of Parrott guns; Omaha, Fifty-seventh Ohio; Sioux City, Eighty-third Indiana; Spread Eagle, One Hundred and Twenty-seventh Illinois; Ed. Walsh, One Hundred and Thirteenth Illinois; Westmoreland, Fifty-fifth Illinois, headquarters Fourth Brigade; Sunny South, Fifty-fourth Ohio; Universe, Sixth Missouri; Robert Allen, commissary-boat.

Third Division, Brigadier-General G. W. MORGAN.—Steamers Empress, division headquarters; Key West, One Hundred and Eighteenth Illinois; Sam Gaty, Sixty-ninth Indiana; Northerner, One Hundred and Twentieth Ohio; Belle Peoria, headquarters Second Brigade, two companies Forty-ninth Ohio, and pontoons; Die Vernon, Third Kentucky; War Eagle, Forty-ninth Indiana (eight companies), and Foster's battery; Henry von Phul, headquarters Third Brigade, and eight companies Sixteenth Ohio; Fanny Bullitt, One Hundred and Fourteenth Ohio, and Lamphere's battery; Crescent City, Twenty-second Kentucky and Fifty-fourth Indiana; Des Moines, Forty-second Ohio; Pembina, Lamphere's and Stone's batteries; Lady Jackson, commissary-boat.

Fourth Division, Brigadier-General FREDERICK STEELE—Steamers Continental, headquarters, escort and battery; John J. Roe, Fourth and Ninth Iowa; Nebraska, Thirty-first Iowa; Key West, First Iowa Artillery; John Warner, Thirteenth Illinois; Tecumseh, Twenty-sixth Iowa; Decatur, Twenty-eighth Iowa; Quitman, Thirty-fourth Iowa; Kennett, Twenty ninth Missouri; Gladiator, Thirtieth Missouri; Isabella, Thirty-first Missouri; D. G. Taylor, quartermaster's stores and horses; Sucker State, Thirty-second Missouri; Dakota, Third Missouri; Tutt, Twelfth Missouri Emma, Seventeenth Missouri; Adriatic, First Missouri; Meteor, Seventy-sixth Ohio; Polar Star, Fifty-eighth Ohio.

At the same time were communicated the following instructions:

156

HEADQUARTERS RIGHT WING, THIRTEENTH ARMY Corps FOREST QUEEN, December 23, 1882.

To Commanders of Divisions, Generals F. STEELE, GEORGE W. MORGAN, A.J. SMITH, and M. L. SMITH

With this I hand to each of you a copy of a map, compiled from the best sources, and which in the main is correct. It is the same used by Admiral Porter and myself. Complete military success can only be accomplished by united action on some general plan, embracing usually a large district of country. In the present instance, our object is to secure the navigation of the Mississippi River and its main branches, and to hold them as military channels of communication and for commercial purposes. The river, above Vicksburg, has been gained by conquering the country to its rear, rendering its possession by our enemy useless and unsafe to him, and of great value to us. But the enemy still holds the river from Vicksburg to Baton Rouge, navigating it with his boats, and the possession of it enables him to connect his communications and routes of supply, east and west. To deprive him of this will be a severe blow, and, if done effectually, will be of great advantage to us, and probably, the most decisive act of the war. To accomplish this important result we are to act our part— an important one of the great whole. General Banks, with a large force, has reinforced General Butler in Louisiana, and from that quarter an expedition, by water and land, is coming northward. General Grant, with the Thirteenth Army Corps, of which we compose the right wing, is moving southward. The naval squadron (Admiral Porter) is operating with his gunboat fleet by water, each in perfect harmony with the other.

General Grant's left and centre were at last accounts approaching the Yalabusha, near Grenada, and the railroad to his rear, by which he drew his supplies, was reported to be seriously damaged. This may disconcert him somewhat, but only makes more important our line of operations. At the Yalabusha General Grant may encounter the army of General Pemberton, the same which refused him battle on the line of the Tallahatchie, which was strongly fortified; but, as he will not have time to fortify it, he will hardly stand there; and, in that event, General Grant will immediately advance down the high ridge between the Big Black and Yazoo, and will expect to meet us on the Yazoo and receive from us the supplies which he needs, and which he knows we carry along. Parts of this general plan are to cooperate with the naval squadron in the reduction of Vicksburg; to secure possession of the land lying between the Yazoo and Big Black; and to act in concert with General Grant against Pemberton's forces, supposed to have Jackson, Mississippi, as a point of concentration. Vicksburg is doubtless very strongly fortified, both against the river and land approaches. Already the gunboats have secured the Yazoo up for twenty-three miles, to a fort on the Yazoo at Haines's Bluff, giving us a choice for a landing-place at some point up the Yazoo below this fort, or on the island which lies between Vicksburg and the present mouth of the Yazoo. (See map [b, c, d], Johnson's plantation.)

But, before any actual collision with the enemy, I purpose, after our whole land force is rendezvoused at Gaines's Landing, Arkansas, to proceed in order to Milliken's Bend (a), and there dispatch a brigade, without wagons or any incumbrances whatever, to the Vicksburg & Shreveport Railroad (at h and k), to destroy that effectually, and to cut off that fruitful avenue of supply; then to proceed to the mouth of the Yazoo, and, after possessing ourselves of the latest and most authentic information from naval officers now there, to land our whole force on the Mississippi side, and then to reach the point where the Vicksburg & Jackson Railroad crosses the Big Black (f); after which to attack Vicksburg by land, while the gun-boats assail it by water. It may be necessary (looking to Grant's approach), before attacking Vicksburg, to reduce the battery at Haine's Bluff first, so as to enable some of the lighter gunboats and transports to ascend the Yazoo and communicate with General Grant. The detailed manner of accomplishing all these results will be communicated in due season, and these general points are only made known at this time, that commanders may study the maps, and also that in the event of non-receipt of orders all may act in perfect concert by following the general movement, unless specially detached.

You all now have the same map, so that no mistakes or confusion need result from different names of localities. All possible preparations as to wagons, provisions, axes, and intrenching-tools, should be made in advance, so that when we do land there will be no want of them. When we begin to act on shore, we must do the work quickly and effectually. The gunboats under Admiral Porter will do their full share, and I feel every assurance that the army will not fall short in its work.

Division commanders may read this to regimental commanders, and furnish brigade commanders a copy. They should also cause as many copies of the map to be made on the same scale as possible, being very careful in copying the names.

The points marked e and g (Allan's and Mount Albans) are evidently strategical points that will figure in our future operations, and these positions should be well studied.

I am, with great respect, your obedient servant,

W. T. SHERMAN, Major-General.

The Mississippi boats were admirably calculated for handling troops, horses, guns, stores, etc., easy of embarkation and disembarkation, and supplies of all kinds were abundant, except fuel. For this we had to rely on wood, but most of the wood-yards, so common on the river before the war, had been exhausted, so that we had to use fence-rails, old dead timber, the logs of houses, etc. Having abundance of men and plenty of axes, each boat could daily procure a supply.

In proceeding down the river, one or more of Admiral Porter's gunboats took the lead; others were distributed throughout the column, and some brought up the rear. We manoeuvred by divisions and brigades when in motion, and it was a magnificent sight as we thus steamed down the river. What few inhabitants remained at the plantations on the river-bank were unfriendly, except the slaves; some few guerrilla-parties infested the banks, but did not dare to molest so, strong a force as I then commanded.

We reached Milliken's Bend on Christmas-day, when I detached one brigade (Burbridge's), of A. J. Smith's division, to the southwest, to break up the railroad leading from Vicksburg toward Shreveport, Louisiana. Leaving A. J. Smith's division there to await the return of Burbridge, the remaining three divisions proceeded, on the 26th, to the mouth of the Yazoo, and up that river to Johnson's plantation, thirteen miles, and there disembarked Steele's division above the mouth of Chickasaw Bayou, Morgans division near the house of Johnson (which had been burned by the gunboats on a former occasion), and M. L. Smith's just below. A. J. Smith's division arrived the next night, and disembarked below that of M. L. Smith. The place of our disembarkation was in fact an island, separated from the high bluff known as Walnut Hills, on which the town of Vicksburg stands, by a broad and shallow bayou-evidently an old channel of the Yazoo. On our right was another wide bayou, known as Old River; and on the left still another, much narrower, but too deep to be forded, known as Chickasaw Bayou. All the island was densely wooded, except Johnson's plantation, immediately on the bank of the Yazoo, and a series of old cotton-fields along Chickasaw Bayou. There was a road from Johnson's plantation directly to Vicksburg, but it crossed numerous bayous and deep swamps by bridges, which had been destroyed; and this road debouched on level ground at the foot of the Vicksburg bluff, opposite strong forts, well prepared and defended by heavy artillery. On this road I directed General A. J. Smith's division, not so much by way of a direct attack as a diversion and threat.

Morgan was to move to his left, to reach Chickasaw Bayou, and to follow it toward the bluff, about four miles above A. J. Smith. Steele was on Morgan's left, across Chickasaw Bayou, and M. L. Smith on Morgan's right. We met light resistance at all points, but skirmished, on the 27th, up to the main bayou, that separated our position from the bluffs of Vicksburg, which were found to be strong by nature and by art, and seemingly well defended. On reconnoitring the front in person, during the 27th and 28th, I became satisfied that General A. J. Smith could not cross the intervening obstacles under the heavy fire of the forts immediately in his front, and that the main bayou was impassable, except at two points—one near the head of Chickasaw Bayou, in front of Morgan, and the other about a mile lower down, in front of M. L. Smith's division.

During the general reconnoissance of the 28th General Morgan L. Smith received a severe and dangerous wound in his hip, which completely disabled him and compelled him to go to his steamboat, leaving the command of his division to Brigadier General D. Stuart; but I drew a part of General A. J. Smith's division, and that general himself, to the point selected for passing the bayou, and committed that special task to his management.

General Steele reported that it was physically impossible to reach the bluffs from his position, so I ordered him to leave but a show of force there, and to return to the west side of Chickasaw Bayou in support of General Morgan's left. He had to countermarch and use the steamboats in the Yazoo to get on the firm ground on our side of the Chickasaw.

On the morning of December 29th all the troops were ready and in position. The first step was to make a lodgment on the foot-hills and bluffs abreast of our position, while diversions were made by the navy toward Haines's Bluff, and by the first division directly toward Vicksburg. I estimated the enemy's forces, then strung from Vicksburg to Haines's Bluff, at fifteen thousand men, commanded by the rebel Generals Martin Luther Smith and Stephen D. Lee. Aiming to reach firm ground beyond this bayou, and to leave as little time for our enemy to reenforce as possible, I determined to make a show of attack along the whole front, but to break across the bayou at the two points named, and gave general orders accordingly. I pointed out to General Morgan the place where he could pass the bayou, and he answered, "General, in ten minutes after you give the signal I'll be on those hills." He was to lead his division in person, and was to be supported by Steele's division. The front was very narrow, and immediately opposite, at the base of the hills about three hundred yards from the bayou, was a rebel battery, supported by an infantry force posted on the spurs of the hill behind. To draw attention from this, the real point of attack, I gave instructions to commence the attack at the flanks.

I went in person about a mile to the right rear of Morgan's position, at a place convenient to receive reports from all other parts of the line; and about noon of December 29th gave the orders and signal for the main attack. A heavy artillery-fire opened along our whole line, and was replied to by the rebel batteries, and soon the infantry-fire opened heavily, especially on A. J. Smith's front, and in front of General George W. Morgan. One brigade (DeCourcey's) of Morgan's troops crossed the bayou safely, but took to cover behind the bank, and could not be moved forward. Frank Blairs brigade, of Steele's division, in support, also crossed the bayou, passed over the space of level ground to the foot of the hills; but, being unsupported by Morgan, and meeting a very severe cross-fire of artillery, was staggered and gradually fell back, leaving about five hundred men behind, wounded and prisoners; among them Colonel Thomas Fletcher, afterward Governor of Missouri. Part of Thayer's brigade took a wrong direction, and did not cross the bayou at all; nor did General Morgan cross in person. This attack failed; and I have always felt that it was due to the failure of General G. W. Morgan to obey his orders, or to fulfill his promise made in person. Had he used with skill and boldness one of his brigades, in addition to that of Blair's, he could have made a lodgment on the bluff, which would have opened the door for our whole force to follow. Meantime the Sixth Missouri Infantry, at heavy loss, had also crossed the bayou at the narrow passage lower down, but could not ascend the steep bank; right over their heads was a rebel battery, whose fire was in a measure kept down by our sharp-shooters (Thirteenth United States Infantry) posted behind logs, stumps, and trees, on our side of the bayou.

The men of the Sixth Missouri actually scooped out with their hands caves in the bank, which sheltered them against the fire of the enemy, who, right over their heads, held their muskets outside the parapet vertically, and fired down So critical was the position, that we could not recall the men till after dark, and then one at a time. Our loss had been pretty heavy, and we had accomplished nothing, and had inflicted little loss on our enemy. At first I intended to renew the assault, but soon became satisfied that, the enemy's attention having been drawn to the only two practicable points, it would prove too costly, and accordingly resolved to look elsewhere for a point below Haines's Bluff, or Blake's plantation. That night I conferred with Admiral Porter, who undertook to cover the landing; and the next day (December 30th) the boats were all selected, but so alarmed were the captains and pilots, that we had to place sentinels with loaded muskets to insure their remaining at their posts.

Under cover of night, Steele's division, and one brigade of Stuart's, were drawn out of line, and quietly embarked on steamboats in the Yazoo River. The night of December 30th was appointed for this force, under the command of General Fred Steele, to proceed up the Yazoo just below Haines's Bluff, there to disembark about daylight, and make a dash for the hills. Meantime we had strengthened our positions near Chickasaw Bayou, had all our guns in good position with parapets, and had every thing ready to renew our attack as soon as we heard the sound of battle above.

At midnight I left Admiral Porter on his gunboat; he had his fleet ready and the night was propitious. I rode back to camp and gave orders for all to be ready by daybreak; but when daylight came I received a note from General Steele reporting that, before his boats had got up steam, the fog had settled down on the river so thick and impenetrable, that it was simply impossible to move; so the attempt had to be abandoned. The rain, too, began to fall, and the trees bore water-marks ten feet above our heads, so that I became convinced that the part of wisdom was to withdraw. I ordered the stores which had been landed to be reembarked on the boats, and preparations made for all the troops to regain their proper boats during the night of the 1st of January, 1863. From our camps at Chickasaw we could hear, the whistles of the trains arriving in Vicksburg, could see battalions of men marching up toward Haines's Bluff, and taking post at all points in our front. I was more than convinced that heavy reenforcements were coming to Vicksburg; whether from Pemberton at Grenada, Bragg in Tennessee, or from other sources, I could not tell; but at no point did the enemy assume the offensive; and when we drew off our rear-guard, on the morning of the 2d, they simply followed up the movement, timidly. Up to that moment I had not heard a word from General Grant since leaving Memphis; and most assuredly I had listened for days for the sound of his guns in the direction of Yazoo City. On the morning of January 2d, all my command were again afloat in their proper steamboats, when Admiral Porter told me that General McClernand had arrived at the mouth of the Yazoo in the steamboat Tigress, and that it was rumored he had come down to supersede me. Leaving my whole force where it was, I ran down to the month of the Yazoo in a small tug boat, and there found General McClernand, with orders from the War Department to command the expeditionary force on the Mississippi River. I explained what had been done, and what was the actual state of facts; that the heavy reenforcements pouring into Vicksburg must be Pemberton's army, and that General Grant must be near at hand. He informed me that General Grant was not coming at all; that his depot at Holly Springs had been captured by Van Dorn, and that he had drawn back from Coffeeville and Oxford to Holly Springs and Lagrange; and, further, that Quinby's division of Grant's army was actually at Memphis for stores when he passed down. This, then, fully explained how Vicksburg was being reenforced. I saw that any attempt on the place from the Yazoo was hopeless; and, with General McClernand's full approval, we all came out of the Yazoo, and on the 3d of January rendezvoused at Milliken's Bend, about ten miles above. On the 4th General McClernand issued his General Order No. 1, assuming command of the Army of the Mississippi, divided into two corps; the first to be commanded by General Morgan, composed of his own and A. J. Smith's divisions; and the second, composed of Steele's and Stuart's divisions, to be commanded by me. Up to that time the army had been styled the right wing of (General Grant's) Thirteenth Army Corps, and numbered about thirty thousand men. The aggregate loss during the time of any command, mostly on the 29th of December, was one hundred and seventy-five killed, nine hundred and thirty wounded, and seven hundred and forty-three prisoners. According to Badeau, the rebels lost sixty-three killed, one hundred and thirty-four wounded, and ten prisoners. It afterward transpired that Van Dorn had captured Holly Springs on the 20th of December, and that General Grant fell back very soon after. General Pemberton, who had telegraphic and railroad communication with Vicksburg, was therefore at perfect liberty to reenforce the place with a garrison equal, if not superior, to my command. The rebels held high, commanding ground, and could see every movement of our men and boats, so that the only possible hope of success consisted in celerity and surprise, and in General Grant's holding all of Pemberton's army hard pressed meantime. General Grant was perfectly aware of this, and had sent me word of the change, but it did not reach me in time; indeed, I was not aware of it until after my assault of December 29th, and until the news was brought me by General

McClernand as related. General McClernand was appointed to this command by President Lincoln in person, who had no knowledge of what was then going on down the river. Still, my relief, on the heels of a failure, raised the usual cry, at the North, of "repulse, failure, and bungling." There was no bungling on my part, for I never worked harder or with more intensity of purpose in my life; and General Grant, long after, in his report of the operations of the siege of Vicksburg, gave us all full credit for the skill of the movement, and described the almost impregnable nature of the ground; and, although in all official reports I assumed the whole responsibility, I have ever felt that had General Morgan promptly and skillfully sustained the lead of Frank Blair's brigade on that day, we should have broken the rebel line, and effected a lodgment on the hills behind Vicksburg. General Frank Blair was outspoken and indignant against Generals Morgan and De Courcey at the time, and always abused me for assuming the whole blame. But, had we succeeded, we might have found ourselves in a worse trap, when General Pemberton was at full liberty to turn his whole force against us. While I was engaged at Chickasaw Bayou, Admiral Porter was equally busy in the Yazoo River, threatening the enemy's batteries at Haines's and Snyder's Bluffs above. In a sharp engagement he lost one of his best officers, in the person of Captain Gwin, United States Navy, who, though on board an ironclad, insisted on keeping his post on deck, where he was struck in the breast by a round shot, which carried away the muscle, and contused the lung within, from which he died a few days after. We of the army deplored his loss quite as much as his fellows of the navy, for he had been intimately associated with us in our previous operations on the Tennessee River, at Shiloh and above, and we had come to regard him as one of us.

On the 4th of January, 1863, our fleet of transports was collected at Milliken's Bend, about ten miles above the mouth of the Yazoo, Admiral Porter remaining with his gunboats at the Yazoo. General John A. McClernand was in chief command, General George W. Morgan commanded the First Corps and I the Second Corps of the Army of the Mississippi.

I had learned that a small steamboat, the Blue Wing, with a mail, towing coal-barges and loaded with ammunition, had left Memphis for the Yazoo, about the 20th of December, had been captured by a rebel boat which had come out of the Arkansas River, and had been carried up that river to Fort Hind.

We had reports from this fort, usually called the "Post of Arkansas," about forty miles above the mouth, that it was held by about five thousand rebels, was an inclosed work, commanding the passage of the river, but supposed to be easy of capture from the rear. At that time I don't think General McClernand had any definite views or plays of action. If so, he did not impart them to me. He spoke, in general terms of opening the navigation of the Mississippi, "cutting his way to the sea," etc., etc., but the modus operandi was not so clear. Knowing full well that we could not carry on operations against Vicksburg as long as the rebels held the Post of Arkansas, whence to attack our boats coming and going without convoy, I visited him on his boat, the Tigress, took with me a boy who had been on the Blue Wing, and had escaped, and asked leave to go up the Arkansas, to clear out the Post. He made various objections, but consented to go with me to see Admiral Porter about it. We got up steam in the Forest Queen, during the night of January 4th, stopped at the Tigress, took General McClernand on board, and proceeded down the river by night to the admiral's boat, the Black Hawk, lying in the mouth of the Yazoo. It must have been near midnight, and Admiral Porter was in deshabille. We were seated in his cabin and I explained my views about Arkansas Post, and asked his cooperation. He said that he was short of coal, and could not use wood in his iron-clad boats. Of these I asked for two, to be commanded by Captain Shirk or Phelps, or some officer of my acquaintance. At that moment, poor Gwin lay on his bed, in a state-room close by, dying from the effect of the cannon shot received at Haines's Bluff, as before described. Porter's manner to McClernand was so curt that I invited him out into a forward-cabin where he had his charts, and asked him what he meant by it. He said that "he did not like him;" that in Washington, before coming West, he had been introduced to him by President Lincoln, and he had taken a strong prejudice against him. I begged him, for the sake of harmony, to waive that, which he promised to do. Returning to the cabin, the conversation was resumed, and, on our offering to tow his gunboats up the river to save coal, and on renewing the request for Shirk to command the detachment, Porter said,

"Suppose I go along myself?" I answered, if he would do so, it would insure the success of the enterprise. At that time I supposed General McClernand would send me on this business, but he concluded to go himself, and to take his whole force. Orders were at once issued for the troops not to disembark at Milliken's Bend, but to remain as they were on board the transports. My two divisions were commanded—the First, by Brigadier-General Frederick Steele, with three brigades, commanded by Brigadier-Generals F. P. Blair, C. E. Hooey, and J. M. Thayer; the Second, by Brigadier-General D. Stuart, with two brigades, commanded by Colonels G. A. Smith and T. Kilby Smith.

The whole army, embarked on steamboats convoyed by the gunboats, of which three were iron-clads, proceeded up the Mississippi River to the mouth of White River, which we reached January 8th. On the next day we continued up White River to the "Cut-off;" through this to the Arkansas, and up the Arkansas to Notrib's farm, just below Fort Hindman. Early the next morning we disembarked. Stuart's division, moving up the river along the bank, soon encountered a force of the enemy intrenched behind a line of earthworks, extending from the river across to the swamp. I took Steele's division, marching by the flank by a road through the swamp to the firm ground behind, and was moving up to get to the rear of Fort Hindman, when General McClernand overtook me, with the report that the rebels had abandoned their first position, and had fallen back into the fort. By his orders, we counter-marched, recrossed the swamp, and hurried forward to overtake Stuart, marching for Fort Hindman. The first line of the rebels was about four miles below Fort Hindman, and the intervening space was densely, wooded and obscure, with the exception of some old fields back of and close to the fort. During the night, which was a bright moonlight one, we reconnoitred close up, and found a large number of huts which had been abandoned, and the whole rebel force had fallen back into and about the fort. Personally I crept up to a stump so close that I could hear the enemy hard at work, pulling down houses, cutting with axes, and building intrenchments. I could almost hear their words, and I was thus listening when, about 4 A. M. the bugler in the rebel camp sounded as pretty a reveille as I ever listened to.

When daylight broke it revealed to us a new line of parapet straight across the peninsula, connecting Fort Hindman, on the Arkansas River bank, with the impassable swamp about a mile to its left or rear. This peninsula was divided into two nearly equal parts by a road. My command had the ground to the right of the road, and Morgan's corps that to the left. McClernand had his quarters still on the Tigress, back at Notrib's farm, but moved forward that morning (January 11th) to a place in the woods to our rear, where he had a man up a tree, to observe and report the movements.

There was a general understanding with Admiral Porter that he was to attack the fort with his three ironclad gunboats directly by its water-front, while we assaulted by land in the rear. About 10 a.m. I got a message from General McClernand, telling me where he could be found, and asking me what we were waiting for. I answered that we were then in close contact with the enemy, viz., about five or six hundred yards off; that the next movement must be a direct assault; that this should be simultaneous along the whole line; and that I was waiting to hear from the gunboats; asking him to notify Admiral Porter that we were all ready. In about half an hour I heard the clear ring of the navy-guns; the fire gradually increasing in rapidity and advancing toward the fort. I had distributed our field-guns, and, when I judged the time had come, I gave the orders to begin. The intervening ground between us and the enemy was a dead level, with the exception of one or two small gullies, and our men had no cover but the few standing trees and some logs on the ground. The troops advanced well under a heavy fire, once or twice falling to the ground for a sort of rest or pause. Every tree had its group of men, and behind each log was a crowd of sharp-shooters, who kept up so hot a fire that the rebel troops fired wild. The fire of the fort proper was kept busy by the gunboats and Morgan's corps, so that all my corps had to encounter was the direct fire from the newly-built parapet across the peninsula. This line had three sections of field-guns, that kept things pretty lively, and several round-shot came so near me that I realized that they were aimed at my staff; so I dismounted, and made them scatter.

As the gunboats got closer up I saw their flags actually over the parapet of Fort Hindman, and the rebel gunners scamper out of the embrasures and run down into the ditch behind. About the same time a man jumped up on the rebel parapet just where the road entered, waving a large white flag, and numerous smaller white rags appeared above the parapet along the whole line. I immediately ordered, "Cease firing!" and sent the same word down the line to General Steele, who had made similar progress on the right, following the border of he swamp. I ordered my aide, Colonel Dayton, to jump on his horse and ride straight up to the large white flag, and when his horse was on the parapet I followed with the rest of my staff. All firing had ceased, except an occasional shot away to the right, and one of the captains (Smith) of the Thirteenth Regulars was wounded after the display of the white flag. On entering the line, I saw that our muskets and guns had done good execution; for there was a horse-battery, and every horse lay dead in the traces. The fresh-made parapet had been knocked down in many places, and dead men lay around very thick. I inquired who commanded at that point, and a Colonel Garland stepped up and said that he commanded that brigade. I ordered him to form his brigade, stack arms, hang the belts on the muskets, and stand waiting for orders. Stuart's division had been halted outside the parapet. I then sent Major Hammond down the rebel line to the right, with orders to stop Steele's division outside, and to have the other rebel brigade stack its arms in like manner, and to await further orders. I inquired of Colonel Garland who commanded in chief, and he said that General Churchill did, and that he was inside the fort. I then rode into the fort, which was well built, with good parapets, drawbridge, and ditch, and was an inclosed work of four bastions. I found it full of soldiers and sailors, its parapets toward the river well battered in, and Porter's gunboats in the river, close against the fort, with their bows on shore. I soon found General Churchill, in conversation with Admiral Porter and General A. J. Smith, and about this time my adjutant-general, Major J. H. Hammond, came and reported that General Deshler, who commanded the rebel brigade facing and opposed to Steele, had refused to stack arms and surrender, on the ground that he had received no orders from his commanding general; that nothing separated this brigade from Steele's men except the light parapet, and that there might be trouble there at any moment. I advised General Churchill to send orders at once, because a single shot might bring the whole of Steele's division on Deshler's brigade, and I would not be responsible for the consequences; soon afterward, we both concluded to go in person. General Churchill had the horses of himself and staff in the ditch; they were brought in, and we rode together to where Garland was standing, and Churchill spoke to him in an angry tone, "Why did you display the white flag!" Garland replied, "I received orders to do so from one of your staff." Churchill denied giving such an order, and angry words passed between them. I stopped them, saying that it made little difference then, as they were in our power. We continued to ride down the line to its extreme point, where we found Deshler in person, and his troops were still standing to the parapet with their muskets in hand. Steele'e men were on the outside. I asked Deshler: "What does this mean? You are a regular officer, and ought to know better." He answered, snappishly, that "he had received no orders to surrender;" when General Churchill said: "You see, sir, that we are in their power, and you may surrender." Deshler turned to his staff-officers and ordered them to repeat the command to "stack arms," etc., to the colonels of his brigade. I was on my horse, and he was on foot. Wishing to soften the blow of defeat, I spoke to him kindly, saying that I knew a family of Deshlers in Columbus, Ohio, and inquired if they were relations of his. He disclaimed any relation with people living north of the Ohio, in an offensive tone, and I think I gave him a piece of my mind that he did not relish. He was a West Point graduate, small but very handsome, and was afterward killed in battle. I never met him again.

Returning to the position where I had first entered the rebel line, I received orders from General McClernand, by one of his staff, to leave General A. J. Smith in charge of the fort and prisoners, and with my troops to remain outside. The officer explained that the general was then on the Tigress, which had moved up from below, to a point in the river just above the fort; and not understanding his orders, I concluded to go and see him in person. My troops were then in possession of two of the three brigades which composed the army opposed to us; and my troops were also in possession of all the ground of the peninsula

163

outside the "fort-proper" (Hindman). I found General McClernand on the Tigress, in high spirits. He said repeatedly: "Glorious! glorious! my star is ever in the ascendant!" He spoke complimentarily of the troops, but was extremely jealous of the navy. He said: "I'll make a splendid report;" "I had a man up a tree;" etc. I was very hungry and tired, and fear I did not appreciate the honors in reserve for us, and asked for something to eat and drink. He very kindly ordered something to be brought, and explained to me that by his "orders" he did not wish to interfere with the actual state of facts; that General A. J. Smith would occupy "Fort Hindman," which his troops had first entered, and I could hold the lines outside, and go on securing the prisoners and stores as I had begun. I returned to the position of Garland's brigade and gave the necessary orders for marching all the prisoners, disarmed, to a pocket formed by the river and two deep gullies just above the fort, by which time it had become quite dark. After dark another rebel regiment arrived from Pine Bluff, marched right in, and was also made prisoners. There seemed to be a good deal of feeling among the rebel officers against Garland, who asked leave to stay with me that night, to which I of course consented. Just outside the rebel parapet was a house which had been used for a hospital. I had a room cleaned out, and occupied it that night. A cavalry-soldier lent me his battered coffee-pot with some coffee and scraps of hard bread out of his nose-bag; Garland and I made some coffee, ate our bread together, and talked politics by the fire till quite late at night, when we lay down on straw that was saturated with the blood of dead or wounded men. The next day the prisoners were all collected on their boats, lists were made out, and orders given for their transportation to St. Louis, in charge of my aide, Major Sanger. We then proceeded to dismantle and level the forts, destroy or remove the stores, and we found in the magazine the very ammunition which had been sent for us in the Blue Wing, which was secured and afterward used in our twenty-pound Parrott guns.

On the 13th we reembarked; the whole expedition returned out of the river by the direct route down the Arkansas during a heavy snow-storm, and rendezvoused in the Mississippi, at Napoleon, at the mouth of the Arkansas. Here General McClernand told me he had received a letter from General Grant at Memphis, who disapproved of our movement up the Arkansas; but that communication was made before he had learned of our complete success. When informed of this, and of the promptness with which it had been executed, he could not but approve. We were then ordered back to Milliken's Bend, to await General Grant's arrival in person. We reached Milliken's Bend January 21st.

McClernand's report of the capture of Fort Hindman almost ignored the action of Porter's fleet altogether. This was unfair, for I know that the admiral led his fleet in person in the river-attack, and that his guns silenced those of Fort Hindman, and drove the gunners into the ditch.

The aggregate loss in my corps at Arkansas Post was five hundred and nineteen, viz., four officers and seventy-five men killed, thirty-four officers and four hundred and six men wounded. I never knew the losses in the gunboat fleet, or in Morgan's corps; but they must have been less than in mine, which was more exposed. The number of rebel dead must have been nearly one hundred and fifty; of prisoners, by actual count, we secured four thousand seven hundred and ninety-one, and sent them north to St. Louis.

CHAPTER XIII.
VICKSBURG.

JANUARY TO JULY, 1888.

164

The campaign of 1863, resulting, in the capture of Vicksburg, was so important, that its history has been well studied and well described in all the books treating of the civil war, more especially by Dr. Draper, in his "History of the Civil War in America," and in Badeau's "Military History of General Grant." In the latter it is more fully and accurately given than in any other, and is well illustrated by maps and original documents. I now need only attempt to further illustrate Badeau's account by some additional details. When our expedition came out of the Arkansas River, January, 18,1863, and rendezvoused at the river-bank, in front of the town of Napoleon, Arkansas, we were visited by General Grant in person, who had come down from Memphis in a steamboat. Although at this time Major-General J. A. McClernand was in command of the Army of the Mississippi, by virtue of a confidential order of the War Department, dated October 21, 1862, which order bore the indorsement of President Lincoln, General Grant still exercised a command over him, by reason of his general command of the Department of the Tennessee. By an order (No. 210) of December 18, 1862, from the War Department, received at Arkansas Post, the Western armies had been grouped into five corps d'armee, viz.: the Thirteenth, Major-General McClernand; the Fourteenth, Major-General George H. Thomas, in Middle Tennessee; the Fifteenth, Major-General W. T. Sherman; the Sixteenth, Major-General Hurlbut, then at or near Memphis; and the Seventeenth, Major-General McPherson, also at and back of Memphis. General Grant when at Napoleon, on the 18th of January, ordered McClernand with his own and my corps to return to Vicksburg, to disembark on the west bank, and to resume work on a canal across the peninsula, which had been begun by General Thomas Williams the summer before, the object being to turn the Mississippi River at that point, or at least to make a passage for our fleet of gunboats and transports across the peninsula, opposite Vicksburg. General Grant then returned to Memphis, ordered to Lake Providence, about sixty miles above us, McPherson's corps, the Seventeenth, and then came down again to give his personal supervision to the whole movement.

The Mississippi River was very high and rising, and we began that system of canals on which we expended so much hard work fruitlessly: first, the canal at Young's plantation, opposite Vicksburg; second, that at Lake Providence; and third, at the Yazoo Pass, leading into the head-waters of the Yazoo River. Early in February the gunboats Indianola and Queen of the West ran the batteries of Vicksburg. The latter was afterward crippled in Red River, and was captured by the rebels; and the Indianola was butted and sunk about forty miles below Vicksburg. We heard the booming of the guns, but did not know of her loss till some days after. During the months of January and February, we were digging the canal and fighting off the water of the Mississippi, which continued to rise and threatened to drown us. We had no sure place of refuge except the narrow levee, and such steamboats as remained abreast of our camps. My two divisions furnished alternately a detail of five hundred men a day, to work on the canal. So high was the water in the beginning of March, that McClernand's corps was moved to higher ground, at Milliken's Bend, but I remained at Young's plantation, laid off a due proportion of the levee for each subdivision of my command, and assigned other parts to such steamboats as lay at the levee. My own headquarters were in Mrs. Grove's house, which had the water all around it, and could only be reached by a plank-walk from the levee, built on posts. General Frederick Steele commanded the first division, and General D. Smart the second; this latter division had been reenforced by General Hugh Ewing's brigade, which had arrived from West Virginia.

At the time of its date I received the following note from General Grant:

MILLIKEN'S BEND, March 16, 1863

General SHERMAN.

DEAR SIR: I have just returned from a reconnoissance up Steele's Bayou, with the admiral (Porter), and five of his gunboats. With some labor in cutting tree-tops out of the way, it will be navigable for any class of steamers.

I want you to have your pioneer corps, or one regiment of good men for such work, detailed, and at the landing as soon as possible.

The party will want to take with them their rations, arms, and sufficient camp and garrison equipage for a few days. I will have a boat at any place you may designate, as early as the men can be there. The Eighth Missouri (being many of them boatmen) would be excellent men for this purpose.

As soon as you give directions for these men to be in readiness, come up and see me, and I will explain fully. The tug that takes this is instructed to wait for you. A full supply of axes will be required.

Very respectfully,

U. S. GRANT, Major-General.

This letter was instantly (8 a.m.) sent to Colonel Giles A. Smith, commanding the Eighth Missouri, with orders to prepare immediately. He returned it at 9.15, with an answer that the regiment was all ready. I went up to Milliken's Bend in the tug, and had a conference with the general, resulting in these orders:

HEADQUARTERS DEPARTMENT OF THE TENNESSEE BEFORE VICKSBURG, March 16, 1863

Major-General W. T. SHERMAN, commanding Fifteenth Army Corps.

GENERAL: You will proceed as early as practicable up Steele's Bayou, and through Black Bayou to Deer Creek, and thence with the gunboats now there by any route they may take to get into the Yazoo River, for the purpose of determining the feasibility of getting an army through that route to the east bank of that river, and at a point from which they can act advantageously against Vicksburg.

Make such details from your army corps as may be required to clear out the channel of the various bayous through which transports would have to ran, and to hold such points as in your judgment should be occupied.

I place at your disposal to-day the steamers Diligent and Silver Wave, the only two suitable for the present navigation of this route. Others will be supplied you as fast as required, and they can be got.

I have given directions (and you may repeat them) that the party going on board the steamer Diligent push on until they reach Black Bayou, only stopping sufficiently long at any point before reaching there to remove such obstructions as prevent their own progress. Captain Kossak, of the Engineers, will go with this party. The other boat-load will commence their work in Steele's Bayou, and make the navigation as free as possible all the way through.

There is but little work to be done in Steele's Bayou, except for about five miles abort midway of the bayou. In this portion many overhanging trees will have to be removed, and should be dragged out of the channel.

Very respectfully,

U. S. GRANT, Major-General.

166

On returning to my camp at Young's Point, I started these two boats up the Yazoo and Steele's Bayou, with the Eighth Missouri and some pioneers, with axes, saws, and all the tools necessary. I gave orders for a part of Stuart's division to proceed in the large boats up the Mississippi River to a point at Gwin's plantation, where a bend of Steele's Bayou neared the main river; and the next day, with one or two stag-officers and orderlies, got a navy-tug, and hurried up to overtake Admiral Porter. About sixty miles up Steele's Bayou we came to the gunboat Price, Lieutenant Woodworth, United States Navy; commanding, and then turned into Black Bayou, a narrow, crooked channel, obstructed by overhanging oaks, and filled with cypress and cotton-wood trees. The gunboats had forced their way through, pushing aside trees a foot in diameter. In about four miles we overtook the gunboat fleet just as it was emerging into Deer Creek. Along Deer Creek the alluvium was higher, and there was a large cotton-plantation belonging to a Mr. Hill, who was absent, and the negroes were in charge of the place. Here I overtook Admiral Porter, and accompanied him a couple of miles up Deer Creek, which was much wider and more free of trees, with plantations on both sides at intervals. Admiral Porter thought he had passed the worst, and that he would be able to reach the Rolling Fork and Sunflower. He requested me to return and use all possible means to clear out Black Bayou. I returned to Hill's plantation, which was soon reached by Major Coleman, with a part of the Eighth Missouri; the bulk of the regiment and the pioneers had been distributed along the bayous, and set to work under the general supervision of Captain Kosaak. The Diligent and Silver Wave then returned to twin's plantation and brought up Brigadier-General Giles A. Smith, with the Sixth Missouri, and part of the One Hundred and Sixteenth Illinois. Admiral Porter was then working up Deer Creek with his iron-clads, but he had left me a tug, which enabled me to reconnoitre the country, which was all under water except the narrow strip along Deer Creek. During the 19th I heard the heavy navy-guns booming more frequently than seemed consistent with mere guerrilla operations; and that night I got a message from Porter, written on tissue-paper, brought me through the swamp by a negro, who had it concealed in a piece of tobacco.

The admiral stated that he had met a force of infantry and artillery which gave him great trouble by killing the men who had to expose themselves outside the iron armor to shove off the bows of the boats, which had so little headway that they would not steer. He begged me to come to his rescue as quickly as possible. Giles A. Smith had only about eight hundred men with him, but I ordered him to start up Deer Creek at once, crossing to the east side by an old bridge at Hill's plantation, which we had repaired for the purpose; to work his way up to the gunboat, fleet, and to report to the admiral that I would come, up with every man I could raise as soon as possible. I was almost alone at Hill's, but took a canoe, paddled down Black Bayou to the gunboat Price, and there, luckily, found the Silver wave with a load of men just arrived from twin's plantation. Taking some of the parties who were at work along the bayou into an empty coal-barge, we tugged it up by a navy-tug, followed by the Silver Wave, crashing through the trees, carrying away pilot-house, smoke-stacks, and every thing above-deck; but the captain (McMillan, of Pittsburg) was a brave fellow, and realized the necessity. The night was absolutely black, and we could only make two and a half of the four miles. We then disembarked, and marched through the canebrake, carrying lighted candles in our hands, till we got into the open cotton-fields at Hill's plantation, where we lay down for a few hours' rest. These men were a part of Giles A. Smith's brigade, and part belonged to the brigade of T. Bilby Smith, the senior officer present being Lieutenant-Colonel Rice, Fifty-fourth Ohio, an excellent young officer. We had no horses.

On Sunday morning, March 21st, as soon as daylight appeared, we started, following the same route which Giles A. Smith had taken the day before; the battalion of the Thirteenth United States Regulars, Major Chase, in the lead. We could hear Porter's guns, and knew that moments were precious. Being on foot myself, no man could complain, and we generally went at the double-quick, with occasional rests. The road lay along Deer Creek, passing several plantations; and occasionally, at the bends, it crossed the swamp, where the water came above my hips. The smaller drummer-boys had to carry their drums on their heads, and most of the men slang their cartridge-boxes around their necks. The soldiers generally were glad to have their general and field officers afoot, but we gave them a fair specimen of marching, accomplishing about twenty-one miles by noon. Of course, our speed was accelerated by the sounds of the navy-guns, which became more and more distinct, though we could see nothing. At a plantation near some Indian mounds we met a detachment of the Eighth Missouri, that had been up to the fleet, and had been sent down as a picket to prevent any obstructions below. This picket reported that Admiral Porter had found Deer Creek badly obstructed, had turned back; that there was a rebel force beyond the fleet, with some six-pounders, and nothing between us and the fleet. So I sat down on the door-sill of a cabin to rest, but had not been seated ten minutes when, in the wood just ahead, not three hundred yards off, I heard quick and rapid firing of musketry. Jumping up, I ran up the road, and found Lieutenant-Colonel Rice, who said the head of his column had struck a small force of rebels with a working gang of negroes, provided with axes, who on the first fire had broken and run back into the swamp. I ordered Rice to deploy his brigade, his left on the road, and extending as far into the swamp as the ground would permit, and then to sweep forward until he uncovered the gunboats. The movement was rapid and well executed, and we soon came to some large cotton-fields and could see our gunboats in Deer Creek, occasionally firing a heavy eight-inch gun across the cotton field into the swamp behind. About that time Major Kirby, of the Eighth Missouri, galloped down the road on a horse he had picked up the night before, and met me. He explained the situation of affairs, and offered me his horse. I got on bareback, and rode up the levee, the sailors coming out of their iron-clads and cheering most vociferously as I rode by, and as our men swept forward across the cotton-field in full view. I soon found Admiral Porter, who was on the deck of one of his iron-clads, with a shield made of the section of a smoke-stack, and I doubt if he was ever more glad to meet a friend than he was to see me. He explained that he had almost reached the Rolling Fork, when the woods became full of sharp-shooters, who, taking advantage of trees, stumps, and the levee, would shoot down every man that poked his nose outside the protection of their armor; so that he could not handle his clumsy boats in the narrow channel. The rebels had evidently dispatched a force from Haines's Bluff up the Sunflower to the Rolling Fork, had anticipated the movement of Admiral Porter's fleet, and had completely obstructed the channel of the upper part of Deer Creek by felling trees into it, so that further progress in that direction was simply impossible. It also happened that, at the instant of my arrival, a party of about four hundred rebels, armed and supplied with axes, had passed around the fleet and had got below it, intending in like manner to block up the channel by the felling of trees, so as to cut off retreat. This was the force we had struck so opportunely at the time before described. I inquired of Admiral Porter what he proposed to do, and he said he wanted to get out of that scrape as quickly as possible. He was actually working back when I met him, and, as we then had a sufficient force to cover his movement completely, he continued to back down Deer Creek. He informed me at one time things looked so critical that he had made up his mind to blow up the gunboats, and to escape with his men through the swamp to the Mississippi River. There being no longer any sharp-shooters to bother the sailors, they made good progress; still, it took three full days for the fleet to back out of Deer Creek into Black Bayou, at Hill's plantation, whence Admiral Porter proceeded to his post at the month of the Yazoo, leaving Captain Owen in command of the fleet. I reported the facts to General Grant, who was sadly disappointed at the failure of the fleet to get through to the Yazoo above Haines's Bluff, and ordered us all to resume our camps at Young's Point. We accordingly steamed down, and regained our camps on the 27th. As this expedition up Deer Creek was but one of many efforts to secure a footing from which to operate against Vicksburg, I add the report of Brigadier-General Giles A. Smith, who was the first to reach the fleet:

HEADQUARTERS FIRST BRIGADE, SECOND DIVISION
FIFTEENTH ARMY CORPS, YOUNGS POINT, LOUISIANA,

March 28, 1863

Captain L. M. DAYTON, Assistant Adjutant-General.

CAPTAIN: I have the honor to report the movements of the First Brigade in the expedition up Steele's Bayou, Black Bayou, and Deer Creek. The Sixth Missouri and One Hundred and Sixteenth Illinois regiments embarked at the mouth of Muddy Bayou on the evening of Thursday, the 18th of March, and proceeded up Steele's Bayou to the mouth of Black; thence up Black Bayou to Hill's plantation, at its junction with Deer Creek, where we arrived on Friday at four o'clock p.m., and joined the Eighth Missouri, Lieutenant-Colonel Coleman commanding, which had arrived at that point two days before. General Sherman had also established his headquarters there, having preceded the Eighth Missouri in a tug, with no other escort than two or three of his staff, reconnoitring all the different bayous and branches, thereby greatly facilitating the movements of the troops, but at the same time exposing himself beyond precedent in a commanding general. At three o'clock of Saturday morning, the 20th instant, General Sherman having received a communication from Admiral Porter at the mouth of Rolling Fork, asking for a speedy cooperation of the land forces with his fleet, I was ordered by General Sherman to be ready, with all the available force at that point, to accompany him to his relief; but before starting it was arranged that I should proceed with the force at hand (eight hundred men), while he remained, again entirely unprotected, to hurry up the troops expected to arrive that night, consisting of the Thirteenth Infantry and One Hundred and Thirteenth Illinois Volunteers, completing my brigade, and the Second Brigade, Colonel T. Kilby Smith commanding.

This, as the sequel showed; proved a very wise measure, and resulted in the safety of the whole fleet. At daybreak we were in motion, with a regular guide. We had proceeded but about six miles, when we found the enemy had been very busy felling trees to obstruct the creek.

All the negroes along the route had been notified to be ready at night fall to continue the work. To prevent this as much as possible, I ordered all able-bodied negroes to be taken along, and warned some of the principal inhabitants that they would be held responsible for any more obstructions being placed across the creek. We reached the admiral about four o'clock p.m., with no opposition save my advance-guard (Company A, Sixth Missouri) being fired into from the opposite side of the creek, killing one man, and slightly wounding another; having no way of crossing, we had to content ourselves with driving them beyond musket-range. Proceeding with as little loss of time as possible, I found the fleet obstructed in front by fallen trees, in rear by a sunken coal-barge, and surrounded, by a large force of rebels with an abundant supply of artillery, but wisely keeping their main force out of range of the admiral's guns. Every tree and stump covered a sharp-shooter, ready to pick off any luckless marine who showed his head above-decks, and entirely preventing the working-parties from removing obstructions.

In pursuance of orders from General Sherman, I reported to Admiral Porter for orders, who turned over to me all the land-forces in his fleet (about one hundred and fifty men), together with two howitzers, and I was instructed by him to retain a sufficient force to clear out the sharp-shooters, and to distribute the remainder along the creek for six or seven miles below, to prevent any more obstructions being placed in it during the night. This was speedily arranged, our skirmishers capturing three prisoners. Immediate steps were now taken to remove the coal-barge, which was accomplished about daylight on Sunday morning, when the fleet moved back toward Black Bayou. By three o'clock p.m. we had only made about six miles, owing to the large number of trees to be removed; at this point, where our progress was very slow, we discovered a long line of the enemy filing along the edge of the woods, and taking position on the creek below us, and about one mile ahead of our advance. Shortly after, they opened fire on the gunboats from batteries behind the cavalry and infantry. The boats not only replied to the batteries, which they soon silenced, but poured a destructive fire into their lines. Heavy skirmishing was also heard in our front, supposed to be by three companies from the Sixth and Eighth Missouri, whose position, taken the previous night to guard the creek, was beyond the point reached by the enemy, and consequently liable to be cut off or captured. Captain Owen, of the Louisville, the leading boat, made every effort to go through the obstructions and aid in the rescuing of the men. I ordered Major Kirby, with four companies of the Sixth Missouri, forward, with two companies deployed. He soon met General Sherman, with the Thirteenth Infantry and One Hundred and Thirteenth Illinois, driving the enemy before them, and opening communication along the creek with the gunboats. Instead of our three companies referred to as engaging the enemy, General Sherman had arrived at a very opportune moment with the two *regiments mentioned above, and the Second Brigade. The enemy, not expecting an attack from that quarter, after some hot skirmishing, retreated. General Sherman immediately ordered the Thirteenth Infantry and One Hundred and Thirteenth Illinois to pursue; but, after following their trace for about two miles, they were recalled.*

We continued our march for about two miles, when we bivouacked for the night. Early on Monday morning (March 22d) we continued our march, but owing to the slow progress of the gunboats did not reach Hill's plantation until Tuesday, the 23d instant, where we remained until the 25th; we then reembarked, and arrived at Young's Point on Friday, the 27th instant.

Below you will find a list of casualties. Very respectfully,

Giles A. SMITH, Colonel Eighth Missouri, commanding First Brigade.

P. S.-I forgot to state above that the Thirteenth Infantry and One Hundred and Thirteenth Illinois being under the immediate command of General Sherman, he can mention them as their conduct deserves.

On the 3d of April, a division of troops, commanded by Brigadier-General J. M. Tuttle, was assigned to my corps, and was designated the Third Division; and, on the 4th of April, Brigadier-General D. Stuart was relieved from the command of the Second Division, to which Major-General Frank P. Blair was appointed by an order from General Grant's headquarters. Stuart had been with me from the time we were at Benton Barracks, in command of the Fifty-fifth Illinois, then of a brigade, and finally of a division; but he had failed in seeking a confirmation by the Senate to his nomination as brigadier-general, by reason of some old affair at Chicago, and, having resigned his commission as colonel, he was out of service. I esteemed him very highly, and was actually mortified that the service should thus be deprived of so excellent and gallant an officer. He afterward settled in New Orleans as a lawyer, and died about 1867 or 1868.

On the 6th of April, my command, the Fifteenth Corps, was composed of three divisions:

The First Division, commanded by Major-General Fred Steele; and his three brigades by Colonel Manter, Colonel Charles R. Wood, and Brigadier-General John M. Thayer.

The Second Division, commanded by Major-General Frank P. Blair; and his three brigades by Colonel Giles A. Smith, Colonel Thomas Gilby Smith, and Brigadier-General Hugh Ewing.

The Third Division, commanded by Brigadier-General J. M. Tuttle; and his three brigades by Brigadier-General R. P. Buckland, Colonel J. A. Mower, and Brigadier-General John E. Smith.

My own staff then embraced: Dayton, McCoy, and Hill, aides; J. H. Hammond, assistant adjutant-general; Sanger, inspector-general; McFeeley, commissary; J. Condit Smith, quartermaster; Charles McMillan, medical director; Ezra Taylor, chief of artillery; Jno. C. Neely, ordnance-officer; Jenney and Pitzman, engineers.

By this time it had become thoroughly demonstrated that we could not divert the main river Mississippi, or get practicable access to the east bank of the Yazoo, in the rear of Vicksburg, by any of the passes; and we were all in the habit of discussing the various chances of the future. General Grant's headquarters were at Milliken's Bend, in tents, and his army was strung along the river all the way from Young's Point up to Lake Providence, at least sixty miles. I had always contended that the best way to take Vicksburg was to resume the movement which had been so well begun the previous November, viz., for the main army to march by land down the country inland of the Mississippi River; while the gunboat-fleet and a minor land-force should threaten Vicksburg on its river-front.

I reasoned that, with the large force then subject to General Grant's orders-viz., four army corps—he could easily resume the movement from Memphis, by way of Oxford and Grenada, to Jackson, Mississippi, or down the ridge between the Yazoo and Big Black; but General Grant would not, for reasons other than military, take any course which looked like, a step backward; and he himself concluded on the river movement below Vicksburg, so as to appear like connecting with General Banks, who at the same time was besieging Port Hudson from the direction of New Orleans.

Preliminary orders had already been given, looking to the digging of a canal, to connect the river at Duckport with Willow Bayou, back of Milliken's Bend, so as to form a channel for the conveyance of supplies, by way of Richmond, to New Carthage; and several steam dredge-boats had come from the upper rivers to assist in the work. One day early in April, I was up at General Grant's headquarters, and we talked over all these things with absolute freedom. Charles A. Dana, Assistant Secretary of War, was there, and Wilson, Rawlins, Frank Blair, McPherson, etc. We all knew, what was notorious, that General McClernand was still intriguing against General Grant, in hopes to regain the command of the whole expedition, and that others were raising a clamor against General Grant in the news papers at the North. Even Mr. Lincoln and General Halleck seemed to be shaken; but at no instant of time did we (his personal friends) slacken in our loyalty to him. One night, after such a discussion, and believing that General McClernand had no real plan of action shaped in his mind, I wrote my letter of April 8, 1863, to Colonel Rawlins, which letter is embraced in full at page 616 of Badeau's book, and which I now reproduce here:

HEADQUARTERS FIFTEENTH ARMY CORPS,
CAMP NEAR VICKSBURG, April 8,1868.

Colonel J. A. RAWLINS, Assistant Adjutant-General to General GRANT.

SIR: I would most respectfully suggest (for reasons which I will not name) that General Grant call on his corps commanders for their opinions, concise and positive, on the best general plan of a campaign. Unless this be done, there are men who will, in any result falling below the popular standard, claim that their advice was unheeded, and that fatal consequence resulted therefrom. My own opinions are:

First. That the Army of the Tennessee is now far in advance of the other grand armies of the United States.

Second. That a corps from Missouri should forthwith be moved from St. Louis to the vicinity of Little Rock, Arkansas; supplies collected there while the river is full, and land communication with Memphis opened via Des Arc on the White, and Madison on the St. Francis River.

Third. That as much of the Yazoo Pass, Coldwater, and Tallahatchie Rivers, as can be gained and fortified, be held, and the main army be transported thither by land and water; that the road back to Memphis be secured and reopened, and, as soon as the waters subside, Grenada be attacked, and the swamp-road across to Helena be patrolled by cavalry.

Fourth. That the line of the Yalabusha be the base from which to operate against the points where the Mississippi Central crosses Big Black, above Canton; and, lastly, where the Vicksburg & Jackson Railroad crosses the same river (Big Black). The capture of Vicksburg would result.

Fifth. That a minor force be left in this vicinity, not to exceed ten thousand men, with only enough steamboats to float and transport them to any desired point; this force to be held always near enough to act with the gunboats when the main army is known to be near Vicksburg—Haines's Bluff or Yazoo City.

Sixth. I do doubt the capacity of Willow Bayou (which I estimate to be fifty miles long and very tortuous) as a military channel, to supply an army large enough to operate against Jackson, Mississippi, or the Black

River Bridge; and such a channel will be very vulnerable to a force coming from the west, which we must expect. Yet this canal will be most useful as the way to convey coals and supplies to a fleet that should navigate the lower reach of the Mississippi between Vicksburg and the Red River.

Seventh. The chief reason for operating solely by water was the season of the year and high water in the Tallahatchie and Yalabusha Rivers. The spring is now here, and soon these streams will be no serious obstacle, save in the ambuscades of the forest, and whatever works the enemy may have erected at or near Grenada. North Mississippi is too valuable for us to allow the enemy to hold it and make crops this year.

I make these suggestions, with the request that General Grant will read them and give them, as I know he will, a share of his thoughts. I would prefer that he should not answer this letter, but merely give it as much or as little weight as it deserves. Whatever plan of action he may adopt will receive from me the same zealous cooperation and energetic support as though conceived by myself. I do not believe General Banks will make any serious attack on Port Hudson this spring. I am, etc.,

W. T. SHERMAN, Major-General.

       This is the letter which some critics have styled a "protest." We never had a council of war at any time during the Vicksburg campaign. We often met casually, regardless of rank or power, and talked and gossiped of things in general, as officers do and should. But my letter speaks for itself—it shows my opinions clearly at that stage of the game, and was meant partially to induce General Grant to call on General McClernand for a similar expression of opinion, but, so far as I know, he did not. He went on quietly to work out his own designs; and he has told me, since the war, that had we possessed in December, 1862, the experience of marching and maintaining armies without a regular base, which we afterward acquired, he would have gone on from Oxford as first contemplated, and would not have turned back because of the destruction of his depot at Holly Springs by Van Dorn. The distance from Oxford to the rear of Vicksburg is little greater than by the circuitous route we afterward followed, from Bruinsburg to Jackson and Vicksburg, during which we had neither depot nor train of supplies. I have never criticised General Grant's strategy on this or any other occasion, but I thought then that he had lost an opportunity, which cost him and us six months' extra-hard work, for we might have captured Vicksburg from the direction of Oxford in January, quite as easily as was afterward done in July, 1863.
       General Grant's orders for the general movement past Vicksburg, by Richmond and Carthage, were dated April 20, 1863. McClernand was to lead off with his corps, McPherson next, and my corps (the Fifteenth) to bring up the rear. Preliminary thereto, on the night of April 16th, seven iron-clads led by Admiral Porter in person, in the Benton, with three transports, and ten barges in tow, ran the Vicksburg batteries by night. Anticipating a scene, I had four yawl-boats hauled across the swamp, to the reach of the river below Vicksburg, and manned them with soldiers, ready to pick up any of the disabled wrecks as they floated by. I was out in the stream when the fleet passed Vicksburg, and the scene was truly sublime. As soon as the rebel gunners detected the Benton, which was in the lead, they opened on her, and on the others in succession, with shot and shell; houses on the Vicksburg side and on the opposite shore were set on fire, which lighted up the whole river; and the roar of cannon, the bursting of shells, and finally the burning of the Henry Clay, drifting with the current, made up a picture of the terrible not often seen. Each gunboat returned the fire as

she passed the town, while the transports hugged the opposite shore. When the Benton had got abreast of us, I pulled off to her, boarded, had a few words with Admiral Porter, and as she was drifting rapidly toward the lower batteries at Warrenton, I left, and pulled back toward the shore, meeting the gunboat Tuscumbia towing the transport Forest Queen into the bank out of the range of fire. The Forest Queen, Captain Conway, had been my flag-boat up the Arkansas, and for some time after, and I was very friendly with her officers. This was the only transport whose captain would not receive volunteers as a crew, but her own officers and crew stuck to their boat, and carried her safely below the Vicksburg batteries, and afterward rendered splendid service in ferrying troops across the river at Grand Gulf and Bruinsburg. In passing Vicksburg, she was damaged in the hull and had a steam-pipe cut away, but this was soon repaired. The Henry Clay was set on fire by bursting shells, and burned up; one of my yawls picked up her pilot floating on a piece of wreck, and the bulk of her crew escaped in their own yawl-boat to the shore above. The Silver Wave, Captain McMillan, the same that was with us up Steele's Bayou, passed safely, and she also rendered good service afterward.

Subsequently, on the night of April 26th, six other transports with numerous barges loaded with hay, corn, freight, and provisions, were drifted past Vicksburg; of these the Tigress was hit, and sunk just as she reached the river-bank below, on our side: I was there with my yawls, and saw Colonel Lagow, of General Grant's staff, who had passed the batteries in the Tigress, and I think he was satisfied never to attempt such a thing again. Thus General Grant's army had below Vicksburg an abundance of stores, and boats with which to cross the river. The road by which the troops marched was very bad, and it was not until the 1st of May that it was clear for my corps. While waiting my turn to march, I received a letter from General Grant, written at Carthage, saying that he proposed to cross over and attack Grand Gulf, about the end of April, and he thought I could put in my time usefully by making a "feint" on Haines's Bluff, but he did not like to order me to do it, because it might be reported at the North that I had again been "repulsed, etc." Thus we had to fight a senseless clamor at the North, as well as a determined foe and the obstacles of Nature. Of course, I answered him that I would make the "feint," regardless of public clamor at a distance, and I did make it most effectually; using all the old boats I could get about Milliken's Bend and the mouth of the Yazoo, but taking only ten small regiments, selected out of Blair's division, to make a show of force. We afterward learned that General Pemberton in Vicksburg had previously dispatched a large force to the assistance of General Bowers, at Grand Gulf and Port Gibson, which force had proceeded as far as Hankinson's Ferry, when he discovered our ostentatious movement up the Yazoo, recalled his men, and sent them up to Haines's Bluff to meet us. This detachment of rebel troops must have marched nearly sixty miles without rest, for afterward, on reaching Vicksburg, I heard that the men were perfectly exhausted, and lay along the road in groups, completely fagged out. This diversion, made with so much pomp and display, therefore completely fulfilled its purpose, by leaving General Grant to contend with a minor force, on landing at Bruinsburg, and afterward at Port Gibson and Grand Gulf.

In May the waters of the Mississippi had so far subsided that all our canals were useless, and the roads had become practicable. After McPherson's corps had passed Richmond, I took up the route of march, with Steele's and Tuttle's divisions. Blair's division remained at Milliken's Bend to protect our depots there, till relieved by troops from Memphis, and then he was ordered to follow us. Our route lay by Richmond and Roundabout Bayou; then, following Bayou Vidal we struck the Mississippi at Perkins's plantation. Thence the route followed Lake St. Joseph to a plantation called Hard Times, about five miles above Grand Gulf. The road was more or less occupied by wagons and detachments belonging to McPherson's corps; still we marched rapidly and reached Hard Times on the 6th of May. Along the Bayou or Lake St. Joseph were many very fine cotton plantations, and I recall that of a Mr. Bowie, brother-in-law of the Hon. Reverdy Johnson, of Baltimore. The house was very handsome, with a fine, extensive grass-plot in front. We entered the yard, and, leaving our horses with the headquarters escort, walked to the house. On the front-porch I found a magnificent grand-piano, with several satin-covered arm-chairs, in one of which sat a Union soldier (one of McPherson's men), with his feet on the keys of the piano, and his musket and knapsack lying on the porch. I asked him what he was doing there, and he answered that he was "taking a rest;" this was manifest and I started him in a hurry, to overtake his command. The house was tenantless, and had been completely ransacked; articles of dress and books were strewed about, and a handsome boudoir with mirror front had been cast down, striking a French bedstead, shivering the glass. The library was extensive, with a fine collection of books; and hanging on the wall were two full-length portraits of Reverdy Johnson and his wife, one of the most beautiful ladies of our country, with whom I had been acquainted in Washington at the time of General Taylor's administration. Behind the mansion was the usual double row of cabins called the "quarters." There I found an old negro (a family servant) with several women, whom I sent to the house to put things in order; telling the old man that other troops would follow, and he must stand on the porch to tell any officers who came along that the property belonged to Mr. Bowie, who was the brother-in-law of our friend Mr. Reverdy Johnson, of Baltimore, asking them to see that no further harm was done. Soon after we left the house I saw some negroes carrying away furniture which manifestly belonged to the house, and compelled them to carry it back; and after reaching camp that night, at Hard Times, I sent a wagon back to Bowie's plantation, to bring up to Dr. Hollingsworth's house the two portraits for safe keeping; but before the wagon had reached Bowie's the house was burned, whether by some of our men or by negroes I have never learned.

At the river there was a good deal of scrambling to get across, because the means of ferriage were inadequate; but by the aid of the Forest Queen and several gunboats I got my command across during the 7th of May, and marched out to Hankiuson's Ferry (eighteen miles), relieving General Crocker's division of McPherson's corps. McClernand's corps and McPherson's were still ahead, and had fought the battle of Port Gibson, on the 11th. I overtook General Grant in person at Auburn, and he accompanied my corps all the way into Jackson, which we reached May 14th. McClernand's corps had been left in observation toward Edwards's Ferry. McPherson had fought at Raymond, and taken the left-hand road toward Jackson, via Clinton, while my troops were ordered by General Grant in person to take the right-hand road leading through Mississippi Springs. We reached Jackson at the same time; McPherson fighting on the Clinton road, and my troops fighting just outside the town, on the Raymond road, where we captured three entire field-batteries, and about two hundred prisoners of war. The rebels, under General Joe Johnston, had retreated through the town northward on the Canton road. Generals Grant, McPherson, and I, met in the large hotel facing the State-House, where the former explained to us that he had intercepted dispatches from Pemberton to Johnston, which made it important for us to work smart to prevent a junction of their respective forces. McPherson was ordered to march back early the next day on the Clinton road to make junction with McClernand, and I was ordered to remain one day to break up railroads, to destroy the arsenal, a foundery, the cotton-factory of the Messrs. Green, etc., etc., and then to follow McPherson.

McPherson left Jackson early on the 15th, and General Grant during the same day. I kept my troops busy in tearing up railroad-tracks, etc., but early on the morning of the 16th received notice from General Grant that a battle was imminent near Edwards's Depot; that he wanted me to dispatch one of my divisions immediately, and to follow with the other as soon as I had completed the work of destruction. Steele's division started immediately, and later in the day I followed with the other division (Tuttle's). Just as I was leaving Jackson, a very fat man came to see me, to inquire if his hotel, a large, frame building near the depot, were doomed to be burned. I told him we had no intention to burn it, or any other house, except the machine-shops, and such buildings as could easily be converted to hostile uses. He professed to be a law-abiding Union man, and I remember to have said that this fact was manifest from the sign of his hotel, which was the "Confederate Hotel;" the sign "United States" being faintly painted out, and "Confederate" painted over it! I remembered that hotel, as it was the supper-station for the New Orleans trains when I used to travel the road before the war. I had not the least purpose, however, of burning it, but, just as we were leaving the town, it burst out in flames and was burned to the ground. I never found out exactly who set it on fire, but was told that in one of our batteries were some officers and men who had been made prisoners at Shiloh, with Prentiss's division, and had been carried past Jackson in a railroad-train; they had been permitted by the guard to go to this very hotel for supper, and had nothing to pay but greenbacks, which were refused, with insult, by this same law-abiding landlord. These men, it was said, had quietly and stealthily applied the fire underneath the hotel just as we were leaving the town.

About dark we met General Grant's staff-officer near Bolton Station, who turned us to the right, with orders to push on to Vicksburg by what was known as the upper Jackson Road, which crossed the Big Black at Bridgeport. During that day (May 16th) the battle of Champion Hills had been fought and won by McClernand's and McPherson's corps, aided by one division of mine (Blairs), under the immediate command of General Grant; and McPherson was then following the mass of Pemberton's army, disordered and retreating toward Vicksburg by the Edwards's Ferry road. General Blair's division had come up from the rear, was temporarily attached to McClernand's corps, taking part with it in the battle of Champion Hills, but on the 17th it was ordered by General Grant across to Bridgeport, to join me there.

Just beyond Bolton there was a small hewn-log house, standing back in a yard, in which was a well; at this some of our soldiers were drawing water. I rode in to get a drink, and, seeing a book on the ground, asked some soldier to hand it to me. It was a volume of the Constitution of the United States, and on the title-page was written the name of Jefferson Davis. On inquiry of a negro, I learned that the place belonged to the then President of the Southern Confederation. His brother Joe Davis's plantation was not far off; one of my staff-officers went there, with a few soldiers, and took a pair of carriage-horses, without my knowledge at the time. He found Joe Davis at home, an old man, attended by a young and affectionate niece; but they were overwhelmed with grief to see their country overran and swarming with Federal troops.

We pushed on, and reached the Big Black early, Blair's troops having preceded us by an hour or so. I found General Blair in person, and he reported that there was no bridge across the Big Black; that it was swimming-deep; and that there was a rebel force on the opposite side, intrenched. He had ordered a detachment of the Thirteenth United States Regulars, under Captain Charles Ewing, to strip some artillery-horses, mount the men, and swim the river above the ferry, to attack and drive away the party on the opposite bank. I did not approve of this risky attempt, but crept down close to the brink of the river bank, behind a corn-crib belonging to a plantation house near by, and saw the parapet on the opposite bank. Ordering a section of guns to be brought forward by hand behind this corn-crib, a few well-directed shells brought out of their holes the little party that was covering the crossing, viz., a lieutenant and ten men, who came down to the river-bank and surrendered. Blair's pontoon-train was brought up, consisting of India-rubber boats, one of which was inflated, used as a boat, and brought over the prisoners. A pontoon-bridge was at once begun, finished by night, and the troops began the passage. After dark, the whole scene was lit up with fires of pitch-pine. General Grant joined me there, and we sat on a log, looking at the passage of the troops by the light of those fires; the bridge swayed to and fro under the passing feet, and made a fine war-picture. At daybreak we moved on, ascending the ridge, and by 10 a.m. the head of my column, long drawn out, reached the Benton road, and gave us command of the peninsula between the Yazoo and Big Black. I dispatched Colonel Swan, of the Fourth Iowa Cavalry, to Haines's Bluff, to capture that battery from the rear, and he afterward reported that he found it abandoned, its garrison having hastily retreated into Vicksburg, leaving their guns partially disabled, a magazine full of ammunition, and a hospital full of wounded and sick men. Colonel Swan saw one of our gunboats lying about two miles below in the Yazoo, to which he signaled. She steamed up, and to its commander the cavalry turned over the battery at Haines's Bluff, and rejoined me in front of Vicksburg. Allowing a couple of hours for rest and to close up the column, I resumed the march straight on Vicksburg. About two miles before reaching the forts, the road forked; the left was the main Jackson road, and the right was the "graveyard" road, which entered Vicksburg near a large cemetery. General Grant in person directed me to take the right-hand road, but, as McPherson had not yet got up from the direction of the railroad-bridge at Big Black, I sent the Eighth Missouri on the main Jackson road, to push the rebel skirmishers into town, and to remain until relieved by McPherson's advance, which happened late that evening, May

18th. The battalion of the Thirteenth United States Regulars, commanded by Captain Washington, was at the head of the column on the right-hand road, and pushed the rebels close behind their parapets; one of my staff, Captain Pitzman, receiving a dangerous wound in the hip, which apparently disabled him for life. By night Blair's whole division had closed up against the defenses of Vicksburg, which were found to be strong and well manned; and, on General Steele's head of column arriving, I turned it still more to the right, with orders to work its way down the bluff, so as to make connection with our fleet in the Mississippi River. There was a good deal of desultory fighting that evening, and a man was killed by the aide of General Grant and myself, as we sat by the road-side looking at Steele's division passing to the right. General Steele's men reached the road which led from Vicksburg up to Haines's Bluff, which road lay at the foot of the hills, and intercepted some prisoners and wagons which were coming down from Haines's Bluff.

All that night McPherson's troops were arriving by the main Jackson road, and McClernand'a by another near the railroad, deploying forward as fast as they struck the rebel works. My corps (the Fifteenth) had the right of the line of investment; McPherson's (the Seventeenth) the centre; and McClernand's (the Thirteenth) the left, reaching from the river above to the railroad below. Our lines connected, and invested about three-quarters of the land-front of the fortifications of Vicksburg. On the supposition that the garrison of Vicksburg was demoralized by the defeats at Champion Hills and at the railroad crossing of the Big Black, General Grant ordered an assault at our respective fronts on the 19th. My troops reached the top of the parapet, but could not cross over. The rebel parapets were strongly manned, and the enemy fought hard and well. My loss was pretty heavy, falling chiefly on the Thirteenth Regulars, whose commanding officer, Captain Washington, was killed, and several other regiments were pretty badly cut up. We, however, held the ground up to the ditch till night, and then drew back only a short distance, and began to counter-trench. On the graveyard road, our parapet was within less than fifty yards of the rebel ditch.

On the 20th of May, General Grant called the three corps commanders together, viz., McClernand, McPherson, and Sherman. We compared notes, and agreed that the assault of the day before had failed, by reason of the natural strength of the position, and because we were forced by the nature of the ground to limit our attacks to the strongest parts of the enemy's line, viz., where the three principal roads entered the city.

It was not a council of war, but a mere consultation, resulting in orders from General Grant for us to make all possible preparations for a renewed assault on the 22d, simultaneously, at 10 a.m. I reconnoitred my front thoroughly in person, from right to left, and concluded to make my real attack at the right flank of the bastion, where the graveyard road entered the enemy's intrenchments, and at another point in the curtain about a hundred yards to its right (our left); also to make a strong demonstration by Steele's division, about a mile to our right, toward the river. All our field batteries were put in position, and were covered by good epaulements; the troops were brought forward, in easy support, concealed by the shape of the ground; and to the minute, viz., 10 a.m. of May 22d, the troops sprang to the assault. A small party, that might be called a forlorn hope, provided with plank to cross the ditch, advanced at a run, up to the very ditch; the lines of infantry sprang from cover, and advanced rapidly in line of battle. I took a position within two hundred yards of the rebel parapet, on the off slope of a spur of ground, where by advancing two or three steps I could see every thing. The rebel line, concealed by the parapet, showed no sign of unusual activity, but as our troops came in fair view, the enemy rose behind their parapet and poured a furious fire upon our lines; and, for about two hours, we had a severe and bloody battle, but at every point we were repulsed. In the very midst of this, when shell and shot fell furious and fast, occurred that little episode which has been celebrated in song and story, of the boy Orion P. Howe, badly wounded, bearing me a message for cartridges, calibre 54, described in my letter to the Hon. E. M. Stanton, Secretary of War. This boy was afterward appointed a cadet to the United States Naval Academy, at Annapolis, but he could not graduate, and I do not now know what has become of him.

After our men had been fairly beaten back from off the parapet, and had got cover behind the spurs of ground close up to the rebel works, General Grant came to where I was, on foot, having left his horse some distance to the rear. I pointed out to him the rebel works, admitted that my assault had failed, and he said the result with McPherson and McClernand was about the same. While he was with me, an orderly or staff-officer came and handed him a piece of paper, which he read and handed to me. I think the writing was in pencil, on a loose piece of paper, and was in General McClernand's handwriting, to the effect that "his troops had captured the rebel parapet in his front," that, "the flag of the Union waved over the stronghold of Vicksburg," and asking him (General Grant) to give renewed orders to McPherson and Sherman to press their attacks on their respective fronts, lest the enemy should concentrate on him (McClernand). General Grant said, "I don't believe a word of it;" but I reasoned with him, that this note was official, and must be credited, and I offered to renew the assault at once with new troops. He said he would instantly ride down the line to McClernand's front, and if I did not receive orders to the contrary, by 3 o'clock p.m., I might try it again. Mower's fresh brigade was brought up under cover, and some changes were made in Giles Smith's brigade; and, punctually at 3 p.m., hearing heavy firing down along the line to my left, I ordered the second assault. It was a repetition of the first, equally unsuccessful and bloody. It also transpired that the same thing had occurred with General McPherson, who lost in this second assault some most valuable officers and men, without adequate result; and that General McClernand, instead of having taken any single point of the rebel main parapet, had only taken one or two small outlying lunettes open to the rear, where his men were at the mercy of the rebels behind their main parapet, and most of them were actually thus captured. This affair caused great feeling with us, and severe criticisms on General McClernand, which led finally to his removal from the command of the Thirteenth Corps, to which General Ord succeeded. The immediate cause, however, of General McClernand's removal was the publication of a sort of congratulatory order addressed to his troops, first published in St. Louis, in which he claimed that he had actually succeeded in making a lodgment in Vicksburg, but had lost it, owing to the fact that McPherson and Sherman did not fulfill their parts of the general plan of attack. This was simply untrue. The two several assaults made May 22d, on the lines of Vicksburg, had failed, by reason of the great strength of the position and the determined fighting of its garrison. I have since seen the position at Sevastopol, and without hesitation I declare that at Vicksburg to have been the more difficult of the two.

Thereafter our proceedings were all in the nature of a siege. General Grant drew more troops from Memphis, to prolong our general line to the left, so as completely to invest the place on its land-side, while the navy held the river both above and below. General Mower's brigade of Tuttle's division was also sent across the river to the peninsula, so that by May 31st Vicksburg was completely beleaguered. Good roads were constructed from our camps to the several landing-places on the Yazoo River, to which points our boats brought us ample supplies; so that we were in a splendid condition for a siege, while our enemy was shut up in a close fort, with a large civil population of men, women, and children to feed, in addition to his combatant force. If we could prevent sallies, or relief from the outside, the fate of the garrison of Vicksburg was merely a question of time.

I had my headquarters camp close up to the works, near the centre of my corps, and General Grant had his bivouac behind a ravine to my rear. We estimated Pemberton's whole force in Vicksburg at thirty thousand men, and it was well known that the rebel General Joseph E. Johnston was engaged in collecting another strong force near the Big Black, with the intention to attack our rear, and thus to afford Pemberton an opportunity to escape with his men. Even then the ability of General Johnston was recognized, and General Grant told me that he was about the only general on that side whom he feared. Each corps kept strong pickets well to the rear; but, as the rumors of Johnston's accumulating force reached us, General Grant concluded to take stronger measures. He had received from the North General J. G. Parker's corps (Ninth), which had been posted at Haines's Bluff; then, detailing one division from each of the three corps d'armee investing Vicksburg, he ordered me to go out, take a general command of all, and to counteract any movement on the part of General Johnston to relieve Vicksburg. I reconnoitred the whole country, from Haines's Bluff to the railroad bridge, and posted the troops thus:

Parke's two divisions from Haines's Bluff out to the Benton or ridge road; Tuttle's division, of my corps, joining on and extending to a plantation called Young's, overlooking

Bear Creek valley, which empties into the Big Black above Messinger's Ferry; then McArthurs division, of McPherson's corps, took up the line, and reached to Osterhaus's division of McClernand's corps, which held a strong fortified position at the railroad-crossing of the Big Black River. I was of opinion that, if Johnston should cross the Big Black, he could by the favorable nature of the country be held in check till a concentration could be effected by us at the point threatened. From the best information we could gather, General Johnston had about thirty or forty thousand men. I took post near a plantation of one Trible, near Markham's, and frequently reconnoitred the whole line, and could see the enemy engaged in like manner, on the east aide of Big Black; but he never attempted actually to cross over, except with some cavalry, just above Bear Creek, which was easily driven back. I was there from June 20th to the 4th of July. In a small log-house near Markham's was the family of Mr. Klein, whose wife was the daughter of Mrs. Day, of New Orleans, who in turn was the sister of Judge T. W. Bartley, my brother-in-law. I used frequently to drop in and take a meal with them, and Mrs. Klein was generally known as the general's cousin, which doubtless saved her and her family from molestation, too common on the part of our men.

One day, as I was riding the line near a farm known as Parson Fog's, I heard that the family of a Mr. Wilkinson, of New Orleans, was "refugeeing" at a house near by. I rode up, inquired, and found two young girls of that name, who said they were the children of General Wilkinson, of Louisiana, and that their brother had been at the Military School at Alexandria. Inquiring for their mother, I was told she was spending the day at Parson Fox's. As this house was on my route, I rode there, went through a large gate into the yard, followed by my staff and escort, and found quite a number of ladies sitting on the porch. I rode up and inquired if that were Parson Fox's. The parson, a fine-looking, venerable old man, rose, and said that he was Parson Fox. I then inquired for Mrs. Wilkinson, when an elderly lady answered that she was the person. I asked her if she were from Plaquemine Parish, Louisiana, and she said she was. I then inquired if she had a son who had been a cadet at Alexandria when General Sherman was superintendent, and she answered yes. I then announced myself, inquired after the boy, and she said he was inside of Vicksburg, an artillery lieutenant. I then asked about her husband, whom I had known, when she burst into tears, and cried out in agony, "You killed him at Bull Run, where he was fighting for his country!" I disclaimed killing anybody at Bull Run; but all the women present (nearly a dozen) burst into loud lamentations, which made it most uncomfortable for me, and I rode away. On the 3d of July, as I sat at my bivouac by the road-side near Trible's, I saw a poor, miserable horse, carrying a lady, and led by a little negro boy, coming across a cotton-field toward me; as they approached I recognized poor Mrs. Wilkinson, and helped her to dismount. I inquired what had brought her to me in that style, and she answered that she knew Vicksburg, was going to surrender, and she wanted to go right away to see her boy. I had a telegraph-wire to General Grant's headquarters, and had heard that there were symptoms of surrender, but as yet nothing definite. I tried to console and dissuade her, but she was resolved, and I could not help giving her a letter to General Grant, explaining to him who she was, and asking him to give her the earliest opportunity to see her son. The distance was fully twenty miles, but off she started, and I afterward learned that my letter had enabled her to see her son, who had escaped unharmed. Later in the day I got by telegraph General Grant's notice of the negotiations for surrender; and, by his directions, gave general orders to my troops to be ready at a moment's notice to cross the Big Black, and go for Joe Johnston.

The next day (July 4, 1863) Vicksburg surrendered, and orders were given for at once attacking General Johnston. The Thirteenth Corps (General Ord) was ordered to march rapidly, and cross the Big Black at the railroad-bridge; the Fifteenth by Mesainger's, and the Ninth (General Parker) by Birdsong's Ferry-all to converge on Bolton. My corps crossed the Big Black during the 5th and 6th of July, and marched for Bolton, where we came in with General Ord's troops; but the Ninth Corps was delayed in crossing at Birdsong's. Johnston had received timely notice of Pemberton's surrender, and was in full retreat for Jackson. On the 8th all our troops reached the neighborhood of Clinton, the weather fearfully hot, and water scarce. Johnston had marched rapidly, and in retreating had caused cattle, hogs, and sheep, to be driven into the ponds of water, and there shot down; so that we had to haul their dead and stinking carcasses out to use the water. On the 10th of July we had driven the rebel army into Jackson, where it turned at bay behind the intrenchments, which had been enlarged and strengthened since our former visit in May. We closed our lines about Jackson; my corps (Fifteenth) held the centre, extending from the Clinton to the Raymond road; Ord's (Thirteenth) on the right, reaching Pearl River below the town; and Parker's (Ninth) the left, above the town.

On the 11th we pressed close in, and shelled the town from every direction. One of Ords brigades (Lauman's) got too close, and was very roughly handled and driven back in disorder. General Ord accused the commander (General Lauman) of having disregarded his orders, and attributed to him personally the disaster and heavy loss of men. He requested his relief, which I granted, and General Lauman went to the rear, and never regained his division. He died after the war, in Iowa, much respected, as before that time he had been universally esteemed a most gallant and excellent officer. The weather was fearfully hot, but we continued to press the siege day and night, using our artillery pretty freely; and on the morning of July 17th the place was found evacuated. General Steele's division was sent in pursuit as far as Brandon (fourteen miles), but General Johnston had carried his army safely off, and pursuit in that hot weather would have been fatal to my command.

Reporting the fact to General Grant, he ordered me to return, to send General Parkes's corps to Haines's Bluff, General Ord's back to Vicksburg, and he consented that I should encamp my whole corps near the Big Black, pretty much on the same ground we had occupied before the movement, and with the prospect of a period of rest for the remainder of the summer. We reached our camps on the 27th of July.

Meantime, a division of troops, commanded by Brigadier-General W. Sooy Smith, had been added to my corps. General Smith applied for and received a sick-leave on the 20th of July; Brigadier-General Hugh Ewing was assigned to its command; and from that time it constituted the Fourth Division of the Fifteenth Army Corps.

Port Hudson had surrendered to General Banks on the 8th of July (a necessary consequence of the fall of Vicksburg), and thus terminated probably the most important enterprise of the civil war—the recovery of the complete control of the Mississippi River, from its source to its mouth—or, in the language of Mr. Lincoln, the Mississippi went "unvexed to the sea."

I put my four divisions into handsome, clean camps, looking to health and comfort alone, and had my headquarters in a beautiful grove near the house of that same Parson Fox where I had found the crowd of weeping rebel women waiting for the fate of their friends in Vicksburg.

The loss sustained by the Fifteenth Corps in the assault of May 19th, at Vicksburg, was mostly confined to the battalion of the Thirteenth Regulars, whose commanding officer, Captain Washington, was mortally wounded, and afterward died in the hands of the enemy, which battalion lost seventy-seven men out of the two hundred and fifty engaged; the Eighty-third Indiana (Colonel Spooner), and the One Hundred and Twenty seventh Illinois (Lieutenant-Colonel Eldridge), the aggregate being about two hundred.

In the assaults of the 22d, the loss in the Fifteenth Corps was about six hundred.

In the attack on Jackson, Mississippi, during the 11th-16th of July, General Ord reported the loss in the Thirteenth Army Corps seven hundred and sixty-two, of which five hundred and thirty-three were confined to Lauman's division; General Parkes reported, in the Ninth Corps, thirty-seven killed, two hundred and fifty-eight wounded, and thirty-three missing: total, three hundred and twenty-eight. In the Fifteenth Corps the loss was less; so that, in the aggregate, the loss as reported by me at the time was less than a thousand men, while we took that number alone of prisoners.

In General Grant's entire army before Vicksburg, composed of the Ninth, part of the Sixteenth, and the whole of the Thirteenth; Fifteenth, and Seventeenth Corps, the aggregate loss, as stated by Badeau, was:

Killed:
.... 243
Wounded:..........

....	095
Missing:	
....	35
Total:	
....	873

Whereas the Confederate loss, as stated by the same author,

Surrendered at Vicksburg	
....	2000
Captured at Champion Hills............	000
Captured at Big Black Bridge	000
Captured at Port Gibson...............	000
Captured with Loring	000
Killed and wounded	0000
Stragglers............................	000
Total................................	6000

Besides which, "a large amount of public property, consisting of railroads, locomotives, cars, steamers, cotton, guns, muskets, ammunition, etc., etc., was captured in Vicksburg."

The value of the capture of Vicksburg, however, was not measured by the list of prisoners, guns, and small-arms, but by the fact that its possession secured the navigation of the great central river of the continent, bisected fatally the Southern Confederacy, and set the armies which had been used in its conquest free for other purposes; and it so happened that the event coincided as to time with another great victory which crowned our arms far away, at Gettysburg, Pennsylvania. That was a defensive battle, whereas ours was offensive in the highest acceptation of the term, and the two, occurring at the same moment of time, should have ended the war; but the rebel leaders were mad, and seemed determined that their people should drink of the very lowest dregs of the cup of war, which they themselves had prepared.

The campaign of Vicksburg, in its conception and execution, belonged exclusively to General Grant, not only in the great whole, but in the thousands of its details. I still retain many of his letters and notes, all in his own handwriting, prescribing the routes of march for divisions and detachments, specifying even the amount of food and tools to be carried along. Many persons gave his adjutant general, Rawlins, the credit for these things, but they were in error; for no commanding general of an army ever gave more of his personal attention to details, or wrote so many of his own orders, reports, and letters, as General Grant. His success at Vicksburg justly gave him great fame at home and abroad. The President conferred on him the rank of major-general in the regular army, the highest grade then existing by law; and General McPherson and I shared in his success by receiving similar commissions as brigadier-generals in the regular army.

But our success at Vicksburg produced other results not so favorable to our cause—a general relaxation of effort, and desire to escape the hard drudgery of camp: officers sought leaves of absence to visit their homes, and soldiers obtained furloughs and discharges on the most slender pretexts; even the General Government seemed to relax in its efforts to replenish our ranks with new men, or to enforce the draft, and the politicians were pressing their schemes to reorganize or patch up some form of civil government, as fast as the armies gained partial possession of the States.

In order to illustrate this peculiar phase of our civil war, I give at this place copies of certain letters which have not heretofore been published:

[Private.]

WASHINGTON, August 29, 1868.

Major-General W. T. SHERMAN, Vicksburg, Mississippi

My DEAR GENERAL: The question of reconstruction in Louisiana, Mississippi, and Arkansas, will soon come up for decision of the Government, and not only the length of the war, but our ultimate and complete success, will depend upon its decision. It is a difficult matter, but I believe it can be successfully solved, if the President will consult opinions of cool and discreet men, who are capable of looking at it in all its bearings and effects. I think he is disposed to receive the advice of our generals who have been in these States, and know much more of their condition than gassy politicians in Congress. General Banks has written pretty fully, on the subject. I wrote to General Grant, immediately, after the fall of Vicksburg, for his views in regard to Mississippi, but he has not yet answered.

I wish you would consult with Grant, McPherson, and others of cool, good judgment, and write me your views fully, as I may wish to use them with the President. You had better write me unofficially, and then your letter will not be put on file, and cannot hereafter be used against you. You have been in Washington enough to know how every thing a man writes or says is picked up by his enemies and misconstrued. With kind wishes for your further success,

I am yours truly,

H. W. HALLECK

[Private and Confidential.]

HEADQUARTERS, FIFTEENTH ARMY CORPS,
CAMP ON BIG BLACK, MISSISSIPPI, September 17 1863
H. W. HALLECK, Commander-in-Chief, Washington, D. C.

DEAR GENERAL: I have received your letter of August 29th, and with pleasure confide to you fully my thoughts on the important matters you suggest, with absolute confidence that you will use what is valuable, and reject the useless or superfluous.

That part of the continent of North America known as Louisiana, Mississippi, and Arkansas, is in my judgment the key to the whole interior. The valley of the Mississippi is America, and, although railroads have changed the economy of intercommunication, yet the water-channels still mark the lines of fertile land, and afford cheap carriage to the heavy products of it.

The inhabitants of the country on the Monongahela, the Illinois, the Minnesota, the Yellowstone, and Osage, are as directly concerned in the security of the Lower Mississippi as are those who dwell on its very banks in Louisiana; and now that the nation has recovered its possession, this generation of men will make a fearful mistake if they again commit its charge to a people liable to misuse their position, and assert, as was recently done, that, because they dwelt on the banks of this mighty stream, they had a right to control its navigation.

I would deem it very unwise at this time, or for years to come, to revive the State governments of Louisiana, *etc.*, or to institute in this quarter any civil government in which the local people have much to say. They had a government so mild and paternal that they gradually forgot they had any at all, save what they themselves controlled; they asserted an absolute right to seize public moneys, forts, arms, and even to shut up the natural avenues of travel and commerce. They chose war—they ignored and denied all the obligations of the solemn contract of government and appealed to force.

We accepted the issue, and now they begin to realize that war is a two-edged sword, and it may be that many of the inhabitants cry for peace. I know them well, and the very impulses of their nature; and to deal with the inhabitants of that part of the South which borders on the great river, we must recognize the classes into which they have divided themselves:

First. The large planters, owning lands, slaves, and all kinds of personal property. These are, on the whole, the ruling class. They are educated, wealthy, and easily approached. In some districts they are bitter as gall, and have given up slaves, plantations, and all, serving in the armies of the Confederacy; whereas, in others, they are conservative. None dare admit a friendship for us, though they say freely that they were at the outset opposed to war and disunion. I know we can manage this class, but only by action. Argument is exhausted, and words have lost their usual meaning. Nothing but the logic of events touches their understanding; but, of late, this has worked a wonderful change. If our country were like Europe, crowded with people, I would say it would be easier to replace this class than to reconstruct it, subordinate to the policy of the nation; but, as this is not the case, it is better to allow the planters, with individual exceptions, gradually to recover their plantations, to hire any species of labor, and to adapt themselves to the new order of things. Still, their friendship and assistance to reconstruct order out of the present ruin cannot be depended on. They watch the operations of our armies, and hope still for a Southern Confederacy that will restore to them the slaves and privileges which they feel are otherwise lost forever. In my judgment, we have two more battles to win before we should even bother our minds with the idea of restoring civil order—*viz.*, one near Meridian, in November, and one near Shreveport, in February and March next, when Red River is navigable by our gunboats. When these are done, then, and not until then, will the planters of Louisiana, Arkansas, and Mississippi, submit. Slavery is already gone, and, to cultivate the land, negro or other labor must be hired. This, of itself, is a vast revolution, and time must be afforded to allow men to adjust their minds and habits to this new order of things. A civil government of the representative type would suit this class far less than a pure military role, readily adapting itself to actual occurrences, and able to enforce its laws and orders promptly and emphatically.

Second. The smaller farmers, mechanics, merchants, and laborers. This class will probably number three-quarters of the whole; have, in fact, no real interest in the establishment of a Southern Confederacy, and have been led or driven into war on the false theory that they were to be benefited somehow—they knew not how. They are essentially tired of the war, and would slink back home if they could. These are the real *tiers etat* of the South, and are hardly worthy a thought; for they swerve to and fro according to events which they do not comprehend or attempt to shape. When the time for reconstruction comes, they will want the old political system of caucuses, Legislatures, etc., to amuse them and make them believe they are real sovereigns; but in all things they will follow blindly the lead of the planters. The Southern politicians, who understand this class, use them as the French do their masses—seemingly consult their prejudices, while they make their orders and enforce them. We should do the same.

Third. The Union men of the South. I must confess I have little respect for this class. They allowed a clamorous set of demagogues to muzzle and drive them as a pack of curs. Afraid of shadows, they submit tamely to squads of dragoons, and permit them, without a murmur, to burn their cotton, take their horses, corn, and every thing; and, when we reach them, they are full of complaints if our men take a few fence-rails for fire, or corn to feed our horses. They give us no assistance or information, and are loudest in their complaints at the smallest excesses of our soldiers. Their sons, horses, arms, and every thing useful, are in the army against us, and they stay at home, claiming all the exemptions of peaceful citizens. I account them as nothing in this great game of war.

Fourth. The young bloods of the South: sons of planters, lawyers about towns, good billiard-players and sportsmen, men who never did work and never will. War suits them, and the rascals are brave, fine riders, bold to rashness, and dangerous subjects in every sense. They care not a sou for niggers, land, or any thing. They hate Yankees *per se*, and don't bother their brains about the past, present, or future. As long as they *have good horses, plenty of forage, and an open country, they are happy. This is a larger class than most men suppose, and they are the most dangerous set of men that this war has turned loose upon the world. They are splendid riders, first-rate shots, and utterly reckless. Stewart, John Morgan, Forrest, and Jackson, are the types and leaders of this class. These men must all be killed or employed by us before we can hope for peace. They have no property or future, and therefore cannot be influenced by any thing, except personal considerations. I have two brigades of these fellows in my front, commanded by Cosby, of the old army, and Whitfield, of Texas. Stephen D. Lee is in command of the whole. I have frequent interviews with their officers, a good understanding with them, and am inclined to think, when the resources of their country are exhausted, we must employ them. They are the best cavalry in the world, but it will tax Mr. Chase's genius for finance to supply them with horses. At present horses cost them nothing; for they take where they find, and don't bother their brains as to who is to pay for them; the same may be said of the cornfields, which have, as they believe, been cultivated by a good-natured people for their special benefit. We propose to share with them the free use of these cornfields, planted by willing hands, that will never gather the crops.*

Now that I have sketched the people who inhabit the district of country under consideration, I will proceed to discuss the future.

A civil government now, for any part of it, would be simply ridiculous. The people would not regard it, and even the military commanders of the antagonistic parties would treat it lightly. Governors would be simply petitioners for military assistance, to protect supposed friendly interests, and military commanders would refuse to disperse and weaken their armies for military reasons. Jealousies would arise between the two conflicting powers, and, instead of contributing to the end of the war, would actually defer it. Therefore, I contend that the interests of the United States, and of the real parties concerned, demand the continuance of the simple military role, till after all the organized armies of the South are dispersed, conquered, and subjugated.

The people of all this region are represented in the Army of Virginia, at Charleston, Mobile, and Chattanooga. They have sons and relations in each of the rebel armies, and naturally are interested in their fate. Though we hold military possession of the key-points of their country, still they contend, and naturally, that should Lee succeed in Virginia, or Bragg at Chattanooga, a change will occur here also. We cannot for this reason attempt to reconstruct parts of the South as we conquer it, till all idea of the establishment of a Southern Confederacy is abandoned. We should avail ourselves of the present lull to secure the strategical points that will give us an advantage in the future military movements, and we should treat the idea of civil government as one in which we as a nation have a minor or subordinate interest. The opportunity is good to impress on the population the truth that they are more interested in civil government than we are; and that, to enjoy the protection of laws, they most not be passive observers of events, but must aid and sustain the constituted authorities in enforcing the laws; they must not only submit themselves, but should pay their share of taxes, and render personal services when called on.

It seems to me, in contemplating the history of the past two years, that all the people of our country, North, South, East, and West, have been undergoing a salutary political schooling, learning lessons which might have been acquired from the experience of other people; but we had all become so wise in our own conceit that we would only learn by actual experience of our own. The people even of small and unimportant localities, North as well as South, had reasoned themselves into the belief that their opinions were superior to the aggregated interest of the whole nation. Half our territorial nation rebelled, on a doctrine of secession that they themselves now scout; and a real numerical majority actually believed that a little State was endowed with such sovereignty that it could defeat the policy of the great whole. I think the present war has exploded that notion, and were this war to cease now, the experience gained, though dear, would be worth the expense.

Another great and important natural truth is still in contest, and can only be solved by war. Numerical majorities by vote have been our great arbiter. Heretofore all men have cheerfully submitted to it in questions left open, but numerical majorities are not necessarily physical majorities. The South, though numerically inferior, contend they can whip the Northern superiority of numbers, and therefore by natural law they contend that they are not bound to submit. This issue is the only real one, and in my judgment all else should be deferred to it. War alone can decide it, and it is the only question now left for us as a people to decide. Can we whip the South? If we can, our numerical majority has both the natural and constitutional right to govern them. If we cannot whip them, they contend for the natural right to select their own government, and they have the argument. Our armies must prevail over theirs; our officers, marshals, and courts, must penetrate into the innermost recesses of their land, before we have the natural right to demand their submission.

I would banish all minor questions, assert the broad doctrine that as a nation the United States has the right, and also the physical power, to penetrate to every part of our national domain, and that we will do it—that we will do it in our own time and in our own way; that it makes no difference whether it be in one year, or two, or ten, or twenty; that we will remove and destroy every obstacle, if need be, take every life, every acre of land, every particle of property, every thing that to us seems proper; that we will not cease till the end is attained; that all who do not aid us are enemies, and that we will not account to them for our acts. If the people of the South oppose, they do so at their peril; and if they stand by, mere lookers-on in this domestic tragedy, they have no right to immunity, protection, or share in the final results.

I even believe and contend further that, in the North, every member of the nation is bound by both natural and constitutional law to "maintain and defend the Government against all its enemies and opposers whomsoever." If they fail to do it they are derelict, and can be punished, or deprived of all advantages arising from the labors of those who do. If any man, North or South, withholds his share of taxes, or his physical assistance in this, the crisis of our history, he should be deprived of all voice in the future elections of this country, and might be banished, or reduced to the condition of a mere denizen of the land.

War is upon us, none can deny it. It is not the choice of the Government of the United States, but of a faction; the Government was forced to accept the issue, or to submit to a degradation fatal and disgraceful to all the inhabitants. In accepting war, it should be "pure and simple" as applied to the belligerents. I would keep it so, till all traces of the war are effaced; till those who appealed to it are sick and tired of it, and come to the emblem of our nation, and sue for peace. I would not coax them, or even meet them half-way, but make them so sick of war that generations would pass away before they would again appeal to it.

I know what I say when I repeat that the insurgents of the South sneer at all overtures looking to their interests. They scorn the alliance with the Copperheads; they tell me to my face that they respect Grant, McPherson, and our brave associates who fight manfully and well for a principle, but despise the Copperheads and sneaks at the North, who profess friendship for the South and opposition to the war, as mere covers for their knavery and poltroonery.

God knows that I deplore this fratricidal war as much as any man living, but it is upon us, a physical fact; and there is only one honorable issue from it. We must fight it out, army against army, and man against man; and I know, and you know, and civilians begin to realize the fact, that reconciliation and reconstruction will be easier through and by means of strong, well-equipped, and organized armies than through any species of conventions that can be framed. The issues are made, and all discussion is out of place and ridiculous. The section of thirty-pounder Parrott rifles now drilling before my tent is a more convincing argument than the largest Democratic meeting the State of New York can possibly assemble at Albany; and a simple order of the War Department to draft enough men to fill our skeleton regiments would be more convincing as to our national perpetuity than an humble pardon to Jeff. Davis and all his misled host.

The only government needed or deserved by the States of Louisiana, Arkansas, and Mississippi, now exists in Grant's army. This needs, simply, enough privates to fill its ranks; all else will follow in due season. This army has its well-defined code of laws and practice, and can adapt itself to the wants and necessities of a city, the country, the rivers, the sea, indeed to all parts of this land. It better subserves the interest and policy of the General Government, and the people here prefer it to any weak or servile combination that would at once, from force of habit, revive sad perpetuate local prejudices and passions. The people of this country have forfeited all right to a voice in the councils of the nation. They know it and feel it, and in after-years they will be the better citizens from the dear bought experience of the present crisis. Let them learn now, and learn it well, that good citizens must obey as well as command. Obedience to law, absolute—yea, even abject—is the lesson that this war, under Providence, will teach the free and enlightened American citizen. As a nation, we shall be the better for it.

I never have apprehended foreign interference in our family quarrel. Of coarse, governments founded on a different and it may be an antagonistic principle with ours naturally feel a pleasure at our complications, and, it may be, wish our downfall; but in the end England and France will join with us in jubilation at the triumph of constitutional government over faction. Even now the English manifest this. I do not profess to understand Napoleon's design in Mexico, and I do not, see that his taking military possession of Mexico concerns us. We have as much territory now as we want. The Mexicans have failed in self-government, and it was a question as to what nation she should fall a prey. That is now solved, and I don't see that we are damaged. We have the finest part of the North American Continent, all we can people and can take care of; and, if we can suppress rebellion in our own land, and compose the strife generated by it, we shall have enough people, resources, and wealth, if well combined, to defy interference from any and every quarter.

I therefore hope the Government of the United States will continue, as heretofore, to collect, in well-organized armies, the physical strength of the nation; applying it, as heretofore, in asserting the national authority; and in persevering, without relaxation, to the end. This, whether near or far off, is not for us to say; but, fortunately, we have no choice. We must succeed—no other choice is left us except degradation. The South must be ruled by us, or she will rule us. We must conquer them, or ourselves be conquered. There is no middle course. They ask, and will have, nothing else, and talk of compromise is bosh; for we know they would even scorn the offer.

I wish the war could have been deferred for twenty years, till the superabundant population of the North could flow in and replace the losses sustained by war; but this could not be, and we are forced to take things as they are.

All therefore I can now venture to advise is to raise the draft to its maximum, fill the present regiments to as large a standard as possible, and push the war, pure and simple. Great attention should be paid to the discipline of our armies, for on them may be founded the future stability of the Government.

The cost of the war is, of course, to be considered, but finances will adjust themselves to the actual state of affairs; and, even if we would, we could not change the cost. Indeed, the larger the cost now, the less will it be in the end; for the end must be attained somehow, regardless of loss of life and treasure, and is merely a question of time.

Excuse so long a letter. With great respect, etc.,

W. T. SHERMAN, Major-General.

General Halleck, on receipt of this letter, telegraphed me that Mr. Lincoln had read it carefully, and had instructed him to obtain my consent to have it published. At the time, I preferred not to be drawn into any newspaper controversy, and so wrote to General Halleck; and the above letter has never been, to my knowledge, published; though Mr. Lincoln more than once referred to it with marks of approval.

HEADQUARTERS FIFTEENTH ARMY CORPS CAMP ON BIG BLACK, September 17, 1863

Brigadier-General J. A. RAWLINS, Acting Assistant Adjutant-General, Vicksburg.

DEAR GENERAL: I inclose for your perusal, and for you to read to General Grant such parts as you deem interesting, letters received by me from Prof. Mahan and General Halleck, with my answers. After you have read my answer to General Halleck, I beg you to inclose it to its address, and return me the others.

I think Prof. Mahan's very marked encomium upon the campaign of Vicksburg is so flattering to General Grant, that you may offer to let him keep the letter, if he values such a testimonial. I have never written a word to General Halleck since my report of last December, after the affair at Chickasaw, except a short letter a few days ago, thanking him for the kind manner of his transmitting to me the appointment of brigadier-general. I know that in Washington I am incomprehensible, because at the outset of the war I would not go it blind and rush headlong into a war unprepared and with an utter ignorance of its extent and purpose. I was then construed unsound; and now that I insist on war pure and simple, with no admixture of civil compromises, I am supposed vindictive. You remember what Polonius said to his son Laertes: "Beware of entrance to a quarrel; but, being in, bear it, that the opposed may beware of thee." What is true of the single man, is equally true of a nation. Our leaders seemed at first to thirst for the quarrel, willing, even anxious, to array against us all possible elements of opposition; and now, being in, they would hasten to quit long before the "opposed" has received that lesson which he needs. I would make this war as severe as possible, and show no symptoms of tiring till the South begs for mercy; indeed, I know, and you know, that the end would be reached quicker by such a course than by any seeming yielding on our part. I don't want our Government to be bothered by patching up local governments, or by trying to reconcile any class of men. The South has done her worst, and now is the time for us to pile on our blows thick and fast.

Instead of postponing the draft till after the elections, we ought now to have our ranks full of drafted men; and, at best, if they come at all, they will reach us when we should be in motion.

I think General Halleck would like to have the honest, candid opinions of all of us, viz., Grant, McPherson, and Sherman. I have given mine, and would prefer, of course, that it should coincide with the others. Still, no matter what my opinion may be, I can easily adapt my conduct to the plane of others, and am only too happy when I find theirs better, than mine.

If no trouble, please show Halleck's letter to McPherson, and ask him to write also. I know his regiments are like mine (mere squads), and need filling up. Yours truly,

W. T. SHERMAN, Major-General.

CHAPTER XIV.
CHATTANOOGA AND KNOXVILLE.

JULY TO DECEMBER, 1863.

After the fall of Vicksburg, and its corollary, Port Hudson, the Mississippi River was wholly in the possession of the Union forces, and formed a perfect line of separation in the territories of our opponents. Thenceforth, they could not cross it save by stealth, and the military affairs on its west bank became unimportant. Grant's army had seemingly completed its share of the work of war, and lay, as it were, idle for a time. In person General Grant went to New Orleans to confer with General Banks, and his victorious army was somewhat dispersed. Parke's corps (Ninth) returned to Kentucky, and afterward formed part of the Army of the Ohio, under General Burnside; Ord's corps (Thirteenth) was sent down to Natchez, and gradually drifted to New Orleans and Texas; McPhersons (Seventeenth) remained in and near Vicksburg; Hurlbut's (Sixteenth) was at Memphis; and mine (Fifteenth) was encamped along the Big Black, about twenty miles east of Vicksburg. This corps was composed of four divisions: Steele's (the First) was posted at and near the railroad-bridge; Blair's (the Second), next in order, near Parson Fox's; the Third Division (Tuttle's) was on the ridge about the head of Bear Creek; and the Fourth (Ewing's) was at Messinger's Ford. My own headquarters were in tents in a fine grove of old oaks near Parson Fox's house, and the battalion of the Thirteenth Regulars was the headquarters guard.

All the camps were arranged for health, comfort, rest, and drill. It being midsummer, we did not expect any change till the autumn months, and accordingly made ourselves as comfortable as possible. There was a short railroad in operation from Vicksburg to the bridge across the Big Black, whence supplies in abundance were hauled to our respective camps. With a knowledge of this fact Mrs. Sherman came down from Ohio with Minnie, Lizzie, Willie, and Tom, to pay us a visit in our camp at Parson Fog's. Willie was then nine years old, was well advanced for his years, and took the most intense interest in the affairs of the army. He was a great favorite with the soldiers, and used to ride with me on horseback in the numerous drills and reviews of the time. He then had the promise of as long a life as any of my children, and displayed more interest in the war than any of them. He was called a "sergeant" in the regular battalion, learned the manual of arms, and regularly attended the parade and guard-mounting of the Thirteenth, back of my camp. We made frequent visits to Vicksburg, and always stopped with General McPherson, who had a large house, and boarded with a family (Mrs. Edwards's) in which were several interesting young ladies. General Grant occupied another house (Mrs. Lum's) in Vicksburg during that summer, and also had his family with him. The time passed very agreeably, diversified only by little events of not much significance, among which I will recount only one.

While, we occupied the west bank of the Big Black, the east bank was watched by a rebel cavalry-division, commanded by General Armstrong. He had four brigades, commanded by Generals Whitfield, Stark, Cosby, and Wirt Adams. Quite frequently they communicated with us by flags of truce on trivial matters, and we reciprocated; merely to observe them. One day a flag of truce, borne by a Captain B...., of Louisville, Kentucky, escorted by about twenty-five men, was reported at Messinger's Ferry, and I sent orders to let them come right into my tent. This brought them through the camps of the Fourth Division, and part of the Second; and as they drew up in front of my tent, I invited Captain B.... and another officer with him (a major from Mobile) to dismount, to enter my tent, and to make themselves at home. Their escort was sent to join mine, with orders to furnish them forage and every thing they wanted. B.... had brought a sealed letter for General Grant at Vicksburg, which was dispatched to him. In the evening we had a good supper, with wine and cigars, and, as we sat talking, B.... spoke of his father and mother, in Louisville, got leave to write them a long letter without its being read by any one, and then we talked about the war. He said: "What is the use of your persevering? It is simply impossible to subdue eight millions of people;" asserting that "the feeling in the South had become so embittered that a reconciliation was impossible." I answered that, "sitting as we then were, we appeared very comfortable, and surely there was no trouble in our becoming friends." "Yes," said he, "that is very true of us, but we are gentlemen of education, and can easily adapt ourselves to any condition of things; but this would not apply equally well to the common people, or to the common soldiers." I took him out to the camp-fires behind the tent, and there were the men of his escort and mine mingled together, drinking their coffee, and happy as soldiers always seem. I asked B.... what he thought of that, and he admitted that I had the best of the argument. Before I dismissed this flag of truce, his companion consulted me confidentially as to what disposition he ought to make of his family, then in Mobile, and I frankly gave him the best advice I could.

While we were thus lying idle in camp on the big Black, the Army of the Cumberland, under General Rosecrans, was moving against Bragg at Chattanooga; and the Army of the Ohio, General Burnside, was marching toward East Tennessee. General Rosecrans was so confident of success that he somewhat scattered his command, seemingly to surround and capture Bragg in Chattanooga; but the latter, reenforced from Virginia, drew out of Chattanooga, concentrated his army at Lafayette, and at Chickamauga fell on Rosecrans, defeated him, and drove him into Chattanooga. The whole country seemed paralyzed by this unhappy event; and the authorities in Washington were thoroughly stampeded. From the East the Eleventh Corps (Slocum), and the Twelfth Corps (Howard), were sent by rail to Nashville, and forward under command of General Hooker; orders were also sent to General Grant, by Halleck, to send what reenforcements he could spare immediately toward Chattanooga.

Bragg had completely driven Rosecrans's army into Chattanooga; the latter was in actual danger of starvation, and the railroad to his rear seemed inadequate to his supply. The first intimation which I got of this disaster was on the 22d of September, by an order from General Grant to dispatch one of my divisions immediately into Vicksburg, to go toward Chattanooga, and I designated the First, General Osterhaus—Steele meantime having been appointed to the command of the Department of Arkansas, and had gone to Little Rock. General Osterhaus marched the same day, and on the 23d I was summoned to Vicksburg in person, where General Grant showed me the alarming dispatches from General Halleck, which had been sent from Memphis by General Hurlbut, and said, on further thought, that he would send me and my whole corps. But, inasmuch as one division of McPherson's corps (John E. Smith's) had already started, he instructed me to leave one of my divisions on the Big Black, and to get the other two ready to follow at once. I designated the Second, then commanded by Brigadier-General Giles A. Smith, and the Fourth, commanded by Brigadier-General Corse.

On the 25th I returned to my camp on Big Black, gave all the necessary orders for these divisions to move, and for the Third (Tittle's) to remain, and went into Vicksburg with my family. The last of my corps designed for this expedition started from camp on the 27th, reached Vicksburg the 28th, and were embarked on boats provided for them. General Halleck's dispatches dwelt upon the fact that General Rosecrans's routes of supply were overtaxed, and that we should move from Memphis eastward, repairing railroads as we progressed, as far as Athens, Alabama, whence I was to report to General Rosecrans, at Chattanooga, by letter.

I took passage for myself and family in the steamer Atlantic, Captain Henry McDougall. When the boat was ready to start, Willie was missing. Mrs. Sherman supposed him to have been with me, whereas I supposed he was with her. An officer of the Thirteenth went up to General McPherson's house for him, and soon returned, with Captain Clift leading him, carrying in his hands a small double-barreled shot gun; and I joked him about carrying away captured property. In a short time we got off. As we all stood on the guards to look at our old camps at Young's Point, I remarked that Willie was not well, and he admitted that he was sick. His mother put him to bed, and consulted Dr. Roler, of the Fifty-fifth Illinois, who found symptoms of typhoid fever. The river was low; we made slow progress till above Helena; and, as we approached Memphis, Dr. Roler told me that Willie's life was in danger, and he was extremely anxious to reach Memphis for certain medicines and for consultation. We arrived at Memphis on the 2d of October, carried Willie up to the Gayoso Hotel, and got the most experienced physician there, who acted with Dr. Roler, but he sank rapidly, and died the evening of the 3d of October. The blow was a terrible one to us all, so sudden and so unexpected, that I could not help reproaching myself for having consented to his visit in that sickly region in the summer-time. Of all my children, he seemed the most precious. Born in San Francisco, I had watched with intense interest his development, and he seemed more than any of the children to take an interest in my special profession. Mrs. Sherman, Minnie, Lizzie, and Tom, were with him at the time, and we all, helpless and overwhelmed, saw him die. Being in the very midst of an important military enterprise, I had hardly time to pause and think of my personal loss. We procured a metallic casket, and had a military funeral, the battalion of the Thirteenth United States Regulars acting as escort from the Gayoso Hotel to the steamboat Grey Eagle, which conveyed him and my family up to Cairo, whence they proceeded to our home at Lancaster, Ohio, where he was buried. I here give my letter to Captain C. C. Smith, who commanded the battalion at the time, as exhibiting our intense feelings:

GAYOSO HOUSE, MEMPHIS, TENNESSEE
October 4, 1863, Midnight

Captain C. C. SMITH, commanding Battalion Thirteenth United States Regulars.

MY DEAR FRIEND: I cannot sleep to-night till I record an expression of the deep feelings of my heart to you, and to the officers and soldiers of the battalion, for their kind behavior to my poor child. I realize that you all feel for my family the attachment of kindred, and I assure you of full reciprocity. Consistent with a sense of duty to my profession and office, I could not leave my post, and sent for the family to come to me in that fatal climate, and in that sickly period of the year, and behold the result! The child that bore my name, and in whose future I reposed with more confidence than I did in my own plan of life, now floats a mere corpse, seeking a grave in a distant land, with a weeping mother, brother, and sisters, clustered about him. For myself, I ask no sympathy. On, on I must go, to meet a soldier's fate, or live to see our country rise superior to all factions, till its flag is adored and respected by ourselves and by all the powers of the earth.

But Willie was, or thought he was, a sergeant in the Thirteenth. I have seen his eye brighten, his heart beat, as he beheld the battalion under arms, and asked me if they were not real soldiers. Child as he was, he had the enthusiasm, the pure love of truth, honor, and love of country, which should animate all soldiers.

God only knows why he should die thus young. He is dead, but will not be forgotten till those who knew him in life have followed him to that same mysterious end.

Please convey to the battalion my heart-felt thanks, and assure each and all that if in after-years they call on me or mine, and mention that they were of the Thirteenth Regulars when Willie was a sergeant, they will have a key to the affections of my family that will open all it has; that we will share with them our last blanket, our last crust! Your friend,

W. T. SHERMAN, Major-general.

Long afterward, in the spring of 1867, we had his body disinterred and brought to St. Louis, where he is now buried in a beautiful spot, in Calvary Cemetery, by the side of another child, "Charles," who was born at Lancaster, in the summer of 1864, died early, and was buried at Notre Dame, Indiana. His body was transferred at the same time to the same spot. Over Willie's grave is erected a beautiful marble monument, designed and executed by the officers and soldiers, of that battalion which claimed him as a sergeant and comrade.

During the summer and fall of 1863 Major-General S. A. Hurlbut was in command at Memphis. He supplied me copies of all dispatches from Washington, and all the information he possessed of the events about Chattanooga. Two of these dispatches cover all essential points:

WASHINGTON CITY, September 15, 1863—5 p.m.

Major-General S. A. HURLBUT, Memphis:

All the troops that can possibly be spared in West Tennessee and on the Mississippi River should be sent without delay to assist General Rosecrans on the Tennessee River.

Urge Sherman to act with all possible promptness.

If you have boats, send them down to bring up his troops.

Information just received indicates that a part of Lee's army has been sent to reenforce Bragg.

H. W. HALLECK, General-in-Chief.

Washington, September 19, 1868—4 p.m.

Major-General S. A. HURLBUT, Memphis, Tennessee:

Give me definite information of the number of troops sent toward Decatur, and where they are. Also, what other troops are to follow, and when.

Has any thing been heard from the troops ordered from Vicksburg?

No efforts must be spared to support Rosecrans's right, and to guard the crossings of the Tennessee River.

H. W. HALLECK, General-in-Chief.

My special orders were to repair the Memphis & Charleston Railroad eastward as I progressed, as far as Athens, Alabama, to draw supplies by that route, so that, on reaching Athens, we should not be dependent on the roads back to Nashville, already overtaxed by the demand of Rosecrans's army.

On reaching Memphis, October 2d, I found that Osterhaus's division had already gone by rail as far as Corinth, and than John E. Smith's division was in the act of starting by cars. The Second Division, then commanded by Brigadier-General Giles A. Smith, reached Memphis at the same time with me; and the Fourth Division, commanded by Brigadier-General John M. Corse, arrived a day or two after. The railroad was in fair condition as far as Corinth, ninety-six miles, but the road was badly stocked with locomotives and cars, so that it took until the 9th to get off the Second Division, when I gave orders for the Fourth Division and wagon-trains to march by the common road.

On Sunday morning, October 11th, with a special train loaded with our orderlies and clerks, the horses of our staff, the battalion of the Thirteenth United States Regulars, and a few officers going forward to join their commands, among them Brigadier-General Hugh Ewing, I started for Corinth.

At Germantown, eight miles, we passed Corse's division (Fourth) on the march, and about noon the train ran by the depot at Colliersville, twenty-six miles out. I was in the rear car with my staff, dozing, but observed the train slacking speed and stopping about half a mile beyond the depot. I noticed some soldiers running to and fro, got out at the end of the car, and soon Colonel Anthony (Silty-sixth Indiana), who commanded the post, rode up and said that his pickets had just been driven in, and there was an appearance of an attack by a large force of cavalry coming from the southeast. I ordered the men to get off the train, to form on the knoll near the railroad-cut, and soon observed a rebel officer riding toward us with a white flag. Colonel Anthony and Colonel Dayton (one of my aides) were sent to meet him, and to keep him in conversation as long as possible. They soon returned, saying it was the adjutant of the rebel general Chalmers, who demanded the surrender of the place. I instructed them to return and give a negative answer, but to delay him as much as possible, so as to give us time for preparation. I saw Anthony, Dayton, and the rebel bearer of the flag, in conversation, and the latter turn his horse to ride back, when I ordered Colonel McCoy to run to the station, and get a message over the wires as quick as possible to Memphis and Germantown, to hurry forward Corse's division. I then ordered the train to back to the depot, and drew back the battalion of regulars to the small earth redoubt near it. The depot-building was of brick, and had been punctured with loop-holes. To its east, about two hundred yards, was a small square earthwork or fort, into which were put a part of the regulars along with the company of the Sixty-sixth Indiana already there. The rest of the men were distributed into the railroad-cut, and in some shallow rifle-trenches near the depot. We had hardly made these preparations when the enemy was seen forming in a long line on the ridge to the south, about four hundred yards off, and soon after two parties of cavalry passed the railroad on both sides of us, cutting the wires and tearing up some rails. Soon they opened on us with artillery (of which we had none), and their men were dismounting and preparing to assault. To the south of us was an extensive cornfield, with the corn still standing, and on the other side was the town of Colliersville. All the houses near, that could give shelter to the enemy, were ordered to be set on fire, and the men were instructed to keep well under cover and to reserve their fire for the assault, which seemed inevitable. A long line of rebel skirmishers came down through the cornfield, and two other parties approached us along the railroad on both sides. In the fort was a small magazine containing some cartridges. Lieutenant James, a fine, gallant fellow, who was ordnance-officer on my staff, asked leave to arm the orderlies and clerks with some muskets which he had found in the depot, to which I consented; he marched them into the magazine, issued cartridges, and marched back to the depot to assist in its defense. Afterward he came to me, said a party of the enemy had got into the woods near the depot, and was annoying him, and he wanted to charge and drive it away. I advised him to be extremely cautious, as our enemy vastly outnumbered us, and had every advantage in position and artillery; but instructed him, if they got too near, he might make a sally. Soon after, I heard a rapid fire in that quarter, and Lieutenant. James was brought in on a stretcher, with a ball through his breast, which I supposed to be fatal.

[After the fight we sent him back to Memphis, where his mother and father came from their home on the North River to nurse him. Young James was recovering from his wound, but was afterward killed by a fall from his horse, near his home, when riding with the daughters of Mr. Hamilton Fish, now Secretary of State.]

The enemy closed down on us several times, and got possession of the rear of our train, from which they succeeded in getting five of our horses, among them my favorite mare Dolly; but our men were cool and practised shots (with great experience acquired at Vicksburg), and drove them back. With their artillery they knocked to pieces our locomotive and several of the cars, and set fire to the train; but we managed to get possession again, and extinguished the fire. Colonel Audenreid, aide-de-camp, was provoked to find that his valise of nice shirts had been used to kindle the fire. The fighting continued all round us for three or four hours, when we observed signs of drawing off, which I attributed to the rightful cause, the rapid approach of Corse's division, which arrived about dark, having marched the whole distance from Memphis, twenty-six miles, on the double-quick. The next day we repaired damages to the railroad and locomotive, and went on to Corinth.

At Corinth, on the 16th, I received the following important dispatches:

MEMPHIS, *October 14, 1863—11 a.m.*

Arrived this morning. Will be off in a few hours. My orders are only to go to Cairo, and report from there by telegraph. McPherson will be in Canton to-day. He will remain there until Sunday or Monday next, and reconnoitre as far eastward as possible with cavalry, in the mean time.

U. S. GRANT, *Major-General.*

WASHINGTON, *October 14, 1863—1 p.m.*

Major-General W. T. SHERMAN, *Corinth*

Yours of the 10th is received. The important matter to be attended to is that of supplies. When Eastport can be reached by boats, the use of the railroad can be dispensed with; but until that time it must be guarded as far as need. The Kentucky Railroad can barely supply General Rosecrans. All these matters must be left to your judgment as circumstances may arise. Should the enemy be so strong as to prevent your going to Athena, or connecting with General Rosecrans, you will nevertheless have assisted him greatly by drawing away a part of the enemy's forces.

H. W. HALLECK, *Major-General.*

On the 18th, with my staff and a small escort, I rode forward to Burnsville, and on the 19th to Iuka, where, on the next day, I was most agreeably surprised to hear of the arrival at Eastport (only ten miles off) of two gunboats, under the command of Captain Phelps, which had been sent up the Tennessee River by Admiral Porter, to help us.

Satisfied that, to reach Athens and to communicate with General Rosecrans, we should have to take the route north of the Tennessee River, on the 24th I ordered the Fourth Division to cross at Eastport with the aid of the gunboats, and to move to Florence. About the same time, I received the general orders assigning General Grant to command the Military Division of the Mississippi, authorizing him, on reaching Chattanooga, to supersede General Rosecrans by General George H. Thomas, with other and complete authority, as set, forth in the following letters of General Halleck, which were sent to me by General Grant; and the same orders devolved on me the command of the Department and Army of the Tennessee.

HEADQUARTERS OF THE ARMY WASHINGTON, D.C., October 16, 1863

Major-General U. S. GRANT, Louisville.

GENERAL: You will receive herewith the orders of the President of the United States, placing you in command of the Departments of the Ohio, Cumberland, and Tennessee. The organization of these departments will be changed as you may deem most practicable. You will immediately proceed to Chattanooga, and relieve General Rosecrans. You can communicate with Generals Burnside and Sherman by telegraph. A summary of the orders sent to these officers will be sent to you immediately. It is left optional with you to supersede General Rosecrans by General G. H. Thomas or not. Any other changes will be made on your request by telegram.

One of the first objects requiring your attention is the supply of your armies. Another is the security of the passes in the Georgia mountains, to shut out the enemy from Tennessee and Kentucky. You will consult with General Meigs and Colonel Scott in regard to transportation and supplies.

Should circumstances permit, I will visit you personally in a few days for consultation.

H. W. HALLECK, General-in-Chief.

HEADQUARTERS OF THE ARMY WASHINGTON, D. C., October 20, 1868.

Major-General GRANT, Louisville.

GENERAL: In compliance with my promise, I now proceed to give you a brief statement of the objects aimed at by General Rosecrans and General Burnside's movement into East Tennessee, and of the measures directed to be taken to attain these objects.

It has been the constant desire of the government, from the beginning of the war, to rescue the loyal inhabitants of East Tennessee from the hands of the rebels, who fully appreciated the importance of continuing their hold upon that country. In addition to the large amount of agricultural products drawn from the upper valley of the Tennessee, they also obtained iron and other materials from the vicinity of Chattanooga. The possession of East Tennessee would cut off one of their most important railroad communications, and threaten their manufactories at Rome, Atlanta, etc.

When General Buell was ordered into East Tennessee in the summer of 1882, Chattanooga was comparatively unprotected; but Bragg reached there before Buell, and, by threatening his communications, forced him to retreat on Nashville and Louisville. Again, after the battle of Perryville, General Buell was urged to pursue Bragg's defeated army, and drive it from East Tennessee. The same was urged upon his successor, but the lateness of the season or other causes prevented further operations after the battle of Stone River.

Last spring, when your movements on the Mississippi River had drawn out of Tennessee a large force of the enemy, I again urged General Rosecrans to take advantage of that opportunity to carry out his projected plan of campaign, General Burnside being ready to cooperate, with a diminished but still efficient force. But he could not be persuaded to act in time, preferring to lie still till your campaign should be terminated. I represented to him, but without avail, that by this delay Johnston might be able to reenforce Bragg with the troops then operating against you.

When General Rosecrans finally determined to advance, he was allowed to select his own lines and plans for carrying out the objects of the expedition. He was directed, however, to report his movements daily, till he crossed the Tennessee, and to connect his left, so far as possible, with General Burnside's right. General Burnside was directed to move simultaneously, connecting his right, as far as possible, with General Rosecrans's left so that, if the enemy concentrated upon either army, the other could move to its assistance. When General Burnside reached Kingston and Knoxville, and found no considerable number of the enemy in East Tennessee, he was instructed to move down the river and cooperate with General Rosecrans.

These instructions were repeated some fifteen times, but were not carried out, General Burnside alleging as an excuse that he believed that Bragg was in retreat, and that General Rosecrans needed no reenforcements. When the latter had gained possession of Chattanooga he was directed not to move on Rome as he proposed, but simply to hold the mountain-passes, so as to prevent the ingress of the rebels into East Tennessee. That object accomplished, I considered the campaign as ended, at least for the present. Future operations would depend upon the ascertained strength and; movements of the enemy. In other words, the main objects of the campaign were the restoration of East Tennessee to the Union, and by holding the two extremities of the valley to secure it from rebel invasion.

The moment I received reliable information of the departure of Longstreet's corps from the Army of the Potomac, I ordered forward to General Rosecrans every available man in the Department of the Ohio, and again urged General Burnside to move to his assistance. I also telegraphed to Generals Hurlbut, Sherman, and yourself, to send forward all available troops in your department. If these forces had been sent to General Rosecrans by Nashville, they could not have been supplied; I therefore directed them to move by Corinth and the Tennessee River. The necessity of this has been proved by the fact that the reinforcements sent to him from the Army of the Potomac have not been able, for the want of railroad transportation, to reach General Rosecrans's army in the field.

In regard to the relative strength of the opposing armies, it is believed that General Rosecrans when he first moved against Bragg had double, if not treble, his force. General Burnside, also, had more than double the force of Buckner; and, even when Bragg and Buckner united, Rosecrans's army was very greatly superior in number. Even the eighteen thousand men sent from Virginia, under Longstreet, would not have given the enemy the superiority. It is now ascertained that the greater part of the prisoners parolled by you at Vicksburg, and General Banks at Port Hudson, were illegally and improperly declared exchanged, and forced into the ranks to swell the rebel numbers at Chickamauga. This outrageous act, in violation of the laws of war, of the cartel entered into by the rebel authorities, and of all sense of honor, gives us a useful lesson in regard to the character of the enemy with whom we are contending. He neither regards the rules of civilized warfare, nor even his most solemn engagements. You may, therefore, expect to meet in arms thousands of unexchanged prisoners released by you and others on parole, not to serve again till duly exchanged.

Although the enemy by this disgraceful means has been able to concentrate in Georgia and Alabama a much larger force than we anticipated, your armies will be abundantly able to defeat him. Your difficulty will not be in the want of men, but in the means of supplying them at this season of the year. A single-track railroad can supply an army of sixty or seventy thousand men, with the usual number of cavalry and artillery; but beyond that number, or with a large mounted force, the difficulty of supply is very great.

I do not know the present condition of the road from Nashville to Decatur, but, if practicable to repair it, the use of that triangle will be of great assistance to you. I hope, also, that the recent rise of water in the

Cumberland and Tennessee Rivers will enable you to employ water transportation to Nashville, Eastport, or Florence.

If you reoccupy the passes of Lookout Mountain, which should never have been given up, you will be able to use the railroad and river from Bridgeport to Chattanooga. This seems to me a matter of vital importance, and should receive your early attention.

I submit this summary in the hope that it will assist you in fully understanding the objects of the campaign, and the means of attaining these objects. Probably the Secretary of War, in his interviews with you at Louisville, has gone over the same ground. Whatever measures you may deem proper to adopt under existing circumstances, you will receive all possible assistance from the authorities at Washington. You have never, heretofore, complained that such assistance has not been afforded you in your operations, and I think you will have no cause of complaint in your present campaign. Very respectfully, your obedient servant,

H. W. HALLECK, General-in-Chief

General Frank P. Blair, who was then ahead with the two divisions of Osterhaus and John E. Smith, was temporarily assigned to the command of the Fifteenth Corps. General Hurlbut remained at Memphis in command of the Sixteenth Corps, and General McPherson at Vicksburg with the Seventeenth. These three corps made up the Army of the Tennessee. I was still busy in pushing forward the repairs to the railroad bridge at Bear Creek, and in patching up the many breaks between it and Tuscumbia, when on the 27th of October, as I sat on the porch of a house, I was approached by a dirty, black-haired individual with mixed dress and strange demeanor, who inquired for me, and, on being assured that I was in fact the man, he handed me a letter from General Blair at Tuscumbia, and another short one, which was a telegraph-message from General Grant at Chattanooga, addressed to me through General George Crook, commanding at Huntsville, Alabama, to this effect:

Drop all work on Memphis & Charleston Railroad, cross the Tennessee and hurry eastward with all possible dispatch toward Bridgeport, till you meet further orders from me.

U. S. GRANT.

The bearer of this message was Corporal Pike, who described to me, in his peculiar way, that General Crook had sent him in a canoe; that he had paddled down the Tennessee River, over Muscle Shoals, was fired at all the way by guerrillas, but on reaching Tuscumbia he had providentially found it in possession of our troops. He had reported to General Blair, who sent him on to me at Iuka. This Pike proved to be a singular character; his manner attracted my notice at once, and I got him a horse, and had him travel with us eastward to about Elkton, whence I sent him back to General Crook at Huntsville; but told him, if I could ever do him a personal service, he might apply to me. The next spring when I was in Chattanooga, preparing for the Atlanta campaign, Corporal Pike made his appearance and asked a fulfillment of my promise. I inquired what he wanted, and he said he wanted to do something bold, something that would make him a hero. I explained to him, that we were getting ready to go for Joe Johnston at Dalton, that I expected to be in the neighborhood of Atlanta about the 4th of July, and wanted the bridge across the Savannah River at Augusta, Georgia, to be burnt about that time, to produce alarm and confusion behind the rebel army. I explained to Pike that the chances were three to one that he would be caught and hanged; but the greater the danger the greater seemed to be his desire to attempt it. I told him to select a companion, to disguise himself as an East Tennessee refugee, work his way over the mountains into North Carolina, and at the time appointed to float down the Savannah River and burn that bridge. In a few days he had made his preparations and took his departure. The bridge was not burnt, and I supposed that Pike had been caught and hanged.

When we reached Columbia, South Carolina, in February, 1865, just as we were leaving the town, in passing near the asylum, I heard my name called, and saw a very dirty fellow followed by a file of men running toward me, and as they got near I recognized Pike. He called to me to identify him as one of my men; he was then a prisoner under guard, and I instructed the guard to bring him that night to my camp some fifteen miles up the road, which was done. Pike gave me a graphic narrative of his adventures, which would have filled a volume; told me how he had made two attempts to burn the bridge, and failed; and said that at the time of our entering Columbia he was a prisoner in the hands of the rebels, under trial for his life, but in the confusion of their retreat he made his escape and got into our lines, where he was again made a prisoner by our troops because of his looks. Pike got some clothes, cleaned up, and I used him afterward to communicate with Wilmington, North Carolina. Some time after the war, he was appointed a lieutenant of the Regular, Cavalry, and was killed in Oregon, by the accidental discharge of a pistol. Just before his death he wrote me, saying that he was tired of the monotony of garrison-life, and wanted to turn Indian, join the Cheyennes on the Plains, who were then giving us great trouble, and, after he had gained their confidence, he would betray them into our hands. Of course I wrote him that he must try and settle down and become a gentleman as well as an officer, apply himself to his duties, and forget the wild desires of his nature, which were well enough in time of war, but not suited to his new condition as an officer; but, poor fellow I he was killed by an accident, which probably saved him from a slower but harder fate.

At Iuka I issued all the orders to McPherson and Hurlbut necessary for the Department of the Tennessee during my absence, and, further, ordered the collection of a force out of the Sixteenth Corps, of about eight thousand men, to be commanded by General G. M. Dodge, with orders to follow as far east as Athens, Tennessee, there to await instructions. We instantly discontinued all attempts to repair the Charleston Railroad; and the remaining three divisions of the Fifteenth Corps marched to Eastport, crossed the Tennessee River by the aid of the gunboats, a ferry-boat, and a couple of transports which had come up, and hurried eastward.

In person I crossed on the 1st of November, and rode forward to Florence, where I overtook Ewing's division. The other divisions followed rapidly. On the road to Florence I was accompanied by my staff, some clerks, and mounted orderlies. Major Ezra Taylor was chief of artillery, and one of his sons was a clerk at headquarters. The latter seems to have dropped out of the column, and gone to a farm house near the road. There was no organized force of the rebel army north of the Tennessee River, but the country was full of guerrillas. A party of these pounced down on the farm, caught young Taylor and another of the clerks, and after reaching Florence, Major Taylor heard of the capture of his son, and learned that when last seen he was stripped of his hat and coat, was tied to the tail-board of a wagon, and driven rapidly to the north of the road we had traveled. The major appealed to me to do something for his rescue. I had no cavalry to send in pursuit, but knowing that there was always an understanding between these guerrillas and their friends who staid at home, I sent for three or four of the principal men of Florence (among them a Mr. Foster, who had once been a Senator in Congress), explained to them the capture of young Taylor and his comrade, and demanded their immediate restoration. They, of course, remonstrated, denied all knowledge of the acts of these guerrillas, and claimed to be peaceful citizens of Alabama, residing at home. I insisted that these guerrillas were their own sons and neighbors; that they knew their haunts, and could reach them if they wanted, and they could effect the restoration to us of these men; and I said, moreover, they must do it within twenty-four hours, or I would take them, strip them of their hats and coats, and tie them to the tail-boards of our wagons till they were produced. They sent off messengers at once, and young Taylor and his comrade were brought back the next day.

Resuming our march eastward by the large road, we soon reached Elk River, which was wide and deep, and could only be crossed by a ferry, a process entirely too slow for the occasion; so I changed the route more by the north, to Elkton, Winchester, and Deckerd. At this point we came in communication with the Army of the Cumberland, and by telegraph with General Grant, who was at Chattanooga. He reiterated his orders for me and my command to hurry forward with all possible dispatch, and in person I reached Bridgeport during the night of November 13th, my troops following behind by several roads. At Bridgeport I found a garrison guarding the railroad-bridge and pontoon bridge there, and staid with the quartermaster, Colonel William G. Le Due (who was my school-mate at How's School in 1836). There I received a dispatch from General Grant, at Chattanooga, to come up in person, leaving my troops to follow as fast as possible. At that time there were two or three small steamboats on the river, engaged in carrying stores up as far as Kelly's Ferry. In one of these I took passage, and on reaching Kelly's Ferry found orderlies, with one of General Grant's private horses, waiting for me, on which I rode into Chattanooga, November 14th. Of course, I was heartily welcomed by Generals Grant, Thomas, and all, who realized the extraordinary efforts we had made to come to their relief. The next morning we walked out to Fort Wood, a prominent salient of the defenses of the place, and from its parapet we had a magnificent view of the panorama. Lookout Mountain, with its rebel flags and batteries, stood out boldly, and an occasional shot fired toward Wauhatchee or Moccasin Point gave life to the scene. These shots could barely reach Chattanooga, and I was told that one or more shot had struck a hospital inside the lines. All along Missionary Ridge were the tents of the rebel beleaguering force; the lines of trench from Lookout up toward the Chickamauga were plainly visible; and rebel sentinels, in a continuous chain, were walking their posts in plain view, not a thousand yards off. "Why," said I, "General Grant, you are besieged;" and he said, "It is too true." Up to that moment I had no idea that things were so bad. The rebel lines actually extended from the river, below the town, to the river above, and the Army of the Cumberland was closely held to the town and its immediate defenses. General Grant pointed out to me a house on Missionary Ridge, where General Bragg's headquarters were known to be. He also explained the situation of affairs generally; that the mules and horses of Thomas's army were so starved that they could not haul his guns; that forage, corn, and provisions, were so scarce that the men in hunger stole the few grains of corn that were given to favorite horses; that the men of Thomas's army had been so demoralized by the battle of Chickamauga that he feared they could not be got out of their trenches to assume the offensive; that Bragg had detached Longstreet with a considerable force up into East Tennessee, to defeat and capture Burnside; that Burnside was in danger, etc.; and that he (Grant) was extremely anxious to attack Bragg in position, to defeat him, or at least to force him to recall Longstreet. The Army of the Cumberland had so long been in the trenches that he wanted my troops to hurry up, to take the offensive first; after which, he had no doubt the Cumberland army would fight well. Meantime the Eleventh and Twelfth Corps, under General Hooker, had been advanced from Bridgeport along the railroad to Wauhatchee, but could not as yet pass Lookout Mountain. A pontoon-bridge had been thrown across the Tennessee River at Brown's Ferry, by which supplies were hauled into Chattanooga from Kelly's and Wauhatchee..

Another bridge was in course of construction at Chattanooga, under the immediate direction of Quartermaster-General Meigs, but at the time all wagons, etc., had to be ferried across by a flying-bridge. Men were busy and hard at work everywhere inside our lines, and boats for another pontoon-bridge were being rapidly constructed under Brigadier-General W. F. Smith, familiarly known as "Baldy Smith," and this bridge was destined to be used by my troops, at a point of the river about four miles above Chattanooga, just below the mouth of the Chickamauga River. General Grant explained to me that he had reconnoitred the rebel line from Lookout Mountain up to Chickamauga, and he believed that the northern portion of Missionary Ridge was not fortified at all; and he wanted me, as soon as my troops got up, to lay the new pontoon-bridge by night, cross over, and attack Bragg's right flank on that part of the ridge abutting on Chickamauga Creek, near the tunnel; and he proposed that we should go at once to look at the ground. In company with Generals Thomas, W. F. Smith, Brannan, and others, we crossed by the flying-bridge, rode back of the hills some four miles, left our horses, and got on a hill overlooking the whole ground about the mouth of the Chickamauga River, and across to the Missionary Hills near the tunnel. Smith and I crept down behind a fringe of trees that lined the river-bank, to the very point selected for the new bridge, where we sat for some time, seeing the rebel pickets on the opposite bank, and almost hearing their words.

Having seen enough, we returned to Chattanooga; and in order to hurry up my command, on which so much depended, I started back to Kelly's in hopes to catch the steamboat that same evening; but on my arrival the boat had gone. I applied to the commanding officer, got a rough boat manned by four soldiers, and started down the river by night. I occasionally took a turn at the oars to relieve some tired man, and about midnight we reached Shell Mound, where General Whittaker, of Kentucky, furnished us a new and good crew, with which we reached Bridgeport by daylight. I started Ewings division in advance, with orders to turn aside toward Trenton, to make the enemy believe we were going to turn Braggs left by pretty much the same road Rosecrans had followed; but with the other three divisions I followed the main road, via the Big Trestle at Whitesides, and reached General Hooker's headquarters, just above Wauhatchee, on the 20th; my troops strung all the way back to Bridgeport. It was on this occasion that the Fifteenth Corps gained its peculiar badge: as the men were trudging along the deeply-cut, muddy road, of a cold, drizzly day, one of our Western soldiers left his ranks and joined a party of the Twelfth Corps at their camp-fire. They got into conversation, the Twelfth-Corps men asking what troops we were, etc., etc. In turn, our fellow (who had never seen a corps-badge, and noticed that every thing was marked with a star) asked if they were all brigadier-generals. Of course they were not, but the star was their corps-badge, and every wagon, tent, hat, etc., had its star. Then the Twelfth-Corps men inquired what corps he belonged to, and he answered, "The Fifteenth Corps." "What is your badge?" "Why," said he (and he was an Irishman), suiting the action to the word, "forty rounds in the cartridge-box, and twenty in the pocket." At that time Blair commanded the corps; but Logan succeeded soon after, and, hearing the story, adopted the cartridge-box and forty rounds as the corps-badge.

The condition of the roads was such, and the bridge at Brown's so frail, that it was not until the 23d that we got three of my divisions behind the hills near the point indicated above Chattanooga for crossing the river. It was determined to begin the battle with these three divisions, aided by a division of Thomas's army, commanded by General Jeff. C. Davis, that was already near that point. All the details of the battle of Chattanooga, so far as I was a witness, are so fully given in my official report herewith, that I need add nothing to it. It was a magnificent battle in its conception, in its execution, and in its glorious results; hastened somewhat by the supposed danger of Burnside, at Knoxville, yet so completely successful, that nothing is left for cavil or fault-finding. The first day was lowering and overcast, favoring us greatly, because we wanted to be concealed from Bragg, whose position on the mountain-tops completely overlooked us and our movements. The second day was beautifully clear, and many a time, in the midst of its carnage and noise, I could not help stopping to look across that vast field of battle, to admire its sublimity.

The object of General Hooker's and my attacks on the extreme flanks of Bragg's position was, to disturb him to such an extent, that he would naturally detach from his centre as against us, so that Thomas's army could break through his centre. The whole plan succeeded admirably; but it was not until after dark that I learned the complete success at the centre, and received General Grant's orders to pursue on the north side of Chickamauga Creek:

HEADQUARTERS MILITARY DIVISION OF THE MISSISSIPPI, CHATTANOOGA, TENNESSEE, Nov. 25, 1863

Major-General SHERMAN.

GENERAL: No doubt you witnessed the handsome manner in which Thomas's troops carried Missionary Ridge this afternoon, and can feel a just pride, too, in the part taken by the forces under your command in taking first so much of the same range of hills, and then in attracting the attention of so many of the enemy as to make Thomas's part certain of success. The neat thing now will be to relieve Burnside. I have heard from him to the evening of the 23d. At that time he had from ten to twelve days' supplies, and spoke hopefully of being able to hold out that length of time.

My plan is to move your forces out gradually until they reach the railroad between Cleveland and Dalton. Granger will move up the south side of the Tennessee with a column of twenty thousand men, taking no wagons, or but few, with him. His men will carry four days' rations, and the steamer Chattanooga, loaded with rations, will accompany the expedition.

I take it for granted that Bragg's entire force has left. If not, of course, the first thing is to dispose of him. If he has gone, the only thing necessary to do to-morrow will be to send out a reconnoissance to ascertain the whereabouts of the enemy. Yours truly,

U. S. GRANT, Major-General.

P. S.-On reflection, I think we will push Bragg with all our strength to-morrow, and try if we cannot cut off a good portion of his rear troops and trains. His men have manifested a strong disposition to desert for some time past, and we will now give them a chance. I will instruct Thomas accordingly. Move the advance force early, on the most easterly road taken by the enemy. U. S. G.

This compelled me to reverse our column, so as to use the bridge across the Chickamauga at its mouth. The next day we struck the rebel rear at Chickamauga Station, and again near Graysville. There we came in contact with Hooker's and Palmer's troops, who had reached Ringgold. There I detached Howard to cross Taylor's Ridge, and strike the railroad which comes from the north by Cleveland to Dalton. Hooker's troops were roughly handled at Ringgold, and the pursuit was checked. Receiving a note from General Hooker, asking help, I rode forward to Ringgold to explain the movement of Howard; where I met General Grant, and learned that the rebels had again retreated toward Dalton. He gave orders to discontinue the pursuit, as he meant to turn his attention to General Burnside, supposed to be in great danger at Knoxville, about one hundred and thirty miles northeast. General Grant returned and spent part of the night with me, at Graysville. We talked over matters generally, and he explained that he had ordered General Gordon Granger, with the Fourth Corps, to move forward rapidly to Burnsides help, and that he must return to Chattanooga to push him. By reason of the scarcity of food, especially of forage, he consented that, instead of going back, I might keep out in the country; for in motion I could pick up some forage and food, especially on the Hiawassee River, whereas none remained in Chattanooga.

Accordingly, on the 29th of November, my several columns marched to Cleveland, and the next day we reached the Hiawassee at Charleston, where the Chattanooga & Knoxville Railroad crosses it. The railroad-bridge was partially damaged by the enemy in retreating, but we found some abandoned stores. There and thereabouts I expected some rest for my weary troops and horses; but, as I rode into town, I met Colonel J. H. Wilson and C. A. Dana (Assistant Secretary of War), who had ridden out from Chattanooga to find me, with the following letter from General Grant, and copies of several dispatches from General Burnside, the last which had been received from him by way of Cumberland Gap:

HEADQUARTERS MILITARY DIVISION OF THE MISSISSIPPI, CHATTANOOGA, TENNESSEE, Nov. 29, 1863

Major-General W. T. SHERMAN

News are received from Knoxville to the morning of the 27th. At that time the place was still invested, but the attack on it was not vigorous. Longstreet evidently determined to starve the garrison out. Granger is on the way to Burnside's relief, but I have lost all faith in his energy or capacity to manage an expedition of the importance of this one. I am inclined to think, therefore, I shall have to send you. Push as rapidly as you can to the Hiawassee, and determine for yourself what force to take with you from that point. Granger has his corps with him, from which you will select in conjunction with the force now with you. In plain words, you will assume command of all the forces now moving up the Tennessee, including the garrison at Kingston, and from that force, organize what you deem proper to relieve Burnside. The balance send back to Chattanooga. Granger has a boat loaded with provisions, which you can issue, and return the boat. I will have another loaded, to follow you. Use, of course, as sparingly as possible from the rations taken with you, and subsist off the country all you can.

It is expected that Foster is moving, by this time, from Cumberland Gap on Knoxville. I do not know what force he will have with him, but presume it will range from three thousand five hundred to five thousand I leave this matter to you, knowing that you will do better acting upon your discretion than you could trammeled with instructions. I will only add, that the last advices from Burnside himself indicated his ability to hold out with rations only to about the 3d of December. Very respectfully,

U. S. GRANT, Major-General commanding,

This showed that, on the 27th of November, General Burnside was in Knoxville, closely besieged by the rebel General Longstreet; that his provisions were short, and that, unless relieved by December 3d, he might have to surrender. General Grant further wrote that General Granger, instead of moving with great rapidity as ordered, seemed to move "slowly, and with reluctance;" and, although he (General Grant) hated to call on me and on my tired troops, there was no alternative. He wanted me to take command of every thing within reach, and to hurry forward to Knoxville.

All the details of our march to Knoxville are also given in my official report. By extraordinary efforts Long's small brigade of cavalry reached Knoxville during the night of the 3d, purposely to let Burnside know that I was rapidly approaching with an adequate force to raise the siege.

With the head of my infantry column I reached Marysville, about fifteen miles short of Knoxville, on the 5th of December; when I received official notice from Burnside that Longstreet had raised the siege, and had started in retreat up the valley toward Virginia. Halting all the army, except Granger's two divisions, on the morning of the 6th, with General Granger and some of my staff I rode into Knoxville. Approaching from the south and west, we crossed the Holston on a pontoon bridge, and in a large pen on the Knoxville side I saw a fine lot of cattle, which did not look much like starvation. I found General Burnside and staff domiciled in a large, fine mansion, looking very comfortable, and in, a few words he described to me the leading events, of the previous few days, and said he had already given orders looking to the pursuit of Longstreet. I offered to join in the pursuit, though in fact my men were worn out, and suffering in that cold season and climate.

Indeed, on our way up I personally was almost frozen, and had to beg leave to sleep in the house of a family at Athens.

Burnside explained to me that, reenforced by Granger's two divisions of ten thousand men, he would be able to push Longstreet out of East Tennessee, and he hoped to capture much of his artillery and trains. Granger was present at our conversation, and most unreasonably, I thought, remonstrated against being left; complaining bitterly of what he thought was hard treatment to his men and himself. I know that his language and manner at that time produced on my mind a bad impression, and it was one of the causes which led me to relieve him as a corps commander in the campaign of the next spring. I asked General Burnside to reduce his wishes to writing, which he did in the letter of December 7th, embodied in my official report. General Burnside and I then walked along his lines and examined the salient, known as Fort Sanders, where, some days before, Longstreet had made his assault, and had sustained a bloody repulse.

Returning to Burnside's quarters, we all sat down to a good dinner, embracing roast-turkey. There was a regular dining table, with clean tablecloth, dishes, knives, forks, spoons, etc., etc. I had seen nothing of this kind in my field experience, and could not help exclaiming that I thought "they were starving," etc.; but Burnside explained that Longstreet had at no time completely invested the place, and that he had kept open communication with the country on the south side of the river Holston, more especially with the French Broad settlements, from whose Union inhabitants he had received a good supply of beef, bacon, and corn meal. Had I known of this, I should not have hurried my men so fast; but until I reached Knoxville I thought his troops there were actually in danger of starvation.

Having supplied General Burnside all the help he wanted, we began our leisurely return to Chattanooga, which we reached on the 16th; when General Grant in person ordered me to restore to General Thomas the divisions of Howard and Davis, which belonged to his army, and to conduct my own corps (the Fifteenth) to North Alabama for winter-quarters.

HEADQUARTERS DEPARTMENT OF THE ARMY OF TENNESSEE,
BRIDGEPORT,
ALABAMA December 19, 1863

Brigadier-General John A. RAWLINS, Chief of Staff to General GRANT, Chattanooga.

GENERAL: For the first time, I am now at leisure to make an official record of events with which the troops under my command have been connected during the eventful campaign which has just closed. Dating the month of September last, the Fifteenth Army Corps, which I had the honor to command, lay in camps along the Big Black, about twenty miles east of Vicksburg, Mississippi. It consisted of four divisions:

The First, commanded by Brigadier-General P. J. Osterhaus, was composed of two brigades, led by Brigadier-General C. R. Woods and Colonel J. A. Williamson (of the Fourth Iowa).

The Second, commanded by Brigadier-General Morgan L. Smith, was composed of two brigades, led by Brigadier-Generals Giles A. Smith and J. A. J. Lightburn.

The Third, commanded by Brigadier-General J. M. Tuttle, was composed of three brigades, led by Brigadier-Generals J. A. Mower and R. P. Buckland, and Colonel J. J. Wood (of the Twelfth Iowa).

The Fourth, commanded by Brigadier-General Hugh Ewing, was composed of three brigades, led by Brigadier-General J. M. Corse, Colonel Loomis (Twenty-sixth Illinois), and Colonel J. R. Cockerill (of the Seventieth Ohio).

On the 22d day of September I received a telegraphic dispatch from General Grant, then at Vicksburg, commanding the Department of the Tennessee, requiring me to detach one of my divisions to march to Vicksburg, there to embark for Memphis, where it was to form a part of an army to be sent to Chattanooga, to reenforce General Rosecrans. I designated the First Division, and at 4 a. m. the same day it marched for Vicksburg, and embarked the neat day.

On the 23d of September I was summoned to Vicksburg by the general commanding, who showed me several dispatches from the general-in-chief, which led him to suppose he would have to send me and my whole corps to Memphis and eastward, and I was instructed to prepare for such orders. It was explained to me that, in consequence of the low stage of water in the Mississippi, boats had arrived irregularly, and had brought dispatches that seemed to conflict in their meaning, and that General John E. Smith's division (of General McPherson's corps) had been ordered up to Memphis, and that I should take that division and leave one of my own in its stead, to hold the line of the Big Black. I detailed my third division (General Tuttle) to remain and report to Major-General McPherson, commanding the Seventeenth Corps, at Vicksburg; and that of General John E. Smith, already started for Memphis, was styled the Third Division, Fifteenth Corps, though it still belongs to the Seventeenth Army Corps. This division is also composed of three brigades, commanded by General Matthias, Colonel J. B. Raum (of the Fifty-sixth Illinois), and Colonel J. I. Alexander (of the Fifty-ninth Indiana).

The Second and Fourth Divisions were started for Vicksburg the moment I was notified that boats were in readiness, and on the 27th of September I embarked in person in the steamer Atlantic, for Memphis, followed by a fleet of boats conveying these two divisions. Our progress was slow, on account of the unprecedentedly low water in the Mississippi, and the scarcity of coal and wood. We were compelled at places to gather fence-rails, and to land wagons and haul wood from the interior to the boats; but I reached Memphis during the night of the 2d of October, and the other boats came in on the 3d and 4th.

On arrival at Memphis I saw General Hurlbut, and read all the dispatches and letters of instruction of General Halleck, and therein derived my instructions, which I construed to be as follows:

To conduct the Fifteenth Army Corps, and all other troops which could be spared from the line of the Memphis & Charleston Railroad, to Athens, Alabama, and thence report by letter for orders to General Rosecrans, commanding the Army of the Cumberland, at Chattanooga; to follow substantially the railroad eastward, repairing it as I moved; to look to my own line for supplies; and in no event to depend on General Rosecrans for supplies, as the roads to his rear were already overtaxed to supply his present army.

I learned from General Hurlbut that General Osterhaus's division was already out in front of Corinth, and that General John E. Smith was still at Memphis, moving his troops and material by railroad as fast as its limited stock would carry them. General J. D. Webster was superintendent of the railroad, and was enjoined to work night and day, and to expedite the movement as rapidly as possible; but the capacity of the road was so small, that I soon saw that I could move horses, mules, and wagons faster by land, and therefore I dispatched the artillery and wagons by the road under escort, and finally moved the entire Fourth Division by land.

The enemy seems to have had early notice of this movement, and he endeavored to thwart us from the start. A considerable force assembled in a threatening attitude at Salem, south of Salisbury Station; and General Carr, who commanded at Corinth, felt compelled to turn back and use a part of my troops, that had already reached Corinth, to resist the threatened attack.

On Sunday, October 11th, having put in motion my whole force, I started myself for Corinth, in a special train, with the battalion of the Thirteenth United States Regulars as escort. We reached Collierville Station about noon, just in time to take part in the defense made of that station by Colonel D. C. Anthony, of the Sixty-sixth Indiana, against an attack made by General Chalmers with a force of about three thousand cavalry, with eight pieces of artillery. He was beaten off, the damage to the road repaired, and we resumed our journey the next day, reaching Corinth at night.

I immediately ordered General Blair forward to Iuka, with the First Division, and, as fast as I got troops up, pushed them forward of Bear Creek, the bridge of which was completely destroyed, and an engineer regiment, under command of Colonel Flag, was engaged in its repairs.

Quite a considerable force of the enemy was assembled in our front, near Tuscumbia, to resist our advance. It was commanded by General Stephen D. Lee, and composed of Roddy's and Ferguson's brigades, with irregular cavalry, amounting in the aggregate to about five thousand.

In person I moved from Corinth to Burnsville on the 18th, and to Iuka on the 19th of October.

Osterhaus's division was in the advance, constantly skirmishing with the enemy; he was supported by General Morgan L. Smith's, both divisions under the general command of Major-General Blair. General John E. Smith's division covered the working-party engaged in rebuilding the railroad.

Foreseeing difficulty in crossing the Tennessee River, I had written to Admiral Porter, at Cairo, asking him to watch the Tennessee and send up some gunboats the moment the stage of water admitted; and had also requested General Allen, quartermaster at St. Louis, to dispatch to Eastport a steam ferry-boat.

The admiral, ever prompt and ready to assist us, had two fine gunboats at Eastport, under Captain Phelps, the very day after my arrival at Iuka; and Captain Phelps had a coal-barge decked over, with which to cross our horses and wagons before the arrival of the ferry-boat.

Still following literally the instructions of General Halleck, I pushed forward the repairs of the railroad, and ordered General Blair, with the two leading divisions, to drive the enemy beyond Tuscumbia. This he did successfully, after a pretty severe fight at Cane Creek, occupying Tuscumbia on the 27th of October.

In the meantime many important changes in command had occurred, which I must note here, to a proper understanding of the case.

General Grant had been called from Vicksburg, and sent to Chattanooga to command the military division of the Mississippi, composed of the three Departments of the Ohio, Cumberland, and Tennessee; and the Department of the Tennessee had been devolved on me, with instructions, however, to retain command of the army in the field. At Iuka I made what appeared to me the best disposition of matters relating to the department, giving General McPherson full powers in Mississippi and General Hurlbut in West Tennessee, and assigned General Blair to the command of the Fifteenth Army Corps; and summoned General Hurlbut from Memphis, and General Dodge from Corinth, and selected out of the Sixteenth Corps a force of about eight thousand men, which I directed General Dodge to organize with all expedition, and with it to follow me eastward.

On the 27th of October, when General Blair, with two divisions, was at Tuscumbia, I ordered General Ewing, with the Fourth Division, to cross the Tennessee (by means of the gunboats and scow) as rapidly as possible at Eastport, and push forward to Florence, which he did; and the same day a messenger from General Grant floated down the Tennessee over Muscle Shoals, landed at Tuscumbia, and was sent to me at Iuka. He bore a short message from the general to this effect: "Drop all work on the railroad east of Bear Creek; push your command toward Bridgeport till you meet orders;" etc. Instantly the order was executed; the order of march was reversed, and all the columns were directed to Eastport, the only place where we could cross the Tennessee. At first we only had the gunboats and coal-barge; but the ferry-boat and two transports arrived on the 31st of October, and the work of crossing was pushed with all the vigor possible. In person I crossed, and passed to the head of the column at Florence on the 1st of November, leaving the rear divisions to be conducted by General Blair, and marched to Rogersville and Elk River. This was found impassable. To ferry would have consumed much time, and to build a bridge still more; so there was no alternative but to turn up Elk River by way of Gilbertsboro, Elkton, etc., to the stone bridge at Fayetteville, where we crossed the Elk, and proceeded to Winchester and Deckerd.

At Fayetteville I received orders from General Grant to come to Bridgeport with the Fifteenth Army Corps, and to leave General Dodge's command at Pulaski, and along the railroad from Columbia to Decatur. I instructed General Blair to follow with the Second and First Divisions by way of New Market, Larkinsville, and Bellefonte, while I conducted the other two divisions by way of Deckerd; the Fourth Division crossing the mountain to Stevenson, and the Third by University Place and Sweden's Cove.

In person I proceeded by Sweden's Cove and Battle Creek, reaching Bridgeport on the night of November 13th. I immediately telegraphed to the commanding general my arrival, and the positions of my several divisions, and was summoned to Chattanooga. I took the first steamboat during the night of the 14th for Belly's Ferry, and rode into Chattanooga on the 16th. I then learned the part assigned me in the coming drama, was supplied with the necessary maps and information, and rode, during the 18th, in company with Generals Grant, Thomas, W. F. Smith, Brannan, and others, to the positions occupied on the west bank of the Tennessee, from which could be seen the camps of the enemy, compassing Chattanooga and the line of Missionary Hills, with its terminus on Chickamauga Creek, the point that I was expected to take, hold, and fortify. Pontoons, with a full supply of balks and chesses, had been prepared for the bridge over the Tennessee, and all things had been prearranged with a foresight that elicited my admiration. From the hills we looked down on the amphitheatre of Chattanooga as on a map, and nothing remained but for me to put my troops in the desired position. The plan contemplated that, in addition to crossing the Tennessee River and making a lodgment on the terminus of Missionary Ridge, I should demonstrate against Lookout Mountain, near Trenton, with a part of my command.

All in Chattanooga were impatient for action, rendered almost acute by the natural apprehensions felt for the safety of General Burnside in East Tennessee.

My command had marched from Memphis, three hundred and thirty miles, and I had pushed them as fast as the roads and distance would admit, but I saw enough of the condition of men and animals in Chattanooga to inspire me with renewed energy. I immediately ordered my leading division (General Ewing's) to march via Shellmound to Trenton, demonstrating against Lookout Ridge, but to be prepared to turn quickly and follow me to Chattanooga and in person I returned to Bridgeport, rowing a boat down the Tennessee from Belly's Ferry, and immediately on arrival put in motion my divisions in the order in which they had arrived. The bridge of boats at Bridgeport was frail, and, though used day and night, our passage was slow; and the road thence to Chattanooga was dreadfully cut up and encumbered with the wagons of the other troops stationed along the road. I reached General Hooker's headquarters during a rain, in the afternoon of the 20th, and met General Grant's orders for the general attack on the next day. It was simply impossible for me to fulfill my part in time; only one division (General John E. Smith's) was in position. General Ewing was still at Trenton, and the other two were toiling along the terrible road from Shellmound to Chattanooga. No troops ever were or could be in better condition than mine, or who labored harder to fulfill their part. On a proper representation, General Grant postponed the attack. On the 21st I got the Second Division over Brown's-Ferry Bridge, and General Ewing got up; but the bridge broke repeatedly, and delays occurred which no human sagacity could prevent. All labored night and day, and General Ewing got over on the 23d; but my rear division was cut off by the broken bridge at Brown's Ferry, and could not join me. I offered to go into action with my three divisions, supported by General Jeff. C. Davis, leaving one of my best divisions (Osterhaus's) to act with General Hooker against Lookout Mountain. That division has not joined me yet, but I know and feel that it has served the country well, and that it has reflected honor on the Fifteenth Army Corps and the Army of the Tennessee. I leave the record of its history to General Hooker, or whomsoever has had its services during the late memorable events, confident that all will do it merited honor.

At last, on the 28d of November, my three divisions lay behind the hills opposite the mouth of the Chickamauga. I dispatched the brigade of the Second Division, commanded by General Giles A. Smith, under cover of the hills, to North Chickamauga Creek, to man the boats designed for the pontoon-bridge, with orders (at midnight) to drop down silently to a point above the mouth of the South Chickamauga, there land two regiments, who were to move along the river-bank quietly, and capture the enemy's river-pickets.

General Giles A. Smith then was to drop rapidly below the month of the Chickamauga, disembark the rest of his brigade, and dispatch the boats across for fresh loads. These orders were skillfully executed, and every rebel picket but one was captured. The balance of General Morgan L. Smith's division was then rapidly ferried across; that of General John E. Smith followed, and by daylight of November 24th two divisions of about eight thousand men were on the east bank of the Tennessee, and had thrown up a very respectable rifle-trench as a tete du pont. As soon as the day dawned, some of the boats were taken from the use of ferrying, and a pontoon-bridge was begun, under the immediate direction of Captain Dresser, the whole planned and supervised by General William F. Smith in person. A pontoon-bridge was also built at the same time over Chickamanga Creek, near its mouth, giving communication with the two regiments which had been left on the north side, and fulfilling a most important purpose at a later stage of the drama. I will here bear my willing testimony to the completeness of this whole business. All the officers charged with the work were present, and manifested a skill which I cannot praise too highly. I have never beheld any work done so quietly, so well; and I doubt if the history of war can show a bridge of that extent (viz., thirteen hundred and fifty feet) laid so noiselessly and well, in so short a time. I attribute it to the genius and intelligence of General William F. Smith. The steamer Dunbar arrived up in the course of the morning, and relieved Ewing's division of the labor of rowing across; but by noon the pontoon-bridge was done, and my three divisions were across, with men, horses, artillery, and every thing.

General Jeff. C. Davis's division was ready to take the bridge, and I ordered the columns to form in order to carry the Missionary Hills. The movement had been carefully explained to all division commanders, and at 1 p.m. we marched from the river in three columns in echelon: the left, General Morgan L. Smith, the column of direction, following substantially Chickamauga Creek; the centre, General, John E. Smith, in columns, doubled on the centre, at one brigade interval to the right and rear; the right, General Ewing, in column at the same distance to the right rear, prepared to deploy to the right, on the supposition that we would meet an enemy in that direction. Each head of column was covered by a good line of skirmishers, with supports. A light drizzling rain prevailed, and the clouds hung low, cloaking our movement from the enemy's tower of observation on Lookout Mountain. We soon gained the foothills; our skirmishers crept up the face of the hills, followed by their supports, and at 3.30 p.m. we had gained, with no loss, the desired point. A brigade of each division was pushed rapidly to the top of the hill, and the enemy for the first time seemed to realize the movement, but too late, for we were in possession. He opened with artillery, but General Ewing soon got some of Captain Richardson's guns up that steep hill and gave back artillery, and the enemy's skirmishers made one or two ineffectual dashes at General Lightburn, who had swept round and got a farther hill, which was the real continuation of the ridge. From studying all the maps, I had inferred that Missionary Ridge was a continuous hill; but we found ourselves on two high points, with a deep depression between us and the one immediately over the tunnel, which was my chief objective point. The ground we had gained, however, was so important, that I could leave nothing to chance, and ordered it to be fortified during the night. One brigade of each division was left on the hill, one of General Morgan L. Smith's closed the gap to Chickamauga Creek, two of General John E. Smith's were drawn back to the base in reserve, and General Ewing's right was extended down into the plain, thus crossing the ridge in a general line, facing southeast.

The enemy felt our left flank about 4 p.m., and a pretty smart engagement with artillery and muskets ensued, when he drew off; but it cost us dear, for General Giles A. Smith was severely wounded, and had to go to the rear; and the command of the brigade devolved on Colonel Topper (One Hundred and Sixteenth Illinois), who managed it with skill during the rest of the operations. At the moment of my crossing the bridge, General Howard appeared, having come with three regiments from Chattanooga, along the east bank of the Tennessee, connecting my new position with that of the main army in Chattanooga. He left the three regiments attached temporarily to Gen. Ewing's right, and returned to his own corps at Chattanooga. As night closed in, I ordered General Jeff. C. Davis to keep one of his brigades at the bridge, one close up to my position, and one intermediate. Thus we passed the night, heavy details being kept busy at work on the intrenchments on the hill. During the night the sky cleared away bright, a cold frost filled the air, and our camp-fires revealed to the enemy and to our friends in Chattanooga our position on Missionary Ridge. About midnight I received, at the hands of Major Rowley (of General Grant's staff), orders to attack the enemy at "dawn of day," with notice that General Thomas would attack in force early in the day. Accordingly, before day I was in the saddle, attended by all my staff; rode to the extreme left of our position near Chickamauga Creek; thence up the hill, held by General Lightburn; and round to the extreme right of General Ewing.

Catching as accurate an idea of the ground as possible by the dim light of morning, I saw that our line of attack was in the direction of Missionary Ridge, with wings supporting on either flank. Quite a valley lay between us and the next hill of the series, and this hill presented steep sides, the one to the west partially cleared, but the other covered with the native forest. The crest of the ridge was narrow and wooded. The farther point of this hill was held by the enemy with a breastwork of logs and fresh earth, filled with men and two guns. The enemy was also seen in great force on a still higher hill beyond the tunnel, from which he had a fine plunging fire on the hill in dispute. The gorge between, through which several roads and the railroad-tunnel pass, could not be seen from our position, but formed the natural place d'armes, where the enemy covered his masses to resist our contemplated movement of turning his right flank and endangering his communications with his depot at Chickamauga Station.

As soon as possible, the following dispositions were made: The brigades of Colonels Cockrell and Alexander, and General Lightburn, were to hold our hill as the key-point. General Corse, with as much of his brigade as could operate along the narrow ridge, was to attack from our right centre. General Lightburn was to dispatch a good regiment from his position to cooperate with General Corse; and General Morgan L. Smith was to move along the east base of Missionary Ridge, connecting with General Corse; and Colonel Loomis, in like manner, to move along the west bank, supported by the two reserve brigades of General John E. Smith.

The sun had hardly risen before General Corse had completed his preparations and his bugle sounded the "forward!" The Fortieth Illinois, supported by the Forty-sixth Ohio, on our right centre, with the Thirtieth Ohio (Colonel Jones), moved down the face of our hill, and up that held by the enemy. The line advanced to within about eighty yards of the intrenched position, where General Corse found a secondary crest, which he gained and held. To this point he called his reserves, and asked for reenforcements, which were sent; but the space was narrow, and it was not well to crowd the men, as the enemy's artillery and musketry fire swept the approach to his position, giving him great advantage. As soon as General Corse had made his preparations, he assaulted, and a close, severe contest ensued, which lasted more than an hour, gaining and losing ground, but never the position first obtained, from which the enemy in vain attempted to drive him. General Morgan L. Smith kept gaining ground on the left spurs of Missionary Ridge, and Colonel Loomis got abreast of the tunnel and railroad embankment on his aide, drawing the enemy's fire, and to that extent relieving the assaulting party on the hill-crest. Captain Callender had four of his guns on General Ewing's hill, and Captain Woods his Napoleon battery on General Lightburn's; also, two guns of Dillon's battery were with Colonel Alexander's brigade. All directed their fire as carefully as possible, to clear the hill to our front, without endangering our own men. The fight raged furiously about 10 a.m., when General Corse received a severe wound, was brought off the field, and the command of the brigade and of the assault at that key-point devolved on that fine young, gallant officer, Colonel Walcutt, of the Forty-sixth Ohio, who fulfilled his part manfully. He continued the contest, pressing forward at all points. Colonel Loomis had made good progress to the right, and about 2 p.m., General John E. Smith, judging the battle to be most severe on the hill, and being required to support General Ewing, ordered up Colonel Raum's and General Matthias's brigades across the field to the summit that was being fought for. They moved up under a heavy fire of cannon and musketry, and joined Colonel Walcutt; but the crest was so narrow that they necessarily occupied the west face of the hill. The enemy, at the time being massed in great strength in the tunnel-gorge, moved a large force under cover of the ground and the thick bushes, and suddenly appeared on the right rear of this command. The suddenness of the attack disconcerted the men, exposed as they were in the open field; they fell back in some disorder to the lower edge of the field, and reformed. These two brigades were in the nature of supports, and did not constitute a part of the real attack.

The movement, seen from Chattanooga (five miles off) with spy-glasses, gave rise to the report, which even General Meiga has repeated, that we were repulsed on the left. It was not so. The real attacking columns of General Corse, Colonel Loomis, and General Smith, were not repulsed. They engaged in a close struggle all day persistently, stubbornly, and well. When the two reserve brigades of General John E. Smith fell back as described, the enemy made a show of pursuit, but were in their turn caught in flank by the well-directed fire of our brigade on the wooded crest, and hastily sought cover behind the hill. Thus matters stood about 3 p.m. The day was bright and clear, and the amphitheatre of Chattanooga sat in beauty at our feet. I had watched for the attack of General Thomas "early in the day." Column after column of the enemy was streaming toward me; gun after gun poured its concentric shot on us, from every hill and spur that gave a view of any part of the ground held by us. An occasional shot from Fort Wood and Orchard Knob, and some musketry-fire and artillery over about Lookout Mountain, was all that I could detect on our side; but about 3 p.m. I noticed the white line of musketry-fire in front of Orchard Knoll extending farther and farther right and left and on. We could only hear a faint echo of sound, but enough was seen to satisfy me that General Thomas was at last moving on the centre. I knew that our attack had drawn vast masses of the enemy to our flank, and felt sure of the result. Some guns which had been firing on us all day were silent, or were turned in a different direction.

The advancing line of musketry-fire from Orchard Knoll disappeared to us behind a spar of the hill, and could no longer be seen; and it was not until night closed in that I knew that the troops in Chattanooga had swept across Missionary Ridge and broken the enemy's centre. Of course, the victory was won, and pursuit was the next step.

I ordered General Morgan L. Smith to feel to the tunnel, and it was found vacant, save by the dead and wounded of our own and the enemy commingled. The reserve of General Jeff. C. Davis was ordered to march at once by the pontoon-bridge across Chickamauga Creek, at its mouth, and push forward for the depot.

General Howard had reported to me in the early part of the day, with the remainder of his army corps (the Eleventh), and had been posted to connect my left with Chickamauga Creek. He was ordered to repair an old broken bridge about two miles up the Chickamauga, and to follow General Davis at 4 a.m., and the Fifteenth Army Corps was ordered to follow at daylight. But General Howard found that to repair the bridge was more of a task than was at first supposed, and we were all compelled to cross the Chickamauga on the new pontoon-bridge at its mouth. By about 11 a.m. General Jeff. C. Davis's division reached the depot, just in time to see it in flames. He found the enemy occupying two hills, partially intrenched, just beyond the depot. These he soon drove away. The depot presented a scene of desolation that war alone exhibits—corn-meal and corn in huge burning piles, broken wagons, abandoned caissons, two thirty-two-pounder rifled-guns with carriages burned, pieces of pontoons, balks and chesses, etc., destined doubtless for the famous invasion of Kentucky, and all manner of things, burning and broken. Still, the enemy kindly left us a good supply of forage for our horses, and meal, beans, etc., for our men.

Pausing but a short while, we passed on, the road filled with broken wagons and abandoned caissons, till night. Just as the head of the column emerged from a dark, miry swamp, we encountered the rear-guard of the retreating enemy. The fight was sharp, but the night closed in so dark that we could not move. General Grant came up to us there. At daylight we resumed the march, and at Graysville, where a good bridge spanned the Chickamauga, we found the corps of General Palmer on the south bank, who informed us that General Hooker was on a road still farther south, and we could hear his guns near Ringgold.

As the roads were filled with all the troops they could possibly accommodate, I turned to the east, to fulfill another part of the general plan, viz., to break up all communication between Bragg and Longstreet.

We had all sorts of rumors as to the latter, but it was manifest that we should interpose a proper force between these two armies. I therefore directed General Howard to move to Parker's Gap, and thence send rapidly a competent force to Red Clay, or the Council-Ground, there to destroy a large section of the railroad which connects Dalton and Cleveland. This work was most successfully and fully accomplished that day. The division of General Jeff. C. Davis was moved close up to Ringgold, to assist General Hooker if needed, and the Fifteenth Corps was held at Grayeville, for any thing that might turn up. About noon I had a message from General Hooker, saying he had had a pretty hard fight at the mountain-pass just beyond Ringgold, and he wanted me to come forward to turn the position. He was not aware at the time that Howard, by moving through Parker's Gap toward Red Clay, had already turned it. So I rode forward to Ringgold in person, and found the enemy had already fallen back to Tunnel Hill. He was already out of the valley of the Chickamauga, and on ground whence the waters flow to the Coosa. He was out of Tennessee.

I found General Grant at Ringgold, and, after some explanations as to breaking up the railroad from Ringgold back to the State line, as soon as some cars loaded with wounded men could be pushed back to Chickamauga depot, I was ordered to move slowly and leisurely back to Chattanooga.

On the following day the Fifteenth Corps destroyed absolutely and effectually the railroad from a point half-way between Ringgold and Graysville, back to the State line; and General Grant, coming to Graysville, consented that, instead of returning direct to Chattanooga, I might send back all my artillery-wagons and impediments, and make a circuit by the north as far as the Hiawasaee River.

Accordingly, on the morning of November 29th, General Howard moved from Parker's Gap to Cleveland, General Davis by way of McDaniel's Gap, and General Blair with two divisions of the Fifteenth Corps by way of Julien's Gap, all meeting at Cleveland that night. Here another good break was made in the Dalton & Cleveland road. On the 30th the army moved to Charleston, General Howard approaching so rapidly that the enemy evacuated with haste, leaving the bridge but partially damaged, and five car-loads of flour and provisions on the north bank of the Hiawassee.

This was to have been the limit of our operations. Officers and men had brought no baggage or provisions, and the weather was bitter cold. I had already reached the town of Charleston, when General Wilson arrived with a letter from General Grant, at Chattanooga, informing me that the latest authentic accounts from Knoxville were to the 27th, at which time General Burnside was completely invested, and had provisions only to include the 3d of December; that General Granger had left Chattanooga for Knoxville, by the river-road, with a steamboat following him in the river; but he feared that General Granger could not reach Knoxville in time, and ordered me to take command of all troops moving for the relief of Knoxville, and hasten to General Burnside. Seven days before, we had left our camps on the other side of the Tennessee with two days' rations, without a change of clothing—stripped for the fight, with but a single blanket or coat per man, from myself to the private included.

Of course, we then had no provisions save what we gathered by the road, and were ill supplied for such a march. But we learned that twelve thousand of our fellow-soldiers were beleaguered in the mountain town of Knoxville, eighty-four miles distant; that they needed relief, and must have it in three days. This was enough—and it had to be done. General Howard that night repaired and planked the railroad-bridge, and at daylight the army passed over the Hiawassee and marched to Athens, fifteen miles. I had supposed rightly that General Granger was about the mouth of the Hiawassee, and had sent him notice of my orders; that General Grant had sent me a copy of his written instructions, which were full and complete, and that he must push for Kingston, near which we would make a junction. But by the time I reached Athens I had better studied the geography, and sent him orders, which found him at Decatur, that Kingston was out of our way; that he should send his boat to Kingston, but with his command strike across to Philadelphia, and report to me there. I had but a small force of cavalry, which was, at the time of my receipt of General Grant's orders, scouting over about Benton and Columbus. I left my aide, Major McCoy, at Charleston, to communicate with this cavalry and hurry it forward. It overtook me in the night at Athens.

On the 2d of December the army moved rapidly north toward Loudon, twenty-six miles distant. About 11 a.m., the cavalry passed to the head of the column, was ordered to push to London, and, if possible, to save a pontoon-bridge across the Tennessee, held by a brigade of the enemy commanded by General Vaughn. The cavalry moved with such rapidity as to capture every picket; but the brigade of Vaughn had artillery in position, covered by earthworks, and displayed a force too respectable to be carried by a cavalry dash, so that darkness closed in before General Howard's infantry got up. The enemy abandoned the place in the night, destroying the pontoons, running three locomotives and forty-eight cars into the Tennessee River, and abandoned much provision, four guns, and other material, which General Howard took at daylight. But the bridge was gone, and we were forced to turn east and trust to General Burnside's bridge at Knoxville. It was all-important that General Burnside should have notice of our coming, and but one day of the time remained.

Accordingly, at Philadelphia, during the night of the 2d of December, I sent my aide (Major Audenried) forward to Colonel Long, commanding the brigade of cavalry at London, to explain to him how all-important it was that notice of our approach should reach General Burnside within twenty-four hours, ordering him to select the best materials of his command, to start at once, ford the Little Tennessee, and push into Knoxville at whatever cost of life and horse-flesh. Major Audenried was ordered to go along. The distance to be traveled was about forty miles, and the roads villainous. Before day they were off, and at daylight the Fifteenth Corps was turned from Philadelphia for the Little Tennessee at Morgantown, where my maps represented the river as being very shallow; but it was found too deep for fording, and the water was freezing cold—width two hundred and forty yards, depth from two to five feet; horses could ford, but artillery and men could not. A bridge was indispensable. General Wilson (who accompanied me) undertook to superintend the bridge, and I am under many obligations to him, as I was without an engineer, having sent Captain Jenny back from Graysville to survey our field of battle. We had our pioneers, but only such tools as axes, picks, and spades. General Wilson, working partly with cut wood and partly with square trestles (made of the houses of the late town of Morgantown), progressed apace, and by dark of December 4th troops and animals passed over the bridge, and by daybreak of the 5th the Fifteenth Corps (General Blair's) was over, and Generals-Granger's and Davis's divisions were ready to pass; but the diagonal bracing was imperfect for, want of spikes, and the bridge broke, causing delay. I had ordered General Blair to move out on the Marysville road five miles, there to await notice that General Granger was on a parallel road abreast of him, and in person I was at a house where the roads parted, when a messenger rode up, bringing me a few words from General Burnside, to the effect that Colonel Long had arrived at Knoxville with his cavalry, and that all was well with him there; Longstreet still lay before the place, but there were symptoms of his speedy departure.

I felt that I had accomplished the first great step in the problem for the relief of General Burnside's army, but still urged on the work. As soon as the bridge was mended, all the troops moved forward. General Howard had marched from Loudon, had found a pretty good ford for his horses and wagons at Davis's, seven miles below Morgantown, and had made an ingenious bridge of the wagons left by General Vaughn at London, on which to pass his men. He marched by Unitia and Louisville. On the night of the 5th all the heads of columns communicated at Marysville, where I met Major Van Buren (of General Burnside's staff), who announced that Longstreet had the night before retreated on the Rutledge, Rogersville, and Bristol road, leading to Virginia; that General Burnside's cavalry was on his heels; and that the general desired to see me in person as soon as I could come to Knoxville. I ordered all the troops to halt and rest, except the two divisions of General Granger, which were ordered to move forward to Little River, and General Granger to report in person to General Burnside for orders. His was the force originally designed to reenforce General Burnside, and it was eminently proper that it should join in the stern-chase after Longstreet.

On the morning of December 6th I rode from Marysville into Knoxville, and met General Burnside. General Granger arrived later in the day. We examined his lines of fortifications, which were a wonderful production for the short time allowed in their selection of ground and construction of work. It seemed to me that they were nearly impregnable. We examined the redoubt named "Sanders," where, on the Sunday previous, three brigades of the enemy had assaulted and met a bloody repulse. Now, all was peaceful and quiet; but a few hours before, the deadly bullet sought its victim all round about that hilly barrier.

The general explained to me fully and frankly what he had done, and what he proposed to do. He asked of me nothing but General Granger's command; and suggested, in view of the large force I had brought from Chattanooga, that I should return with due expedition to the line of the Hiawasaee, lest Bragg, reenforced, might take advantage of our absence to resume the offensive. I asked him to reduce this to writing, which he did, and I here introduce it as part of my report:

HEADQUARTERS OF THE OHIO KNOXVILLE, December 7, 1863

Major-General W. T. SHERMAN, commanding, etc.

GENERAL: I desire to express to you and your command my most hearty thanks and gratitude for your promptness in coming to our relief during the siege of Knoxville, and I am satisfied your approach served to raise the siege. The emergency having passed, I do not deem, for the present, any other portion of your command but the corps of General Granger necessary for operations in this section; and, inasmuch as General Grant has weakened the forces immediately with him in order to relieve us (thereby rendering the position of General Thomas less secure), I deem it advisable that all the troops now here, save those commanded by

208

General Granger, should return at once to within supporting distance of the forces in front of Bragg's army. In behalf of my command, I desire again to thank you and your command for the kindness you have done us.

I am, general, very respectfully, your obedient servant,

A. E. BURNSIDE, Major-General commanding.

Accordingly, having seen General Burnside's forces move out of Knoxville in pursuit of Longstreet, and General Granger's move in, I put in motion my own command to return. General Howard was ordered to move, via Davis's Ford and Sweetwater, to Athena, with a guard forward at Charleston, to hold and repair the bridge which the enemy had retaken after our passage up. General Jeff. C. Davis moved to Columbus, on the Hiawaesee, via Madisonville, and the two divisions of the Fifteenth Corps moved to Tellico Plains, to cover movement of cavalry across the mountains into Georgia, to overtake a wagon-train which had dodged us on our way up, and had escaped by way of Murphy. Subsequently, on a report from General Howard that the enemy held Charleston, I diverted General Ewing's division to Athena, and went in person to Tellico with General Morgan L. Smith's division. By the 9th all our troops were in position, and we held the rich country between the Little Tennessee and the Hiawasaee. The cavalry, under Colonel Long, passed the mountain at Tellico, and proceeded about seventeen miles beyond Murphy, when Colonel Long, deeming his farther pursuit of the wagon-train useless, returned on the 12th to Tellico. I then ordered him and the division of General Morgan L. Smith to move to Charleston, to which point I had previously ordered the corps of General Howard.

On the 14th of December all of my command in the field lay along the Hiawassee. Having communicated to General Grant the actual state of affairs, I received orders to leave, on the line of the Hiawassee, all the cavalry, and come to Chattanooga with the rest of my command. I left the brigade of cavalry commanded by Colonel Long, reenforced by the Fifth Ohio Cavalry (Lieutenant-Colonel Heath)—the only cavalry properly belonging to the Fifteenth Army Corps—at Charleston, and with the remainder moved by easy marches, by Cleveland and Tyner's Depot, into Chattanooga, where I received in person from General Grant orders to transfer back to their appropriate commands the corps of General Howard and the division commanded by General Jeff. C. Davis, and to conduct the Fifteenth Army Corps to its new field of operations.

It will thus appear that we have been constantly in motion since our departure from the Big Black, in Mississippi, until the present moment. I have been unable to receive from subordinate commanders the usual full, detailed reports of events, and have therefore been compelled to make up this report from my own personal memory; but, as soon as possible, subordinate reports will be received and duly forwarded.

In reviewing the facts, I must do justice to the men of my command for the patience, cheerfulness, and courage which officers and men have displayed throughout, in battle, on the march, and in camp. For long periods, without regular rations or supplies of any kind, they have marched through mud and over rocks, sometimes barefooted, without a murmur. Without a moment's rest after a march of over four hundred miles, without sleep for three successive nights, we crossed the Tennessee, fought our part of the battle of Chattanooga, pursued the enemy out of Tennessee, and then turned more than a hundred and twenty miles north and compelled Longstreet to raise the siege of Knoxville, which gave so much anxiety to the whole country. It is hard to realize the importance of these events without recalling the memory of the general feeling which pervaded all minds at Chattanooga prior to our arrival. I cannot speak of the Fifteenth Army Corps without a seeming vanity; but as I am no longer its commander, I assert that there is no better body of soldiers in America than it. I wish all to feel a just pride in its real honors.

To General Howard and his command, to General Jeff. C. Davis and his, I am more than usually indebted for the intelligence of commanders and fidelity of commands. The brigade of Colonel Bushbeck, belonging to the Eleventh Corps, which was the first to come out of Chattanooga to my flank, fought at the Tunnel Hill, in connection with General Ewing's division, and displayed a courage almost amounting to rashness. Following the enemy almost to the tunnel-gorge, it lost many valuable lives, prominent among them Lieutenant-Colonel Taft, spoken of as a most gallant soldier.

In General Howard throughout I found a polished and Christian gentleman, exhibiting the highest and most chivalric traits of the soldier. General Davis handled his division with artistic skill, more especially at the moment we encountered the enemy's rear-guard, near Graysville, at nightfall. I must award to this division the credit of the best order during our movement through East Tennessee, when long marches and the necessity of foraging to the right and left gave some reason for disordered ranks:

Inasmuch as exception may be taken to my explanation of the temporary confusion, during the battle of Chattanooga, of the two brigades of General Matthias and Colonel Raum, I will here state that I saw the whole; and attach no blame to any one. Accidents will happen in battle, as elsewhere; and at the point where they so manfully went to relieve the pressure on other parts of our assaulting line, they exposed themselves unconsciously to an enemy vastly superior in force, and favored by the shape of the ground. Had that enemy come out on equal terms, those brigades would have shown their mettle, which has been tried more than once before and stood the test of fire. They reformed their ranks, and were ready to support General Ewing's division in a very few minutes; and the circumstance would have hardly called for notice on my part, had not others reported what was seen from Chattanooga, a distance of nearly five miles, from where could only be seen the troops in the open field in which this affair occurred.

I now subjoin the best report of casualties I am able to compile from the records thus far received:

Killed; Wounded; and Missing.............. 1949

No report from General Davis's division, but loss is small.

Among the killed were some of our most valuable officers: Colonels Putnam, Ninety-third Illinois; O'Meara, Ninetieth Illinois; and Torrence, Thirtieth Iowa; Lieutenant-Colonel-Taft, of the Eleventh Corps; and Major Bushnell, Thirteenth Illinois.

Among the wounded are Brigadier-Generals Giles A. Smith, Corse, and Matthias; Colonel Raum; Colonel Waugelin, Twelfth Missouri; Lieutenant-Colonel Partridge, Thirteenth Illinois; Major P. I. Welsh, Fifty-sixth Illinois; and Major Nathan McAlla, Tenth Iowa.

Among the missing is Lieutenant-Colonel Archer, Seventeenth Iowa.

My report is already so long, that I must forbear mentioning acts of individual merit. These will be recorded in the reports of division commanders, which I will cheerfully indorse; but I must say that it is but justice that colonels of regiments, who have so long and so well commanded brigades, as in the following cases, should be commissioned to the grade which they have filled with so much usefulness and credit to the public service, viz.: Colonel J. R. Cockerell, Seventieth, Ohio; Colonel J. M. Loomis, Twenty-sixth Illinois; Colonel C. C. Walcutt, Forty-sixth Ohio; Colonel J. A. Williamson, Fourth Iowa; Colonel G. B. Raum, Fifty-sixth Illinois; Colonel J. I. Alexander, Fifty-ninth Indiana.

My personal staff, as usual, have served their country with fidelity, and credit to themselves, throughout these events, and have received my personal thanks.

Inclosed you will please find a map of that part of the battle-field of Chattanooga fought over by the troops under my command, surveyed and drawn by Captain Jenney, engineer on my staff. I have the honor to be, your obedient servant,

W. T. SHERMAN, Major-General commanding.

[General Order No. 68.]

WAR DEPARTMENT ADJUTANT-GENERAL'S OFFICE WASHINGTON, February 21, 1884

Joint resolution tendering the thanks of Congress to Major-General W. T. Sherman and others.

Be it resolved by the Senate and House of Representatives of the United States of America in Congress assembled, That the thanks of Congress and of the people of the United States are due, and that the same are hereby tendered, to Major-General W. T. Sherman, commander of the Department and Army of the Tennessee, and the officers and soldiers who served under him, for their gallant and arduous services in marching to the relief of the Army of the Cumberland, and for their gallantry and heroism in the battle of Chattanooga, which contributed in a great degree to the success of our arms in that glorious victory.

Approved February 19, 1864. By order of the Secretary of War:

E. D. TOWNSEND, Assistant Adjutant-General.

On the 19th of December I was at Bridgeport, and gave all the orders necessary for the distribution of the four divisions of the Fifteenth Corps along the railroad from Stevenson to Decatur, and the part of the Sixteenth Corps; commanded by General Dodge, along the railroad from Decatur to Nashville, to make the needed repairs, and to be in readiness for the campaign of the succeeding year; and on the 21st I went up to Nashville, to confer with General Grant and conclude the arrangements for the winter. At that time General Grant was under the impression that the next campaign would be up the valley of East Tennessee, in the direction of Virginia; and as it was likely to be the last and most important campaign of the war, it became necessary to set free as many of the old troops serving along the Mississippi River as possible. This was the real object and purpose of the Meridian campaign, and of Banks's expedition up Red River to Shreveport during that winter.

CHAPTER XV.
MERIDIAN CAMPAIGN.

JANUARY AND FEBRUARY, 1864.

The winter of 1863-'64 opened very cold and severe; and it was manifest after the battle of Chattanooga, November 25, 1863, and the raising of the siege of Knoxville, December 5th, that military operations in that quarter must in a measure cease, or be limited to Burnside's force beyond Knoxville. On the 21st of December General Grant had removed his headquarters to Nashville, Tennessee, leaving General George H. Thomas at Chattanooga, in command of the Department of the Cumberland, and of the army round about that place; and I was at Bridgeport, with orders to distribute my troops along the railroad from Stevenson to Decatur, Alabama, and from Decatur up toward Nashville.

General G. M. Dodge, who was in command of the detachment of the Sixteenth Corps, numbering about eight thousand men, had not participated with us in the battle of Chattanooga, but had remained at and near Pulaski, Tennessee, engaged in repairing that railroad, as auxiliary to the main line which led from Nashville to Stevenson, and Chattanooga. General John A. Logan had succeeded to the command of the Fifteenth Corps, by regular appointment of the President of the United States, and had relieved General Frank P. Blair, who had been temporarily in command of that corps during the Chattanooga and Knoxville movement.

At that time I was in command of the Department of the Tennessee, which embraced substantially the territory on the east bank of the Mississippi River, from Natchez up to the Ohio River, and thence along the Tennessee River as high as Decatur and Bellefonte, Alabama. General McPherson was at Vicksburg and General Hurlbut at Memphis, and from them I had the regular reports of affairs in that quarter of my command. The rebels still maintained a considerable force of infantry and cavalry in the State of Mississippi, threatening the river, whose navigation had become to us so delicate and important a matter. Satisfied that I could check this by one or two quick moves inland, and thereby set free a considerable body of men held as local garrisons, I went up to Nashville and represented the case to General Grant, who consented that I might go down the Mississippi River, where the bulk of my command lay, and strike a blow on the east of the river, while General Banks from New Orleans should in like manner strike another to the west; thus preventing any further molestation of the boats navigating the main river, and thereby widening the gap in the Southern Confederacy.

After having given all the necessary orders for the distribution, during the winter months, of that part of my command which was in Southern and Middle Tennessee, I went to Cincinnati and Lancaster, Ohio, to spend Christmas with my family; and on my return I took Minnie with me down to a convent at Reading, near Cincinnati, where I left her, and took the cars for Cairo, Illinois, which I reached January 3d, a very cold and bitter day. The ice was forming fast, and there was great danger that the Mississippi River, would become closed to navigation. Admiral Porter, who was at Cairo, gave me a small gunboat (the Juliet), with which I went up to Paducah, to inspect that place, garrisoned by a small force; commanded by Colonel S. G. Hicks, Fortieth Illinois, who had been with me and was severely wounded at Shiloh. Returning to Cairo, we started down the Mississippi River, which was full of floating ice. With the utmost difficulty we made our way through it, for hours floating in the midst of immense cakes, that chafed and ground our boat so that at times we were in danger of sinking. But about the 10th of January we reached Memphis, where I found General Hurlbut, and explained to him my purpose to collect from his garrisons and those of McPherson about twenty thousand men, with which in February to march out from Vicksburg as far as Meridian, break up the Mobile & Ohio Railroad, and also the one leading from Vicksburg to Selma, Alabama. I instructed him to select two good divisions, and to be ready with them to go along. At Memphis I found Brigadier-General W. Sooy Smith, with a force of about twenty-five hundred cavalry, which he had by General Grant's orders brought across from Middle Tennessee, to assist in our general purpose, as well as to punish the rebel General Forrest, who had been most active in harassing our garrisons in West Tennessee and Mississippi. After staying a couple of days at Memphis, we continued on in the gunboat Silver Cloud to Vicksburg, where I found General McPherson, and, giving him similar orders, instructed him to send out spies to ascertain and bring back timely information of the strength and location of the enemy. The winter continued so severe that the river at Vicksburg was full of floating ice, but in the Silver Cloud we breasted it manfully, and got back to Memphis by the 20th. A chief part of the enterprise was to destroy the rebel cavalry commanded by General Forrest, who were a constant threat to our railway communications in Middle Tennessee, and I committed this task to Brigadier-General W. Sooy Smith. General Hurlbut had in his command about seven thousand five hundred cavalry, scattered from Columbus, Kentucky, to Corinth, Mississippi, and we proposed to make up an aggregate cavalry force of about seven thousand "effective," out of these and the twenty-five hundred which General Smith had brought with him from Middle Tennessee. With this force General Smith was ordered to move from Memphis straight for Meridian, Mississippi, and to start by February 1st. I explained to him personally the nature of Forrest as a man, and of his peculiar force; told him that in his route he was sure to encounter Forrest, who always attacked with a vehemence for which he must be prepared, and that, after he had repelled the first attack, he must in turn assume the most determined offensive, overwhelm him and utterly destroy his whole force. I knew that Forrest could not have more than four thousand cavalry, and my own movement would give employment to every other man of the rebel army not immediately present with him, so that he (General Smith) might safely act on the hypothesis I have stated.

Having completed all these preparations in Memphis, being satisfied that the cavalry force would be ready to start by the 1st of February, and having seen General Hurlbut with his two divisions embark in steamers for Vicksburg, I also reembarked for the same destination on the 27th of January.

On the 1st of February we rendezvoused in Vicksburg, where I found a spy who had been sent out two weeks before, had been to Meridian, and brought back correct information of the state of facts in the interior of Mississippi. Lieutenant-General (Bishop) Polk was in chief command, with headquarters at Meridian, and had two divisions of infantry, one of which (General Loring's) was posted at Canton, Mississippi, the other (General French's) at Brandon. He had also two divisions of cavalry—Armstrong's, composed of the three brigades of Ross, Stark, and Wirt Adams, which were scattered from the neighborhood of Yazoo City to Jackson and below; and Forrest's, which was united, toward Memphis, with headquarters at Como. General Polk seemed to have no suspicion of our intentions to disturb his serenity.

Accordingly, on the morning of February 3d, we started in two columns, each of two divisions, preceded by a light force of cavalry, commanded by Colonel E. F. Winslow. General McPherson commanded the right column, and General Hurlbut the left. The former crossed the Big Black at the railroad-bridge, and the latter seven miles above, at Messinger's. We were lightly equipped as to wagons, and marched without deployment straight for Meridian, distant one hundred and fifty miles. We struck the rebel cavalry beyond the Big Black, and pushed them pell-mell into and beyond Jackson during the 6th. The next day we reached Brandon, and on the 9th Morton, where we perceived signs of an infantry concentration, but the enemy did not give us battle, and retreated before us. The rebel cavalry were all around us, so we kept our columns compact and offered few or no chances for their dashes. As far as Morton we had occupied two roads, but there we were forced into one. Toward evening of the 12th, Hurlbut's column passed through Decatur, with orders to go into camp four miles beyond at a creek. McPherson's head of column was some four miles behind, and I personally detached one of Hurlbut's regiments to guard the cross-roads at Decatur till the head of McPherson's column should come in sight. Intending to spend the night in Decatur, I went to a double log-house, and arranged with the lady for some supper. We unsaddled our horses, tied them to the fence inside the yard, and, being tired, I lay down on a bed and fell asleep. Presently I heard shouts and hallooing, and then heard pistol-shots close to the house. My aide, Major Audenried, called me and said we were attacked by rebel cavalry, who were all around us. I jumped up and inquired where was the regiment of infantry I had myself posted at the cross-roads. He said a few moments before it had marched past the house, following the road by which General Hurlbut had gone, and I told him to run, overtake it, and bring it back. Meantime, I went out into the back-yard, saw wagons passing at a run down the road, and horsemen dashing about in a cloud of dust, firing their pistols, their shots reaching the house in which we were. Gathering the few orderlies and clerks that were about, I was preparing to get into a corn-crib at the back side of the lot, wherein to defend ourselves, when I saw Audenried coming back with the regiment, on a run, deploying forward as they came. This regiment soon cleared the place and drove the rebel cavalry back toward the south, whence they had come.

It transpired that the colonel of this infantry regiment, whose name I do not recall, had seen some officers of McPherson's staff (among them Inspector-General Strong) coming up the road at a gallop, raising a cloud of duet; supposing them to be the head of

McPherson's column, and being anxious to get into camp before dark, he had called in his pickets and started down the road, leaving me perfectly exposed. Some straggling wagons, escorted by a New Jersey regiment, were passing at the time, and composed the rear of Hurlbut's train. The rebel cavalry, seeing the road clear of troops, and these wagons passing, struck them in flank, shot down the mules of three or four wagons, broke the column, and began a general skirmish. The escort defended their wagons as well as they could, and thus diverted their attention; otherwise I would surely have been captured. In a short time the head of McPherson's column came up, went into camp, and we spent the night in Decatur.

The next day we pushed on, and on the 14th entered Meridian, the enemy retreating before us toward Demopolis, Alabama. We at once set to work to destroy an arsenal, immense storehouses, and the railroad in every direction. We staid in Meridian five days, expecting every hour to hear of General Sooy Smith, but could get no tidings of him whatever. A large force of infantry was kept at work all the time in breaking up the Mobile & Ohio Railroad south and north; also the Jackson & Selma Railroad, east and west. I was determined to damage these roads so that they could not be used again for hostile purposes during the rest of the war. I never had the remotest idea of going to Mobile, but had purposely given out that idea to the people of the country, so as to deceive the enemy and to divert their attention. Many persons still insist that, because we did not go to Mobile on this occasion, I had failed; but in the following letter to General Banks, of January 31st, written from Vicksburg before starting for Meridian, it will be seen clearly that I indicated my intention to keep up the delusion of an attack on Mobile by land, whereas I promised him to be back to Vicksburg by the 1st of March, so as to cooperate with him in his contemplated attack on Shreveport:

HEADQUARTERS DEPARTMENT OF THE TENNESSEE VICKSBURG, January 31, 1864

Major-General N. P. BANKS, commanding Department of the Gulf, New Orleans.

GENERAL: I received yesterday, at the hands of Captain Durham, aide-de-camp, your letter of the 25th inst., and hasten to reply. Captain Durham has gone to the mouth of White River, en route for Little Rock, and the other officers who accompanied him have gone up to Cairo, as I understand, to charter twenty-five steamboats for the Red River trip. The Mississippi River, though low for the season, is free of ice and in good boating order; but I understand that Red River is still low. I had a man in from Alexandria yesterday, who reported the falls or rapids at that place impassable save by the smallest boats. My inland expedition is now moving, and I will be off for Jackson and Meridian to-morrow. The only fear I have is in the weather. All the other combinations are good. I want to keep up the delusion of an attack on Mobile and the Alabama River, and therefore would be obliged if you would keep up an irritating foraging or other expedition in that direction.

My orders from General Grant will not, as yet, justify me in embarking for Red River, though I am very anxious to move in that direction. The moment I learned that you were preparing for it, I sent a communication to Admiral Porter, and dispatched to General Grant at Chattanooga, asking if he wanted me and Steele to cooperate with you against Shreveport; and I will have his answer in time, for you cannot do any thing till Red River has twelve feet of water on the rapids at Alexandria. That will be from March to June. I have lived on Red River, and know somewhat of the phases of that stream. The expedition on Shreveport should be made rapidly, with simultaneous movements from Little Rock on Shreveport, from Opelousas on Alexandria, and a combined force of gunboats and transports directly up Red River. Admiral Porter will be able to have a splendid fleet by March 1st. I think Steele could move with ten thousand infantry and five thousand cavalry. I could take about ten thousand, and you could, I suppose, have the same. Your movement from Opelousas, simultaneous with mine up the river, would compel Dick Taylor to leave Fort De Russy (near Marksville), and the whole combined force could appear at Shreveport about a day appointed beforehand.

I doubt if the enemy will risk a siege at Shreveport, although I am informed they are fortifying the place, and placing many heavy guns in position. It would be better for us that they should stand there, as we might make large and important captures. But I do not believe the enemy will fight a force of thirty thousand men, acting in concert with gunboats.

I will be most happy to take part in the proposed expedition, and hope, before you have made your final dispositions, that I will have the necessary permission. Half the Army of the Tennessee is near the Tennessee River, beyond Huntsville, Alabama, awaiting the completion of the railroad, and, by present orders, I will be compelled to hasten there to command it in person, unless meantime General Grant modifies the plan. I have now in this department only the force left to hold the river and the posts, and I am seriously embarrassed by the promises made the veteran volunteers for furlough. I think, by March 1st, I can put afloat for Shreveport ten thousand men, provided I succeed in my present movement in cleaning out the State of Mississippi, and in breaking up the railroads about Meridian.

I am, with great respect, your obedient servant,

W. T. SHERMAN, Major-General, commanding.

The object of the Meridian expedition was to strike the roads inland, so to paralyze the rebel forces that we could take from the defense of the Mississippi River the equivalent of a corps of twenty thousand men, to be used in the next Georgia campaign; and this was actually done. At the same time, I wanted to destroy General Forrest, who, with an irregular force of cavalry, was constantly threatening Memphis and the river above, as well as our routes of supply in Middle Tennessee. In this we failed utterly, because General W. Sooy Smith did not fulfill his orders, which were clear and specific, as contained in my letter of instructions to him of January 27th, at Memphis, and my personal explanations to him at the same time. Instead of starting at the date ordered, February 1st, he did not leave Memphis till the 11th, waiting for Warings brigade that was ice-bound near Columbus, Kentucky; and then, when he did start, he allowed General Forrest to head him off and to defeat him with an inferior force, near West Point, below Okalona, on the Mobile & Ohio Railroad.

We waited at Meridian till the 20th to hear from General Smith, but hearing nothing whatever, and having utterly destroyed the railroads in and around that junction, I ordered General McPherson to move back slowly toward Canton. With Winslow's cavalry, and Hurlbut's infantry, I turned north to Marion, and thence to a place called "Union," whence I dispatched the cavalry farther north to Philadelphia and Louisville, to feel as it were for General Smith, and then turned all the infantry columns toward Canton, Mississippi. On the 26th we all reached Canton, but we had not heard a word of General Smith, nor was it until some time after (at Vicksburg) that I learned the whole truth of General Smith's movement and of his failure. Of course I did not and could not approve of his conduct, and I know that he yet chafes under the censure. I had set so much store on his part of the project that I was disappointed, and so reported officially to General Grant. General Smith never regained my confidence as a soldier, though I still regard him as a most accomplished gentleman and a skillful engineer. Since the close of the war he has appealed to me to relieve him of that censure, but I could not do it, because it would falsify history.

Having assembled all my troops in and about Canton, on the 27th of February I left them under the command of the senior major-general, Hurlbut, with orders to remain till about the 3d of March, and then to come into Vicksburg leisurely; and, escorted by Winslow's cavalry, I rode into Vicksburg on the last day of February. There I found letters from General Grant, at Nashville, and General Banks, at New Orleans, concerning his (General Banks's) projected movement up Red River. I was authorized by the former to contribute aid to General Banks for a limited time; but General Grant insisted on my returning in person to my own command about Huntsville, Alabama, as soon as possible, to prepare for the spring campaign.

About this time we were much embarrassed by a general order of the War Department, promising a thirty-days furlough to all soldiers who would "veteranize"—viz., reenlist for the rest of the war. This was a judicious and wise measure, because it doubtless secured the services of a very large portion of the men who had almost completed a three-years enlistment, and were therefore veteran soldiers in feeling and in habit. But to furlough so many of our men at that instant of time was like disbanding an army in the very midst of battle.

In order to come to a perfect understanding with General Banks, I took the steamer Diana and ran down to New Orleans to see him. Among the many letters which I found in Vicksburg on my return from Meridian was one from Captain D. F. Boyd, of Louisiana, written from the jail in Natchez, telling me that he was a prisoner of war in our hands; had been captured in Louisiana by some of our scouts; and he bespoke my friendly assistance. Boyd was Professor of Ancient Languages at the Louisiana Seminary of Learning during my administration, in 1859-'60; was an accomplished scholar, of moderate views in politics, but, being a Virginian, was drawn, like all others of his kind, into the vortex of the rebellion by the events of 1861, which broke up colleges and every thing at the South. Natchez, at this time, was in my command, and was held by a strong division, commanded by Brigadier-General J. W. Davidson. In the Diana we stopped at Natchez, and I made a hasty inspection of the place. I sent for Boyd, who was in good health, but quite dirty, and begged me to take him out of prison, and to effect his exchange. I receipted for him; took him along with me to New Orleans; offered him money, which he declined; allowed him to go free in the city; and obtained from General Banks a promise to effect his exchange, which was afterward done. Boyd is now my legitimate successor in Louisiana, viz., President of the Louisiana University, which is the present title of what had been the Seminary of Learning. After the war was over, Boyd went back to Alexandria, reorganized the old institution, which I visited in 1866 but the building was burnt down by an accident or by an incendiary about 1868, and the institution was then removed to Baton Rouge, where it now is, under its new title of the University of Louisiana.

We reached New Orleans on the 2d of March. I found General Banks, with his wife and daughter, living in a good house, and he explained to me fully the position and strength of his troops, and his plans of action for the approaching campaign. I dined with him, and, rough as I was—just out of the woods—attended, that night, a very pleasant party at the house of a lady, whose name I cannot recall, but who is now the wife of Captain Arnold, Fifth United States Artillery. At this party were also Mr. and Mrs. Frank Howe. I found New Orleans much changed since I had been familiar with it in 1853 and in 1860-'61. It was full of officers and soldiers. Among the former were General T. W. Sherman, who had lost a leg at Port Hudson, and General Charles P: Stone, whom I knew so well in California, and who is now in the Egyptian service as chief of staff. The bulk of General Banks's army was about Opelousas, under command of General Franklin, ready to move on Alexandria. General Banks seemed to be all ready, but intended to delay his departure a few days to assist in the inauguration of a civil government for Louisiana, under Governor Hahn. In Lafayette Square I saw the arrangements of scaffolding for the fireworks and benches for the audience. General Banks urged me to remain over the 4th of March, to participate in the ceremonies, which he explained would include the performance of the "Anvil Chorus" by all the bands of his army, and during the performance the church-bells were to be rung, and cannons were to be fired by electricity. I regarded all such ceremonies as out of place at a time when it seemed to me every hour and every minute were due to the war. General Banks's movement, however, contemplated my sending a force of ten thousand men in boats up Red River from Vicksburg, and that a junction should occur at Alexandria by March 17th. I therefore had no time to wait for the grand pageant of the 4th of March, but took my departure from New Orleans in the Diana the evening of March 3d.

On the next day, March 4th, I wrote to General Banks a letter, which was extremely minute in conveying to him how far I felt authorized to go under my orders from General Grant. At that time General Grant commanded the Military Division of the Mississippi, embracing my own Department of the Tennessee and that of General Steele in Arkansas, but not that of General Banks in Louisiana. General Banks was acting on his own powers, or under the instructions of General Halleck in Washington, and our assistance to him was designed as a loan of ten thousand men for a period of thirty days. The instructions of

March 6th to General A. J. Smith, who commanded this detachment, were full and explicit on this point. The Diana reached Vicksburg on the 6th, where I found that the expeditionary army had come in from Canton. One division of five thousand men was made up out of Hurlbut's command, and placed under Brigadier-General T. Kilby Smith; and a similar division was made out of McPherson's and Hurlbut's troops, and placed under Brigadier-General Joseph A. Mower; the whole commanded by Brigadier-General A. J. Smith. General Hurlbut, with the rest of his command, returned to Memphis, and General McPherson remained at Vicksburg. General A. J. Smith's command was in due season embarked, and proceeded to Red River, which it ascended, convoyed by Admiral Porter's fleet. General Mower's division was landed near the outlet of the Atchafalaya, marched up by land and captured the fort below Alexandria known as Fort De Russy, and the whole fleet then proceeded up to Alexandria, reaching it on the day appointed, viz., March 17th, where it waited for the arrival of General Banks, who, however, did not come till some days after. These two divisions participated in the whole of General Banks's unfortunate Red River expedition, and were delayed so long up Red River, and subsequently on the Mississippi, that they did not share with their comrades the successes and glories of the Atlanta campaign, for which I had designed them; and, indeed, they did not join our army till just in time to assist General George H. Thomas to defeat General Hood before Nashville, on the 15th and 16th of December, 1864.

General Grant's letter of instructions, which was brought me by General Butterfield, who had followed me to New Orleans, enjoined on me, after concluding with General Banks the details for his Red River expedition, to make all necessary arrangements for furloughing the men entitled to that privilege, and to hurry back to the army at Huntsville, Alabama. I accordingly gave the necessary orders to General McPherson, at Vicksburg, and continued up the river toward Memphis. On our way we met Captain Badeau, of General Grant's staff, bearing the following letter, of March 4th, which I answered on the 10th, and sent the answer by General Butterfield, who had accompanied me up from New Orleans. Copies of both were also sent to General McPherson, at Vicksburg:

[Private.]

NASHVILLE, TENNESSEE, March 4, 1864

DEAR SHERMAN: The bill reviving the grade of lieutenant-general in the army has become a law, and my name has been sent to the Senate for the place.

I now receive orders to report at Washington immediately, in person, which indicates either a confirmation or a likelihood of confirmation. I start in the morning to comply with the order, but I shall say very distinctly on my arrival there that I shall accept no appointment which will require me to make that city my headquarters. This, however, is not what I started out to write about.

While I have been eminently successful in this war, in at least gaining the confidence of the public, no one feels more than I how much of this success is due to the energy, skill, and the harmonious putting forth of that energy and skill, of those whom it has been my good fortune to have occupying subordinate positions under me.

There are many officers to whom these remarks are applicable to a greater or less degree, proportionate to their ability as soldiers; but what I want is to express my thanks to you and McPherson, as the men to whom, above all others, I feel indebted for whatever I have had of success. How far your advice and suggestions have been of assistance, you know. How far your execution of whatever has been given you to do entitles you to the reward I am receiving, you cannot know as well as I do. I feel all the gratitude this letter would express, giving it the most flattering construction.

The word you I use in the plural, intending it for McPherson also. I should write to him, and will some day, but, starting in the morning, I do not know that I will find time just now. Your friend,

U. S. GRANT, *Major-General.*

NEAR MEMPHIS, March 10, 1864

General GRANT.

DEAR GENERAL: I have your more than kind and characteristic letter of the 4th, and will send a copy of it to General McPherson at once.

You do yourself injustice and us too much honor in assigning to us so large a share of the merits which have led to your high advancement. I know you approve the friendship I have ever professed to you, and will permit me to continue as heretofore to manifest it on all proper occasions.

You are now Washington's legitimate successor, and occupy a position of almost dangerous elevation; but if you can continue as heretofore to be yourself, simple, honest, and unpretending, you will enjoy through life the respect and love of friends, and the homage of millions of human beings who will award to you a large share for securing to them and their descendants a government of law and stability.

I repeat, you do General McPherson and myself too much honor. At Belmont you manifested your traits, neither of us being near; at Donelson also you illustrated your whole character. I was not near, and General McPherson in too subordinate a capacity to influence you.

Until you had won Donelson, I confess I was almost cowed by the terrible array of anarchical elements that presented themselves at every point; but that victory admitted the ray of light which I have followed ever since.

I believe you are as brave, patriotic, and just, as the great prototype Washington; as unselfish, kind-hearted, and honest, as a man should be; but the chief characteristic in your nature is the simple faith in success you have always manifested, which I can liken to nothing else than the faith a Christian has in his Saviour.

This faith gave you victory at Shiloh and Vicksburg. Also, when you have completed your best preparations, you go into battle without hesitation, as at Chattanooga—no doubts, no reserve; and I tell you that it was this that made us act with confidence. I knew wherever I was that you thought of me, and if I got in a tight place you would come—if alive.

My only points of doubt were as to your knowledge of grand strategy, and of books of science and history; but I confess your common-sense seems to have supplied all this.

Now as to the future. Do not stay in Washington. Halleck is better qualified than you are to stand the buffets of intrigue and policy. Come out West; take to yourself the whole Mississippi Valley; let us make it dead-sure, and I tell you the Atlantic slope and Pacific shores will follow its destiny as sure as the limbs of a tree live or die with the main trunk! We have done much; still much remains to be done. Time and time's influences are all with us; we could almost afford to sit still and let these influences work. Even in the seceded States your word now would go further than a President's proclamation, or an act of Congress.

For God's sake and for your country's sake, come out of Washington! I foretold to General Halleck, before he left Corinth, the inevitable result to him, and I now exhort you to come out West. Here lies the seat of the coming empire; and from the West, when our task is done, we will make short work of Charleston and Richmond, and the impoverished coast of the Atlantic. Your sincere friend,

W. T. SHERMAN

We reached Memphis on the 13th, where I remained some days, but on the 14th of March received from General Grant a dispatch to hurry to Nashville in person by the 17th, if possible. Disposing of all matters then pending, I took a steamboat to Cairo, the cars thence to Louisville and Nashville, reaching that place on the 17th of March, 1864.

I found General Grant there. He had been to Washington and back, and was ordered to return East to command all the armies of the United States, and personally the Army of the Potomac. I was to succeed him in command of the Military Division of the Mississippi, embracing the Departments of the Ohio, Cumberland, Tennessee, and Arkansas. General Grant was of course very busy in winding up all matters of business, in transferring his command to me, and in preparing for what was manifest would be the great and closing campaign of our civil war. Mrs. Grant and some of their children were with him, and occupied a large house in Nashville, which was used as an office, dwelling, and every thing combined.

On the 18th of March I had issued orders assuming command of the Military Division of the Mississippi, and was seated in the office, when the general came in and said they were about to present him a sword, inviting me to come and see the ceremony. I went back into what was the dining-room of the house; on the table lay a rose-wood box, containing a sword, sash, spurs, etc., and round about the table were grouped Mrs. Grant, Nelly, and one or two of the boys. I was introduced to a large, corpulent gentleman, as the mayor, and another citizen, who had come down from Galena to make this presentation of a sword to their fellow-townsman. I think that Rawlins, Bowers, Badeau, and one or more of General Grant's personal staff, were present. The mayor rose and in the most dignified way read a finished speech to General Grant, who stood, as usual, very awkwardly; and the mayor closed his speech by handing him the resolutions of the City Council engrossed on parchment, with a broad ribbon and large seal attached. After the mayor had fulfilled his office so well, General Grant said: "Mr. Mayor, as I knew that this ceremony was to occur, and as I am not used to speaking, I have written something in reply." He then began to fumble in his pockets, first his breast-coat pocket, then his pants, vest; etc., and after considerable delay he pulled out a crumpled piece of common yellow cartridge-paper, which he handed to the mayor. His whole manner was awkward in the extreme, yet perfectly characteristic, and in strong contrast with the elegant parchment and speech of the mayor. When read, however, the substance of his answer was most excellent, short, concise, and, if it had been delivered by word of mouth, would have been all that the occasion required.

I could not help laughing at a scene so characteristic of the man who stood prominent before the country; and to whom all had turned as the only one qualified to guide the nation in a war that had become painfully critical. With copies of the few letters referred to, and which seem necessary to illustrate the subject-matter, I close this chapter:

HEADQUARTERS DEPARTMENT OF THE TENNESSEE
STEAMER DIANA (UNDER WEIGH), March 4, 1864

Major-General N. P. BANKS, commanding Department of the Gulf, New Orleans.

GENERAL: I had the honor to receive your letter of the 2d instant yesterday at New Orleans, but was unable to answer, except verbally, and I now reduce it to writing.

I will arrive at Vicksburg the 6th instant, and I expect to meet there my command from Canton, out of which I will select two divisions of about ten thousand men, embark them under a good commander, and order him:

1st. To rendezvous at the mouth of Red River, and, in concert with Admiral Porter (if he agree), to strike Harrisonburg a hard blow.

2d. To return to Red River and ascend it, aiming to reach Alexandria on the 17th of March, to report to you.

3d. That, as this command is designed to operate by water, it will not be encumbered with much land transportation, say two wagons to a regiment, but with an ample supply of stores, including mortars and heavy rifled guns, to be used against fortified places.

4th. That I have calculated, and so reported to General Grant, that this detachment of his forces in no event is to go beyond Shreveport, and that you will spare them the moment you can, trying to get them back to the Mississippi River in thirty days from the time they actually enter Red River.

The year is wearing away fast, and I would like to carry to General Grant at Huntsville, Alabama, every man of his military division, as early in April as possible, for I am sure we ought to move from the base of the Tennessee River to the south before the season is too far advanced, say as early as April 15th next.

I feel certain of your complete success, provided you make the concentration in time, to assure which I will see in person to the embarkation and dispatch of my quota, and I will write to General Steele, conveying to him my personal and professional opinion that the present opportunity is the most perfect one that will ever offer itself to him to clean out his enemies in Arkansas.

Wishing you all honor and success, I am, with respect, your friend and servant,

W. T. SHERMAN, Major-General.

HEADQUARTERS DEPARTMENT OF THE TENNESSEE
VICKSBURG, March 6, 1864

Brigadier-General A. J. SMITH, commanding Expedition up Red River, Vicksburg, Mississippi.

GENERAL: By an order this day issued, you are to command a strong, well-appointed detachment of the Army of the Tennessee, sent to reinforce a movement up Red River, but more especially against the fortified position at Shreveport.

You will embark your command as soon as possible, little encumbered with wagons or wheeled vehicles, but well supplied with fuel, provisions, and ammunition. Take with you the twelve mortars, with their ammunition, and all the thirty-pound Parrotts the ordnance-officer will supply. Proceed to the mouth of Red River and confer with Admiral Porter. Consult with him, and in all the expedition rely on him implicitly, as he is the approved friend of the Army of the Tennessee, and has been associated with us from the beginning. I have undertaken with General Banks that you will be at Alexandria, Louisiana, on or before the 17th day of March; and you will, if time allows, cooperate with the navy in destroying Harrisonburg, up Black River; but as I passed Red River yesterday I saw Admiral Porter, and he told me he had already sent an expedition to Harrisonburg, so that I suppose that part of the plan will be accomplished before you reach Red River; but, in any event, be careful to reach Alexandria about the 17th of March.

General Banks will start by land from Franklin, in the Teche country, either the 6th or 7th, and will march via Opelousas to Alexandria. You will meet him there, report to him, and act under his orders. My understanding with him is that his forces will move by land, via Natchitoches, to Shreveport, while the gunboat-fleet is to ascend the river with your transports in company. Red River is very low for the season, and I doubt if any of the boats can pass the falls or rapids at Alexandria. What General Banks proposes to do in that event I do not know; but my own judgment is that Shreveport ought not to be attacked until the gunboats can reach it. Not that a force marching by land cannot do it alone, but it would be bad economy in war to invest the place with an army so far from heavy guns, mortars, ammunition, and provisions, which can alone reach Shreveport by water. Still, I do not know about General Banks's plans in that event; and whatever they may be, your duty will be to conform, in the most hearty manner.

My understanding with General Banks is that he will not need the cooperation of your force beyond thirty days from the date you reach Red River. As soon as he has taken Shreveport, or as soon as he can spare you, return to Vicksburg with all dispatch, gather up your detachments, wagons, tents, transportation, and all property pertaining to so much of the command as belongs to the Sixteenth Army Corps, and conduct it to Memphis, where orders will await you. My present belief is your division, entire, will be needed with the Army of the Tennessee, about Huntsville or Bridgeport. Still, I will leave orders with General, Hurlbut, at Memphis, for you on your return.

I believe if water will enable the gunboats to cross the rapids at Alexandria, you will be able to make a quick, strong, and effective blow at our enemy in the West, thus widening the belt of our territory, and making the breach between the Confederate Government and its outlying trans-Mississippi Department more perfect.

It is understood that General Steele makes a simultaneous move from Little Rock, on Shreveport or Natchitoches, with a force of about ten thousand men. Banks will have seventeen thousand, and you ten thousand. If these can act concentrically and simultaneously, you will make short work of it, and then General Banks will have enough force to hold as much of the Red River country as he deems wise, leaving you to bring to General Grant's main army the seven thousand five hundred men of the Sixteenth Corps now with you. Having faith in your sound judgment and experience, I confide this important and delicate command to you, with certainty that you will harmonize perfectly with Admiral Porter and General Banks, with whom you are to act, and thereby insure success.

I am, with respect, your obedient servant,

W. T. SHERMAN, Major-General commanding.

HEADQUARTERS DEPARTMENT OF THE TENNESSEE
MEMPHIS, March 14, 1864

Major General McPHERSON, commanding, etc, Vicksburg, Mississippi

DEAR GENERAL: I wrote you at length on the 11th, by a special bearer of dispatches, and now make special orders to cover the movements therein indicated. It was my purpose to await your answer, but I am summoned by General Grant to be in Nashville on the 17th, and it will keep me moving night and day to get there by that date. I must rely on you, for you understand that we must reenforce the great army at the centre (Chattanooga) as much as possible, at the same time not risking the safety of any point on the Mississippi which is fortified and armed with heavy guns. I want you to push matters as rapidly as possible, and to do all you can to put two handsome divisions of your own corps at Cairo, ready to embark up the Tennessee River by the 20th or 30th of April at the very furthest. I wish it could be done quicker; but the promise of those thirty-days furloughs in the States of enlistment, though politic, is very unmilitary. It deprives us of our ability to calculate as to time; but do the best you can. Hurlbut can do nothing till A. J. Smith returns from Red River. I will then order him to occupy Grenada temporarily, and to try and get those locomotives that we need here. I may also order him with cavalry and infantry to march toward Tuscaloosa, at the same time that we move from the Tennessee River about Chattanooga.

I don't know as yet the grand strategy of the next campaign, but on arrival at Nashville I will soon catch the main points, and will advise you of them..

Steal a furlough and run to Baltimore incog.; but get back in time to take part in the next grand move.

Write me fully and frequently of your progress. I have ordered the quartermaster to send down as many boats as he can get, to facilitate your movements. Mules, wagons, etc., can come up afterward by transient boats. I am truly your friend,

W. T. SHERMAN, Major-General commanding.

[Special Field Order No. 28.]

HEADQUARTERS DEPARTMENT OF THE TENNESSEE MEMPHIS, March 14, 1864

1. Major-General McPherson will organize two good divisions of his corps (Seventeenth) of about five thousand men, each embracing in part the reenlisted veterans of his corps whose furloughs will expire in April, which he will command in person, and will rendezvous at Cairo, Illinois, and report by telegraph and letter to the general commanding at department headquarters, wherever they may be. These divisions will be provided with new arms and accoutrements, and land transportation (wagons and mules) out of the supplies now at Vicksburg, which will be conveyed to Cairo by or before April 15th.

4. During the absence of General McPherson from the district of Vicksburg, Major-General Hurlbut will exercise command over all the troops in the Department of the Tennessee from Cairo to Natchez, inclusive, and will receive special instructions from department headquarters.

By order of Major-General W. T. Sherman:

L. M. DAYTON, Aide-de-Camp.

APPENDIX TO VOLUME I.
CHICKASAW BAYOU.

Report of Brigadier-General G. W. Morgan.

HEADQUARTERS THIRD DIVISION, RIGHT WING, THIRTEENTH ARMY CORPS, STEAMER EMPRESS, January 8, 1868.

Major J. H. HAMMOND, Chief of Staff:

SIR: On the 1st instant, while pressed by many arduous duties, I was requested to report to the commanding general the operations of my division during the affair of the 27th, the action of the 28th, and the battle of the 29th ult.

I had not received the report of subordinate commanders, nor had I time to review the report I have the honor to submit.

Herewith I have the honor to forward these reports, connected with which I will submit a few remarks.

Brigadier-General Blair speaks of having discovered, while on his retreat from the enemy's works, a broad and easy road running from the left of my position to the enemy's lines. The road is neither broad nor easy, and was advanced over by De Courcey when leading his brigade to the charge. The road General Blair speaks of is the one running from Lake's Landing and intersecting with the Vicksburg road on the Chickasaw Bluffs. Its existence was known to me on the 28th ult., but it was left open intentionally by the enemy, and was commanded by a direct and cross fire from batteries and rifle-pits. The withdrawal of his brigade from the assault by Colonel De Courcey was justified by the failure of the corps of A. J. Smith, and the command of Colonel Lindsey, to advance simultaneously to the assault. Both had the same difficulties to encounter—impassable bayous. The enemy's line of battle was concave, and De Courcey advanced against his centre—hence he sustained a concentric fire, and the withdrawal of Steele from the front of the enemy's right on the 28th ult. enabled the enemy on the following day to concentrate his right upon his centre.

I regret to find, from the report of Brigadier-General Thayer, some one regiment skulked; this I did not observe, nor is it mentioned by General Blair, though his were the troops which occupied that portion of the field. As far as my observation extended, the troops bore themselves nobly; but the Sixteenth Ohio Infantry was peerless on the field, as it had ever been in camp or on the march. Lieutenant-Colonel Kershner, commanding, was wounded and taken prisoner. He is an officer of rare merit, and deserves to command a brigade. Lieutenant-Colonel Dieter, commanding the Fifty-eighth Ohio, was killed within the enemy's works; and Lieutenant-Colonel Monroe, Twenty-second Kentucky, was struck down at the head of his regiment.

I again express my profound acknowledgments to Brigadier-Generals Blair and Thayer, and Colonels De Conrcey, Lindsey, and Sheldon, brigade commanders. Also to Major M. C. Garber, assistant quartermaster; Captain S. S. Lyon, acting topographical engineer; Lieutenant Burdick, acting ordnance officer; Lieutenant Hutchins, acting chief of staff; Lieutenants H. G. Fisher and Smith, of Signal Corps; Lieutenant E. D. Saunders, my acting assistant adjutant-general; and Lieutenants English and Montgomery, acting aides-de-camp, for the efficient services rendered me.

Nor can I close this report without speaking in terms of high praise of the meritorious and gallant services of Captains Foster and Lamphier. Their batteries silenced several of the enemy's works, and throughout the operations rendered good service. My sincere acknowledgments are also due to Captain Griffith, commanding First Iowa Battery, and Captain Hoffman, commanding Fourth Ohio Battery.

I am, sir, very respectfully, your obedient servant,

GEORGE W. MORGAN, Brigadier-General Volunteers.

CINCINNATI, February 8, 1876.

MY DEAR GENERAL: Regarding the attack at Chickasaw Bayou, my record shows the position of Steele on the left; Morgan to his right; Morgan L. Smith to his right, and A. J. Smith on the extreme right; the latter not expected to accomplish much more than a diversion, the result to come from the three other divisions, Morgan having the best opportunity. Saturday night they were in position; you were at Lake's plantation, right and rear of Morgan.

The attack for lodgment on the hills was ordered for Sunday morning, December 28th. I was sent to A. J. Smith before daylight, and returned to you soon after. You were with Morgan. You had fully explained to him the importance of his success, and that he should be present with the attacking column, which was to be a part of his division, supported by the remainder, and by Blair's brigade of Steele's division cooperating. The attack was to be simultaneous, by the four divisions, on a signal.

Morgan's answer to you was that, when the signal was given, he would lead his attack, and with his life he would be on the bluffs in fifteen minutes. He seemed of positive knowledge, and as sure of success. You then retired to a central point, to be in easy communication with Steele and Morgan L. Smith. The attack was made, and developed, in the case of Steele, M. L. Smith, and A. J. Smith, that to cross the bayou was impossible, if opposed by any force, and in each they were by a strong one. Morgan's attacking force succeeded *in getting across the causeway and marsh, but he did not go with it, nor support it with more men, and a large number were captured from Blair's brigade after gaining the enemy's last line of works covering the bayou. At the time everybody blamed and criticised Morgan with the failure. You felt from the advance of his attack it must be successful, and, as it pushed forward, you sent me to urge on M. L. Smith, as Morgan was over, and he, Smith, must aid by persistent attack, and give Morgan as good a chance as could be to make his lodgment....*

I am, etc., L. M. DAYTON Late Colonel of the Staff, now of Cincinnati, Ohio General W. T. SHERMAN, St. Louis, Missouri

[COPY.]

" . . . . The expedition was wonderfully well provided with provisions, transportation, and munitions, and even axes, picks, and shovels, so much in use later in the war, evidenced the forethought that governed this force. The boats, from their open lower deck construction, proved admirable for transports, but their tinder-box construction made fire-traps of them, requiring unremitting vigilance. These points were well understood, and the readiness with which the troops adapted themselves to circumstances was a constant source of wonder and congratulations.

"The fleet collected at Friar's Point for final orders, and there the order of sailing was laid down with great minuteness, and private instructions issued to commanders of divisions, all of whom had personal interviews with the commanding general, and received personal explanations on pretty much every point involved. Our headquarters boat, the Forest Queen, was not very comfortable, nor well provided, but General Sherman submitted cheerfully, on the grounds of duty, and thought Conway a fine fellow. I was only able to concede that he was a good steamboat captain....

"Our camp appointments were Spartan in the extreme, and in their simplicity would have met the demands of any demagogue in the land. The nights were cold and damp, and General Sherman uncomfortably active in his preparations, so that the assistant adjutant-general had no very luxurious post just then. We were surrounded with sloughs. The ground was wet, and the water, although in winter, was very unwholesome. Many of our men, to this day, have reminders of the Yazoo in ague, fevers, and diseases of the bowels. Cavalry was useless. One battalion of Illinois cavalry was strongly suspected of camping in the timber, until time passed enough to justify the suspicion of having been somewhere. Really the strength of Vicksburg was in being out of reach of attack....

"My orders were to learn and report what was going on on the right, particularly to try and form an idea of the enemy's force in front of M. L. Smith's division, and at the sand-bar. Leaving my horse close in the rear of the Sixth Missouri, when the fire became too heavy for riding, I succeeded, by taking frequent cover, in reaching unhurt the verge of the bayou among the drift-logs. There, by concert of action with Lieutenant-Colonel Blood, of the Sixth Missouri, his regiment, and the Thirteenth Regular Infantry, kept up a heavy fire on everything that showed along the levee and earthworks in front. The enemy were behind the embankment, not over one hundred and fifty yards across the bayou. Several officers, including Colonel Blood, Colonel Kilby Smith, and myself, managed, by getting on the piles of drift, to see over the levee through the cleared fields beyond, even to the foot of the bluff. The chips and twigs flew around lively enough, but we staid up long enough to make sure that the enemy had as many men behind the levee as could get cover. We saw, also, a line of rifle-pits in the rear, commanding the rear of the levee, and still beyond, winding along the foot of the bluff, a road worn by long use deep into the side-hill, and with the side next us strengthened with a good earthwork, affording a covered line of communication in the rear. The fire of our men was so well maintained that we were able to see all these things, say a minute or more. Some of those who ventured were wounded, but those mentioned and myself escaped unhurt. I advised that men enough to hold the position, once across—say three hundred—should make a rush (protected as our lookout had been by a heavy fire) across the sand-bar, and get a footing under the other bank of the bayou, as the nucleus of an attacking force, if General Sherman decided to attack there, or to make a strong diversion if the attack was made at the head of Chickasaw Bayou, in front of Morgan. General A. J. Smith, commanding First and Second Divisions, approved of this.

While returning to General Sherman, I passed along the Second and part of the Third Division. On the left of the Second I found a new Illinois regiment, high up in numbers, working its way into position. The colonel, a brave but inexperienced officer, was trying to lead his men according to the popular pictorial idea, viz., riding in advance waving his sword. I was leading my horse, and taking advantage of such cover as I could find on my course, but this man acted so bravely that I tried to save him. He did not accept my expostulations with very good grace, but was not rough about it. While I was begging him to dismount, he waved his sword and advanced. In a second he was shot, through the chest, and dropped from his horse, plucky to the last. He died, I was told, within the hour. Many of the regiments were new and inexperienced, but as a rule behaved well. The fire along the bayou was severe, but not very fatal, on account of the cover. I was constantly asked what news from Grant, for from the moment of our arrival in the Yazoo we were in expectation of either hearing his guns in the rear, or of having communication with him. This encouraged the men greatly, but the long waiting was disappointing, as the enemy was evidently in large force in the plenty of works, and a very strong position. Careful estimates and available information placed their force at fifteen to twenty thousand men. I returned to headquarters about the middle of the afternoon, and made my report to the general. We were busy till after midnight, and again early in the morning of the 29th, in preparing orders for the attack. These were unusually minute in detail. It seemed as though no contingency was left unprovided for. Urgent orders and cautions as to rations and ammunition were given. Drawings of the line of attack, orders for supports, all and everything was foreseen and given in writing, with personal explanations to commanders of divisions, brigades, and even commanders of regiments. Indeed, the commanding general, always careful as to detail, left nothing to chance, and with experienced and ordinate officers we would have succeeded, for the troops were good. The general plan involved a feint on our left toward Haines's Bluff, by the navy, under Admiral Porter, with whom we were in constant communication, while between him and General Sherman perfect harmony existed. On the right a demonstration by A. J. Smith was to be made. The Second Division (Stuart's) was to cross the sand-bar, and the Third (General Morgan's) was to cross on a small bridge over the dough at the head of Chickasaw Bayou, and, supported by Steele, was to push straight for the Bluff at the nearest spur where there was a battery in position, and to effect a lodgment there and in the earthworks. General Sherman gave his orders in person to Morgan and Steele. I understood Morgan to promise that he would lead his division in person, and he seemed to expect an easy victory, and expressed himself freely to that effect. The aides were sent out, until I was left alone with the general and a couple of orderlies. He located himself in a position easy of access, and the most convenient afforded to the point of attack. He directed me to see what I could, and report if I met anything that he should know. I galloped as fast as possible to the right, and found part of the Sixth Missouri pushing over the sand-bar covered by the Thirteenth Regulars with a heavy fire. We supposed, if once across, they could get up the bank and turn the levee against the enemy, and left with that impression. Being in heavy timber, I was not quite sure of my way back to the general, his location being new, and therefore pushed full gallop for Morgan's front, catching a good many stray shots from the sharpshooters behind the levee, as I was compelled to keep in sight of the bayou to hold direction. Something over half-way along Morgan's division front, the commander of a Kentucky regiment hailed me and said he must have support, as he was threatened by a masked battery, and the enemy was in force in his front, and might cross any moment. I answered, rather shortly, 'How the devil do you know there is a masked battery? If you can't get over, how can the rebels get at you?' He insisted on the battery, and danger. I finally told him the bayou was utterly impassable there, but, if he insisted the enemy could cross, I would insist on an advance on our side at that point. Hurrying on to make up lost time, I soon reached Morgan. He was making encouraging speeches in a general way, but stopped to ask me questions as to Steele's rank, date of commission, etc. I was very much disturbed at this, fearing want of harmony, and rode on to Steele, whom I found cursing Morgan so fiercely that I could not exactly make out the source of the trouble, or reason why; but saw want of concert clearly enough. I hastened back to General Sherman, and endeavored to impress my ideas on him and my fears; but, while he admitted the facts, he could not be made to believe that any jealousy or personal quarrel could lead to a failure to support each other, and a neglect of duty. The signal for attack had already been given, and the artillery had opened, when I left him again for Morgan's front. I found Morgan where I left him, and the troops advancing. I had understood that he was to lead his division, and asked about it, but, getting no satisfaction, pushed for the front, crossing the slough at the little bridge at the head of the bayou. I found the willows cut off eighteen inches or two feet long, with sharp points above the mud, making it slow and difficult to pass, save at the bridge. I overtook the rear of the advance about two or three hundred feet up the gentle slope, and was astonished to find how small a force was making the attack. I was also surprised to find that they were Steele's men instead of Morgan's. I also saw several regiments across the bayou, but not advancing; they were near the levee. A heavy artillery and infantry fire was going on all this time. While making my way along the column, from which there were very few falling back, a shell burst near me, and the concussion confused me at the time and left me with a headache for several months. When I got my wits about me again I found a good many coming back, but the main part of the force was compact and keeping up the fight. I did not get closer to the woods than about five hundred feet, and found that a large number had penetrated into the enemy's works. When our men fell back, very few ran, but came slowly and sullenly, far more angry than frightened. I found General Frank Blair on foot, and with him Colonel Sea, of Southwest Missouri, and learned that Colonel Thomas Fletcher, afterward Governor of Missouri, was captured with many of his men. They both insisted there on the spot, with those around us, that if all the men ordered up had gone up, or even all that crossed the bayou had moved forward, we could have readily established ourselves in the enemy's works. I was firmly of the same opinion at the time on the ground; and, an entrance effected, we could have brought the whole force on dry ground, and had a base of operations against Vicksburg—though probably, in view of later events, we would have had to stand a siege from Pemberton's army. After explanations with Blair, I rode to where the men were, who had crossed the bayou, but had not advanced with the others. I found them to be De Courcey's brigade; of Morgan's division, which General Sherman supposed to be in advance. In fact, it was the intended support that made the attack. A correspondence and controversy followed between General Blair and Colonel De Courcey, most of which I have, but nothing came of it. On reaching the bayou, I found that Thayer's brigade, of Steele's division, had in some way lost its direction and filed off to the right. Remembering the masked battery, I suspected that had something to do with the matter, and, on following it up, I learned that the Kentucky colonel before mentioned had appealed for aid against the masked battery and invisible force of rebels, and that a regiment had been ordered to him. This regiment, filing off into the timber, had been followed by Thayer's brigade, supposing it to be advancing to the front, and thus left a single brigade to attack a superior force of the enemy in an intrenched and naturally strong position. By the time the mistake could be rectified, it was too late. Our loss was from one hundred and fifty to two hundred killed, and about eleven hundred prisoners and wounded. During the afternoon I went with a flag of truce, with reference to burying the dead. I saw between eighty and one hundred of our men dead, all stripped. There were others closer into the enemy's works than I was allowed to go. On going later to where the Sixth Missouri crossed, I found that they were under the bank, and had dug in with their hands and bayonets, or anything in reach, to protect themselves from a vertical fire from the enemy overhead, who had a heavy force there. With great difficulty they were withdrawn at night. Next day arrangements were made to attempt a lodgment below Haines's Bluff: This was to be done by Steele's command, while the rest of the force attacked again where we had already tried. During the day locomotives whistled, and a great noise and fuss went on in our front, and we supposed that Grant was driving in Pemberton, and expected firing any moment up the Yazoo or in the rear of Vicksburg. Not hearing this, we concluded that Pemberton was throwing his forces into Vicksburg. A heavy fog prevented Steele from making his movement. Rain began to fall, and our location was not good to be in after a heavy rain, or with the river rising. During the night (I think) of January, 1, 1863, our troops were embarked, material and provisions having been loaded during the day. A short time before daylight of the 2d, I went by order of the general commanding, to our picket lines and carefully examined the enemy's lines, wherever a camp-fire indicated their presence. They were not very vigilant, and I once got close enough to hear them talk, but could understand nothing. Early in the morning I came in with the rear-guard, the enemy advancing his pickets and main guards only, and making no effort at all to press us. Once I couldn't resist the temptation to fire into a squad that came bolder than the rest, and the two shots were good ones. We received a volley in return that did come very close among us, but hurt none of my party. Very soon after our rear-guard was aboard, General Sherman learned from Admiral Porter that McClernand had arrived at the mouth of the Yazoo. He went, taking me and one other staff-officer, to see McClernand, and found that, under an order from the President, he had taken command of the Army of the Mississippi. He and his staff, of whom I only remember two- Colonels Scates and Braham, assistant adjutant-general and aide-de-camp—seemed to think they had a big thing, and, so far as I could judge, they had just that. All hands thought the country expected them to cut their way to the Gulf; and to us, who had just come out of the swamp, the cutting didn't seem such an easy job as to the new-comers. Making due allowance for the elevation they seemed to feel in view of their job, everything passed off pleasantly, and we learned that General Grant's communications had been cut at Holly Springs by the capture of Murphy and his force (at Holly Springs), and that he was either in Memphis by that time or would soon be. So that, everything considered, it was about as well that we did not get our forces on the bluff's of Walnut Hill."

The above statement was sent to General Sherman in a letter dated "Chicago, February 5,1876," and *signed "John H. Hammond." Hammond was General Sherman's assistant adjutant-general at the Chickasaw Bayou.*

J. E. TOURTELOTTE, *Colonel and Aide-de-Camp.*

On 29th December, 1862, at Chickasaw Bayou, I was in command of the Thirty-first Missouri Volunteer Infantry, First Brigade, First Division, Fifteenth Army Corps (Blair's brigade). Colonel Wyman, of the Thirteenth Illinois Volunteer Infantry, having been killed, I was the senior colonel of the brigade. General Blair rode up to where my regiment lay, and said to me:

"We are to make a charge here; we will charge in two lines; your regiment will be in the first line, and the Twenty-ninth (Cavender's) will support you. Form here in the timber, and move out across the bayou on a double-quick, and go right on to the top of the heights in your front." He then told me to await a signal. I then attempted to make a reconnaissance of the ground over which we would have to charge, and rode out to the open ground in my front, and saw that there was water and soft mud in the bayou, and was fired upon by the sharp-shooters of the enemy, and turned and went back into the woods where my command lay. Soon after that General Blair came near me, and I told him there was water and mud in the bayou, and I doubted if we could get across. He answered me that General Morgan told him there was no water nor mud to hinder us. I remarked that I had seen it myself, and General Morgan, or any one else, could see it if he would risk being shot at pretty lively. I then told General Blair that it was certain destruction to us if we passed over the abatis upon the open ground where there had once been a corn-field; that we could never reach the base of the hill. He turned to me and said, "Can't you take your regiment up there?" I told him, "Yes, I can take my regiment anywhere, because the men do not know any better than to go," but remarked that old soldiers could not be got to go up there. General Blair then said, "Tom, if we succeed, this will be a grand thing; you will have the glory of leading the assault." He then went on to say that General Morgan's division would support us, and they were heroes of many battles, and pointed to the Fifty-eighth Ohio, then forming in the rear of the Thirteenth Illinois on my right, and said: "See these men? They are a part of Morgan's division, and are heroes of many battles." I laughingly said that they might be heroes, but the regiment did not number as many as one of my companies. He again assured me we would be supported by Morgan's division, and all I had to do was to keep right on and "keep going till you get into Vicksburg." I took my position in advance of my regiment and awaited the signal. When we heard it, we raised a shout, and started at a double-quick, the Thirteenth Illinois on my right. I saw no troops on my left. When we emerged from the woods, the enemy opened upon us; crossing the bayou under fire, and many of the men sinking in the mud and water, our line was very much disordered, but we pretty well restored it before reaching the abatis. Here we were greatly disordered, but somewhat restored the line on reaching the plateau or corn-field. The Twenty-ninth Missouri came on, gallantly supporting us. The Thirteenth Illinois came out upon the corn-field, and the Fifty-eighth Ohio followed close upon it. There was firing to my left, and as I afterward learned was from the Fourth Iowa of Thayer's brigade (and I believe of Steele's division). I was struck and fell, and my regiment went back in great disorder. The fire was terrific. I saw beyond the Thirteenth Illinois, to my right, a disordered line, and learned afterward it was the Sixteenth Ohio. When I was taken from the field by the enemy and taken into Vicksburg, I found among the wounded and prisoners men and officers of the Sixteenth and Fifty-eighth Ohio, and of the Twenty-ninth and Thirty-first Missouri, and Thirteenth Illinois. After I was exchanged and joined my command, General Blair laughingly remarked to me that I had literally obeyed his order and gone "straight on to Vicksburg." He lamented the cutting to pieces of our force on that day. We talked the whole matter over at his headquarters during the siege of Vicksburg. He said that if the charge had been made along our whole line with the same vigor of attack made by his brigade, and if we had been supported as Morgan promised to do, we might have succeeded. I dissented from the opinion that we could even then have succeeded. I asked him what excuse Morgan gave for failing to support us, and he said that Colonel or General De Courcey was in some manner to blame for that, but he said Morgan was mistaken as to the nature of the ground and generally as to the feasibility of the whole thing, and was responsible for the failure to afford us the support he had promised; that he and General Sherman and all of them were misled by the statements and opinions of Morgan as to the situation in our front, and Morgan was, on his part, deceived by the reports of his scouts about other matters as well as the matter of the water in the bayou.

THOMAS C. FLETCHER

ARKANSAS POST.

Extracts from Admiral Porter's Journal.

Sherman and I had made arrangements to capture Arkansas Post.

On the 31st of December, while preparing to go out of the Yazoo, an army officer called to see me, and said that he belonged to General McClernand's staff, and that the general was at the mouth of the Yazoo River, and desired to see me at once. I sent word to the general that if he wished to see me he could have an opportunity by calling on board my flag-ship.

A few moments after I had heard the news of McClernand'a arrival, I saw Sherman pulling about in a boat, and hailed him, informing him that McClernand was at the mouth of the Yazoo. Sherman then came on board, and, in consequence of this unexpected news, determined to postpone the movement out of the Yazoo River, and let McClernand take that upon himself.

General McClernand took my hint and came on board the flag-ship, but I soon discovered that any admiral, Grant, Sherman, or all the generals in the army, were nobody in his estimation. Sherman had been at McClernand's headquarters to see him and state the condition of affairs, and he then suggested to the latter the plan of going to Arkansas Post.

I had a number of fine maps hanging up in my cabin, and when McClernand came on board he examined them all with the eye of a connoisseur. He then stated to me as a new thing the plan he proposed!!! of going to Arkansas Post and stirring up our troops, which had been "demoralized by the late defeat" (Sherman was present, looking daggers at him). I answered, "Yes, General Sherman and myself have already arranged for going to Arkansas Post." Sherman then made some remark about the disposition of the troops in the coming expedition, when McClernand gave him rather a curt answer. McClernand then remarked, "If you will let me have three gunboats, I will go and take the place." Now General McClernand had about as much idea of what a gunboat was, or could do, as the man in the moon. He did not know, the difference between an ironclad and a "tin-clad." He had heard that gunboats had taken Fort Henry, and that was all he knew about them. I said to him: "I'll tell you what I will do, General McClernand. If General Sherman goes in command of the troops, I will go myself in command of a proper force, and will insure the capture of the post." McClernand winced under this, and Sherman quietly walked off into the after-cabin. He beckoned me to come there, while McClernand was apparently deeply engaged in studying out a chart, making believe he was interested, in order to conceal his temper. Sherman said to me: "Admiral, how could you make such a remark to McClernand? He hates me already, and you have made him an enemy for life."

"I don't care," said I; "he shall not treat you rudely in my cabin, and I was glad of the opportunity of letting him know my sentiments." By this time, General McClernand having bottled up his wrath, or cooled down, I went in to him and we discussed the matter. He consented that Sherman should go in command of the troops, and the interview ended pleasantly enough.

The above extracts from Admiral Porter's journal were sent by the admiral to General Sherman, inclosed in a letter dated "Washington, May 29, 1875," and signed "David D. Porter."

228

J. E. TOURTELOTTE.

After leaving the Yazoo, the Army of the Mississippi rendezvous was at Milliken's Bend. During the night of January 4th or 5th, General McClernand came on board the Forest Queen, and with General Sherman went to the Black Hawk flag-boat. There an interview took place, during which the expedition to Arkansas Post took shape. General Sherman having asked leave to take the post, and Admiral Porter having decided to go along, McClernand thought best to go with his entire army, although the enemy were supposed to have only about four or five thousand men, and the fort was little more than a large earthwork commanding the river.

General Sherman's command was then entitled the Second Corps, Army of the Mississippi, and was comprised of the First Division, Blair's, Hovey's, and Thayer's brigades, commanded by Steele; and the Second Division, commanded by David Stuart, with Colonels Giles A. and Kilby Smith commanding brigades.

Our fleet was convoyed by three ironclads and several other gunboats. The weather was bitterly cold for that latitude; we were four days getting into the Arkansas River, which we entered by the White River cut-off; and my recollection is, that our passing the mouth of the main river deceived the enemy as to our destination. The entrance through the cut-off was feasible by reason of high water, and I think made our appearance a surprise to the force at the post. We disembarked on the morning of the 10th of January. Stuart's division first encountered the enemy behind an earthwork about four miles from the fort, running across the solid ground from the river to a swamp. General Sherman in person took Steele's division, and followed a road leading to the rear of the earthwork just mentioned. We had got fairly under way when the rebels fell back to the fort, and McClernand, coming up, ordered us to fall back, and march up the river. It seemed to me then, and afterward, that it would have been better to have marched straight to the rear of the fort, as we started to do. We soon overtook Stuart and closed in, General Sherman on the right, Morgan's force on the left, reaching to the river, where the gunboats were, while Sherman reached from the road which connected the post with the back country, toward where the earthworks reached the river above the fort, and threatened their communications with Little Rock. The night was cold and cloudy, with some snow. There were a good many abandoned huts to our rear, but our forces in position lay on the frozen ground, sheltered as best they could, among the bushes and timber. We were so close that they could have reached us any time during the night with light artillery. The gun-boats threw heavy shells into the fort and behind the earthworks all night, keeping the enemy awake and anxious. The heavy boom of the artillery was followed by the squeak, squeak of Admiral Porter's little tug, as he moved around making his arrangements for the morrow. The sounds were ridiculous by comparison. General Sherman and staff lay on the roots of an old oak-tree, that kept them partly clear of mud. The cold was sharp, my right boot being frozen solid in a puddle in the morning. About half-past two or three o'clock, General Sherman, with another and myself, crept in as close as possible and reconnoitred the position. The general managed to creep in much closer than the rest of us—in fact, so close as to cause us anxiety. The enemy worked hard all night on their abatis and intrenchments, and in the morning we found a ditch and parapet running clear across the point on which the post was situated. This point was cut by a road from the back country, across which was a heavy earthwork and a battery. This road was at the extremity of our left. General McClernand kept his head-quarters on his boat, the Tigress. He came up in the morning to a place in the woods in our rear. One of his staff, a cavalry-officer, climbed a tree to report movements; but from that point there was very little to be seen. Between ten and eleven o'clock the fire opened from the fleet, and we opened along the whole line from infantry and field-guns. Our men soon worked in close enough to keep down the fire of the enemy to a very marked degree.

After reporting to General Sherman, and while explaining the position of the fleet, the smoke-stacks and flags appeared above the fort. What firing was going on in our immediate front ceased. A good many rebels were in plain sight, running away from the fort and scattering. While we were still surprised, the cry was raised that a white flag was hung out. I did not see it, but in a few minutes saw others along the line, and just as the general started for the fort I saw the flag not far from the white house, near the parapet. Orders were given to cease firing. Captain Dayton was sent to the fort where the first flag was raised. Some shots were fired and some men hurt after this. The first rebel officer we encountered was Colonel or General Garland, *commanding brigade, who was ordered to put his men in line and stack arms, which was done. I was directed to pass along the line to the right, and cause the prisoners to stack arms and form our men in line, just outside the work. This I did till I reached Deshler's brigade, on our extreme right, or nearly so, and who was opposed to the right of Steele's force. Steele's men had rushed up to the very foot of the parapet, and some were on it, though they did not fire. The commander of the enemy (Deshler) refused to obey my orders to stack arms, and asked a good many questions as to "how it happened;" said he was not whipped, but held us in check, etc. I told him there were eight or nine thousand men right there, that a shot from me, or a call, would bring down on him, and that we had entire possession of the place. After sending officer two officers from the nearest troops to explain the condition to Steele, and to warn every officer they met to pass the word for everybody to be on the sharp lookout, I arranged with Deshler to keep quiet until I could bring his own commander, or orders from him. Returning to General Sherman, I found a party of young rebel officers, including Robert Johnston's son (rebel Senate) and Captain Wolf, quartermaster, of New Orleans, who declined to surrender except to gentlemen. Some German Missouri soldiers didn't relish the distinction, and were about clubbing them over the head, when I interfered and received their surrender. Hurrying back to the general, I reported the dangerous condition of things. He and General Churchill, commanding officer of the enemy, started for Deshler's brigade; meeting Garland, a quarrel and some recrimination followed between him and Churchill, as to where the fault of the surrender belonged, which was rather promptly silenced by General Sherman, who hurried to the scene of trouble. There, after some ill-natured talk, Deshler ordered his men to lay down their arms. I rode into the fort, and found the parapet badly torn up by the fire from the fleet. On going to the embrasure where I had seen the gun while on the river-bank talking to Captain Shirk, the piece was found split back about eighteen inches, and the lower half of the muzzle dropped out. A battered but unexploded shell lying with the piece explained that it must have struck the gun in the muzzle, almost squarely. On passing along the inside I saw from the torn condition of the earthworks how tremendous our fire was, and how the fire of the enemy was kept down. The fire of the navy had partly torn down the side of the fort next the river. A good many sailors were in the fort. General A. J. Smith, Admiral Porter, and General Burbridge were there—all in high spirits, but in some contention as to who got in first. Toward dark, or nearly so, an Arkansas regiment came in as reenforcements, but surrendered without any trouble. About the same time General Sherman received orders to put General A. J. Smith in charge of the fort, and stay outside with his men. As his troops were nearly all inside, and had four-fifths of the prisoners in charge, these orders were not very clear, and the general left for headquarters to find out what was meant. I went on collecting arms, and as our men were scattering a good deal and were greatly excited, I took the precaution to pass along the line and march the prisoners far enough from the stacked arms to be out of temptation. I was especially urged to this by hearing several rebel officers speak of their guns being still loaded. It was dark before all the prisoners were collected and under guard, including the regiment that arrived after the fight. I am confident that all the prisoners were under guard by General Sherman's troops.*

Everything being secure, the staff-officers, all of whom had been busily engaged, scattered to compare notes and enjoy the victory. I found my way onboard the Tigress, where every one was greatly excited, and in high feather regarding our victory, the biggest thing since Donelson. I also obtained some food and small comforts for a few rebel officers, including young Johnston, Wolfe, and the Colonel Deshler already mentioned. Then hunted up General Sherman, whom I found sitting on a cracker-boa in the white house already mentioned, near where the white flag first appeared. Garland was with him, and slept with him that night, while the rest of us laid around wherever we could. It was a gloomy, bloody house, and suggestive of war. Garland was blamed by the other Confederate officers for the white flag, and remained with us for safety. Next day was very cold. We worked hard at the lists of prisoners—nearly five thousand in number—all of whom were sent to St. Louis, in charge of our inspector-general, Major Sanger. Our loss was less than one hundred. The enemy, although behind intrenchments, lost more than double what we did. Their wounded were much worse hurt than ours, who were mostly hit around the head and arms.

The losses were nearly all in General Sherman's wing of the army. The loss in the fleet amounted to little, but their service was very valuable, and deserved great credit, though they received little. There was a good deal of sympathy between our part of the forces and the fleet people, and I then thought, and still think, if we had been on the left next the river, that in connection with the tremendous fire from the navy, we could have carried the work in an hour after we opened on it. Their missiles traversed the whole fortification, clear through to the hospitals at the upper end, and I stood five minutes in rifle-range of the fort next the river—not hit, and but seldom shot at, and no one hit near me.

On the 18th we embarked, in a snow-storm; collected at Napoleon, which seemed to be washing away; and steamed to Milliken's Bend, were we arrived on January 21st, and soon after went to Young's plantation, near Vicksburg.

The above statement from General Hammond was received by General Sherman, inclosed in a letter dated "Chicago, February 5, 1876" and signed "John H. Hammond," who was adjutant-general to General Sherman during the winter of 1862-'83.

J. E. TOURTELLOTTE

CINCINNATI, *February 3, 1876*

MY DEAR GENERAL: At Arkansas Post the troops debarked from steamer January 9th, from one o'clock to dark, in the vicinity of Notrib's farm, and on the 10th moved out to get position; Steele to the right, crossing the low ground to the north, to get a higher ground, avoid crowding the moving columns, and gain the left (our right) and rear of the "post," and the river-bank above the post. Stuart took the river-road the movement commencing at 11 o'clock a.m.. After crossing the low ground covered with water, you were called back with Steele, as Stuart had driven out the enemy's rifle-trench pickets, this giving more and feasible room for moving. Stuart was pushed forward, and by dark he and Steele were well up to their expected positions. Before daylight on the 11th you directed me to accompany you for a personal inspection of the ground to your front, which we made on foot, going so far forward that we could easily hear the enemy at work and moving about. Discovering the open fields, you at once directed Steele to move to the right and front, and pushed Stuart out so as to fully command them and the field-work of the enemy extending from the fort, to prevent farther strengthening, as it was evident these works were the product of a recent thought. Stuart and Steele were prompt in taking position, but Morgan's command (not under your control) did not seem to work up, or keep in junction with you. At ten o'clock you sent me to McClernand to ascertain why the delay of attack. He attributed it to Admiral Porter, which was really unjust. The attack began at 1 p.m., by Admiral Porter, and the sound of his first gun had not died till your men were engaged—Wood's, Barrett's, and the Parrott batteries and infantry. It was lively for a time, and Stuart pushed clear up to the enemy's rifle-trenches, and forced them to keep sheltered. Hammond was mostly with Steele; Sanger sent to McClernand, and McCoy, myself, and John Taylor were with you and Stuart. At about half-past three I got your permission to go to Giles Smith's skirmish-line, and, thinking I saw evidence of the enemy weakening, I hurried back to you and reported my observations. I was so confident that a demand for it would bring a surrender, that I asked permission to make it, and, as you granted me, but refused to let another member of your staff, at his request, go with me, I rode directly down the road with only an orderly. Colonel Garland, commanding a brigade, was the first officer I saw, to whom, for you, I made the demand. All firing ceased at once, or in a few moments. I sent the orderly back to you, and you rode forward. It was then four o'clock.

During the attack, nobody seemed to think McClernand had any clear idea of what or how it was to be done. During the day he gave you no directions, nor came where you were; he was well to the rear, with his "man up a tree," who in the capacity of a lookout gave McClernand information, from which he based such instructions as he made to his subordinates. He was free to express himself as being a man of "destiny," and his "star" was in the ascendance. I am, etc.,

L. M. DAYTON, *late Colonel of the Staff, now of Cincinnati, Ohio.*

General W. T. SHERMAN.

MERIDIAN CAMPAIGN.

[Special Field Orders, No. 11.]

HEADQUARTERS DEPARTMENT OF THE TENNESSEE
MEMPHIS, January 27, 1864

V. The expedition is one of celerity, and all things must tend to that. Corps commanders and staff-officers will see that our movements are not encumbered by wheeled vehicles improperly loaded. Not a tent, from the commander-in-chief down, will be carried. The sick will be left behind, and the surgeons can find houses and sheds for all hospital purposes.

VI. All the cavalry in this department is placed under the orders and command of Brigadier-General W. S. Smith, who will receive special instructions.

By order of Major-General W. T. SHERMAN

L. M. DAYTON, Aide-de-Camp.

NOTE.-That same evening I started in a steamboat for Vicksburg.
W. T. S.
St. Louis, 1885.

HEADQUARTERS DEPARTMENT OF THE TENNESSEE
MEMPHIS, January 27, 1864

Brigadier-General W. S. SMITH, commanding Cavalry, etc., present.

DEAR GENERAL: By an order issued this day I have placed all the cavalry of this department subject to your command. I estimate you can make a force of full seven thousand men, which I believe to be superior and better in all respects than the combined cavalry which the enemy has in all the State of Mississippi. I will in person start for Vicksburg to-day, and with four divisions of infantry, artillery, and cavalry move out for Jackson, Brandon, and Meridian, aiming to reach the latter place by February 10th. General Banks will feign on Pascagoula and General Logan on Rome. I want you with your cavalry to move from Colliersville on Pontotoc and Okolona; thence sweeping down near the Mobile & Ohio Railroad, disable that road as much as possible, consume or destroy the resources of the enemy along that road, break up the connection with Columbus, Mississippi, and finally reach me at or near Meridian as near the date I have mentioned as possible. This will call for great energy of action on your part, but I believe you are equal to it, and you have the best and most experienced troops in the service, and they will do anything that is possible. General Grierson is with you, and is familiar with the whole country. I will send up from Haines's Bluff an expedition of gunboats and transports combined, to feel up the Yazoo as far as the present water will permit. This will disconcert the enemy. My movement on Jackson will also divide the enemy, so that by no combination can he reach you with but a part of his force. I wish you to attack any force of cavalry you meet and follow them southward, but in no event be drawn into the forks of the streams that make up the Yazoo nor over into Alabama. Do not let the enemy draw you into minor affairs, but look solely to the greater object to destroy his communication from Okolona to Meridian, and thence eastward to Selma. From Okolona south you will find abundance of forage collected along the railroad, and the farmers have corn standing in the fields. Take liberally of all these, as well as horses, mules, cattle, etc. As a rule, respect dwellings and families as something too sacred to be disturbed by soldiers, but mills, barns, sheds, stables, and such like things use for the benefit or convenience of your command. If convenient, send into Columbus, Mississippi, and destroy all machinery there, and the bridge across the Tombigbee, which enables the enemy to draw the resources of the east side of the valley, but this is not of sufficient importance to delay your movement. Try and communicate with me by scouts and spies from the time you reach Pontotoc. Avoid any large force of infantry, leaving them to me. We have talked over this matter so much that the above covers all points not provided for in my published orders of to-day. I am, etc.,

W. T. SHERMAN, Mayor-General, commanding.

MEMPHIS, TENNESSEE, *January 27, 1864.*

Brigadier-General J. P. HATCH, in charge of Cavalry Bureau, St. Louis, Missouri.

SIR: Your favor of the 21st inst. is just received. Up to the present time eight hundred and eighteen horses have arrived here since Captain Hudson's visit to St. Louis. I wrote you upon his return several days ago that it would not be necessary to divert shipments to this point which could not reach us before February 1st. We shall certainly get off on our contemplated expedition before that time. The number of horses estimated for in this department by its chief quartermaster was two thousand, and this number, including those already sent, will, I think, completely mount all the dismounted cavalry of this department. Recruits for cavalry regiments are arriving freely, and this will swell our requisitions for a couple of months to come. I will as far as possible procure horses from the regions of country traversed by our cavalry.

Yours truly, W. SOOY SMITH, Brigadier-General,

Chief of Cavalry, Military Division of the Mississippi.

MEMPHIS, TENNESSEE, *January 28, 1864*

Brigadier-General GEORGE CROOK, commanding Second Cavalry Division, Huntsville, Alabama.

I start in about three days with seven, thousand men to Meridian via Pontotoc. Demonstrate on Decatur, to hold Roddy.

W. SOOY SMITH, Brigadier-General, Chief of Cavalry, Military Division of the Mississippi.

MAYWOOD, ILLINOIS, *July 9,1875*
General W. T. SHERMAN, Commander-in-Chief, United States Army.

SIR: Your letter of July 7th is just received.

Your entire statement in the "Memoirs" concerning my part in the Meridian campaign is incorrect.

You overstate my strength, placing it at seven thousand effective, when it was but six. The nominal strength of my command was seven thousand.

You understate the strength of my enemy, putting Forrest's force at four thousand. On our return to Nashville, you stated it, in General Grant's presence, to have been but twenty-five hundred. Before and during my movement I positively knew Forrest's strength to be full six thousand, and he has since told me so himself.

Instead of delaying from the 1st to the 11th of February for "some regiment that was ice-bound near Columbus, Kentucky," it was an entire brigade, Colonel Waring's, without which your orders to me were peremptory not to move. I asked you if I should wait its arrival, and you answered: "Certainly; if you go without it, you will be, too weak, and I want you strong enough to go where you please."

The time set for our arrival at Meridian, the 10th of February, had arrived before it was possible for me, under your orders, to move from Memphis, and I would have been entirely justifiable if I had not started at all. But I was at that time, and at all times during the war, as earnest and anxious to carry out my orders, and do my full duty as you or any other officer could be, and I set out to make a march of two hundred and fifty miles into the Confederacy, having to drive back a rebel force equal to my own. After the time had arrived for the full completion of my movement, I drove this force before me, and penetrated one hundred and sixty miles into the Confederacy—did more hard fighting, and killed, wounded, and captured more of the enemy than you did during the campaign—did my work most thoroughly, as far as I could go without encountering the rebel cavalry set loose by your return from Meridian, and brought off my command, with all the captured property and rescued negroes, with very small loss, considering that inflicted on the enemy, and the long-continued and very severe fighting. If I had disobeyed your orders, and started without Waring's brigade, I would have been "too weak," would probably have been defeated, and would have been subjected to just censure. Having awaited its arrival, as I was positively and distinctly ordered to do, it only remained for me to start upon its arrival, and accomplish all that I could of the work allotted to me. To have attempted to penetrate farther into the enemy's country, with the cavalry of Polk's army coming up to reenforce Forrest, would have insured the destruction of my entire command, situated as it was. I cannot now go into all the particulars, though I assure you that they make the proof of the correctness of my conduct as conclusive as I could desire it to be. I was not headed off and defeated by an inferior force near West Point. We had the fighting all our own way near West Point, and at all other points except at Okalona, on our return, when we had the worst of it for a little while, but finally checked the enemy handsomely, and continued our return march, fighting at the rear and on both flanks, repulsing all attacks and moving in perfect order. And so my movement was not a failure, except that I did not reach Meridian as intended, for the reason stated, and for many more which it is not necessary for me to detail here. On the other hand, it was a very decided success, inflicting a terrible destruction of supplies of every kind, and a heavy loss of men upon the enemy. You should have so reported it in the beginning. You should so amend your report, and "Memoirs" now. This, and no less than this, is due from one soldier to another. It is due to the exalted position which you occupy, and, above all, it is due to that truthfulness in history which you claim to revere. If you desire it, I will endeavor to visit you, and in a friendly manner "fight our battles o'er again," and endeavor to convince you that you have always been mistaken as to the manner in which my part in the "Meridian campaign" was performed. But I will never rest until the wrong statements regarding it are fully and fairly corrected. Yours truly,

WILLIAM SOOY SMITH

HEADQUARTERS ARMY OF THE UNITED STATES
St. Louis, Missouri, July 11, 1875.

General J. D. WEBSTER, Chicago, Illinois

DEAR GENERAL: General W. Sooy Smith feels aggrieved and wronged by my account of his part in the Meridian campaign, in my "Memoirs," pages 394, 395, and properly appeals to me for correction. I have offered to modify any words or form of expression that he may point out, but he asks me to completely change the whole that concerns him. This, of course, I will not do, as his part was material to the whole, and cannot be omitted or materially altered without changing the remainder, for his failure to reach Meridian by February 10th was the reason for other movements distant from him. I now offer him, what seems to me fair and liberal, that we submit the points at issue to you as arbitrator. You are familiar with the ground, the coincident history, and most, if not all, the parties.

I propose to supply you with

1. Copy of my orders placing all the cavalry under General Smith's orders (with returns).

2. My letter of instructions to him of January 27th.

3. My official report of the campaign, dated Vicksburg, March 7, 1864.

4. General W. Sooy Smith's report of his operations, dated Nashville, Tennessee, March 4, 1864.

After reading these, I further propose that you address us questions which we will answer in writing, when you are to make us a concise, written decision, which I will have published in close connection with the subject in controversy. If General Smith will show you my letter to him of this date, and also deliver this with his written assent, I will promptly furnish you the above documents, and also procure from the official files a return of the cavalry force available at and near Memphis on the date of my orders, viz., January 27, 1864.

With great respect, your friend and servant,

W. T. SHERMAN, General.

NOTE:—General Smith never submitted his case to the arbitration offered. The whole will be made clear by the publication of the official records, which are already in print, though not yet issued. His orders were in writing, and I have no recollection of the "peremptory" verbal orders to which he refers, and quotes as from me.

ST. Louis, Missouri, 1895. W. T. S.

MAYWOOD, ILLINOIS, July 14, 1875.

General W. T. SHERMAN, Commander-in-Chief, etc.

DEAR GENERAL: Your letter of the 11th of July reaches me just as I am starting to spend the first vacation I have ever allowed myself —in the Territories, with my wife and son.

It indicates a spirit of fairness from which we have better things than an arbitration to hope for. Though, if we should reach such a necessity, there is no one living to whom our differences might more properly be referred than to General Webster. I make no objection to your writing your "Memoirs," and, as long as they refer to your own conduct, you are at liberty to write them as you like; but, when they refer to mine, and deal unjustly with my reputation, I, of right, object.

Neither do I wish to write my "Memoirs," unless compelled to do so to vindicate my good name. There were certain commands which were to make up mine. These, Waring's brigade included, were spoken of by us in the long conversation to which you refer. This brigade we knew was having a hard time of it in its movement from Columbus to Memphis. I asked you if I should move without it if it did not arrive, and you answered me as stated in my last letter to you. Those who immediately surrounded me during the painful delay that occurred will inform you how sorely I chafed under the restraint of that peremptory order.

In the conversation that occurred between us at Nashville, while all the orders, written and verbal, were still fresh in your memory, you did not censure me for waiting for Waring, but for allowing myself to be encumbered with fugitive negroes to such an extent that my command was measurably unfit for active movement or easy handling, and for turning back from West Point, instead of pressing on toward Meridian. Invitations had been industriously circulated, by printed circulars and otherwise, to the negroes to come into our lines, and to seek our protection wherever they could find it, and I considered ourselves pledged to receive and protect them. Your censure for so doing, and your remarks on that subject to me in Nashville, are still fresh in my memory, and of a character which you would now doubtless gladly disavow.

But we must meet and talk the whole matter over, and I will be at any trouble to see you when I return.

Meantime I will not let go the hope that I will convince you absolutely of your error, for the facts are entirely on my side. Yours truly,

WILLIAM SOOY SMITH

Printed in the USA
CPSIA information can be obtained
at www.ICGtesting.com
LVHW012317230324
775357LV00020B/456